Wild Vanilla

Pacific Island Stories

by

Peter Thomson

for
Bolivia's Eternal Princess

from

Parador

July 5, 2018

Exordium

Acknowledgements, book references, translations, quotation sources and supplementary comments are presented in the Travellers' Notes at volume's end.

The manuscript of *Wild Vanilla* was completed in Sydney, Australia in 2009. *Wild Vanilla* is the second book in a trilogy on island life that began with the 1999 publication of *Kava in the Blood*. A third book will cover the author's experience as the Permanent Representative of Fiji to the United Nations.

Artwork by Viti Makawa, gratefully incorporating contributions by Chong (facing pg. 1), Jessie Peterson (pg. 92 & 200), Dorothy Kearsley (pg. 92), Marc Rambeau (pg. 296) and Andy Bell (pg. 404).

Book design and production by Marijcke Thomson.
Proof-reading by Merlyn Cassidy.

2nd Kindle version published 2015

Peter Thomson, 418 E59 St, New York, NY10022, USA

M

Omnia vincit amor

Contents

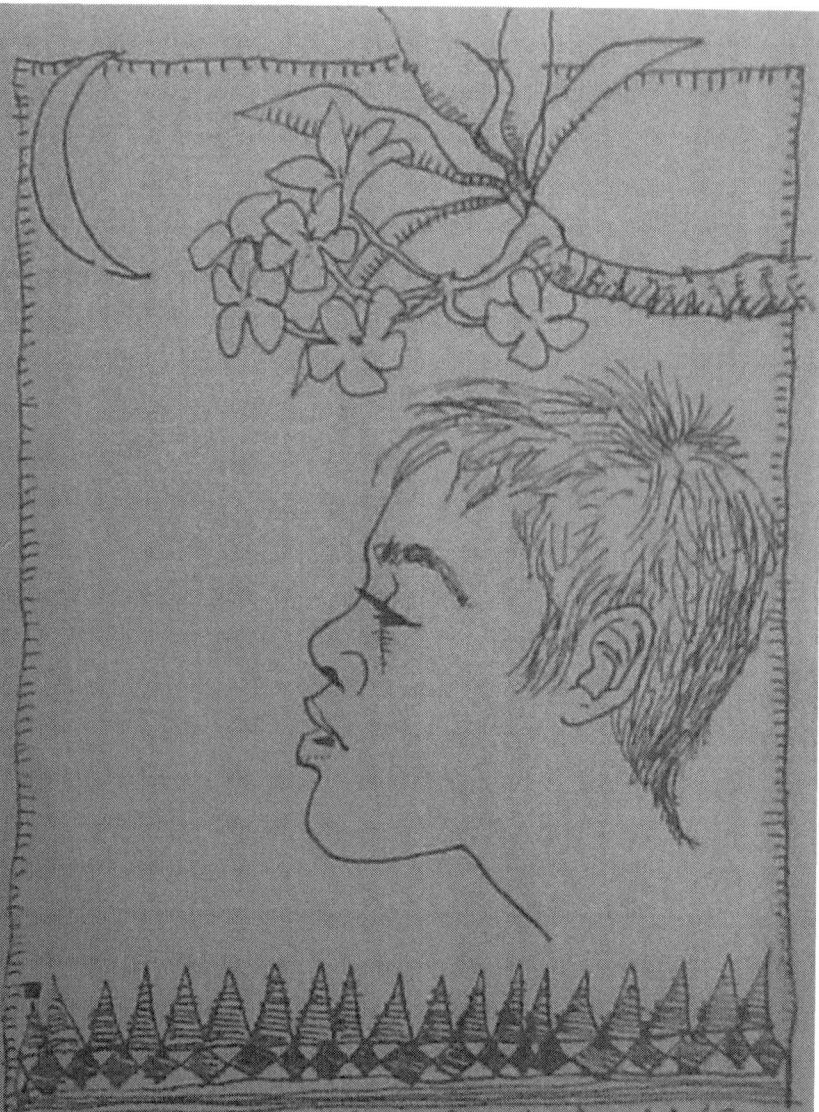

DEAR MARIJCKE & LE BLANC —
THANK YOU SO MUCH ONCE AGAIN
FOR YOR ISLAND HOSPITALITY RAOUL

The Moon over Matsushima

Dear Companion,

Here is an account of the journey so far. There is so much we have in common I might have written these stories in the first person plural, 'not unto us alone'. But our little variances have their moments, so in the singular let them be.

As you well know, my friend, life is a journey. From fluky moments of conception, to vibrant sappy days, fleeting perceptions lead on to tottering denouement. We follow the fate of all things: whole races, religions, civilizations, flowering and fading into eternity's dusk. Even great continents expire when their tectonic course is run. But how wonderful of our kind to have figured out how the journey of all things proceeded in the aeons before the first travellers set forth, and to imagine what will be when the last of us has vanished and time goes surging on to inexplicable end. No doubt you will remind me, that this is but our version of reality.

You also have told me, there's little original in the thoughts we arrive at. The same forage we hunt and gather has known consumption, extraction, expulsion, so many times before. Yet still we delight in this path, in the divine wrestle, squinting at the light. We are vectors of the continuity and everything learnt in the days since we wandered from the plains of the Serengeti lies within us; even the viruses that have shaped us into what we have become.

To illustrate your point: it occurred to me that when the second paragraph of this epistle insisted on its existence, it was in spirit if not in form, nothing but a regurgitation of something Basho calligraphied over three hundred years ago. And just as all our wine-soaked ideas are derived from those of our betters, that creaky old Japanese poet-monk pulled his from passing eddies of the same stream of inheritance. Thus lack of originality is no cause for deflation, rather one of elation; for with the debt thus acknowledged, the bond of shared consciousness fortifies the spirit.

That brings us to one more preamble. In the course of these Pacific Island ambulations, I will call on your innate generosity to allow me two indulgences. Firstly, I will interpose relevant vignettes from the pens of other chroniclers of the journey. Fired in from the past, their succinct missiles will brighten my plodding prose. I promise this device is no lazy ruse, for in every case, during some quiet dalliance along the way, the splash of their arrival caused profound ripples across ponds of reflection. In fact, in sharing them with you, I confess there is an element of unburdening.

Since we are just setting forth, here is one of those pond-ripplers sent from the seventeenth century musings of Basho. The traveller's high priest, he begins the account of his own journey on narrow roads to northern Japan with these words,

> There came a day when the clouds drifting along aroused a wanderlust in me, and I set off on a journey to roam along the seashores. I returned to my hut on the riverbank last autumn, and by the time I had swept away the cobwebs, the year was over. But when spring came with its misty skies, the god of temptation possessed me with a longing to pass the barrier at Shirakawa, and the road gods beckoned, and I could not set my mind to anything. So I mended my breeches, put new cords on my hat, and as I burned moxa on my knees to make them strong, I was already dreaming of the moon over Matsushima.[1]

The second indulgence I beg is that of including in this traveller's journal a few stories that are not exactly mine. While they come from my pen, they're not at first glance about my personal journey, for they cover subjects as divergent as what it was to find violent death in the Tarawa tide, or to have suffered a leper's life on the exile's island of Makogai.

One of the stories follows the progress of northern writers swanning through our islands on South Sea sabbaticals. Another recalls the unusual fortunes of some Fiji beachcombers of old. There is among them a report on the strange expectations imposed on small Pacific states by the constructs of

Westphalian world order; while another explores the cosmology of evangelists, home-grown and imported, so plentiful in the Pacific Islands today. Divergent as these subjects may appear, you and I are closely connected to them all; for in their curious ways, they have had their play on the many turns of this journey, and we would not be who we are without them.

I will soon break from this monologue, for I promised you an interesting diversion early in the piece, but first let me get us through the gate and stepping along the way. Some back-story demands to be covered for the sake of those who are not familiar with where I'm coming from, so for a moment or two more I appeal for your patience while I clear a few things up.

Firstly I must deal with this issue of being a fifth-generation Fijian and being white. Well actually when I look in the mirror nowadays, the only white things I see are my eyeballs and what little remains of my hair. Thanks to a combination of long exposure to tropical sun, high blood pressure and the effects of various fermentations and distillations of grain, cane and fruit, my skin colour is essentially various shades of pink and red. And there is the pity of it, for if only I'd picked up some Micronesian, Polynesian or Melanesian genes along the way, regardless of how much whisky got sampled, I would have at the very least foregone this rosaceous appearance.

'Mais … il est BLANC!'

That was the exclamation of a lady of substance upon first meeting me; a *café au lait* woman of Tahitian origin who for reasons I won't go into, having heard accounts of me over the years, had expectations. The scene was a waterfront mansion in Auckland, the cast a conclave of elegant notables of that city. Mutual friends had mentioned my deep-etched Fijian origins, so she'd comfortably assumed I too was of an attractive shade of coffee.

To have so disappointed her on that first and last meeting, was something I held lightly against myself at the time, but there was little I could do to rectify the situation. Thus, emphatic impressions concluded, and with a

3

hint of fraudulence exposed, the Papeete princess drifted away in a cloud of cigarette smoke.

Do you remember the old Fiji coins with holes in their middles? Silver pennies and halfpennies, perforated in their minting so they could be strung on twine: prosaic and somehow eternal objects, there was a day when slapping one of these on a worn wooden counter could produce a sweet ice-block pierced by a stick. During the decade I sojourned in Sydney town, if I'd got one of those coins for every time I was party to the following repartee, I could've spanned the harbour bridge with my penny-string.

The mid-Pacific accent can be hard to place, so more often than not, the listener poses the question, 'Where you from, mate?'

'Fiji.'

A pregnant pause while the interrogator takes a second look, and then, 'Oh yeah? Well you don't look much like a Fijian! Ha, ha, ha, hah.'

Another pause, slight umbrage taken, and the riposte, 'Well, for that matter you don't look much like an Australian.'

Further pause, while deep umbrage registers on the features of the Anglo-Celtic-Greek-Jewish-Italian-Chinese-Lebanese inquisitor.

Silly stuff, I suppose. I had long thought that the longevity of the racial prejudices that shape so many peoples' lives came down in the end to an imperious numbers game. Tyrannies of the majority reward themselves with bully comfort and worse in the golden age of democracy; such is the potency of demography. I wrote about this in *Kava in the Blood*, in fact the book was infused with the subject. But now I see there's a lot more to it than just numbers, and I see how the willingness to include, and the desire to be included, are so available and so essential for a more wholesome experience of the journey.

Under the Gothic spandrels and turrets of Westminster Palace, these last few decades, how glorious it has been to see members of the House of Lords, in miniver robes of crimson and gold, whose facial features and deep brown skin announce the certainty of their West African heritage. Exodus, movement of Jah people! From the Serengeti to the ever-biding stars, our journey down the road of creation goes ever on.

Anyway, yes, though a Fijian by birth and upbringing, my genetic code derives from European forbears, from people who long ago felt the urge to leave off their continental wanderings and travel in boats to the islands now called Britain. How they got from those northern islands to Fiji, I'll summarise for you in just two pages of that promised back-story.

The first generation of my Fiji family was that of Captain William Scott Petrie and his wife Emma. I once stood by his grave at Lovonilase cemetery along the inner shores of Suva Harbour, and I recall his since-lost headstone marking the 1888 date of his death and his rank of Master Mariner. I'd heard from one of Captain Petrie's granddaughters that he'd run away to sea as a lad, from the braw Scottish port of Arbroath, and that brine was in his blood. Though his life would lie before the mast, he must have been possessed of sufficient degree of Scottish charm and sureness, for the lady he wooed and wed was of gentler farming stock, one of the Howards of Buckinghamshire.

That same granddaughter related how Emma Howard was up in London staying with her aunt, the spouse of a member of parliament, when she met William. She said the only place our forbears could make love was on the dining-room table. How could she have known such a thing? Her grandmother told her. Wonderful the way life's intimacies so often skip a generation, for I imagine Emma would never have confided that detail to her daughters. Wonderful also to think of the possibility that one of those daughters, their first-born, my great-grandmother Maud Wilhelmina, might have been conceived in such a manner; and that without that passionate affair between a salty Scot and an English lady, I would have no story to tell, for I would not be.

What storms of moments William and Emma must have passed through on their long passage under sail to Fiji. Writing those words has placed a rather daunting weight on my imagination, bringing to mind some others from a favourite novel, *Gilead*, in which an ailing father writes to his son of their deceased loved one.

> I wish I could give you the memory I have of your mother that day. I wish I could leave you certain of the images in my mind, because they are so beautiful that I hate to think they will be extinguished when I am. Well, again this life has its own mortal loveliness. And memory is not strictly mortal in its nature, either. It is a strange thing after all, to be able to return to a moment, when it can hardly be said to have any reality at all, even in its passing. A moment is such a slight thing, I mean, that it's abiding is a most gracious reprieve.[2]

You know, the Petrie granddaughter of whom I wrote, my high-spirited informant, has been gone from this world some three decades now. How is it then that I recall her words with such certainty? Because I am an itinerant keeper of logs, have long made a habit of interviewing my fellow travellers, and for four decades now have filled travel and family journals with scribblings.

While others are out on deck participating in the great adventure, the scribbler is sequestered in a cabin attempting to record snatches of light and time. But this curtailment, this time out from life's direct experience, observing tiresome oscillations of pen and ink, has its occasional reward. For in times of nodding contemplation, when 'old and grey and full of sleep', smoky memories are kindled from all these chronicles of moments. Faded pages combust into once familiar flames, building to a blaze of gracious reprieves.

Beg pardon, dear companion. I'm already over a page into my family's voyage to Fiji and there's little chance I can fit the rest into the promised pair. If you permit, I'll press on, just an extra page or two, quickly now.

In the early 1870s, the Petries set sail for the Antipodes. Confronted by unrelenting Atlantic storms, Emma's first sea voyage was nearly her last; for such was the violent *mal de mer* of the Buckinghamshire bride, she was unable to keep down any sustenance for days on end. Hopes for her survival were dwindling, when somewhere near the Cape of Good Hope the boat's cook witnessed a wave strand a silver sprat on the pitching deck. He fell on the wriggling fish and carried it to his galley, where he fried it 'til it was blistered and burnt. This frizzled morsel he presented to Emma and she stomached it, thereby turning her head to survival; for like Boswell's journal, a little was diffused into a considerable portion, and our Fiji family became possible.

The Petries dwelt for a while in the New Zealand port of Lyttelton, where a daughter was born to them; and then in the Rocks, Sydney's nautical quarter of the day, where another daughter was born. Finally they were Fiji-bound, some time in the late 1870s, where with their daughters Maud, Dora and Florence, a home was established in Levuka, the clapboard mariner's town that was then the capital of Fiji. A son, John, was born to Emma in Levuka in 1880, but the wee bairn did not survive the day, and was buried on a hillside overlooking the Koro Sea.

In 1887 the family moved to Fiji's new capital of Suva, where a bigger harbour and broad hinterland offered space for development. Working out of Suva and Mago Island, Captain Petrie skippered his sailing ship *Westward Ho* through the Islands, with much of his work related to the carriage of plantation labourers from the New Hebrides and the Solomons back to Fiji. He was no blackbirder, and if ever he set sail for Melanesia on a labour run, there was always a government agent on board to supervise conditions. With Fiji now a British colony and Gladstone in London's seat of power, government agents were required to keep records of all labour-recruiting voyages out of Fiji.

In 1888, at the age of forty-five, the Master Mariner, 'sundered far from Scotia's shore', died of typhoid. Emma buried him at Lovonilase. Never remarrying, she lived a widow's life for almost half a century. Her three daughters married men who made their careers in Fiji: Dora to Sir Hugh Ragg, a Suva-born entrepreneur known as the founder of the Fiji tourism industry; Florence to another Scot, Robert Boyd, one of the colony's most respected native lands commissioners; and Maud to my great-grandfather Herbert Ambler.

Ambler was of an ecclesiastic family, English landed-gentry, some of whom had tried their hands in the gold rushes of Australia. He arrived in Fiji as part of a botanical expedition bound for the Solomon Islands, but the goal was not attained, as the expedition fell apart in Suva. All was not lost, for the rough-hewn colony of Fiji took his fancy, as did the charms of the young Suva woman he met there. Herbert married Maud and settled down in Extension, the prosaically named adjunct of downtown Suva.

They called Ambler 'The Captain', not because he had a nautical background, but because he served as such in the pre-WW1 Fiji Defense Force. An 1894 Supreme Court of Fiji jury-list in my possession shows he was a commission agent in Suva, and *The Cyclopedia of Fiji* informs me Captain Ambler was town clerk of the capital until 1903. He sired five Suva children, and then disaster struck. Shortly after the birth of her last child in 1901, Maud died. Then three months after the young mother's death, the fourth of the children died, with Herbert following them seven years later to the common Ambler grave at Lovonilase.

One of the surviving Ambler children was my mother's mother, Constance, a Suva girl born and bred. Let Wordsworth introduce her thus,

> I but repay a gift which I myself
> Received at others' hands; for, though now old
> Beyond the common life of man, I still
> Remember them who loved me in my youth.[3]

It is in part my sense of fealty to her, and to my mother, that I have been provoked into long recording of Fiji stories. From skinny infancy to bearded university days, my Suva grandmother loved me, and I loved her right back. When I was suckling milk bottles, it was she who found I did better on goat's milk. When I was run over by a car, a cream Ford Consul at the corner of Catalina and Hutson streets, it was in her bed at Suva Point that I lay while awaiting a doctor's scrutiny. When the extended family was traveling overseas, and she shared a bed with a couple of my other infant siblings and me, it was me who would ask her to roll on her side to quell her rumbling snores.

Wittingly or not, she filled my head with Fijian detail: from the times of her orphaned youth before the outbreak of the Great War, of her marriage to the young English radio engineer Bill Kearsley, and of their life together in the Amalgamated Wireless stations in the northern islands of Vanua Levu and Taveuni, until they settled underneath the wireless masts at Kaunimakoni[4] on the Vatuwaqa foreshore of Suva.

I grew up in Connie Kearsley's extended Fiji family, for in those days most of her cousins and their offspring, as well as her own six children and their many kids, were all still living in Suva. Connie's daughters were vivacious, dark-haired beauties, described by one writer as 'an arresting line'. [5]

There was a time in the late sixties when her son Peter Kearsley was an elected member of Legislative Council, sitting opposite the nominated members amongst who were my father, the leader of government business on the Council, and her other Suva son-in-law, Charles Gurd, the director of medical services. On reflection, those were the denouement days for many of the Fiji European families who had founded their little town on the shores of Suva Harbour; for when Fiji became independent in 1970, the capital went into rapid development mode, and Suva was no longer theirs.

When my grandmother was widowed and I was a wandering university student needing a place to doss in Suva, it was to her couch in a humble Gordon Street flat that I would make my way. Those were good times of gin and tonic, Scrabble and listening to the old Fiji stories through the smoke of our cigarettes. But the inevitable came to pass, the day when for the first time as a man I learnt what it was to sob from the very pit, the day we laid her body to rest beneath the drooping *baka* trees of Lovonilase.

Connie's fourth child was my mother Nancy Marguerite Kearsley, she who lies buried on the shores of Loch Feochan in Argyll, Scotland. She wrote the words for her gravestone. They read,

> Lady Thomson
> née Nancy Kearsley
> born Suva Fiji 1921
> died at Sonas, Ardentallen 1988
> Loving wife of

Sir Ian Thomson
and proud mother of
Andrew, Peter, John,
David, Richard, Mark,
Sally and Douglas

In the eulogy he delivered at her Loch Feochan funeral, Sir Robert Sanders described my mother as 'instant sunshine', and 'a true daughter of Fiji, so much loved, with friends among all races and at all levels of society', who held at the very heart of her life, giving it great strength and meaning, her marriage to my father. Sir Robert caught it well. I could add descriptions of sparky dynamism, of a consummate hostess and constant provider, of one who was ever a giver and embracer. There was the way she held together an international web of family and friends, a web that shuddered at her death, and denied her charm, surrendered to the dissolutions of distance.

I could tell you stories, my friend, of her Taveuni childhood, or her wartime job with Naval Air Transport handling the flying boats that touched down in Laucala Bay from far-off America and Australia; or of the years she gave to the Fiji Girl Guides, of which she became president later in life, the YWCA, of which she was vice-president, and a long line of Fiji charities; but 'instant sunshine' will suffice.

As they say, we're all someone's sons and daughters, and as with most of us, I loved my mother more than I could possibly say. But she's been gone some two decades, so let's move on with the story. I know that sounds inadequate, but it'll have to do for now. And she would want it that way, for there's so much more to relate about her Fiji family, because now the great-great-great grandchildren of William and Emma Petrie are creating Fiji offspring. But you've got to lift pen from paper somewhere, so let it be here.

HONIARA

BRITISH SOLOMON ISLANDS

BRITISH SOLOMON ISLANDS

BRITISH SOLOMON ISLANDS

Getting Off the Rock

Yes, I was island-born, under trees too heavy with blossom. Night air was close, perfumed with petal scent, upturned earth and wood-smoke. On still, humid nights, when space was hollowed out, sounds were borrowed from far across the harbour, the clunk of an oar on wooden hull, the idle slap of wavelets on the face of a somnolent beach. By and by the night-breeze came, like fresh water to sea-salty lips, soothing through creaking bamboo groves, fluttering in the poppadum leaf-litter under the breadfruit trees, lulling you back to sleep.

On daytime's shaded shore you whittled at bleached driftwood, dawdled, dreaming of small things. Stringing broken shells and seeds that shone, you stooped to the crunch of coral sand, to the symmetry of fallen flowers, to offerings of curious flotsam. In translucence you swam, skinny jetsam suspended in sapphire and liquid silk.

Further out, where the reef frothed and rumbled at ocean, the rip ran moiré, boiling when it neared *daveta*, the deep narrow passage where coral canyons fell to shadows that wavered deep. And beyond the *daveta*, like bright blue mercury stirring, lay the spread of ocean's vastitude.[6]

Horizon is the islander's pale, the vanishing point over which the smoke of departing ships dissipates into sunset, fading like missed opportunity. Once more you are left behind on the rock, your life marked by that insular legacy of isolation. And each time a ship slipped away from Suva wharf, little by little as the years passed by, you realise now there was an accumulating part of you on the stern deck, waving goodbye.

You had homespun ideas of the places those ships were bound; you'd seen all the pictures in the battered magazines at Sital's, the barber saloon on the tidal banks of Nubukalou Creek where Suva boys went for their short-back-and-sides.

Marooned on the Suva wharf, the crimson-tuniced army band played its last notes and began packing away its triangles and tubas. Sodden strips of pink and green streamers hung despondently from the edge of the wharf, or drifted out in the liner's wake marking the marine pathway to the reef's main passage.

So you shrugged and turned your face from the sea, to where on the high volcanic island of Viti Levu, there was all the boon of nature's bounty. Yes, we were still the lucky ones. We could return to green valleys where tall forests filled with birdcall, to the echo and splash of falling water, where laughter beckoned, bouncing along stream-slicked rocks, to be lost a while more to the lotus.

That was the way it was for us on the volcanic islands; but those highs are not the lot of all Pacific Islanders. The rocks of the atoll-dwellers are semi-submerged, for they exist on the tips of the raggedy coral crowns of submarine mountains. The land is hardly land at all. At high tide, seawater bubbles up into inland lakes and salt-burnt crops are grown in sand. Pigs and chickens jostle with humans above the high-water mark, scavenging below it when low tide bares the reef. Atoll foliage is restricted to a narrow line of scrappy casuarina, spiked pandanus, breadfruit and of course the symbiotic coconut tree, without which there would be no people there at all. Like desert nomads or arctic hunters, atoll-dwellers are humanity at its precarious edge.

I stayed on Funafuti atoll in Tuvalu, in the days before that country's name was forever linked to the perils of rising sea levels. Funafuti; if you're not affected by rock fever, it's a charming place, peopled with laughter and hospitality. Coconut palms surround every house, line every lane, framing the sky with flickering fronds. Delicate white terns hover between the emerald fronds, observing islanders clambering among the coconut crowns, intricate in their adjustment of toddy-bottles that tap the sap of the tree's sugar-rich flowers. The coral-sand yards of the palm-thatched houses are swept clean with brooms made from the spines of coconut leaves.

Invited to dine with a Funafuti family, torchless you leave the palm grove of your waterside abode, to walk down white--sand avenues glowing bright in the moonlight. In humble realms of island hospitality, dinner is served and you discover again the melding of lagoon's harvest with succulent cream of coconut. From root to crown, *Cocos nucifora* is a wondrous marvel of Nature.

Atoll nights are thick with spirits, best avoided as they are usually evil. The spirits can be blamed when life goes awry, when island transgressions are made; for in the obvious transparency of atoll life, who would commit a heinous act, if not under the spell of malevolent spirits?

The Funafuti spirits showed scant interest in my wandering presence, so I felt free to walk alone along those starlit sandy paths. I liked to stroll north, up to where the breadth of the island narrowed to a stone's toss from one shore to the other. Here you could not avoid the vulnerability of atoll life, the precarious creativity of coral, sand and ocean current, caught up like a narrow ecological raft wrecked on a ragged reef. One giant wave and you were atoll jetsam, food for the pelagic fish upon whose relatives you'd so recently dined.

Along that narrow Tuvaluan isthmus, the black dome of equatorial night was hung with all manner of heavenly lights arcing up and over. Crossing the dark parting of the waters, with surf hanging at your shoulder, you saw how the sky was lifted higher by ocean's heaving. To one side, with starlight-flashing crests, the rollers crashed and fizzed on the shore reef, driven on by nocturnal trade winds all the way from South America. To the other, the swollen lagoon spilled through reefs on night's dim horizon, out to where the Pacific rolled away to Asia.

Lifting from the rush and swill of sucking reef, your eyes fixed on the fleeing firmament. And marooned under that untenable starscape, if you began contemplating the impending tragic consequences of anthropogenically-created sea-level rise, you could be quite undone by your solitude.

Under siege from the lonesome swell, it is necessary to hold on tight to the spinning rock if you're to maintain your place. The rock revolves under your puckered feet, turning endlessly over; the porous rock and all the liquid mass in awesome orbit, around a sun that is now somewhere deep down below. As you fly through space in the Funafuti dark, hanging on out there in your nanocorner of a churning universe, appalled by infinity, longing for clarity, you must trust with the blindest of faith to gravity.

It's not just the atolls that isolate; small high islands can be lonely too. If you've ever seen Pitcairn you may know what I mean. I called there two or three times on ocean voyages with my parents in the 1950s, and it's hard to imagine any inhabited island more remote, more lonely, than this mutineer's refuge.

On approach, the rock rises from heaving seas like a tropical Alcatraz. Cresting rolling aquatic hills, the islanders came out to our cargo ships in longboats, working through blue marine valleys towards where we idled. Rope-nets were draped over the sides of our vessels and the islanders clambered up, descendants of Bligh-flogged English seamen and their stolen Tahitian women.

They sold us fresh fruit and flying fish carved of *miro* wood, then loaded precious stores of flour, sugar and fuel down into their whaleboats. On one such occasion, wallowing out there in the ocean blue, we lowered an American to the plunging longboats, one Luis Marden of the National Geographic magazine, on his way to discovering the underwater wreck of the *Bounty*.

The deep-down throb of ship's engines sounded and we were underway again, making course for Panama. But still I have those childhood pictures fixed in the fading albums of my mind. I see the Pitcairners, huddled down there in their boats, left to ocean's cradle, watching us go. And then, before the long pull back to the lonely island, songs of farewell rose from the waves, hymns, and finally the bittersweet, improbable, far-off strains of *In the Sweet Bye and Bye*.

So you're stuck on a rock, where do you go from that realisation? Succumb to the lotus-eating limits of a lush internment, or plot escape to the daunting freedoms of the wide, wide world? Questions of loyalty arise; but then comes the insight that leaving somewhere else was how every islander got here in the first place. Whether on voyaging canoes long ago or in the sailing ships of later years, the gods of wanderlust sent them on their way and drew them hence.

When its in your blood, an island home is like laudanum, heightening senses, lulling fears, beguiling logic, all conspiring to create euphoric dependency. When you're away from it, you crave the aroma of its fecund soil, the addictive scent of night flowers, the soporific sounds of home. And ever after, across the void of sundering seas, in your mind's eye you can read like braille the silhouette of your harbour-town.

In my case, Suva-born fingers run over the lump of the Mau massif, falcon-roosted Voma, the cocks-comb range of Korobasabasaga, the double hump of Korobaba, and our iconic volcanic plug, Joske's Thumb. Neither aging brain nor life on the road can erase this rugged outline: an ever faithful constant, stirring intimations of wistful love.

But if the physical islands must by definition be romantic, there is folly in transposing that romance onto islanders; for like everyone else, they're just people trying to get by. Itinerant scribes, novelists, scriptwriters, shirts wet with the sweat of unrequited tropical nights, have long had it otherwise: the bittersweet of elusive romance being the dominant theme.

Man swims forever in sunset waters to the unattainable allure of island woman. In fantasy's ripe tide, savage peaks thrust from forests fringing the limpid harbour, as a ship sails in from long oceanic deprivations. Waterfalls gush from high cleavages, wetting rocky island flanks. Nut-heavy palms dangle and loll as canoes paddle about, heavy with fruit and suggestion. On the jutting wooden pier, there is a hip-swaying troupe of dancers, portraying what is explained as a polite display of warm welcome.

How often for foreign man, exotic woman and exotic island are one. And yet at the very same time, what is often in the mind of island woman is the exotic prospect of leaving the island! But enough of this daydreaming, my friend, I sense you want something more tangible; so here is a story of how my Suva sister-in-law found her way off the rock.

When pirates arrive, the hackles of island boys go up nearly as fast as the eyebrows of island girls. One day back in 1983, two pirates stepped ashore in Suva. Their golden locks fell on broad shoulders draped in outlandish garb. Golden too were their earrings, their smiles pure pearl, lips rubescent and from their tongues rang the melody of cultivated English vowels.

They swung their cutlasses about the nightclubs and cafés of Victoria Parade and soon their shoulders were draped with more than silken garb. Word got around. These pirates were not gay. They were looking for a boat and they had resources. They weren't saying, but few could now doubt, they were also casting about for female shipmates.

Still there was plenty of speculation: were they drug traffickers, gunrunners, escaped criminals, Lord Lucan in drag? More word got around: they were none of these, they were in fact true adventurers, trained as such in English public schools, and they had marvelous purpose. Once they'd procured an appropriate boat, they were going to sail from Fiji waters, make for the remote island groups of Banks and Santa Cruz, ride the Iron Bottom Sound to Guadalcanal, on and on to Vella Lavella, New Georgia, and off to deepest, darkest Melanesia. And their mission? Upon reaching deepest, darkest Melanesia, they would summon up all the piratical skills of their public school training, to rediscover a fabled tribe of monkey-tailed people.

Okay, let us take a short break. Monkey-tailed people? Cynics may mock, but I have my suspicions the pirates were onto something. Back in the dark ages when I was attending university in Auckland, social anthropology was in fashion. It was a rather languid pursuit, but one in which it was easy enough to pass exams. I chose it as one of my majors, and I distinctly remember reading then of an endogamous tribe inhabiting the sands of Arabia, whose members all possessed hands and feet. Nothing special about that, except that on each of these appendages there dangled six digits. I recall that infanticide ensured no five-digited interlopers polluted the tribe. With considerably less degree of certainty, I feel I may have come across reference to a tribe dwelling somewhere in South East Asia, or perhaps Melanesia. It too was secretive and jealous of its tribal peculiarity: that of sporting spectacularly elongated coccyxes. Thereby hangs a tale!

Fortified by this dubious scholarship, the reader may now be glad to learn that the pirates achieved success in the procurement of a boat. It so happened that a Suva friend of mine had built a yacht that was capable of crossing the ocean. He'd made the yacht for an overseas client, who'd seemed healthy enough when the order was placed, but had carked it when it came time to pay the bill. The pirates stepped into the breach, forked over sufficient doubloons to cover my friend's costs, then drove the yacht deep within the mangroves of one of our local estuaries in order to modify it for the expedition ahead.

The mangrove modifications meant the pirates now had limited time to carouse the gin-joints of Victoria Parade. But still they searched for that which young men have craved since time began. The gaze of one of the pirates had fallen upon my wife's sister, then employed at our venerable museum; a beautiful creature, with a penchant for marine studies and firm resolve to be quit of the rock of her birth before too much more of life passed her by. She was without doubt a winning prospect for the Melanesian run.

The other pirate ran the swagger of his eye across the Suva field, and was reputedly impressed by another of my sisters-in-law, my double-sister-in-law in fact. That may ring a little Appalachian, so let me explain. One of my younger brothers married one of my wife's younger sisters, a tidy classification, anthropologically sound, with no consequent implications of six digit hands or elongated coccyxes.

The brother in question got wind of the pirate's show of interest and the aforementioned hackles began to rise higher. One evening the two sisters were in Suva's picturesque Cable & Wireless building with the latter two of the pirates. With many a wink, he was making an overseas phone-call to England, intent on persuading an uncle to part with sufficient funds to allow the mangrove modifications to continue. The two sisters-in-law were in the telephone booth with him. Meanwhile, down the coconut wireless, word flew along Victoria Parade and fell upon the ears of my brother.

Though slighter in build than the pirate, this brother was described as being 'like a wire' and played first grade rugby for Kadavu, one of the toughest team in the Suva competition. He entered the Cable & Wireless building in a white rage, grabbed the pirate by the collar and connected his fist upon the pirate's head with such force that the mariner spun half way down the considerable length of the highly polished red-tile floor of the Cable & Wireless lobby. The husband and wife departed, leaving the other sister to transport the dazed pirate up to the Colonial War Memorial Hospital to have his head-wound stitched. That is the extent of my brother's involvement in this story, and as for the pirate, he took it all in his magnificent stride.

Next that pirate's gaze fell upon a local beauty of mixed Polynesian, Chinese and European descent. Her young life had been subjected to far more burdens than most, but in looks and nature she was highly blessed. Not particularly drawn to the thought of life on the ocean waves, she was nevertheless keen to be quit of the rock. The pirates conferred with the girls. There was a problem: the local beauty's guardians were not expected to approve of the pirates or their adventure. As for my sister-in-law, her father was a sensible man and had flat-forbidden her to depart on the pirate ship.

And so a cunning plan was devised. The girls would not leave Fiji with the pirates; they would wait until they received word from Honiara, on the island of Guadalcanal. As soon as their fiddling in the Suva mangroves was over, the pirates would hasten thence by sea. Thereafter, upon receiving the signal from Honiara, the girls would resort immediately to the South Pacific's considerable advances in civil aviation.

Since those piratical days I have visited Honiara twice; once before, and once after the emergencies that paralysed the Solomon Islands in the first two years of the twenty-first century. Those tragic times were not the first time, nor will they be the last, when a perfectly viable country falls to its knees under the weight of ethnic hatred and a rich vein of political incompetence.

On my first visit to Guadalcanal I'd read the warning signs. At the airport terminal a large sign in stark red letters: WARNING! Chewing and Spiting of Betelnut is Prohibited within the Terminal Building. I certainly had no intention of being spiteful about betelnut.

Driving into Honiara I saw warning signs everywhere. A tree with heavy wooden sign nailed to it: Keep Your Hands Off From This Coconuts. At the Honiara cultural centre, a bush with no flowers had a laminated paper notice tied to it: Keep Your Hands Off Of These Flowers. The dilapidated cultural centre was closed, its renovations complete according to a sign dedicating it to the ever-lasting friendship between Korea and the Solomon Islands. The centre's swimming pool was a half-empty pit of emerald sludge, home to glumly mating cane-toads and clouds of malarial mosquitoes.

In those times, apart from the rickety wood-and-iron Chinatown across the river, where you could find the Yik Yuk Store and Pretty Store II, the Honiara townscape was low on aesthetic merit. It came down to one long street without pavements, lined by scrappy two-storied concrete blockhouses.

Taking a look around, you could see what Honiara could so easily be, for all the blessings of the Pacific are at its doorstep: live coral reefs right there on the foreshore, at its back, hills bright-hued with flamboyant and Pride-of-India.

But those were tense times and the town's eyes had little interest in Nature's bounty. Its street was full of dark-eyed young men, chewing betelnut, suspicious and watchful, waiting for something to arrive. It arrived a year after my visit, when Honiara became a closed town, patrolled by the paramilitary Malaita Eagle Force, while the rest of the island fell under the gun of the Honiara freedom fighters. Freedom from what? Well may you ask.

I stayed at a waterfront hotel named for Avaro de Mendaña, who sailed over here from Peru in 1568. With his armoured soldiers and Franciscan friars he came to establish Christian settlement in the islands. He failed in that mission, but the Spaniards did leave the place with something lasting, for it was they who named the islands for wise King Solomon.

Now here we were, over four hundred years after Mendaña's clanking conquistadors, and there was urgent need for a dose of Solomon's wisdom.

Ethnocentric madness was about to break over these beautiful islands, provoked by guns coming down from Bougainville's little war to the northwest, and the sight of politicians busy at selling their souls, along with the nation's assets, for pieces of silver.

From the verandah of my Honiara hotel room, I looked down on the coastal indent where the two Suva girls made their rendezvous with the pirates, for it was precisely to this slip of water that the pirate-ship had made its tortuous way from Suva. Here the weary pirates stowed their sails and threw down the anchor, a short row from the collection of sheds housing the yacht club of Honiara.

By the time of their arrival in the Solomons, the pirates were in disarray. They'd fallen out, in a way that only those confined-to-each-other's-company-on-a-small-boat-for-months-on-end can do. The medicine cabinet of the pirate ship had been emptied, the galley was gutted, the engine was broken, in fact the only remaining bright spot was the imminence of the arrival of the Suva maidens. About this juncture, it would be fair to surmise that the secrets of the monkey-tailed tribe were destined to remain secure.

The girls had packed their life-belongings into the bags that accompanied them on their flight from Suva. They'd checked over everything they would need for wherever their travels might take them: passports, short life's savings, only their favourite clothes, treasured knick-knacks, lucky charms, photographs of their loved ones and the island they were finally leaving behind. Yes, they were off the rock, heading down life's broad main and the Solomons were just a start.

Arriving in Honiara, they stowed their bags on the pirate ship, and rowed ashore for a celebratory drink at the yacht club. Clad in flimsy sarongs, barefoot on the beach with their buccaneers, they sipped at draughts of freedom.

I needed a closer look at the sipping spot, so I left my hotel verandah and walked around to the hub of Honiara's yachting scene. Heavy security at the entrance signed me in as a visitor, and I walked into the open-walled clubhouse.

Though lapped by the waves of Iron Bottom Sound, there wasn't a lot nautical about the place. It looked more like a watering hole for the sellers, dealmakers and contractors of the rip-it-all-down timber industry. Half the rest of town seemed to be in there, smoking, yarning, drinking rum and beer; a mixture of chocolate Melanesians and red-faced whities. The TV hanging from the ceiling was playing a cricket test between New Zealand and Australia. Clutching SolBrew lagers in neoprene holders, a semi-circle of overweight drinkers watched on, the red uglies snarling endorsement whenever an Australian batsman hit a run.

I took my SolBrew out onto the yacht club jetty, looking up the coast towards Tulagi and the passage the Americans had called The Slot. Back in 1942 the US Navy was operating out there in support of troops of the Allied forces who were in combat with the imperial forces of Nippon in the steaming forests of Guadalcanal. And it was out there that the navy took one of its greatest ever poundings. Each night the so-called Tokyo Express came screaming down The Slot, the Japanese navy proving itself adept with deadly effect at night fighting. But the Japanese took a hammering too; they lost the equivalent of an entire peacetime fleet to Solomon waters and the rusting hulks from those nautical battles still litter the Honiara waterfront.

Standing out on the yacht club jetty, the only ship I could see moving out there now was a monolithic Japanese car-carrier, come to offload second and third-hand Japanese cars on the islanders. A local fisherman, paddling a tiny outrigger-canoe, pitched up and down in the giant carrier's wake.

Turning back to the yacht club shed, I imagined the Suva girls quaffing their celebratory drinks. Then, somewhat ruefully, I considered the short shrift the road-gods had cooked up for them. Even as the young women lifted elbows in toasts to the adventures ahead, the distracted sailors became aware of a turn for the worse in the weather.

But weather-eyes were dulled, for like Ulysses strapped to his mast, the Englishmen were bedazzled by the beauty of their shipmates-to-be. All the while at their backs, the sea began jumping to a crazy dance, the wind running up with such force that rowing back to the yacht was soon impossible. A fast-moving hurricane had torn down The Slot like the ghost ships of the Tokyo Express, unleashing itself on the undefended shores of Honiara.

With the full weight of the predicament descending upon them, the pirates rolled their eyes to the racing clouds and cursed the heavens as only desperate men can do. There was naught to be done now but look on with tortured gaze. Through the searing lash of wind and horizontal rain, they saw how the storm came on, lifting up their bark, staving it in, shattering that worthy Suva hull and driving it to the depths of Iron Bottom Sound.

Thus came to a definitive end the search for the monkey-tailed people. When the Solomon storm passed off to the east and the ocean's surge abated, the flotsam-line of Honiara's storm-eroded beach was searched and found to bear nothing of value. The battered foursome were left with naught but their lives and the sarongs wrapped wet about their bodies.

Well might the pirates have done an Othello, foaming at the mouth, and by and by broken out in savage madness at what pernicious fate had devised. But forget them, what of the girls? Surely this meteorological twist of fate had delivered them the worst of journeys' beginnings. Like the departed storm, the shocked curses and tears abated. But what were they to do, now that all their worldly possessions were blown away?

It was a time to consider the lilies of the field, and along the shores of Guadacanal could be heard,

> In accents clear and still,
> Above the storms of passion,
> The murmurs of self-will.[7]

Good-hearted Honiara people came forward and found ways to help them out of the place with spirits intact. In truth, it took my sister-in-law a while to rebound from the loss of all her worldly goods; but all was not in vain, for she was off the rock and, fueled anew by murmuring self-will, went on from there to many a better thing. She has a Buddhist bent and now sits on high benches in the halls of Australia's academia.

As for the local beauty, she and her pirate flew out of Honiara to a retreat in Bali to undertake recuperation, eventually making their way on to his London home. He being a true adventurer was not much at hand, so she set to exploring England and before too long found herself married to a wealthy English Lord, for whom she produced fine heirs. All who have met her since say she is quite the paragon of what a lady should be. She too was well off the rock.

Her Honiaran pirate, he who crossed the floor of the Cable & Wireless building spinning on his back, also came through to better things. He evolved into something of an adventurer-celebrity, featured in glossy magazines and television networks that devoured up his discourse with greedy ear; until, strangest of all these fates, as a result of some royal marital readjustments, he became the brother-in-law of the future King of England.

And thus our story endeth, dear friend, if I remember King Harry's words aright: with all the while the gentlemen of England still a-bed, crisp-sheeted, thinking themselves fortunate they were neither in the phone-booths of Suva nor the storms of Honiara, and no doubt holding their manhoods however it pleaseth them.[8]

MENU

Avocats Britannia

———

Selle d'Agneau Dubarry
Petits Pois au Beurre
Pommes Fondants

———

Salade

———

Bombe Glacée aux Mangoes

DIMANCHE, LE 31 OCTOBRE, 1982   SUVA

Yo-ho-ho

Travellers all, we have a mentor in Robert Louis Stevenson, he who in the adversity of frail health took to the high roads by donkey and sailed in schooners to far islands; he who advised old and young that 'we are on our last cruise', and gave us the dictum of the road: that to travel hopefully is a better thing than to arrive, and the true success is to labour.

Noqu i tau, my dear companion, if you happen to notice my bias in most things to do with RLS, it is because my Scottish father imprinted it so in my boyhood days.[9] Ian Thomson, what a man he was! 'One out of the box,' they say of him. With rarely a hard word uttered, he led by example, a do-as-I-do man, and it was our privilege to follow. His seven sons and one daughter will all attest to that.

Within the bosom of family, from the tone of his voice when he read us our bedtime stories, his love for the books of RLS was obvious.

> Fifteen men on The Dead Man's Chest -
> Yo-ho-ho, and a bottle of rum!
> Drink and the devil had done for the rest -
> Yo-ho-ho, and a bottle of rum![10]

Yo-ho-ho brings on another gracious reprieve! I ken a mellow voice as my father reads on, filtering down through the fluttered years, I still hear it clear, that soft brogue of a middle class Scot.

Now I recall my siblings hunkered around, all ears, in bunks and beds in Raicakau, the wood-planked ramble of a house that was home during the golden years of a Suva childhood. We are silent because our father has told us to be so and because we too love the moment and the story. Our white cotton mosquito nets are tucked in and the room is dark except for the pool of light by the window where he reads. Outside, under the blazing starscape, fruit bats whistle and screech, flapping rubbery wings among the broad scratchy leaves of the breadfruit trees. The infant siblings are already asleep in one of the other communal bedrooms and Dad is reading to the 'big boys', though none of us has yet crossed the frontier of puberty.

From past readings, we have become well acquainted with the rum-quaffing mutineers of the *Hispaniola* and know the rough voices our father has chosen for each of them. But he has reserved a most sympathetic voice for the character of Doctor Livesey, and we pick up right away who is speaking as he questions our young hero, the narrator Jim Hawkins,

> 'Is this Ben Gunn a man?' he asked.
> "I do not know, sir,' said I. 'I'm not very sure whether he's sane.'
> 'If there's doubt about the matter, he is,' returned the doctor. 'A man who has been three years biting his nails on a desert island, Jim, can't expect to appear as sane as you or me. It doesn't lie in human nature. Was it cheese you said he had a fancy for?'
> 'Yes, sir, cheese,' I answered.
> 'Well, Jim,' says he, 'just see the good that comes of being dainty in your food. You've seen my snuff-box, haven't you? And you never saw me take snuff; the reason being that in my snuff-box I carry a piece of Parmesan cheese – a cheese made in Italy, very nutritious. Well that's for Ben Gunn!'

When the chapter comes to an end, and the book is being closed for another night, one of us will plead for just a few more pages, for we know we can usually squeeze a weary encore from our reader. And then when our wish had been consummated, the reading light is doused and Dad's footsteps fade off across the creaking boards to join our mother at the far end of the house.

There is much to consider here on the edge of sleep: three years on a desert island would have been tough going, eating nothing but berries and the occasional goat. And then there was that English doctor's snuff-box. But much more mysterious than snuff was the cheese called Parmesan, for in those Fiji days, the only cheese we had any experience of at all was the rubbery processed cheese shipped up from Australia in Kraft's little blue boxes. Clearly the wider world held much in store.

All things are connected and through his great uncle, David McCaig, my father had a very tenuous connection with RLS. There is this from a Glasgow Herald cutting in my possession, faded now for it dates from 1932,

> An acquaintance of Robert Louis Stevenson died in Glasgow yesterday in the person of David McCaig, Barrland Street, who sailed in Pacific waters for many years and was marine superintendent at Sydney for the Union Steamship Company of New Zealand. He retired from that post 22 years ago and returned to Glasgow, his native city, where he had begun his career as a marine engineer.

David McCaig, who was 88 years of age when he died, sailed for 40 years between Sydney, Samoa and San Francisco. During Robert Louis Stevenson's residence in Samoa, the two Scots became acquainted. Thereafter whenever McCaig landed in Samoa he'd be carrying with him various requirements of the novelist, obtained on his behalf in Sydney or San Francisco.

In the early years of the Union Steamship Company, it was Glaswegians like David McCaig who endured the throb and hiss of the engine rooms powering the rolling steamers across the seven seas. They delivered vessels from the shipyards of the Clyde to Antipodean harbours, and if it was their want, many stayed on to keep those engines turning.

David McCaig sailed out in 1879 as chief engineer of the *Rotomahana*. In his wake were five of his nephews, all to be engineers in the company's fleet, one of them chief of the *Maunganui* and the *Tahiti*, another the *Monowai's* chief. I must now give you a taste, my friend, of the pride they had in their ships, for in the Pacific these sleek ocean-crossers were marvels of the age.

When they ordered the *Rotomahana*, Union Steamships wanted a ship that would be far in advance, in terms of speed and appointments, of any other in

29

the inter-colonial trade. Thus she was the first merchant steamer in the world to be built of mild steel and be fitted with bilge keels, the results of which became apparent when she earned the sobriquet 'Greyhound of the Pacific'.

Her well-raked funnel and masts, her shapely clipper-ship bow with its handsome figurehead a Maori princess, a jib boom and decorative scroll-work all gave her the appearance of a graceful steam yacht. For some years, like most of the company's early steamers, she was rigged with yards on her foremast and carried a good spread of canvas with favourable winds. The Glasgow newspapers at the time of her trials described the *Rotomahana* as the 'finest specimen of the shipbuilder's and engineer's skill ever turned out by W. Denny and Brothers at Dumbarton.'

On her steaming trials over the measured mile off Skelmorlie, at her loaded draught displacement of 2425 tons, the *Rotomahana* attained an average speed of more than 15½ knots. Leaving London on August 8, 1879, the *Rotomahana*, commanded by Captain T. Underwood, her chief engineer Mr David McCaig, made the fastest passage out to New Zealand recorded up to that time and for some years after.[11]

As the finest and fastest passenger ship in Australasian waters, the *Rotomahana* would have been a grand sight swinging at anchor off the palm-fringed shores of Levuka, Suva and Apia. High up on verdant Samoan hill-slopes, looking out from his Vailima verandah, I've no doubt RLS would have been uplifted whenever he spied the *Rotomahana* steaming up the Upolu coast, rounding the aquamarine passage into Apia's harbour.

Saddling up his favourite horse Jack, the writer would have wasted no time in plodding down through coconut plantations to the Apia beach to meet his marine compatriot and take delivery of those 'various requirements'. And sometimes, I surmise, McCaig would have hired a horse and cart and taken the trouble to lug the requested chattels up the rutted road to Vailima.

A century later, on my own trek to Vailima, it was easy to imagine my forbear on the verandah in an easy chair, shooting the breeze with Tusitala, sharing in the spirit of a too-distant homeland. 'Whisky and freedom gang th'gither,' Burns told us, and as Scots they'd have shared a wee dram, and they'd have known their whisky too. RLS expressed it thus,

The king o' drinks, as I conceive it, Talisker, Isla or Glenlivet!

In his retirement years back in Glasgow, the grizzled *Rotomahana* chief had so many mariner's tales to tell that eventually they'd have been but half-listened to by those whose fate it was to never leave the banks o' Clyde. But there was one in his wider family in whom he had a most faithful disciple.

McCaig's grandnephew was young Ian Thomson and the boy could not hear enough of those South Sea yarns. On *dreich* Glasgow days, with a coal fire reeking in the *lum*[12], there was sunshine in the old man's memories, crashing surf on coral reefs, great green volcanic islands with harbours crossed by fruit-filled canoes. And of all those fragrant harbours, said David McCaig, one was the finest of all. 'There's one place on earth ye'll have tae see, laaddie. Gi'e me back my years and thaat's where'd I spend my life, on the shores of Suva harbour, in the bonnie isles o' Fiji.'

When my father graduated with a masters degree from Glasgow University at the age of twenty-one, he was summoned to the Colonial Office in London to be informed he'd been chosen as an administrative cadet in His Majesty's Colonial Service. When asked where he'd prefer to be posted, his reply was emphatic, 'Fiji.'

'Where else?'

'Only Fiji.'

He was advised to return north of the border to think again, for postings to Fiji were rare and the Colonial Office positions to be filled were in Africa and Asia. But a few months later the moving finger twirled and his fate was writ. In January 1941, a convoy set sail for New Zealand via the Panama Canal and on board the cargo vessel *Taranaki* was a keen young Scotsman, following his destiny to Fiji.

With war raging in Europe and U-boats taking their dread toll on Allied shipping, the convoy took the high road to Panama, amongst the icebergs of the northern Atlantic. As they skirted the wintry coasts of Greenland and Labrador, my father was assigned to look-out duties, perched out on the flying-bridge with a pair of binoculars stuck to his frigid face, scanning bleak seas for periscopes.

Back in Scotland was his older sister Helen, with whom he enjoyed a deep friendship. They did not know it then, but with all the world's oceans dividing, they would see little of each other thereafter. She wrote in her diary on 16th March 1941, 'The war is so serious and never so depressing with my dear wee brother so far far away.' He was on that day, about as far away from Scotland as you could be on this planet, for three days earlier he'd finally arrived in Fiji, having picked up passage from Auckland to Suva on the SS *Mariposa*.

Over four decades of Fiji fortune lay ahead of him, and I use the word fortune in the sense of a life well lived, not in the pecuniary sense, for accumulation of personal assets was never his goal. In that regard, in remembrance of his chosen way, the memorial window erected to him and my mother in St Andrews Church in Suva in 2008, reflects a lesson from the sermon on the mount that he held dear,

> No man can serve two masters: for either he will hate the one, and love the other; or else he will hold to the one, and despise the other. Ye cannot serve God and mammon. Therefore I say unto you, take no thought for your life, what ye shall eat, or what ye shall drink; nor yet for your body what ye shall put on ... consider the lilies of the field, how they grow; they toil not, neither do they spin. And yet I say unto you, that even Solomon in all his glory was not arrayed like one of these.[13]

In essence, from the time he made his life-shaping choices in Glasgow until his last day on this earth, my father's bright enthusiasm, fused in the commonality of man, was inspiring. A generous, diligent, trustworthy man, he was utterly genuine in caring for the welfare of others and was ever considerate of their opinions. His was a character and a life governed by a quiet Christian faith.

When young Ian Thomson stepped down the gangplank onto the Suva Wharf in 1941, his Fiji career commenced as *aide de camp* to the Colony's governor, at a time when Government House was on a war footing. Many years later in times of peace, he would be back at Government House acting on a number of occasions as independent Fiji's governor-general and commander-in-chief.

In the interim, as a district officer and divisional commissioner he was to spend his days and nights in little boats attending to duties in the outer islands, or tramping muddy tracks to meetings in the villages of the hill country. He would become a recognised authority on Fijian custom, language and tribal land holdings, and would eventually be chosen to lead government business in the Colony's legislative council.

After Fiji's independence in 1970, he was made the chairman of the Fiji sugar industry, and of the coconut industry, and of the country's economic development board. Then as chairman of Air Pacific, he would steer the national airline out of insolvency into many years of prosperity. Throughout this great Fiji adventure, he was married to a beautiful Suva lady, who bore their eight children, all of whom adored him 'til his dying day.

But first Ian Thomson had to survive active service in the Pacific War. In December 1941, in the weeks before Japan attacked Pearl Harbour, he was accompanying Sir Harry Luke, Governor of Fiji, on a tour of the Line Islands in the governor's boat, the RCS *Viti*.[14] As well as his Fijian gubernatorial duties, Sir Harry was Britain's High Commissioner for the Western Pacific, which gave him administrative responsibility for the Solomon Islands, the New Hebrides, the Gilbert and Ellice Islands, the Line Islands and Pitcairn Island.

Receiving reports of Japanese naval activity in the area, Sir Harry and his young *aide de camp* boarded a lumbering seaplane at Canton Island to fly back to Fiji. It was thus that my father flew on what turned out to be the last of the southbound flights of the Pan American Airways clipper service, for the following day Japan's forces struck Honolulu.[15]

With the outbreak of the Pacific War, and having completed military officer's training prior to his departure from Scotland, my father requested a transfer to the Fiji Infantry Regiment. His wish was granted, and while this is not the place for a full description of his war service, as I write these words I'm looking at an extract from the Fiji Times of 10th September 1946 describing the presentation to him of the MBE (Mil). There is a faded photo too of a parade on Suva's palm-fringed Albert Park, the Grand Pacific Hotel in the background, the befeathered governor on a plinth, leaning forward to pin the gong on my father's twenty-six year old chest. The extract reads,

> This award is officially stated to be for devotion to duty on active service. During the five months the 3rd Battalion, Fiji Infantry Regiment, served at Bougainville, this officer held the appointment of Adjutant. From March to June 1944, the battalion carried out five major operations and Lieutenant Thomson carried out his duties with the greatest credit, coolness and bravery.

On 17th April 1944, during an action on the East-West Trail, Torokina, he contributed largely to the rallying of a portion of the battalion under fire. At Mawaraka, Bougainville, during a unit operation, at considerable personal risk, he established communication with an advance company when communications by wireless had been lost.

What that citation doesn't mention is the ferocity of the jungle fighting at Mawaraka, where Sukanaivalu won his posthumous VC, and of how the 3rd Battalion had to withdraw to the beach at dusk to be uplifted by American landing crafts, all in the heat of battle. My father was then twenty-four years old and it fell to him to organise that beach evacuation, by which some six hundred battle-wearied men made it safely onto the landing craft. The young adjutant was the last man off the beach.[16]

On his return from the Solomons campaign, he was fluent in the Fijian language and was a made-man within the Fijian hierarchy. The dominant

Fijian of the twentieth century, Ratu Sir Lala Sukuna, had overseen the recruitment of the 3rd Battalion of the Fiji Infantry Regiment and had personally given my father's entry the nod. It was fitting that towards the end of Ratu Sukuna's life, on his retirement from the chairmanship of the Native Lands Commission, the custodian of Fijian communal land rights, Ratu Sukuna did Ian Thomson the honour of selecting him as his replacement.[17]

Early in my father's military service, he had been second-in-command of C Co, 3 Bn, FIR, with Ratu Edward Cakobau in command. They shared a tent and went through the thick and thin of military life in Fiji and Bougainville, with a lifetime's friendship ensuing on the back of that wartime service, their district administration days, the raising of bevies of sons, working together on the Native Lands Commission, and thereafter in the governing of Fiji in the years that approached and followed the country's independence. When my parents married in Suva in 1945, Ratu Edward represented my father's Scottish parents at the wedding and spoke for them. Though he was the son of the king of Tonga and a Fijian lady of the very highest rank, Ratu Edward claimed in his speech that he was Scotch, by absorption. And when Ratu Sir Edward Cakobau, by then the Deputy Prime Minister of independent Fiji, passed away in 1973, my father went to the chiefly island of Bau to deliver the eulogy at his old friend's funeral.

A week before my father died in his eighty-ninth year, I received an email from him in which he talked about dear Fijian friends who had predeceased him. In the email his shorthand mention of their names is explained as follows: 'Ratu Tui' refers to Ratu Edward Cakobau, 'Ratu JLVS' refers to Ratu Lala Sukuna, 'Ratu GKC' to Ratu George Cakobau, and 'Ratu PKG' to Ratu Penaia Ganilau,

> Ratu Tui was like an elder brother to me. He and Adi Lala's father[18] opened a lot of doors for me into understanding the ways of Fijian society. I owe much to their friendship and willingness to speak their minds to me about their thoughts concerning Fijian progress. I came to understand why leaders like Ratu JLVS wanted time – years – for Fijian society to adjust to the ways of the capitalist

world. I took it as a great compliment when Deryck Scarr, in his biography of Ratu Sukuna, said that Ratu JLVS had selected me to succeed him because I thought as he did. For that I have to thank both Ratu GKC and Ratu Tui. Of course to that duo I must add my friendship with Ratu PKG, who is aptly described by you in *Kava in the Blood* as the type of guy you would follow to the ends of the Earth.

Ian Thomson's life was captured within these great friendships, forged as they were in the furnace of war and beaten true on many anvils of peace.

1966 was a tumultuous year for my parents. My father was by then acting as chief secretary and leader of government business in Fiji's legislative assembly and he regarded his commitment to Fiji's progress as his life's work. But the winds of change were blowing him off course, for decisions were being made in far-away London with the result that he would be posted to the Caribbean to govern the British Virgin Islands.

In Fiji there was outrage that someone so experienced in the administration and customs of the country should be replaced by an Englishman with no background at all in the Islands. On 15th November, the Fiji Times ran an editorial headlined 'Cause for Strong Protest' describing the 'shock and dismay' the people of Fiji felt at the news,

> It is particularly deplorable that this should happen at the time when the colony is starting out on a new era of responsible self-government, when Mr Thomson's detailed knowledge of Fiji, the respect and affection he commands from every section of the community, and his proved administrative ability can be of inestimable value.

> It is therefore an act of folly on the part of the Colonial Office to remove at this stage a man so uniquely qualified to interpret the wishes and attitudes of the people of Fiji, and so clearly fitted to be a member of a harmonious and effective Government team.

The Fijian language paper Nai Lalakai ran a similar editorial and Ratu KKT Mara, who upon Independence Day in 1970 became Fiji's prime minister, delivered a remarkable letter to the Colony's governor, saying that Fiji's governing parliamentary party had directed by unanimous vote that he address the governor regarding my father's posting,

> In common with the vast majority of people of all races in this country, we have learned with deep dismay that Mr Thomson is likely to be transferred from Fiji. We of course remind ourselves that Mr Thomson is a civil servant; and that matters concerning his appointment, transfer, or promotion are rightly reserved to Your Excellency and the Secretary of State, and in certain circumstances to Her Majesty The Queen.
>
> The concern we feel so strongly relates to Mr Thomson's function as a cog in the parliamentary machine. His long and successful experience at the centre of government and in the districts fits him incomparably, in our view, to assist us in the challenging task of providing effective government under the new constitution. That the challenge will be successfully met we have not the slightest doubt, but the task will be made measurably more difficult if Mr Thomson's very considerable talents as an administrator and adviser are not at our disposal.
>
> We wish to convey to Your Excellency our strong conviction that his transfer at this transitional period would be most inopportune, and against the best interests of the government and the country. We therefore respectfully seek Your Excellency's intervention to secure that Mr Thomson remain in Fiji as a member of the government team, to which we regard him as being for the time being indispensable.[19]

That was quite a vote of confidence, but no doubt in London the Secretary of State for the Colonies, upon receipt of the text of this letter, would have seen to it that my father's transfer from Fiji was expedited with immediate effect. This was a time when Britain was jettisoning ties with remaining colonies, and men of Thomson's ilk, the tried and true of the old order, were not the new brooms London wanted for the severing task at hand. At this stage my father was still only 46 years of age.

At the fringe of these events, the incoming commander of the Fiji Military Forces, a well-liked Kiwi soldier, was making his introductory rounds in Suva,

> I enjoyed our call on the Chief Secretary, Ian Thomson, a Scot who had married into a well-known Fiji family and who endeared himself to the Fijians by serving with the 3rd Battalion of the Fiji Regiment in the Solomons. Ian totally identified himself with Fiji and was one of the most popular colonial servants, with all races, I met during my tour in Fiji. Unfortunately, he was only holding the appointment of Chief Secretary on a temporary basis pending the arrival of Peter Lloyd, the son of the Head of the Colonial Office. Ian Thomson had been advised that he was to be posted to the Virgin Islands, which caused some amusement among the locals as the Thomson family included six sons![20]

This reference to the happy interlude lying ahead of us in the West Indies requires only the correction that we were seven, not six, sons, and that demographically speaking, there were about as many virgins left in the BVI on our departure as there were on our arrival.

We took up residence in Government House, Road Town, British Virgin Islands in early 1967. Road Town is strung along the shores of a bay cutting deep into the hills of Tortola, the balmy island of turtle doves so-named by Christopher Columbus when he sailed through in 1493. When we lived there, before the days of financial centres, mass tourism and the loss of harbour to civic reclamations, the narrow main road followed the harbour foreshore, winding under the frangipani and flamboyants around the base of the rocky point upon which Government House was built.

From the white stucco verandahs of Government House, one looked out over two ancient cannon, great thickets of pink and mauve bougainvillea, and across the shaded tennis court to the blue-on-blue reaches of the Sir Francis Drake Channel. On the far side of the channel lay the flat-topped bulk of the original Dead Chest Island on which the pirate Blackbeard marooned fifteen men. Yo-ho-ho and a bottle of rum!

This was a very different place to the Pacific Islands. For one thing there were no indigenes left, and the islands and their place-names carried the nomenclature of the incoming cultures of imperial quests, religious imagery, piracy and slavery. The islands of Jost Van Dyke named for the Dutch pirate, Virgin Gorda named for the pregnant virgin, and the tumbled rock isle of Fallen Jerusalem come to mind, as do the nautically derived Pull and Be Damm' Point, Man o' War Hill and Free Bottom.

I wrote the words 'happy interlude' because along with my siblings, we had a good time living it up in the Caribbean. I was between school and university and spent most of my days in the BVI studying the finer points of rum-fueled jump-ups, funji music and the risqué lyrics of The Mighty Sparrow.

But for my father, for the first time in his career, work was unfulfilling. He applied himself with all his usual diligence and enthusiasm, but he had become used to a public service where the link between government officers and the community was trustful and committed to the communal good. He found that absent in the BVI, where it appeared the ethos was every man for himself.

Shortly after Fiji's independence in 1970, Prime Minister Mara came to the Caribbean to meet my father and invite him back to service in Fiji. So, at the age of fifty-one, Ian Thomson resigned as the Caribbean's last permanent and pensionable officer of Her Majesty's Colonial Service, and returned home to Fiji.

He died suddenly on 13th March 2008 in Edinburgh. We buried him next to my mother on the shores of Loch Feochan on the wild coast of Argyll in a large piece of Taveuni tapa cloth. On the other side of the world, when the stipulated *vaka bogi drau* was up, we held a memorial service for him in St

Andrews, the Suva church in which he had served as an elder for so many decades of his living years.[21]

The Fiji Times ran an editorial headlined 'Salute to Sir Ian'.[22] Calling him a true son of Fiji, the editorial talked of his patient integrity, the great love and affection he had for the common people of Fiji, and the 'tremendous and deserved respect' they bestowed on him. Obituaries fulsome in praise were carried in the Sydney Morning Herald, the New Zealand Herald, the Scotsman, the Glasgow Herald and The Times of London. In a tribute published in the Fiji Times, the former vice-president of Fiji, Ratu Joni Madraiwiwi, wrote,

> Sir Ian personified the best in the British colonial civil servant. In manner and bearing he was princely, with an approachability that was as reassuring as it was genuine. It was complemented by a voice that evoked dignity and gravitas. Among Fijians, Sir Ian was said to embody *nai vakarau vakaturaga*, the chiefly manner asserted by so many yet practiced by only a few.

I will end here, for a son should not write his father's biography, especially when in sixty years of filial devotion, that father never once gave cause for a blink in the gaze of respect and adoration in which he was held. I will leave off now with a footnote: to those that aspire to high standards of human decency within public service, there is this advice from Goethe,

> That which thy fathers have bequeathed to thee, earn it anew if thou wouldst possess it.

Verata · Matanola · Namatakula · Namuya · Black Rock · Queens Road · Namaka · Kings Road ·
Tunania · Bilo Battery · Nalletua Cave · Korovisilou · Yanuca · Vaileva ·
Serua · Navroga · Sanaei · Vuda · Thkavesi · Vunimago · Navuso ·
Lovonilase · Laucala Bay · Jotualevu · Wailoaloa · Martintar ·
Nabukalou Creek · Turner's Bridge · Raiwaqa · Bay of Islands · Domain · Bekana ·
Valuna Hill · Nukubalavu · Korobaba · Lodoni · Qoresala · Ellington Wharf ·
Valelevu · Raiwaqau · Makoro · Mabua · Joske's Thumb ·
Matawa Bay · Keiyasi · Tamavua · Colo-i-Suva · Sawani · Vainimala ·
Yaqara · Tokoriki · Koro · Tuvana · Komo · Tavuki · Nasau · Buca Bay ·
Tavua · Vinisea · Fulaga · Yadua · Sonaisali · Matamanoa · Komo ·
Yatuwaqa · Muanivatu · Batiki · Kanacea · Malolo · Naomia · Matagi ·
Lavulavu · Namaka · Bureta · Waiyele · Matei · Nausori Highlands · Oneata ·
Albert Park · Prince Charles Park · Lawaqa · Thomson Park · Churchill Park ·
Mamanuca · Yasawa Islands · Matacawalevu · Vidawai · Nalasna · Taorm ·
Taunovo · Waln Bay · Pacific Harbour · Vatukoula · Lobano · Naimolimoli · Kese ·
Wainimakutu · Walbagi · Korobasabasaga Range · Medrausucu · Naitata ·
Sonasau · Mana · Toloya · Ogea · Naca · Navunidabi · Nacoqo · Tokotoko ·
Viseisei · Cevai-ra · Sotoya · Wainuna · Navola · Mosquito Island · Waikitolevu ·
Salialevu · Bouma · Soqulu · Vunidawa · Des Voeux Peak · Wairiki · Yacata ·
Maralyawa · Namuamua · Nakavika · Nailuaba · Yadua · Yaqeta · Kaibu ·
Ringgold Islands · Nanuku Passage · Lomaithoro · Cobia ·
Nabouwalu · Seaqaqa · Udu Pt · Yaqotaki ·
Qamea · Makogai · Waiqele · Taveuni ·
Vunidawa · Mt Victoria · Laucala ·
Waigani · Nakelo · Vanivaivai ·
Nadarivatu · Rakiraki · Lomary ·
Waldina · Wainimala · Tavua ·
Wainikoroiluva · Waimanu-i ·
Namosi · Nailesini · Tailevu ·
Frigate Passage · Rewa River ·
Rat Tail Passage · Cakaudrove ·
Lomaiviti · Macuata ·
Koro Sea · Bligh Water ·
Vanua Levu · Viti Levu · Kia ·
Matololailai · Rotuma ·
Nakabasaga · Yasawa ·
Kabara · Ono Ilau · Waya ·
Makuluva · Toberua · Gabi ·
Boqa · Makaluva · Nairai ·
Kadavu · Ono · Vatu Lele ·
Levuka · Savusavu · Bua ·
Naqelelevu · Cikobia ·
Lakeba · Nayau · Vanua Vatu ·
Ovalau · Koro · Wakaya · Gau ·
Lami · Wainadoi · Namosi · Gau ·
Sabeto · Nadi · Cuvu · Sigatoka · Korotogo ·
Lautoka · Ba · Vaileka · Korovou · Nausori · Narinu · Samabula · Wai ·
Cumming St · Thomson St · Mark St · Waimanu Rd · Gordon St · Macgregor Rd ·
Berkeley Crescent · Domain Rd · Cakobau Hill · Nasese Rd · Richards Rd ·
Vatureikuke · Nacoa · Bulileka · Malau · Naduri · Labasa · Brokoti · Siberia ·
Waiyevo · Nagelesele · Waitavala · Jomosomo · Qeleni · Vuna · Wainaqara ·
Deuba · Nailoaitou · Velwaluka · Nagaributa · Nabukavesi · Nagara · Nau ·
Braiba · Nasere · Muanikau · Narova · Veiuto · Flagstaff · Maigagi · Suva ·

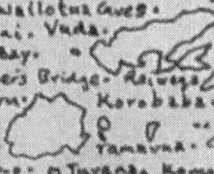

Galib
Vanua
Vomo
Bau
Ra
Koro
Mago
Moturiki
Kavoleau

Inwrought With Affection

Have you heard of the Fiji Mermaid? If you followed the American TV show *X Files*, you might have seen the episode in which one such features. One hundred and fifty years ago, BT Barnum beguiled the people of North America with his sensational 'Feejee Mermaid', thereby spawning a shoal of sideshow imitations. The original was in reality the upper body of a monkey attached to the tail of a fish; but no matter, the Feejee Mermaid has since worked itself into the American lexicon as the epitome of carny oddities, the doyen of those dusty fakes lurking at the rear of curiosity shops.

The Feejee Mermaid! Bravo BT, but why Fiji? It seems that somewhere along the way Fiji got the reputation of being fantastic, in the whimsical sense. Maybe we inadvertently brought it upon ourselves, so far away from the rest of the world we thought what we did went unnoticed. But occasionally it was. By way of example, in 1975 when I was a postgraduate student at Cambridge University, fellow students brought this story on the front page of the Guardian newspaper of January 25th to my attention.

LOVE AND LUNCH

> Gold miners in Fiji want a 30-minute midday 'sex break.' Their union secretary said yesterday that a husband exhausted at the end of the day could not fulfill his marital obligations. Bachelors were not included in the claim. 'We don't want to overdo this,' he said.

I thought that sounded pretty rational, but those pesky Cantabrians reckoned otherwise and you can only imagine how they overworked it.

The newspapers back home weren't making it any easier. The Fiji Sun won Punch magazine's prize for Headline of the Year for a brain-exploding effort in 1977. Rapprochement between Egypt and Israel was underway, when

President Sadat undertook his historic surprise visit to Israel. Lasting world peace was becoming a distinct possibility. This stunning good news was announced by The Fiji Sun in a banner headline covering half the newspaper's front page in black ink,

SADAT FLIES TO EGYPT

I've always thought Fiji was fantastic, even when an army coup in 1987 meant I had to fantasise about it through the bars of a prison cell. But then you already know, my friend, as one who has gone forth and multiplied, that the relationship with home is always going to be complex. Stay or leave, love or loathe, stagnate or change, these delicate balances are coupled with the inevitable demise of most every material thing you love.

Be that as it may, Fiji is always the greatest place on this planet, and in my mind I'm in the grinning rugby stands with all those others who love it, chanting, 'Fiji, Fiji, Fiji!'

I was born in the first half of the last century, into an empire upon which the sun supposedly never set. But India had gained her independence the previous year, and even if it was to take colonies like Fiji another two decades to don the full trappings of nationhood, the game was well and truly up for the British Empire by the time I made my appearance. The golden years of my youth seem at times to have been side-lit by a sun that sat just above the horizon. Considering that slanting light, it's not clear to me what caused my love for Fiji to be so intense. Was it the setting of the colonial culture within which my family had lived for so many generations, or was it the rising of the brave new nation in whose opening acts I was to play out my minor roles?

When I read these words from the pen of Mary Ann Evans, they take me back with a rush to a Suva house called Raicakau,

> A human life, I think, should be well rooted in some spot of a
> native land, where it may get the love of tender kinship for the

face of the earth, for the labours men go forth to, for the sounds and accents that haunt it, for whatever will give that early home a familiar, unmistakable difference amidst the future widening of knowledge: a spot where the definiteness of early memories may be inwrought with affection and kindly acquaintance with all neighbours, even to the dogs and donkeys, may spread, not by sentimental effort and reflection, but as a sweet habit of the blood.[23]

Raicakau was a rambling wooden bungalow set amongst the breadfruit, hibiscus and bamboo at the end of Berkeley Crescent in the Government Domain. It looked out over the pendulous point of Suva's oceanic setting, and as its Fijian name denotes, had a panoramic view of the main sea reef. Equally it could have been named Rorogocakau[24], for lying at rest under your mosquito net on a still tropic evening, the distant rumble of rollers discovering the adamancy of Suva's broad coral reef was the white noise of night.

That house was a place of vibrant life. When we sat down to dinner at Raicakau it would be rare for only my seven siblings to be seated at the long table of the back verandah. Around steaming pots of beef stew, *dalo* and *rourou* there would be an ever-changing cast of relatives, houseguests and neighbourhood kids. Children from small families in Suva would complain to their parents that it wasn't fair, for at the Thomson's house there was a party every night. And it was a one-for-all and all-for-one kind of place, kept that way by the overview of my parents and the Fijian domestic staff who were like strict but loving elder sisters to us kids.

Raicakau was the neighbourhood headquarters for the construction of tinboats, made of disused corrugated-iron, liberated from the tips of Public Works Department building sites. It provided the space and amenities for 'glassing' the cotton lines of our kites for subsequent kite fights; for experiments in parachute-jumping with each boy holding the corner of a *voivoi* mat and leaping in tandem from the roof; for breaking up the savage fights of rival dogs and separating love-knotted dogs by chucking on buckets of water; for trapping mongoose by the chook-house; for making cubbies in the attic or under the house or up in the neighbour's massive *baka* tree; for

45

touch-rugby on the front lawn, or cowboys and indians on the back lawn and in amongst the bamboo groves of the gully below; throwing sticks for mangoes, grating coconuts, climbing for guavas, getting stung by hornets; for getting wounds patched up with mercurochrome or iodine after stone-throwing fights with our enemies at the other end of Domain, or after taking spills from the home-made box-cars we raced down hot, pot-holed roads. The back verandah of Raicakau was the place where we chowed piles of baked *duruka* with butter and salt, or eggplant fritters with Worcestershire sauce, or fried breadfruit with tomato and chili salsa, or did our homework, drew pictures, played 'last card' and traded stamp collections.

The kitchen and pantry were in a separate house connected to the back verandah by a short breezeway. When meals were not in preparation in the kitchen, it was a place where fragrant guava jelly was being boiled or strained in slow-dripping muslin bags. In there, oven trays filled with chocolate fudge or pink and white coconut-ice lay cooling, and banana cakes, pungent with aromas of nutmeg and ginger, sat on wire racks upon a smooth-worn kitchen table.

Here too there was the inexhaustible *talanoa* of the domestic staff to listen to. This story-telling could be heard out on the *voivoi* mats in the marbled shade of the creaking bamboo thickets, as these patient women slowly sorted and folded the sun-dried laundry. There you could lie among the sweet smell of fresh cotton and hear of the complicated lineage of an obscure relative from Naselai, or tenth-hand reports of a juicy local scandal, or the plot of a film someone had seen at the Regal theatre and retold many times, or most riveting of all, the latest exploits of the famous robber and serial prison-escapee, Sairusi Naibogibogi.

At the foot of Cakobau Hill, four minutes jog from Raicakau, was Albert Park, scene of the annual Hibiscus Festival and of epic Saturday matches between the various rugby clubs we supported: Gaunavou, Lomavata and Army. From Albert Park, Victoria Parade ran along the harbour-front, past our foreshore grammar school, next to the cream columns of Carnegie Library, the old wooden town hall and the latticed verandahs of the Cable & Wireless building, to a small beach shadowed by over-hanging *ivi* trees. You'd walk this beach, sorting through the flotsam, before clambering up the seawall at the other end, by the old fire station, next to which lay your destination, the Regal Theatre. Whether it was Steve Reeves in *Hercules Unchained* or Kirk Douglas in *Spartacus*, the 'main boy' of these movies would be the talk of the town for months after 'the show'.

Inwrought with affection! There's hardly an island in Fiji the mention of which fails to conjure a memory, sentiment, or story in my mind's eye, hardly a curve in Viti Levu's circuminsular road that won't jog the brain into reminiscing on rich experience. It is an unspeakably sad feature of the human condition that these memories die with us; a feature that makes me wish to linger as a roadside ghost in order to point out to passing cars such locations as the creek at Nasigasigalaca where Burt Lancaster's long-boat from the movie *His Majesty O'Keefe* slowly rotted away, or the beach at Sovi Bay where the Japanese imperial forces had planned to make their amphibious landing during World War Two. My shade would extol the view of the island of Beqa that my mother most treasured, or the cliff at Mau over which her car tumbled during the war. It would signal the creek at Lobau where I helped build a bridge through the swamp to the village; the turn-off to Vunaniu where I oversaw the construction of a seawall and an Irish crossing; the roadside gut in the reef at Baravi where I first went spear-fishing; the ruins of Korolevu Hotel where I first drank a rum and Coke; that house where so-and-so was conceived, that tree near Saweni where Bizzo died in a late-night car-crash, or that slope past Nabukavesi where cousin Mark was killed in another smash. Recounting stories of how it was back when, my ghostly guide would prevail on you to take the side-road to beloved Naitonitoni, out through soft green ricefields to where tall palms will ever dance along the breezy foreshore. Every turn and every one of us has a story, but peace be upon you friend, for all things must pass.

Here is a vignette that comes to mind whenever I drive through the Serua Hills between Naboutini and Korovisilou. There's a particular hill in that section we call Matanipusi, meaning the face of the cat. I know the hill so well, having driven up it a thousand times or more when I was the Government's district officer for that section of coast in the early 1970s, back in the days when the mighty Queen's Road was little more than a winding gravel track.

The famous Australian artist Brett Whiteley painted an interpretation of Matanipusi, a fabulous canvas he called *The Green Mountain (Fiji)*. He lived nearby at Navutulevu in 1969. The Matanipusi canvas holds a voluptuous bulge of green, draped with Fiji's peculiarly tall and slender coconut palms, under a clear blue sky. A honeyeater has been disturbed from its nest and rises like a shuttlecock over the green mountain. In a corner of the canvas the artist has scribbled some notes, including the following evocative passage,

> As soon as I saw the green mountain I hurried down to the hut in a state of ecstasy to get my paints to do quickly something with the glimpse.
> The love
> The whisper of peace
> The aspirational air …
> … Soon, the bird came back to warm her eggs, she dropped-in-down-out of the sky like a velvet dart and landed on her nest with a monumental calm that echoed down the valley …

Some say Whiteley is the best painter Australia has produced and I wouldn't disagree with them. He would have stayed in Fiji for much longer and had brave plans to do so, but a drug bust sent him on his way. In a letter from Fiji mailed to his friend Ning, Whiteley wrote,

> O you wait till you see the pictures I have made for you all. You want some love, right? Then these visions here on my wall are for simmering and glow-gloating over. Menace has been neglected categorically. They are quintessences, like stars in the sense of 'my celestial body normally seen as a point of light.' These pictures are the purest manifestation of Good I've yet made and they hang around where perfume is born. They want for nothing.
>
> Everything is such a sort of stoned state. I can't tell you about life here. I walk around with a bunch of violets in my hand and a sledgehammer and a grain of sand in my head. I am happy.[25]

So far so good; but Barry Pearce, the head curator of Australian art at the Art Gallery of New South Wales, had this to say on the Fiji interlude in the book *Brett Whiteley Art & Life,*

> Hiring a barn in Suva, Whiteley presented an exhibition of his paintings which stirred a lot of positive local interest. The intention was to go back to Sydney, raise some money, and arrange permanent immigration to Fiji. However, as with many colonial outposts, officials harboured deeply reactionary attitudes, especially to such an off-beat family. Whiteley had talked to someone about drugs, and at 7am the morning after the opening, the apartment was raided by police. They found some opium that Whiteley had purchased from a Chinese man two days before. He was arrested, and the Whiteleys were told to get out of Fiji as soon as possible.

One wonders how many colonial outposts Mr Pearce inhabited in order to experience the 'deeply reactionary attitudes' of their officialdom. Setting aside the fact that the Whiteley exhibition wasn't held in a barn, but in the McGowan bulk-store in the centre of Suva's business district, the salient point of Whiteley's opium bust is how lucky he was to be dealing with Fiji officialdom and not the lawmen of Australia.

What happened in Suva was that a close friend of my family's, one of those 'reactionary' colonial officials referred to, who was privy to what was about to come down on Whiteley and had an understanding of the ways of certain artistic temperaments, got hold of the artist and tipped him off. In the absence of the medium of telephones, he went so far as to drive for over two hours down the long coast road, over the green mountain of Matanipusi, past the whisper of peace and the simmering visions, to advise the artist on a course of action. His message was that if he fronted at the Magistrates Court in Suva, paid a 50 pound fine and left the country within twenty-four hours, the powers-that-be would hold back the heavy hand of the law.

With alacrity, that's exactly what Whiteley did. If the offence had ocurred in Australia at the time, let alone somewhere like modern-day Singapore or

Indonesia, Mr Pearce would have had decades in which to conduct his book interviews with the artist, through the bars of a Sydney gaol.

While I admit that story's hardly autobiographical, it does demonstrate how most of us can be pricked into defending the honour of our heritage. Fiji mermaids and fantasies about deeply reactionary colonial outposts have little to do with Fiji; they exist in ephemeral mind-castles built in dingy sideshows of carnival Americana, or in high-falutin' art salons of Sydney. Fiji has its fantasies, plenty of them, all the way from the Fidji fragrance by Guy Laroche to the befuddling pronouncements of some of our politicians. But few people in Fiji have heard of mermaids or care too much if a family is 'off-beat' or not.

Mention of Matanipusi and my time as a district officer in the 1970s allows me to cut to the chase on the autobiographical back-story. Between the golden days of Raicakau and knocking up and down Matanipusi in the course of my district duties, there was boarding school in New Zealand and England, that rum-soaked Caribbean interlude, a rather grueling three years putting myself through university in Auckland the hard way, and then recruitment by the Fiji Government as an administrative officer at the beginning of 1972, barely a year after the country's attainment of independence.

After the briefest of induction courses, I found myself posted as district officer to the Navua district on the south coast of Viti Levu, taking in the provinces of Serua and Namosi and the fire-walking island of Beqa. In those days, the extent of roading in the district was the narrow gravel road running along the south coast; while access to the many villages of the mountainous interior was up the rapids of the Navua River in an outboard-powered punt, followed by days of trudging a muddy network of hill-tracks.

Our district centre, the riverside metropolis of Navua, had yet to receive the benefits of electrical power. Thus nights were lit by the soft glow of candles, by the kerosene-soaked wicks of hurricane lanterns, or for those who could afford, by Colemans benzene pressure-lamps. My bottom-of-the-ladder salary meant I could not afford, and I was happy with my lot, for I never particularly liked the too-bright tension in those hissing pressure lamps.

I've written in some detail about those Navua times in *Kava in the Blood,* so I won't repeat myself here; but I would like to record some memories of a person who was integral to them. When I took up duties as the district officer in Navua, the *roko* in charge of the provincial administration of Serua and Namosi, was a portly chief from an island province.[26] He was not much given to perambulation, which was a pity as many of the villages of these provinces were only accessible by walking tracks. Luckily for me, his two assistant *roko* were dynamic men: Ratu Leone Matanitobua with responsibilities for Namosi, and Meli Ramacake (pronounced Rama-thaké) who looked after Serua province. For three years, hardly a day passed when I was not in the company of one of these two men.

It is of Meli that I would like to say something here. His family had long relations with mine, both Meli and his father having been in the Fiji Infantry Regiment during the time my father served in it. After the Pacific War, Meli's father had insisted on women from his Tailevu village of Visama coming to work as domestic staff for my parents, and this arrangement continued for over two decades. In the course of those early years, my brothers and I spent a lot of time in Visama village and there were many young people of Visama, apart from those in my parents' employ, who spent extended time in the various Thomson households.

I was a bachelor when I arrived at Navua in 1972 and as district officer I was heir to a large colonial bungalow on the beachfront at the government station of Naitonitoni. Meli was a bachelor too and was housed in a dingy little room at the back of the old riverside provincial office. I invited him to move into the Naitonitoni house with me, he accepted, and even though I married Marijcke the following year, Meli remained a welcome house-guest until I departed the district three years later.

Like his father before him, Meli had been the regimental sergeant-major of Fiji's army. He had joined the army as an eighteen year old and in 1944 went with the same band of men as my father, to do battle with the Imperial Japanese Army in the jungles of Bougainville.

By Fijian standards, Meli was short-to-medium in stature. He had a small head with a high intelligent brow and was usually encountered with a sly smile on his dial, or teasing quip just waiting to slip from his lips. He had what I can best describe as a sweet nature.

They say old soldiers never die and Meli was a real old soldier. Be it around a kava bowl or a jug of beer at the Navua Farmers Club, he was always up for a drink and a sing-song. Very occasionally someone brought a bottle of Scotch to Naitonitoni as a *sevusevu*,[27] and we would handle it with all due care, for there was no way our combined pay-packets could afford such an extravagance.

Once a month he'd take the Friday afternoon bus up to Suva and get hammered at the Union Club. He'd return to Naitonitoni on Monday morning with sweat pouring from his forehead and would always have with him a big bag of beef bones purchased at the butchery near the Suva bus-stand. These he'd ask our housekeeper Nanise to boil up in a big pot, with an onion or two, and we'd be sipping on his recovery soup for the next few days.

Meli was no delegator. He took it on himself to carry the can, and it was always in safe hands. He wouldn't have claimed to be a leader, being more comfortable as a facilitator, an advice-giver and the reliable logistics man who got things done.

In our first year of working together, Hurricane Bebe decimated our part of Fiji, its floods taking out bridges that had stood for half a century, while its winds flattened villages and totally destroyed the villagers' food-crops. It was a time when people showed their true colours, and Meli's were those of commitment to duty, capability and courage.

I have two mental pictures of him that show those colours. The first is from the day the hurricane hit. Its peak winds had yet to engulf us, but days of torrential rain had turned the flatlands of the Navua coast, from Lobau to Galoa, into a giant flood. The Navua River was a mad red torrent, spiked with great clumps of tall bamboo and huge rainforest trees dislodged from landslides in the gorges up-river, all spiraling and thrusting by in nine foot surge-waves.

I judged the river uncrossable, but we were fretting about the fate of the Deuba and Vuibau villagers whose homes lay across the river, down in the delta where the flooded river was colliding with the rising sea. Meli volunteered to investigate and he found an intrepid Navua boatman who was prepared to carry him across.

I had misgivings and at the last moment asked him not to go. Climbing into bow of the flat-bottomed punt, he told me not to worry, he'd be back before nightfall. The driver pulled the rip-chord to fire up the outboard engine and they were off, whipped down-river by the flood's race, quickly disappearing behind rearing waves, driving rain and the hurtling hurricane debris.

That scene is stark in my mind because over the next few hours, with wind-gusts screaming and darkness threatening, there were times when I thought that might be the last sight I would have of Meli. But he returned at last light with news of the delta people, and the sober conclusion that no further crossings of the river should be attempted until the worst of the flood was past.

The second picture is of his face looking up at me through the downdraught of a Royal New Zealand Air Force helicopter. For a year after Hurricane Bebe, we coordinated the delivery of emergency food supplies, medicine, tents and planting material to the badly-affected villages of the interior, and at the early emergency stage of this operation, we had the assistance of RNZAF helicopters. Seated on sacks of flour and sugar, I would hang on in the back of the chopper as the pilot slalomed up the Navua river gorge under low canopies of thick cloud, with me giving directions to the villages of the day over the intercom.

Back in Navua, Meli would be getting the next load ready, checking through charts of village requirements based on comprehensive damage assessments our district team had carried out in the days after the hurricane.

Meli was happy to have the RNZAF around; it put him back in touch with his old military life, and it certainly made our job a lot easier. So there he was at every landing and takeoff, the competent one, his face squinting up in the downdraught, knowing he was vital a cog, trusting to friendship and the common cause.

Well, that was Meli, and that was me, and when Marijcke arrived, there were three of us, living under the tall palms of Naitonitoni with their leaves streaming day and night in the trade-wind's blow, with the lagoon at our doorstep and the jade hills of Beqa sitting out there on the crisply blue horizon. They were wonderful, Spartan days. Thank God for our gardener, Jai Kumar, and the kitchen-garden of eggplant and Chinese cabbage he created to supplement our diet of bone-soups and the occasional crab or *nuqa* snagged in the fish-trap we hung from the jetty. [28]

Meli now lies buried a few paces from my grandparents' graves at Lovonilase. I was overseas when he passed away and was thus unable to say the graveside words I've harboured since.

Moce mada sweet Meli, I'm so grateful you were my mentor and my friend back in our Naitonitoni days. How 'bout one more time I sing that song you liked to play on the ukulele for Marijcke and me. Remember how you used to play it when we sat out on the seawall in front of our haunted home. It finished up like this,

> We three
> We'll wait for you
> Even 'til eternity.[29]

The Dawn Anchor-Watch

As you well know my friend, there are many places that will never hear the scuff of our footsteps. I suspect the time is just not there for us to find our way to Tristan da Cunha, and the days are certainly gone when we might have bathed in the Aral Sea, or trudged the tropical snows of Kilimanjaro in search of stray leopards. You and I will not stand on a South Georgia cliff-top with a white storm coming in, or cross the high pass of Karakoram with whisky in our flasks. Let's face it, dear companion, these places are now beyond the pale; for until we bend them otherwise, time's limitations are obdurate.

The obduracy of distance must also be considered. As you know, I was brought up on an island, a cluster of islands in fact, set far out in the ocean's expanse, in the days when air travel was rare for a human being and the height of telecommunications was a hand-delivered telegram. Thus you will appreciate what I mean when I say horizon's containment was the extent of our lot.

Held up by the sea and squashed flat by the weight of the sky, that line of limit circumscribed island life, defining what you could and could not experience. Within its limitations, just as a prisoner knows every crack and bump of his cell, introspection of your given environment was intense; so that even in these days of reminisce, when so many more who shared those times have gone than remain, traveling through the islands still brings on a pester of memories.

For the great majority of us in that island world, beyond the intensity of the tangible there was one terrain which was part of you, but always exterior to your outstretching experience. I'm referring to the outliers of the archipelago, the outpost islands, the tips of sea-mounts, marooned out there somewhere in the wash of the great ocean. You could only imagine the outliers, for there were no photos or traveller's tales, only names in resolute positions on the national map. They seemed like forlorn sentinels posted on far perimeters, and like Neptune and Pluto they were of your given world, but were so physically marginal to it, there was but faint chance you'd ever set foot on one these islands.

For Fiji, the lonely sentinel of the southwest is Ceva i Ra, a coral cay unknown to humanity before its discovery in 1838 by HMS *Conway*. Over four hundred kilometres of wallowing ocean lie between it and the next Fijian island, and such is the islet's exposure to tides and storms that even the hardy coconut palm has received no refuge there.

Occupied by seabirds and the occasional shipwrecked sailor, 'alone on a wide, wide sea', Ceva i Ra became Fijian territory during colonial times. But it emerged from maritime obscurity in the 1980s when Fiji became the first country in the world to ratify the UN Convention on the Law of the Sea. The convention provided for exclusive economic zones extending two hundred kilometres from national boundaries out into the high seas. Thus it was that Ceva i Ra delivered the windfall of huge swathes of oceanic rights to Fiji, rights pertaining not just to all creatures great and small swimming thereabouts, but to whatever minerals might litter the seafloor thereunder.

My former boss, the late Ratu Sir Penaia Ganilau, the ultimate governor-general and inaugural president of Fiji, was not the kind of man to leave solitary sentinels uninspected. In 1985, while still serving as the country's deputy prime minister, he took one of the Fiji Navy's patrol boats on the long voyage south to Ceva i Ra, only to become embroiled in a violent storm system sweeping in from the west. Huge rollers smashed the bridge and one of the ship's two engines was put out of action.

A 'May Day' call went out and survival chances took on a bleak outlook as all on board were put on stand-by to abandon ship. Ratu Penaia told me that at that moment, a giant shark came astern of the vessel. His hereditary chieftainship was *Na Turaga na Tui Cakau*, the Lord of the Reefs, and the shark god Dakuwaqa had long-protected his noble clan. The huge shark did not quell the storm, but it gave Ratu Penaia, and perhaps through him the captain and crew, the confidence to see it through.

Ratu Penaia later wrote to Fiji's naval commander praising the exemplary behavior of the skipper and his crew throughout the stormy crisis. The captain of the ship on that southern trip was Lieutenant Frank Bainimarama, who would go on to become prime minister of Fiji.[30]

I thought the grueling experience of these two leaders of men would be the closest I would ever get to Ceva i Ra, in a vicarious sense; but if we live on in the lives of our children, then my son has since taken me to the island. In 2009 the following email message popped up on my computer screen,

> Good morning from Ceva i Ra. I have managed to sneak this email into the daily weather downloads. We are currently anchored off Conway Reef upon which Ceva i Ra sits, having arrived at dawn yesterday after a rough thirty-eight hour crossing from Viti Levu.
>
> Ceva i Ra is providing shelter from strong southerlies, so we've been able to get the tender down and go for a snorkeling excursion. The marine life is amazing and unusually curious of us, having seldom if ever seen man. Sea turtles, octopus and countless reef fish are in abundance. There is a relatively recent shipwreck on the reef that we explored - a Chinese vessel called the *San Sang*.
>
> It was too rough yesterday to get the tender onto the little island that sits above the reef. From here one can see that it consists of a sandy beach with low vegetation serving as a nursery for hundreds of booby chicks. We should be able to get ashore at high tide today as the wind has dropped overnight.
>
> I am on the dawn anchor-watch and the sun is starting to rise as I type these words. It is coming out of the ocean on the port side of the bridge, complementing the bright full moon on the starboard side. We are having a great adventure.

My son went ashore that day at high tide and scooped a few handfuls of sand from the beach to indulge his arm-chaired father. The sand sits now in a glass bowl upon my table, tangible to me, even if it seems to have come from a place as distant as the outer rings of Saturn.

I had the good fortune in life to get to know the northeast outliers of Fiji in the 1970s during my time as a district officer in the civil service of Fiji. When the district of Macuata was my bailiwick, I was able to requisition government vessels to carry me to the outlying islands of Kia and Cikobia in the course of census, electoral and rural development duties.

Kia lies in a northerly bulge in the Great Sea Reef, the 300 kilometre-long coral bastion that delineates the northern reaches of Fiji. This high volcanic island had a strategic position in the tribal wars that played out along the Macuata coast in the nineteenth century, and physical evidence of those warlike times can still be found on Kia.

At the island's summit there lies an overgrown ring-ditch, surrounding what was once a defensive hill-fort. I ascended to it in 1976, and in the pages of the Fiji Sun newspaper the following week, there was a photo of my sweating form next to a nineteenth century naval cannon found in the undergrowth of the defensive ditch. After scraping it clean with a cane-knife, with the help of my Fijian companions we restored this unaccounted-for war relic to what we presumed to be its former position on a rock wall overlooking the sea approaches to Kia.

Some one hundred kilometres to the northeast of Kia, beyond the shelter of any protecting reefs and fully exposed to every mood of wind and ocean, lies the island of Cikobia.[31] Na Ciri Kalia is its original name, 'the up-turned canoe', for so it looks: a long, narrow limestone hull abandoned in the lonely sea. It is populated by hardy islanders descended from a blend of Fijian voyagers and elopers from the Polynesian island of Futuna, away over the northern horizon.

On my visits to Cikobia, I always found the people and their isolated island to be bursting with wellbeing, or what Fijians call *sautu*.[32] Their rich food gardens were on the southern half of the island, for the northern half of the twelve kilometre-long island is covered in forbidding limestone rock, rearing to sea-cliffs rising a hundred metres from the crashing surf.

Cikobia has no anchorage, so my visits there involved being dropped on the southern tip of the island, with the Marine Department boat, usually the *Cagi mai Ra*, returning to the shelter of northern Vanua Levu for the duration of my stay on the island. On one such visit, Ratu Sir George Cakobau kindly authorised my use of the *Ramarama*, the governor-general's motor-yacht. At the designated end of my visit, the *Ramarama* returned from her overnight anchorage on the Vanua Levu coast, and on a whim I asked the captain to take the elders of the island for a joyride around Cikobia. Though they'd lived on Cikobia all their lives, most of these old men had never circumnavigated the island.

It was a bright blue day with a great rolling swell coming in from the southeast as we set off in the sea-tracks of Abel Tasman up the island's northeast coast. Motoring up the weather coast, with those high limestone cliffs rising from the thumping rollers, we got in amongst great shoals of silvery skipjack with yellow-fin tuna leaping through. In a flash all our lines went out, and for the next half hour the public purse was allowed to drain a little in favour of the kitchens of Kia, as the *Ramarama* worked her way back and forth amongst the hungry tuna.

When I was the district officer on the verdant monolith of Taveuni from 1976 to 1978, my district took in many outer islands, including administrative responsibility for the Ringgold Islands. The latter were named for Lieutenant-Commander Ringgold of the brig *Porpoise*, part of the United States Exploring Expedition that surveyed and charted Fiji waters in 1840.

The Ringgolds are comprised of the various islands of Budd Reef, notably the sea-breached volcanic cone of Cobia, the remote atoll of Naqelelevu, and the bird island of Nukubasaga. The devious clutter of reefs within and around the Ringgolds, borders the deep seaway of Nanuku Passage, Fiji's northeastern exit to Samoa and North America, and those Ringgold reefs have brought grief to many a mariner approaching Fiji through this passage.

Tasman and his fellow Dutch mariners were the first Europeans to enter Fiji waters in 1643, aboard Tasman's flagship the war yacht *Heemskerck*, accompanied by the quick-sailing flute *Zeehaen*. The first island they sighted was humble Nukubasaga, thus making it the premier Fiji island to ever be fixed on written charts. The Dutch were sailing in hurricane season, and rain-squalls caused poor visibility as they felt their way through the reef-pocked waters of northern Taveuni. The mariners were nearly wrecked on the Ringgold reefs now known as the Heemskerck Shoals, but the tides and fate ran in their favour and they came across.

Faced with foul weather, no apparent anchorage and uncertainty of position in dangerous seas, Tasman decided to be quit of his discovery without setting foot ashore or meeting a single Fijian, possibly to his benefit, for reports by later mariners were to result in Fiji's early name of the Cannibal Islands. Thus the Dutchmen sailed off northwards, around Cikobia, their log noting the island's sea-smashed cliffs. With that they were clear of Fiji waters and bound for Batavia.

So these outlying Fiji reefs are seductive, baneful sirens. To this day, mariners will make their way with great competence through the seven seas of this world before sailing into Fiji waters, at which point they will drive their vessel onto the nearest jagged reef. Sadly, the pounding of oceanic swells will usually then reduce their nautical pride and joy to splinters. The evidence litters the reefs of Fiji and in my life I have learned of many a foundering account, have inspected shattered hulls below and above water, and met plenty of sailors who've been the victims of such Fiji shipwrecks.

I remember one poor soul, a young, bearded American to whom we gave shelter in Taveuni in 1977. He was delivered to us dazed in the dead of night, shortly after wiping out the yacht he'd sailed single-handedly from California all the way to the Nanuku Passage. We helped him salvage what he could from his wreckage on Taveuni's south-east coast the next day, then found him safe passage on to Suva.

One of America's most favourite sailors, Jack London, sailed in on the *Snark* in 1909. He also came through the northeastern gateway of Nanuku Passage, and he too came close to shipwreck on the reefs of the Ringgolds. Jack's first act on arrival in Suva was to sack his incompetent skipper; his second act being to buy some decent charts from the offices of the Fiji Times.

My favourite nautical yarn is *The Saga of Cimba,* the haunting story of a small bluenose schooner sailed by young Richard Maury in the early 1930s from the vessel's home in Nova Scotia through a great Atlantic storm to Bermuda, Grand Turk and Jamaica.[33] *Cimba* made the Pacific through the lakes and locks of Panama's canal, and then Maury's descriptions of her transit from the Galapagos to the Marquesas, and on to Tahiti and Samoa, are of ocean sailing at its most lyrical. Upon arrival in Fiji, *Cimba* did the done thing and wrecked herself on Suva's weather-reef.

It was in the dead of night, approaching Suva from the south, when *Cimba* became engulfed in a torrential tropical downpour. Maury had a circle of visibility of only ten feet, so he turned the helm south of west to find sea-room. The vessel was powered only by sail, for the engine had died. Some time later he thought he heard a sound above the roar of the rain. The sound came from astern and he peered into the watery dark.

> The downpour was deafening, solid. The sound did not return. But as I wiped the rain from my eyes I saw the ghost of foam.

> I moved for the anchors and was passing the mainmast when the ship struck on reef. The deck dropped underfoot, the fore-boom drove against my shoulder – and I had fallen through the companion onto Taggart, sprawled over the chart. There was a loud roar; the cabin heeled, a barrelful of sea foamed over the hatchway, and in one heap the sleeping passengers, bunk-boards, blankets, and the gear fell to pin us underneath. The sound of coral ripping the underbody followed. There was deafening concussion, and as the hull skidded over shoal I found the companion and made the deck, the others behind. But there was no deck left – only a

steep incline piling out of the surf. The sails were in the sea, the lee rigging under, the nearest land two miles off.

Some days later, *Cimba* was salvaged with the help of the pupils of my old grammar school, who were given the day off lessons to man the ropes. Thereafter she was auctioned and became the property of my long-deceased uncle, Towser Lazarus. Thus it is that my old copy of *The Saga of Cimba* is festooned with faded photos of my mother and her beautiful sisters in bathing suits, perched about the decks and rigging of the resurrected schooner from far-off Nova Scotia.

In 1870, George Herbert, 13th Earl of Pembroke and Montgomery, and Dr George Kingsley of the famous English literary and adventuring family, sailed through Polynesia in the schooner *Albatross*. Though something of a forgotten read today, *South Sea Bubbles*, the eloquent and quite humorous account of their voyage, was a massive bestseller in its time.[34]

They were feted wherever they dropped anchor in the South Pacific, and after immersing themselves in the delights of the Society Islands, Rarotonga and Samoa, the voyagers made for Fiji. Coming in from Samoa, the *Albatross* naturally proceeded in the direction of Nanuku Passage in order to skirt the Ringgold Islands. But in the dead of night, in the grip of a heavy gale, *terra firma* made a sudden and dread appearance. The Earl describes it thus,

> At about ten o'clock, as I was dozing off, I felt a sudden shock, a terrible lurch, and long trembling grind. The doctor shouted to me that we had struck, but it needed not that nor the cries on deck to tell me what had happened. I rushed out of my cabin to get on deck, when a heavier lurch and crash sent me slithering right across the saloon under the table. I scrambled up again and made for the companion, Mitchell appearing from his cabin with a hurried, 'What's the matter?'
>
> 'You may say your prayers now,' replied I, with a ghastly grin, 'For the game's up with us.' We climbed on deck and found ourselves

in about as awe-inspiring a position as could be imagined: the vessel lying almost on her beam-ends, the foam flying over her in a white cloud, every sea lifting her up and bringing her down again with a sickening crash, that made the cabin-floor heave like an earthquake, and her whole frame tremble, the scream of the wind sounding even above the roar of the surf, and all these horrors magnified by an intense darkness. The doctor and I said, 'Good-bye,' indeed at that moment I don't think anybody but the skipper expected to live ten minutes.

They survive the night, and at the gloom of dawn through driving rain they make out the low silhouette of the islet of Nukubasaga, the very same that Tasman had charted two centuries before. The schooner's three lifeboats carry the passengers and crew over to the island, where they set up camp in miserable conditions. It is October and they are caught up in what we call in Fiji a *bogi walu*, a tropical depression of wind and heavy rain that usually takes about eight nights to pass.

Nukubasaga is an uninhabited flat coral key less than half a mile long and the droll Earl is deeply underwhelmed by his sojourn on the island. Under a leaking sail rigged as a canopy, his state of mind is journalised,

> How can one do any fine writing, sitting on a brandy case, with the rain coming down in long perpendicular rods, not drops, which break on one's head and trickle down one's nose onto the paper; stopping every fifteen seconds to take revenge on a dozen or so of mosquitoes that are grazing coolly on one's hands; whereby one spills ink, drops the book, and loses the pen, which is discovered some time after planted two inches deep in mud like a young tree: one can't even grumble fluently under such conditions.

A sodden week passes and the weather clears sufficiently for the shipwrecked sailors to make a run for Taveuni in the lifeboats. They are careful to stay well clear of the other Ringgold Islands, for their nautical manual, *The South Pacific Directory*, describes the inhabitants of the Ringgolds as 'the most ferocious cannibals'. Two days and a fearful night are spent in the overladen boats, amongst fierce tidal rips and jagged reefs, before the comparative safety of Taveuni is made and a vessel found to bear them from their watery nightmare.

The Earl's experience, first his complete seduction by Pacific Island charms, and then his ardent desire to be completely quit of the Fiji island upon which he'd been so rudely pitched, is not an unfamiliar drift. It must be confessed that island life can be limiting. Think of Benn Gunn or Napoleon. But while it's true the romantic balloon is ever awaiting a prick, happily for the dreamers there's always someone puffing up another.

The Earl leaves Nukubasaga in a mordant light, and I can't allow it to remain that way; for from several visits to it in my District Officer days, I'm witness to the fact that on most days this bird-nesting island is a place of magical beauty, all the more so for its remoteness. For a rather ornithological description of a more typical day, let us depart Nukubasaga with the words of another peripatetic scribbler, Max Lacrosse. He too lingered on that coral island and afterwards imagined a pair of lovers sitting on Nukubasaga's beach who,

> ... looked out over the marinescape's overlapping shades of blue: from the duck-egg hue of the foreshore, through turquoise to aquamarine, to streaks of kingfisher blue bordering the royal blue of the vast Pacific Ocean flashing its peacock breast. Overhead, bird city was oscillating in a feathered frenzy of feeding, fighting and mating. Masked boobies, red-footed boobies and brown boobies were diving like kamikaze fighters into a shoal of fish out by the passage. They looked up in time to catch pretty snow-white fairy terns smartly dodge a cruising, black man-o'war, a frigate bird with its long hooked beak and crimson neck pouch dangling like a flabby red scrotum.[35]

When we consider the multiple hazards of the sea, what usually comes to mind are wild storms, whirlpools, wily currents and adamant rocks. Then there are the sunderings of hulls by whale-strike or, more invidiously, submerged cargo containers and proliferating sea-junk. A friend of mine, at sea in a tiny sailboat out of Fiji, heading north to the tiny French territory of Futuna, met a very different kind of hazard.

This sailboat had no engine and only a foot of freeboard. She was a mere nineteen feet from the end of the sprit set in her canoe-stern to the tip of her bow-sprit. If you measure that out on your floor, you'll see she was mighty small for ocean crossings. There was just enough space in the hull for one person to curl up in to sleep, and this is what you did when you were not on watch. The division of watches was not a complicated affair as the sailboat's full complement was the American skipper and my friend Lynda Miller. By that stage of her life, Lynda had sailed most of the Caribbean and a fair hunk of the Pacific too, on rather larger sailboats.

Late in the afternoon, somewhere out in the ocean north of Fiji's Udu Point, Lynda had to wake the skipper, for they were approaching something she'd not seen before. It looked like a huge oil slick was coming at them over the water. Before they knew it, with night coming on, the current and wind had their little boat engulfed in what proved to be a great sea-drift of volcanic pumice.

All night the densely-packed pumice ground against the sides of the tiny yacht and when dawn broke, the hapless sailors looked around to see they were marooned, from horizon to horizon, in a grinding ocean of floating grey rocks. The wind had fallen away in the night and for the next four days they were to be completely becalmed in this surreal, sea-clogged scene.

The ocean had been transformed into what looked like a gigantic parking lot. They plunged their arms over the side into the pumice and pushed down, but could feel no clear water below.

> Day after day, day after day,
> We stuck, nor breath nor motion;
> As idle as a painted ship
> Upon a painted ocean.[36]

On day three, a low swell rolled in from the southeast and the parking lot began an undulating motion that threw dollops of pumice onto the yacht.

These dollops arrived at such a constant rate that the scuppers became blocked, as a result of which the deck began flooding and the little sloop fell in danger of sinking. Thus for the remainder of the ordeal, the main activity aboard was clearing the pumice from the decks, so that the mariners' hands were turned raw by constant handling of the abrasive rock.

The longed-for day eventually came when a breeze allowed them to sail clear of the great drift and they found their way on to Futuna. On returning to Fiji they were told their Sargassian experience had been caused by a submarine volcano in Tongan waters spewing forth the mass of wandering rocks that had engulfed them.

The dread of every sailor is the sinking of his vessel out in the deep, deep sea. If like the *Titanic* some of the lifeboats have been lowered before the ship plunges to fathomless depths, there's a good chance some of you will survive. If there are no lifeboats, but there's been sufficient time to don lifejackets, as you lower yourself into ocean's embrace you give yourself a fighting chance. That ray of hope is contingent on the rescue boats showing up sooner than the sharks. If there were flares on your vessel and you managed to grab them before it sank, you imagine you would be able to attract the attention of whatever other boats are out on the ocean. I have a friend whose boat went down in rough seas way out in the Pacific Ocean, and he and his Fijian companion had neither lifeboat, nor life-jackets, nor flares.

John Morgan is a Suva building contractor. His family is from New Zealand, but he was brought up in Fiji. Back in the early 1990s, he worked for a local tuna-fishing company, his job being a supervisory one, shore-based in Suva. On a cool July day, in the middle of what passes for winter in Fiji, a radio message was received that one of the company's fishing vessels *Antwan* was disabled to the north of Solo lighthouse. The lighthouse is about thirty-five miles south of Suva, across open ocean in the full face of the prevailing southeast trade-winds.

It was decided that the disabled boat should be towed back to base, so John set off from Suva in the company of Manasa Bulivou, a relieving skipper for the fishing fleet. Their vessel, *Alley Cat*, was twenty-five feet in length, a twin-hulled aluminium work-boat powered by two brand-new ninety horse-power Evinrude outboards. It had a half-cabin forward, while over the helm there was a Bimini top held in place by aluminium extrusions.

I've not met Manasa Bulivou, but John tells me he's a good man, softly spoken and very religious. A photograph of him at the time shows a well-built Fijian of average height, with a broad smile and thick mustache. He was then thirty-eight years old and John was twenty-eight. As for John, I concur with what anyone in Fiji will say of him if you ask. 'John, yeah John, he's a good guy, a stand-up guy.'

They cleared Suva passage at five in the afternoon and plotted their course on the GPS. The weather was fine, seas were moderate and the boat was coping well as they set off south at about fifteen to twenty knots. By the time they were in the vicinity of Solo lighthouse, wind conditions had stiffened and seas had come up to rough. There was still a bit of daylight and they spotted the lighthouse. As they did so, they realised their course had taken them too far to the west, so they began working their way up to the northeast to attempt the rendezvous with *Antwan*.

Manasa was up forward, with John at the helm, when the Fijian captain turned to see the *Alley Cat's* stern low in the water. 'We're sinking!' he cried. John slowed the engines, grabbed a bucket, ran astern to the starboard pontoon, opened the hatch and saw there was water to the brim. He began bailing, calling to Manasa to radio the Suva office.

Manasa got through on the radio, saying, 'We've sighted the Solo lighthouse and we are sinking!'

A crackling reply came back, 'Say again.'

Manasa gave the radio to John who said, 'Mayday! Mayday! Mayday! We're sinking five miles north of Solo lighthouse.' There was no point in saying more, for the radio's flat battery signal chose that moment to alight, leaving the hapless pair silent in a sinking boat, uncertain whether their distress message had been registered or not.

They looked about them. The sun had set and it was fast getting dark; all around lay nothing but the kicking ocean. Their search for flares and life-jackets was in vain, so they began emptying two twenty-litre drums of fuel to use as flotation devices. Halfway through the process of emptying petrol from the drums, the boat flipped to one side, sending them flying. The next thing they knew, *Alley Cat* had turned turtle and they were submerged in Neptune's watery embrace.

They surfaced, spluttering, clutching their half empty drums, unhurt except for cuts to John's hands. To their dismay, they found that only the upturned bow of the boat was now clear of the surface. They clung onto the drums and swam around assessing their situation. The lids of the petrol drums had been lost in the capsize, along with most else in the boat, so to keep them buoyant every few minutes they would be forced to lift the drums into the air to empty them of seawater. John realised there was a limit to how many times their bodies would let them do that. They had no food or water to sustain them. They were thirty miles from home, out in the open sea, with no certainty their distress message had been understood, and even if it had been, whether any rescuer could find them in the dark. As the night came down upon them, John's outlook darkened with it.

Half an hour after sinking he said, 'That's it, we're fucked.'

But John says at that moment Manasa 'put him right', telling him not to worry, that it was in God's hands now. He said God would guide them home, 'Don't you worry, John'.

So they paddled about in the dark, clutching their leaking drums, emptying them again and again, just riding the swell and lingering by the slosh of the protruding bow. Rather than dwell on their perilous lot, they kept their spirits up by setting new targets hour by hour. They discussed what time the rescue vessels would be departing Suva and what time they would be reach the vicinity of Solo. They conjectured whether the *Alley Cat* would remain afloat in the choppy night-sea, and noted how it sank inch by inch if they attempted to mount the boat's protrusion. So they kept off it and when the wind came up further, and the night deepened, they hunkered in the lee of the pitching bow for the small semblance of shelter it suffered them.

Their next challenge arose at about nine that night, when the petrol leaked out of the *Alley Cat's* breather tanks and formed a broad slick about them. Both men were afflicted with burning sensations so painful they could no longer linger by the boat. So they swam out into the swell with their drums; but once out there beyond the stinging slick, in the dark of night, the tug of current and the slosh of wind-driven waves, the sense of peril was overwhelming, forcing them to kick back to the precarious safety of the upturned hull. Thereafter they 'just stuck it', bearing the pain of the petrol eating into their skin until eventually it dissipated in the waves.

Around eleven o'clock that night they began getting very cold. Both men were shivering uncontrollably and the sound of chattering teeth resounded in their skulls. So they huddled together and hugged each other until the chattering stopped. They discovered that if they huddled tight for ten-minute spells, they were good for another forty minutes of swimming. Thus they survived the night, treading water as they raised those damned drums over and over and over to drain them of seawater.

At dawn they expected to hear the sound of rescue boats, but as the hours ticked by they saw no sign of anyone searching for them. A plane flew overhead, whether just a scheduled flight to Kadavu or a search plane was unclear to them. The sun had come up on a beautiful South Pacific day with the trade-winds sweeping below clear skies and the deep blue ocean plunging about them. At about ten o'clock they were getting desperately thirsty, so John decided to dive into the submerged hull to see if there was anything drinkable trapped within.

After half a dozen dives, he had retrieved a long polypropylene anchor rope and a battered twenty-litre drum, full of petrol. The latter he emptied over his head, at the cost of further burns to his skin, and secured the lid so that they now had a sealed flotation device. In the course of these dives, he was repeatedly hitting his head on an industrial eskie that had slipped its place on the deck and was caught up in the boat's aluminium awning. It eventually dawned on him that the eskie was worth the effort of salvaging. Manasa agreed and John went for it.

It took him a while to free the cool-box. He had to go down the side of the submerged boat, get his feet against the aluminium extrusion holding the awning in place and tug away at the eskie 'til his breath gave out. Luckily John wasn't inside the boat or in any way caught up in it when he eventually freed the box. For when it did come free, the eskie shot straight to the surface and *Alley Cat* plunged to the depths of Davy Jones's locker.

John surfaced to find Manasa had grabbed the bobbing eskie, so they secured the lidded drum to it with the propylene rope. The lidless drums had been lost in the *melêê*, but now flotsam was popping up from the lately departed *Alley Cat*. They grabbed a broomstick that came up, thinking they might use it as a signaling device, and then, oh joy, up floated two bottles of liquid. The first was a one and a half litre Coca-Cola bottle, half-filled with water so old it had green moss growing in it. The second was a two litre unopened bottle of French mineral water with a metal cap. John opened the latter with his teeth and they both took heavy swigs, after which John forced the cap back on and secured the bottle inside his jacket.

They contemplated the eskie. It was a plastic commercial fishing box, 1.7 metres long, six hundred millimetres wide and seven hundred millimetres high, with no lid. Next they tried to board the box, for it was a luxurious prospect to think they might huddle inside it out of the wind and sea. But with its flat bottom and the cajoling of the oceans, there was no way both men could climb in. So after half an hour of desperate floundering, they gave up trying and with no further reason to stay where they were, they began swimming in the vague direction of home, pushing their eskie before them.

Soon after setting off for Suva, a small Cessna aeroplane flew directly overhead, so low they could see its rivets and the wheels folded under its belly. This gave them hope that a search effort was underway and they kicked on with new resolve. But as the hours passed they neither heard nor saw any search-and-rescue vessels and old doubts returned. John acknowledges that he was getting 'pretty pissed off' that no-one was out looking for them.

By about four in the afternoon, Manasa's lips were so puffed up and red, and his face so swollen, that his eyelids were squeezed shut and he could not see. Manasa badly needed to get out of the water, so John held the box steady while his Fijian companion clambered in. Thereafter they had a routine, as Manasa put it, 'one hour one fellah inside, one hour one fellah outside'.

During his paddling shift late that afternoon, John describes hearing the exhilarating sound of a boat engine,

> You couldn't see it because of the three or four foot swells, and you had to wait 'til you were on top of a wave and then you had to wait for the boat that was making the engine sound to actually be on top of a wave so that you could see it. And when we did see it, it was probably two hundred metres ahead of us. We yelled and screamed at him. He was a Fijian guy standing in the back of his Yamaha punt, standing up holding onto his throttle, just heading for Suva. We yelled and screamed at him more, but he didn't hear us. Then the dusk came, then darkness again.

Throughout their ordeal, Manasa led them in morning and evening devotions and John recited what he remembered of the Lord's Prayer. With every turn of fortune, Manasa assured his comrade,

> John, God is with us. Don't you be afraid. We'll live. Don't you worry. God knows I got a family and I have to go and look after them. You got a family too, you should go back and look after your duty.

When John says they may be on their last duty, Manasa replies,

> John, that means you lose hope. Never lose hope. When you stay with God, you don't lose hope. God is with us here and we'll get back home safely. Don't you worry.

They swam on through the night keeping to their hourly rotations. The southeasterly wind was helping them in the direction of home and when the quarter-moon set at three o'clock, they could see the orange glow of

Suva's lights. The stars were thick above them and there were fishing boats moving by, all too far to see the human flotsam or hear their desperate cries.

By this stage lack of fresh water had become critical to their survival. The bottle of French mineral water had provided only that first thirst-quenching swig, for when John put the bottle into his jacket for safe-keeping, seawater seeped in through the metal cap, making the contents undrinkable. The green mossy water in the Coca-Cola bottle was barely potable and all they could do with it was have a little gargle and let a tiny bit trickle down their throats. In spite of the lack of water, John says he continued to pee as he swam, in consequence of all the brine sloshing into his body through his ears, nose and mouth.

Around dawn the weather turned for the worse. The wind swung around to a strong easterly and with Suva tantalisingly close, they were now being pushed away from their destination. The seas came up with the wind and they began traveling towards the strong currents that all Fiji mariners know swirl to the north and south of the island of Beqa. To their left the mountains of the mainland, Viti Levu, were passing by and great squalls of driving rain marched over the sea from the east. When a heavy squall hit, John lifted his head from the tide to try and drink from the flying rain.

> By the time the fresh water rinsed your hair out and washed your face out from all the salt … I just had my tongue out exposed to the rain, and I had my eyes closed, and then waves would hit your head and you'd take a whole lot of salt water into your mouth. So trying to get a drink of rainwater is very hard while you're floating in the ocean, very difficult, don't recommend that one.

The situation in the eskie wasn't much better. Manasa tried holding up the emptied French mineral water bottle as a catcher, but they only got a few drips of rainwater in that. Life in the eskie wasn't without seawater either. They could stretch out to rest, but the box had a leak and filled steadily with brine. When John was in the eskie, he'd wait for the water level inside the box to reach his ears and once it got to that level he'd have to start bailing with scooped hands.

74

That morning Manasa did a two-hour stint in the water from eleven to one. In the deteriorated weather conditions he found he was warmer in the water than in the box, so John got a good two-hour rest. The seas kept up rough, with big whitecaps surfing in at them every few minutes, picking them up and pushing them to the east, so he was grateful for that extra rest.

They swapped places at one o'clock and as John swam along beside the box he was wondering whether he should kick towards Beqa, wondering how they might cope with the surf on Beqa's coral reef, thinking about that reef in the dark, for night would have fallen again by the time they got there … when he heard the sound of a heavy diesel engine ahead. He listened and concluded the boat was heading in their direction, making due west into the sea while they were drifting due east.

From the vantage of the eskie, Manasa saw one of the Fiji Navy's patrol boats smashing into the swell and their hearts lifted. But they soon reasoned that visibility from the boat would be poor in the day's foul weather, and worse, they saw that on its present course the boat would pass well to the Beqa side of them. If they were going to be spotted, they had to try and get onto its bow, so John began frantically swimming, pulling the box, crabbing it across the wind in the direction of Beqa.

> We actually got there at one stage, we could see him coming. I stopped paddling for a couple of minutes because we were on his bow. And then he must have altered course slightly, maybe four or five degrees. He kept on steaming and he was too close by then for us to move across his bow. I tried to get Manasa to stand up in the eskie, but again it was not very stable and that thing fell over and the broom went one way and the bottle of water went the other way and was blown away in the wind. We really did try and attract their attention. We screamed and yelled and I whistled. By the time I started swimming the eskie across again, they passed us by about four hundred metres away. That was quite hard. We whistled and yelled at the Navy boat and they just kept on going by. There was no one on deck. It was a rat-shit day, it was windy, overcast, raining every now and again and I don't blame anyone for not being on deck.

John swallowed his disappointment and began kicking for Beqa, quietly setting himself a new target. He knew they couldn't survive the night without fresh water and the nearest place they'd find that now was Beqa. A big container boat loomed up and sailed past. They waved madly at its giant blue bulk, expecting little and receiving nothing in return. John kicked on towards his new goal.

He was nearing the end of his two-hour shift, when again they heard the throb of the big Detroit diesels of the Navy boat. John calculated bearings and saw that this time the boat's course was taking it to the Viti Levu side of them, so he made a desperate about-turn and began working the box back the way they had come, across the path of wave and current. It was the swim of his life, grimly expending the last of his energy.

> I was hoping and hoping I'd get there or they'd see us. And you could see them a mile away maybe, hear them coming and coming. I was still swimming it and pulling it, crabbing it across, pulling it, pulling it, and hoping and hoping, but I never actually got onto the bow, even though I thought that was the only way they were going to see us, to run right over the top of us. And they kept getting closer and I kept yelling at Manasa, 'Wave the broom, wave the broom, keep waving the broom, wave the broom.' And that's what they saw.

> It must have been the best sound in the world when the skipper saw us and came off the throttle. Just hearing that and seeing the bow sink into the water, just dropping his throttle right down to idle, and putting it in gear again, and making slow ahead … directly for us. There was a lot of screaming and yelling from us when we saw them coming toward us, quite a bit of emotion there.

Manasa says,

> I cry that time. I so thank God. When I saw that boat come back I pray let them come back, we want to stay with our families tonight.

John is a wiser man today. Flares - never go to sea without flares and all the other maritime safety devices available. When I asked him how he survived the ordeal, he says without hesitation it was Manasa's complete faith in God's will that pulled them through. Throughout their ordeal it was plain as the stars above that his Fijian companion was never in fear or in doubt, for he truly believed he was in the palm of God's hand.

> Yeah, his strength was God. Well, I was deriving my strength from his strength. It didn't worry him, God had given him strength. 'Don't worry John, we can float here all month, we can float here for thirty days …'

> My other strength I think was the little things. Mum used to recite *The Little Red Hen* story. Just little by little. It's like the labourer's theory, I call it, when you've got a big stack of timber to move and you go 'Shit, I don't want to do this.' But one by one, you just switch off, one by one you take a plank off, and then little by little you start seeing what you've done and where it's going and then the stack's no longer that big. And that's what I was thinking out there. We just had to keep going, just little by little. Sure we're not going to get there in the next couple of hours, but little by little we were getting there.[37]

Heaven Lies About Us

Upon careful reflection, I consider my greatest contribution to human progress was the liberation of Marijcke Rolls from the confines of Suva's Convent of St Joseph. I'm pleased to report that Miss Rolls, she whose love for my pilgrim soul has sustained our long life upon the road, was a willing party to the adventure. The liberation required the sort of conviction and resolve that only young love can provide. She was only seventeen, and long after I was running scared of nuns.

On the day we married, Alma Wardell, the hostess of the women's programme on our national radio, played a song she dedicated to the lady who was about to become my mother-in-law. The song's chorus laments,

Too young to be married,
Too young to be free,
Too young to be married,
But what could they do?
They were gonna have a ba-by.[38]

Yes, we were gonna, two in fact, but the babies didn't arrive until three and five years later. This is a good point at which to insert another fundamental of island life. The cast of the soap opera is limited, with the script drawn from gossip under the mango tree.

Marijcke hadn't always lived in Suva. She was born in Pokfulam on the rocky slopes of Hong Kong, where her parents resided for a couple of years. They say that from the first, Marijcke made them laugh, and please don't think me sloppy when I say that I've long-since witnessed how she lifts peoples' hearts.

Her mother was Loelie, a highly intelligent autodidact, mad as the cowboy-hat she wore around town, maternal source of the six beautiful Rolls Girls and of her last child, a son. Marijcke was her second-born and of that Hong Kong birth, Loelje once wrote me,

> She burst into the world a few days ahead of schedule. Even before she was fully emerged into the world, she was shouting with rage and hunger for life. She was still yelling as they put her in my arms – a tiny girl with a mop of black hair and furious dark eyes. We eyed each other for the first time – there it was, 'love at first sight' on my part. Marijcke gave one last shout, waving a minute fist and was quiet but wide-awake, glaring around with those glittery eyes. It was so funny I burst into laughter - so that was the first time.

At times it seems the outrage we witness in a baby's surfacing from its mother's amniotic world, is retained from an earlier crossing over, from reluctance at returning, or regret of departure, be it the womb or the palace beyond. Where had she come from I wonder? What palace of souls sent her hence?

> Our birth is but a sleep and a forgetting:
> The soul that rises with us, our life's Star,
> Hath had elsewhere its setting,
> And cometh from afar:
> Not in entire forgetfulness,
> And not in utter nakedness,
> But trailing clouds of glory do we come
> From God, who is our home:
> Heaven lies about us in our infancy![39]

By the time she was seven months old, Marijcke was living in Fiji. To be precise, she was residing in a seaside cottage at Beach Road on the southern end of the Suva peninsula, and for the next sixteen years, her home was never more than a mile away from that cottage of her Suva beginnings - she was a Suva Point stripling, a Muanikau maiden, a St Josephs girl, until she fell in love with me and moved to the Fijian countryside.

I spent a good part of my youth in the same leafy precinct of Suva, so that we share our touchstones, our compass points coincide, roots entwine with ease. We break into the local accents of our home town, sing the old Fiji songs, imitate radio announcers long since gone from this world, and still absently cuss with the Fijian and Hindi words overheard in our formative years.

We know the flavour of the hard-boiled corncobs that used to be sold at the Suva bus-stand. She will remind me of the merits of the various Chinese lollies and home-made ice-blocks you could buy for a penny or two over the worn boards of Nasese Store. We can summon taste recreations of the Coconut Frond's parcels of tinned-fish curry wrapped in soft roti, or curry goat with puri served on the tin plates of Cumming Street lodges.

We have concise mind-maps that give the whereabouts of mango, tamarind and guava trees that could be pillaged by youthful hands. They show the corners and connotations of our neighbourhood: the Goat Track's short-cut into town, the abandoned Veiuto gun-emplacements with their obscene charcoal scrawlings, the scent of roadside frangipani and the stench of tyre-flattened cane-toads, the glimpse of a mongoose in full flight across a pot-holed road, a giant Sunderland seaplane lumbering over the treetops, and all the stops and turns of the open-sided Nasova bus. There is the particular smell of the buses, the body odour mixed with coconut oil, and flashing by the open window, the cobalt iridescence of the harbour, and during Christmas holidays the coral red brilliance of flamboyant trees: the shared minutiae of arcane reference points, essential keys for reading those ephemeral maps.

The Suva seawall runs from where Nubukalou Creek empties into the port, around the peninsula to the breakwater of the RNZAF base at Laucala Bay. That seawall was a big feature of our lives. There you lingered to watch tin boats paddling under Turner's Bridge, or to follow the movements of *belo* and fisherwomen as they worked the shallows with their darting beaks and hand-held nets.[40] It was the place to go for sunset walks, to woo and court where *baka* trees drooped towards the tide.

On the leeward side of the peninsula, across the sheltered harbour, the sun sank in outrageous lightshows over the craggy mountain ranges of Namosi. But on the peninsula's windward coast, facing the rising sun and the brunt of the southeast trades, the eye was drawn to the low islets of Nukulau and Makaluva, out where current and wind pushed ocean swell to thunder and die on broad coral reefs.

In our youth, Laucala Bay was the stretch of water onto which the TEAL Solent flying boats would descend, lumbering in from Auckland before setting off on the long Coral Route to Samoa, Aitutaki and Tahiti. Laucala Bay was home to the imposing bulk of the other great breed of flying boats, the Sunderlands, which could be seen hauled up for maintenance at the RNZAF hangar. As they did in the air, on the hard the Sunderlands revealed elegantly sculptured hulls. Back in the water they tugged sluggishly at the mooring-buoys of a flotilla that was anchored behind the bay's doglegged breakwater. My Suva cousins, Jane and Susan Lazarus, both married RNZAF officers of that Sunderland fleet.

Our mind-maps show where on sunny weekends we sailed out across Laucala Bay to Nukulau Island to picnic and snorkel along reef's edge. They also show where, in Christmases past, we'd spend a week or more, further out on the coral island of Makuluva, cohabiting with the creatures of the seething reef.

On the western side of Suva Harbour lies the Bay of Islands, into which are crammed the islets of Admiralty, Cave, Mosquito and Snake. Mosquito Island has a narrow sand beach and was the place to sail to from the Royal Suva Yacht Club, or set off from in water-skis to slalom between the islands. Marijcke and her mother were both gun skiers and when the foreshore hotel managed to get water-skiing banned from the bay, Marijcke gave them a cheeky parting shot by drenching the hotel's waterfront dining room with a glistening aqua-wall thrown up from a high-speed slalom.

During the hot rainy season from November to March, Suva days can be sauna-like, so that swimming in cool fresh water is called for. If we could lay our hands on some wheels, we'd drive out of town and venture up to the reservoir at Wailoku, or out to the gravel-banked river at Sawani, or climb to waterfalls in the rain-forests of Colo-i-Suva and Nabukavesi. The trek was always worth the effort, for those waterfall pools were sweet and clear, as refreshing as the happy splashings of the old Fijian song *Sisili mai Wainadoi*.

When any Suva kids of our generation get together these days, reminiscing is bound to bring up the movie theatres of our youth. There were Saturday matinees and double-features at the Regal, Phoenix or the New Lilac theatres; one shilling downstairs, two shillings upstairs. Mr Crawford supervised the lobby of the blue-tiled Phoenix with the attention to detail of a circus impresario. Even for the matinees he would be decked out in a white shirt and black bowtie, with his Roy Orbison glasses and oiled hair swept-back and dyed the blackest of jet. Mr Crawford would don a tuxedo for gala evenings.

The New Lilac, rising on a hillside corner like the gateway citadel to the run-down precinct of Toorak, was not as modern as the Phoenix, but had a funkier appeal. If your pocket-money stretched far enough, you went up to the Lilac's verandah kiosk, hanging out high above Toorak Road, to buy a local soda and a packet of roasted peanuts or hot peas to munch through the cartoons and the Coming Attractions. If you had a sweet tooth, orange Jaffas were a popular choice, and when you looked around the audience before lights were dimmed, you could see many an orange-lipped kid who'd carefully sucked the colouring from their orbs of candy-coated chocolate. Before the main show began, as soon as the lights went down, everyone stood to attention while *God Save the Queen* reverberated tinnily from the sound system.

Marijcke says there were two times in her life when she was indelibly struck with the thought that things might never be as good again. The first was when she was a little girl in Suva and she and her older sister Joan were eating coconut toffees. These were so delicious, she was moved to tell Joan that they would never taste anything as wonderful as those toffees did at that moment, and the sensation has lasted for fifty years.

The second was when she was at a matinee at the New Lilac and she and her sisters were seated in a row passing around their hot peas and Crunchy

Bars, settling down as the velvet curtains drew back and the MGM lion let out its silencing roar, when she was gripped with a sense of complete joy and the thought that life was perfect. It was the thrill of the insight that was memorable, not the movie, which would have been one of her corny childhood favourites: a beach-bunny Gidget movie, an Elvis musical, or perhaps *The Sound of Music.*

Getting home from Saturday matinees, you could cut down Marks Street with its Chinese shop-fronts piled high with Hong Kong trinkets, cakes of shocking colours and neatly stacked pearly-white pyramids of steam-buns. Falling from the shutters of the second stories of Marks Street, would come the clatter and smoke of crowded mah jong parlours. Those mind-maps are so clear and true.

If you went instead down Waimanu Road, you passed rows of Gugerati shops with the crisp smell of bolts of fabric emitting from the dim interiors, along with the rubbery rattle of treadle sewing-machines where the tailors were hard at work. Leather aromas and cobblers' muted hammerings came from the bootmakers' dens, cinnamon and star anise from the spice-sellers, and pungent masala from the *vale ni kana* cafes. All these mingled with sandalwood incense smoking at the finer shops' doorways and the intervention of diesel smoke whenever a wood-paneled bus worked its way up the hill to Toorak and beyond.

Thomson boys walked home from town, but Rolls girls took the Nasese bus. Offices were open on Saturday mornings in those days, so if a bus-fare was required, to acquire the requisite pennies Marijcke would climb the steps at the corner of Thomson and Cumming Streets to where her father ran Southern Pacific Insurance. From there she would wander by the inter-island boats where they jostled at Princes Wharf, cross the reeking boards of the copra shed, push through the pungency of the market, purchase a tight little newspaper-cone of hot peas, and board the wooden bus with its roll-down canvas windows for the joyous ride home.

Years passed by, Suva's old wooden buildings, with their broad worn boards of long looping floors, like Morris Hedstrom's in Pratt Street and Joong

Hing Loong on Thomson Street, gave way to concrete and car-parks. The dancing at the Yacht Club 'balls' moved with the times from foxtrot and jive, to shaking and stomping. Brylcream, Connie Francis and Cliff Richard were suddenly *passé*.

Slowly the Hibiscus Festival lost its magical appeal. When we were kids the festival was the great highlight of the year, even though most every festival was flooded by days of solid rain. The combination of that torrential Suva rain and thousands of bare feet treading by the festival's food stalls, kava dens and the chugging carnival rides, would churn Albert Park's grassy surface into a great pudding of mud, liberally impregnated with discarded mango pips and corn cobs. I've only to look down at my toes to conjure the sight and feel of that mud squirming up between them like smooth extrusions of chocolate mousse.

Then boy met girl and the beginnings of shared lifetime began falling into place. Now the matter of under-aged survival at the Golden Dragon nightclub arose. Past a bouncer as broad as five of us, forking over the entry charge to Mr Jansen Ho, and up the stairs, pushing through the tight, fecund swill of drinking and dancing, coloured beams spinning and flashing on sweating brown skin, strobe lights blinking on frizzy afros, dodging the fights, involving knives only if the crew of a Korean or Taiwanese fishing boat was in town. Our goal was to sit over by the band, for the Dragon Band was the best around, with Rupeni on bass and Wise on lead guitar doing virtuoso covers of overseas hits.

Now we are in the twenty-first century and Marijcke and I still find ourselves back in our home town every year or so. When we drive by old Naiqaqi and spot the Golden Dragon, it's hard to conceive that forty years ago up that steep stairway was the epicentre of Suva night-life.

On a recent trip to Suva, a Fiji senator happened to meet Marijcke and her sister Joan at Wahley's Butchery and they began talking about the old days. The Suva Pony Club came up, for both their families were at some time members of that modest equine institution. The senator joked that neither family really fitted at the club.

'Our family wasn't white enough,' she said, 'And yours was too bohemian.'

Marijcke was yet in her last year at the convent when I moved down the coast to Navua to commence my time in the service of the Fiji government. I'd just graduated from Auckland University and had traded over the footloose student life for a career of public service. I was not long in my post as the district officer at Navua, when one day I was driving over the broad boards of Navua bridge in my pick-up truck. It was the old bridge that would soon be swept away in the Hurricane Bebe flood, narrow, with a clattering wooden deck, so that vehicles crossed it slowly and overtaking was not an option.

On this occasion there was a modest sedan ahead, driving very slowly, and as I came up behind it, the car slowed further when the driver spotted me in his rear-vision mirror. He was a priest from the Catholic mission down the coast at Lomary, and his car was crammed 'til it bulged with Suva nuns. The priest must have uttered my name, for the carload turned as one in my direction. The neatly-framed facial expressions, fixed forever in the aspic of my mind, ranged from outraged pique to vinegary perplexity. I had nowhere to turn and nothing to do, but sit it out and whistle a happy tune. Since one of their convent girls was part-time cohabiting with me, the cause of the sisters' ire was clear enough.

All through that year, Marijcke would leave St Josephs on a Friday afternoon, get on the Galoa bus in her blue and white school uniform, and come down the coast to spend the weekend with me. You've got to picture the old Queens Road running between Suva and Navua in those days: a narrow, deeply-corrugated way, winding around and over the coastal hills, through scrappy forests and along the edges of sultry mangrove swamps. The fact that the Taunovo buses of SS Singh had no glass windows, just a flapping roll of canvas if you were lucky, was very relevant on the journey; for if it was raining you arrived wet and splattered with red clay. If it was not raining, each time another vehicle passed by, the bus passengers would be enveloped in a dense cloud of choking dust. On such days, you descended from the bus leaving a dust-trail behind you, brushing the stuff from your eyebrows and slapping it from your shoulders and clothes. Even if you wrapped your head in a turban, as most people did, the first thing you had to do on arrival was wash the dust from your hair.

On its way down the coast, SS Singh's bus would divert out across the Navua delta to turn around at the end of the disused jetty beside my Naitonitoni house. Here the prevailing wind would have the tall coconut palms of the District Officer's compound swaying and bending in a dance of welcome. A broad lawn, a chicken-run and a collection of gnarled frangipanis and flame trees lay between my rambling quarters and the Navua court-house, with my office tacked to the rear of the latter. The covered front-verandah of the courthouse, where I posted notices of marriage, government pronouncements and other matters of bureaucratic trivia, doubled as the Naitonitoni bus-stop.

Nearly forty years have passed since then, but I have only to close my eyes to see Marijcke stepping down from the rickety blue bus and crossing the lawn to the house. That vision fills me forever with such pride in her resolve and joy for her casual beauty. We cared little if Suva tongues wagged; for us there was only certitude and delight in the shared life that was stretching ahead.

The Fijian newspaper Nai Lalakai covered a project I was involved with at that time, the construction of a seawall to protect the foreshore of Vunaniu village. To illustrate the story, Nai Lalakai showed a photo of me with Marijcke by my side standing on the wall. They captioned the photo, '*Na turaga* na *DO kei na i wati ni DO*' – the District Officer and the wife of the District Officer. Since we were then far from married, this threw more tizz into certain sections of Suva society. I cut the story from the newspaper and stuck it in a photo album for the amusement of our grandchildren in years to come.

Marijcke and I married in 1973 and then, like my forebears, we spent most of the next fifteen years living in various placcs around Fiji. Marijcke flew to Suva from Labasa and Taveuni respectively to give birth to our son and daughter. The way things were going back then, it seemed that like my fore-mentioned forebears, there was no question we would end our days in the ground at Lovonilase. However in 1987 there was an ethno-nationalist revolution of sorts and the installation of a military government persuaded

87

us to try our hands at a variety of alternate locations over that ever-daunting horizon. Meanwhile our daughter has been living back in Suva for a decade now, the sixth generation of our family to live there, showing again that once you're of it, you're never really quit of the rock.

Thus it was that, looking for our way in the world, we took up residence in New Zealand at the end of 1987. With our children enrolling in Auckland schools and a startling cost of living kicking in, Marijcke and I went looking for work. She answered an advertisement in the NZ Herald placed by the fledgling Cuisine magazine, calling for someone who could sell ice to Eskimos. She convinced them she could and thus began a publishing career that has since scaled impressive heights in Australia.

Home is the marital bed, the hearth of life, where bliss and wholeness dwell. If I day-dream well, I remember every one of our beds, especially that first one in the shade of the wooden shutters in the far corner of the Naitonitoni house, with the slip-slap of wavelets at our beachy doorstep. Then there were the two Government-issue beds we pushed together in Vatureikuka, with the rustle of a copse of giant teak trees at the window, their waggling leaves the size of dinner plates. At Vatureikuka we lay down under the canopy of a pink mosquito net, festooned from a heavy frame I'd fashioned from bamboo trunks cut from the compound. Beside that bed was our first-born's cot, the nocturnal gurgles of its occupant stirring our hearts with wonder and love.

Next, in Taveuni, was the wide podium of a bed I hammered together from packing cases, stacked with pandanus mats, and set at the window of what was once the island's courthouse. From it, we had only to incline our heads to see the whole flank of the great garden isle swoop from cloud-capped rainforest, down to where the flow of the Somosomo Strait tugged at the black-rocked shore.

When we moved back to the capital, living back at Suva Point, there was the complicated assembly of an antique Chinese edifice of a bed that Marijcke's uncle had acquired when he lived in Java. We had a little cottage by the bay, opposite the very one where Marijcke's Suva days began and just around the corner from the bungalow in which my mother had been born. Our bedroom in the cottage was completely filled by that ornate Javanese bed, with its high-paneled sides and richly carved bedposts and canopy.

When the winds of a *bogi walu* set the tall palms to eight nights of frenzied thrashing, with thunderous rain crashing onto the cottage's clapboard flanks, we'd set sail in our snug Javanese ark.[41] Two by two that sturdy bark carried us through the night, for we were now cuddled by the perfection of all perfections, our baby daughter and infant son. Cocooned in that water-logged shelter, with the roof's thin tin thundering defiance at night-sky's torrent, we were heading for who knows where, trusting to the flow of a predestined course, for heaven lay about us.

Then we were away from the islands in wintry England, and there was that bed at Wolfson College in Cambridge, its window set among the squirrel-runs of the college treetops. Some years later there was a bedroom in Tokyo, in a shoji-screened house in Meguro-ku, where the bed looked beyond a balcony to a flickering bamboo grove. On weekend mornings a-bed, over the roof-tiles of the compound gates and stone steps curving through high azalea banks, rose the nasal chants of wandering street vendors, '*Satsumo imo, satsumo imo! Furio shimbun, furio shimbun!*'[42]

In Auckland, in the house by the harbour-shimmer of Waitemata, we placed our bed so that it faced the tree in the courtyard we had created. It was the same courtyard I'd dreamed up when I lay with the mozzies, festering in the army camp's prison in Suva after the second *coup d'état* of 1987. In the depression of that military cell, the courtyard was the vision that came to me, when for the first time I envisaged an alternative to our Fiji path. It was a place where a spreading tree's branches would shade a ground of crushed white shell, from whence a narrow road would descend to a spinnaker-billowing harbour. It was as I had seen it, a place where we celebrated under the light-filled boughs, with wine and good food, with guitars and dancing, where we saw our children grow to adulthood in a world of respect and happiness.

Having at the beginning of this tale somewhat taken in vain the name of the nuns of St Josephs, I'd like to praise the results of their toils. Most of those St Josephs girls are a credit to Sister Immaculata and her fellow brides of Christ. Sisters, those Catholic girls rock, they have an edge.

As for me, I was brought up in the Church of Scotland and went to a dour Presbyterian boarding school in New Zealand for three years. Our headmaster, Reverend Adam Macfarlan, would hand out cigars to the boys of the 1st XV when they beat the rugby team of Sacred Heart, the local Catholic college for boys.

I like to pipedream. Who doesn't, I suppose? When I consider the Catholic-Presbyterian strife that's still going through its death-throes in Northern Ireland, I think of my own experience and give thanks. And in my pipe-dreams I believe I've hit on a highly-unlikely-to-be-adopted solution to such troubles. Large tax-breaks, so large they'll make the average citizen salivate, could be given as incentives to any Ulstermen or Ulsterwomen who marry into the opposing faith. The same social engineering policy could be applied to Jews and Muslims in Palestine, or anywhere else that sectarian hatred poisons life!

There's a discernible difference in perspective that comes with an upbringing in one faith or another, a range of inherent outlooks that underlie your life whatever philosophical positions you may choose in adulthood. I know for example that Catholic girls have some very different perspectives to Presbyterian boys, and from where I sit, those differences bring a spice to a partnership that would be poorer without it.

As for the children of such 'mixed' marriages; having looked into the hearts of both their parents, I wager there's little hope for the fostering of religious intolerance in their lives. Love conquers all.

How do we love? If I remember right, dear friend, the list of love that Elizabeth Barrett Browning gave us tells of eight ways, and she covers a lot of ground when she wrote,

I love thee to the depth and breadth and height
My soul can reach, when feeling out of sight
For the ends of Being and ideal Grace.

Dare we add more? I think we should; for like the minutiae of those Suva mind-maps, it is the collection of scattered fragments that make love's jigsaw whole. There is for example the love bound up in the maternal and paternal experience. EBB doesn't mention that variety, yet the continuity of love that is passed on from parent to child to grandchild is the binding at our core, the heartbeat of our society.

Then there is that sustaining love which makes humdrum days comfortable and brings fulfillment to mundane domestic tasks when love for others guides the hand. Food without love is just victuals, but prepared with love for family and friends it transcends biology and is a medium of joy for shared lives.

Consider too the love that can be exchanged with just a glance. That is a mercurial thing, the commitment that shows in just one look, an exchange affirming purpose and giving solace for all the worldly woes of the journey.

Then there is the ardour of the sensual world and love's consummation in gorgeous entwinements. Zeus came to Danae in a gush of golden rain and was gone, but sweet passion endures in the arms of true love and understanding.

Most intriguing is the mysterious love that lies deep within. This is the love that is more than the linking of our lives, the love that hints of things that 'cometh from afar', of not entire forgetfulness from whence we came and one day hope to return. And I give thanks that all these loves have been realised in my life, only because of an elegant hand that has held mine through all these adult years of my life.

Where You Cannot Come Again

I promised to keep the stories rolling, my friend, so here's another one. It is a jumbled tale, one from the years that I have spent here in Sydney town. It came to life at the back of a Darlinghurst café, at a cramped corner table made my own for half a decade. By way of introduction, the story meanders around the streets of Darlinghurst, before jumping back to some island entities my boyhood imagination held onto: beachcombers you could call them, the Old Hands as they were once known in Fiji.

Here a snigger, there a slather, come for a gander through the steam of our sleazy quarter. The indifferent wheels of the urban machine turn and turn. Primping poseurs, horny voyeurs, the slick operators, lowlife aspirers and bold hierarchy of harm-bringers buzz about our civic attraction like blow-flies in bling. Their grubby bedfellows, the junkies and soon-to-be junkies, the wild-eyed and soon-to-be-sad-eyed, hang out on street-corners or jiggle anxiously up Surrey Street.

In the great southern metropolis, we live a stone's throw from the tour-bus mecca of Kings Cross. We're told only great cities can sustain world-class dives like ours. Inexplicably, airline magazines and city brochures promote the strip as a reason to come and visit the Great Southern Land.

For five years now, I've meandered most days to the café at the end of our block. Up the middle of the street I go, fed up with dodging the dog-shit dotting the pavements of Darlinghurst. Around here people have mutts in preference to children: the snake-eyed heavies with their war-dogs, the homeless their canine duvets, gay chaps touting dapper yappers, the coiffeur of a miniature schnauzer matters, apparently. Meanwhile, Chihuahua-man likes to have his liquor from the comfort of a brown bag. He meanders benignly by, paper-bagged bottle in one hand, in the other the leads of his scuttling brace of rat-dogs.

At my café I am in the flow, but not of it. No man is an island, I tell myself again, but I can't quite force myself into the city's water, can't quite lose this feeling of being washed up like a castaway on concrete. I keep an eye on the curb-combers, noting their restless gait, the way they scour the gutters for jettisoned coins and the flotsam of spent cigarettes. I see the poise of their pauses, seasoned hunters and gatherers they peer deep into sticky trash cans and winkle forth sustenance.

Still, I endeavor to observe without judgement, as the occasional enlightened observer did of the inhabitants of the Pacific Islands when the tall-masted ships first sailed in. I try to understand what I'm part of here in Sydney, not judging, just recording the customs of this strange new shore.

I find the native women intriguing. Such is their dedication to self-expression, they wear scant clothing, baring bellies and lower-backs even in the chill of dark winter. Tattooing is a widespread custom, particularly on the body parts just described, though I must confess the level of art-istry is disappointing. One may observe swallows, roses, butterflies and the occasional abstract motif attempting the elaborate aesthetics of the original Polynesian art.

Evidence of the deliberate piercing of various body parts with metal rings and bolts is also widespread: tongues, eyebrows, nipples to name a few, with little explanation forthcoming as to the purpose of this custom. I've yet to discover evidence of magico-religious significance in these acts of self-mutilation.

Dyeing of hair is a seasonal ritual practiced by both men and women, per-haps as a right of passage or in response to the dull urban pallor of concrete and tar. I've observed the favoured colours this season to be pale custard and a puce shade of purple.

At the end of the street is a dark-skinned woman about my age, a true indigene of this continent, one of the more genteel and well-spoken of the people frequenting these by-ways. She is a tireless worker. Through five summers and five winters now, I've watched her incessant toil, admiring her

94

manner and the fortitude of her purpose, as she stops every second passer-by to humbly enquire if they might spare her some change.

Most days I see the bantam tough-guy strutting by, making his way to work. He's a street-side spruiker for one of the clubs along the strip. Every day he looks like he's drunk the bar dry the night before, face puffed up, grimacing a bit, and I feel for him as he must be a few years older than me. His shirt is carefully unbuttoned, open to the top of a wrinkled but still-taught belly. People laugh behind their hands when he passes, for his legs move in short struts and he has an exaggerated, shoulder-rolling swagger, like he's the featherweight champion of the world. I once asked the patron of my café why this guy was so cocky and he told me to take a look at the inner leg of his trousers the next time he wandered by. Root my boot! The bantam spruiker's hung like a lazy donkey.

There's a tall man with a white goatee and long white hair tied back in a pony tail. He wears silver chains, a white singlet, white sandshoes and the shortest white shorts. That he is a retired pirate is confirmed by the white eye-patch strung across his face.

Another silver-bearded local is less pleased with himself and the rest of us. Every day he sits on a bench beside the old sandstone church, a pile of empty beer bottles accumulating at his side. He grumbles at passers-by, his face getting redder and angrier by the hour, and we veer away from him as we pass, lest he hurls a bottle in our direction. Eventually he gets to his feet and lurches through the churchyard in a shambling rage, bellowing across the traffic at us all, 'It's wrong! It's fucking wrong!'

Through it all, on a mattress under the bridge at the other end of our street, lives a hermit. They built a motorway around him, but he lives there still, with all his worldly goods stacked about him as concisely as if he was confined to a raft adrift on a lonely ocean. Snowy beard wispy on his chest, he sits upright in his bedding. It took a while to place him, until I recalled that book I had as a wee Fiji boy; within it a picture of old Rip Van Winkle. Most times I pass his roadside shelter, Mr Van Winkle's gaze is transfixed on something intangible in the middle distance, mouth in a tight little 'o', like a perplexed poet stuck on an absent word, a hair's breadth away from it for the rest of his days.

I was once close to a man who hangs out somewhere here in the city. He lives alone now. He is so disaffected with the ways of his fellow man that he sees but little of us and I have codenamed him Coriolanus. There was a time when he was a big man back in the Islands; he was put up in exalted places and his judgements were often sought to right the wrongs and reshape many lives that had gone awry.

And Coriolanus was once a famous raconteur, known for a wit so keen that his tales of the foibles of man, embellished by his mastery of all our Island accents, would fill rooms with head-shaking laughter. But those foibles became more than provocative to him and his derision of them became over-bearing. Now he is an urban hermit, avoided by family and friends; for the scathing attacks of his troubled wit have driven them all away.

Coriolanus is not alone. Around these parts, artists and writers lurk in ascetic lairs, scratching at walls with burnt sticks. Now and then they emerge to blink at the sun, to wonder at the changes and the tedious lack of change. They have thoughts that flash like light on night-water and try to explain, inadequately. They contemplate the curbside castaways shuffling out there in the weather, patrolling the messy shores of the urban island, all the holed-up hermits and lost details of street-sleepers. Many know the turns of the obscured path, the dead-end diversions they were not meant to take. They must control their immigrant ire, tend to the ache of exile and reconcile with this marooning in a life unexpected.

I had a friend in Fiji called Monty Whippy. He was a classmate at Suva Boys Grammar and I remember him still as a boy that nature favoured. His first name arose from the timing of our birth a few years after the Second World War; his surname deriving from that of Fiji's first white settler, a Nantucket sailor by the name of David Whippy.

From about 1800 onwards, there were white men living in Fiji, beachcombers mostly, men washed ashore from ships wrecked on the coral reefs of the cannibal isles. Old Mr Derrick, Fiji's geographer-historian, told us that in early nineteenth century Fiji,

> Low whites and runaway sailors, many of them the dregs of the shipping ports of Europe, gained a standing and a place far beyond their merits, which were few.[43]

But with Whippy's marooning in 1822, a new era began. With little but nature to his name, he set himself up as a trustworthy trader on the beach at Levuka. *Bêche-de-mer*[44] was his stock in trade, until he developed a boat-building business, and was eventually appointed a vice-consul for the USA. Whippy never returned to America, he lived out his days in the Islands, siring many children from his three Fijian wives.

All the way from Nantucket to Fiji came a lesser-known blow-in, William Cary, whale harpooner, twenty-one years of age. In 1825, he was on board the whaler *Oeno* when she was wrecked on remote Vatoa, one of the islands scattered about Fiji's southeast. The captain and twenty of his crew made it to shore, where they were hospitably received by the Vatoans. But things turned bad when eighty warriors arrived in canoes from the nearby island of Ono.

Cary had the smarts to hide in a cave before the Ono men began their slaying of the *Oeno's* captain and crew. The young harpooner would have been murdered too, when starvation eventually drove him from his hiding place, had not the chief of Vatoa intervened by adopting Cary as his son.

For the next nine years, at a time when the outside world's contact with Fiji was still quite tenuous, Cary was passed from house to house of the great chiefs of eastern Fiji as a pet white boy. In the process he learned the language and the customs of the Islands, and his surviving written account of the adventure proves he learnt well. As the years passed, he had more than novelty value, for with his acquired knowledge he could serve as an intermediary between the Fijian chiefs and the captains of ships scouring Fiji for *bêche-de-mer*.

In such pursuits Cary employed his time, until 1834, twelve years after the shipwreck, when he was able to secure passage on a Salem schooner and make the long journey home to Nantucket. It was then that the Fates delivered William Cary their cruelest blow; for instead of being swept up in a joyful homecoming, his account of the end of the *Oeno* and his lone survival was met with hostile distrust, particularly from the relatives of his slaughtered shipmates.

A short time after Cary's return, the Nantucket Inquirer published a story about a white youth reported to be captive in Tonga. The captain of a visiting ship was said to have seen the boy, but had been unable to free him from the Tongans. Nantucket speculation quickly turned to wishful consensus that the captive castaway was the youth Barzillai Swain of the ill-fated *Oeno*. Cary insisted it could not be; Swain was dead, for there'd been no survivors on Vatoa other than himself. But how could he prove his word, when the murders were perpetrated by a band of cannibal warriors on an isolated island at the other end of the world? The prodigal son hung his head and slunk away from his Nantucket home.

Yet, anyone familiar with the geography, culture and languages of eastern Fiji would, like me, find Cary's account full of fascinating detail, ringing true in every respect. Would that one of us could have stood up for the returned castaway in Nantucket's court of public opinion! David Whippy could have done it, but he was no longer of that Quaker's world; he was living out his days on a far-off South Sea island, amid the fast-expanding Whippy tribe.

Incredibly, when you consider the breadth of the South Pacific, the two Nantucket men came across each other in passing vessels. The sole survivor of the *Oeno* was sailing on an ocean-going canoe with the high chief of Lau, heading for the kingly island of Bau, when they were approached by another sailing canoe. As the canoe came closer, Cary was amazed to see a white man amongst its passengers, the first he'd seen since the demise of his shipmates. Of this meeting, Cary wrote:

> As they came alongside our canoe the white man reached out his hand and addressed me by name. I was dumb with astonishment. At last he said, 'Don't you know David Whippy?'

'Yes,' I answered. 'I formerly knew him. He was a townsman of mine and an old playmate.'
'Well,' said he, 'I am that David Whippy.'[45]

When you think of the long road home and how William Cary was received when he got there, there's little doubt Whippy's way was the better course. 'Love the one you're with,' he might have said. He rightly surmised that the parable of the prodigal son was risky history, and that Nantucket's knacker-yard would have long since claimed the fatted calf.

And like the Whippy clan, now spread wide around the South Pacific, there is a common Antipodean inheritance in that story. For all our migrant forbears, each one indentured to precarious fate and fortune, the day came when they saw that one too many sunsets had flickered on the doors of their departures, and that the homeward path was gone in the wash of all tides past.

'No man is an Island, entire of itself.' Suva Grammar school-kids, we scratched our heads and chewed our pens, having been set the task of saying something sensible on the aphorism. John Donne scribbled these words back in the seventeenth century, his devotional continuing with,

> Any man's death diminishes me, because I am involved in Mankind; and therefore never send to know for whom the bell tolls; it tolls for thee.

In our classroom, Donne's lines seemed a bit extreme at first. But then, unless you were one who clung to mentalities of the saved and the damned, the chosen and the unchosen, you were persuaded to come round to his reasoning. Since those salad Suva days, subsequent knowledge of DNA must have lifted the quality of classroom debates; and observing the global progress of killer-acronyms like WMD and HIV, it must now be a lot more difficult to deny the logic of Donne.

His words prod us to know more about those of whom we are a part: not just the famous and the glamorous, not just the big noters of humanity present and heroically past; but down the ladder through the middling people, the much-like-us and the littler guys, to the losers, the remittance men, the castaways, the fallen-from-grace and all the other beach-combing bums. And when we find that we, like they, are creatures of outrageous circumstance, to what extent are we all defined by where our will, or lack thereof, takes us from there? You'd hope the answer to that question would be, 'All the way.'

Shipwrecked on a reef far from home, shipmates slain by cannibals, alone in a strange new land, what do you do? Howl at the moon and scrape a hole in the sand, or become like Robinson Crusoe and start with the thatching? By the way, if you happen to meet the natives, it's unlikely they'll provide a humble Man Friday to assist with your daily chores. Much more likely you'll be impressed by the accuracy of their spear chucking, as you quickly assume the aspect of an expiring porcupine.

Or is it the lack of compatible company that'll do you in? No one to discuss the cricket scores with, you wander your rock like a tormented Caliban, 'hissed into madness by the cloven tongues of adders.'

Or is it the diet? There are berries that taste like goat droppings, sea-slugs and other lagoon-slitherings, and falling from the sky, the occasional rancid sea-fowl. When Jim Hawkins found Ben Gunn, after he'd been marooned on a rock for three long years, the reformed pirate blurted out the greatest of his many torments, 'Many's the long night,' sez 'ee, 'I've dreamed of cheese - toasted mostly.'

If you do happen to get on with the locals, conditions can be quite copasetic. But you must be prepared to contend with the sanction of your former peers if ever you're discovered in your adopted setting. In 1840, Commodore Wilkes, the US Navy Commodore responsible for David Whippy's elevation to vice-consul rank, was in Fiji with his exploring expedition. Wilkes discovered that forty years after their arrival, dissolute white beachcombers were still finding favour in the courts of Fijian chiefs. Apparently they had their uses as menders of muskets and casters of bullets, but basically they were just hanging out, living a life far removed from the exigencies of service before the mast.

Wilkes came across one such character in the chiefly capital of Rewa, where the high chief's cup-bearer was someone the Commodore describes as 'a worthless Englishman'. The man's name was James Housman, known to the Fijians as Jimmy, and Wilkes says of him,

> Few would have distinguished him from a native, so closely was he assimilated to them in ideas and feelings, as well as crouching before the chiefs, his mode of sitting and slovenly walk. [46]

In this matter Housman has a good degree of sympathy from me. Setting aside the prickly relations between the English and the not-so-recently-enfranchised Americans, there is a discordant note to Commander Wilke's critique. Would not a Fijian living in Washington be expected to adopt American dress and manners, show deference to the President and be seated and generally deport himself in an American way? I would have thought so. Maybe worthless Jimmy was just a little ahead of his time; for today Fiji is full of semi-naked tourists chilling out and doing their best to go native.

Levuka, the old capital of Fiji, was a wild town in the middle of the nine-teenth century, and you can return there in the pages of Brewster's book, *The King of the Cannibal Isles*. By the time the author arrived in Fiji in 1870, Whippy's little Levuka settlement had been transformed into the free-port focus of every thirsty mariner then plying Oceania. The seat of government during King Cakobau's precarious reign, Levuka was at its zenith when Brewster disembarked. For those were the rough and roaring days before Fiji was ceded to the British Crown.

At that time Levuka was one of the most important trading towns between San Francisco and Sydney, a crap-shooting magnet for mutineers, deserters, gun-runners, blackbirders, debt-absconders and the other fragrant members of the cut-and-run fraternity. Brewster describes the relish of his arrival,

The harbour was dense with brigs, schooners, ketches and cutters from all parts of Melanesia and Polynesia, and the beach was thronged with the natives of the hundreds of isles to which our mosquito fleet traded …there were three large hotels, the Levuka, the Criterion and the Royal, and a host of small pubs.[47]

At the time of Brewster's arrival, the Kingdom of Fiji's government was loose at best, lack of revenue being the main problem. Since Levuka was the kingdom's main urban conglomeration and as alcohol consumption was the town's leading activity, it was just a matter of time before a financial genius hit on the idea of adding a liquor tax to the harbour dues, court fines and land taxes that were underwhelming the government's coffers. This fiscal innovation caused otherwise worthy citizens to turn to home-distilling.

Taxes, damned taxes, coupled with incompatible interpretations of the Constitution of Fiji by immigrant lawyers and judges, and the consternations of a deeply divided and confused populace, were a harbinger of things to come in the next two centuries of Fiji's progress. King Cakobau knew about *coups d'état*, he'd perpetrated a beauty back in 1837 to gain control of Bau. So in 1873 the king put the inconvenience of law to one side, dissolved the Legislative Assembly and told his ministers to carry on regardless. Eyes were rolled, words were said … and people went back to business.

Throughout these rugged times, a judicial system was maintained and a criminal code, initially based on that of the Kingdom of Hawaii, was seen to function. Brewster recalls the wheels of justice turning at the time in its unique way, giving as an example the condemning and hanging of a man on the beach at Levuka. The hanged man was a Filipino seaman by the name of Looey, who'd killed a shipmate. Technically it is correct to say that Looey was a hanged man; but the noose in which he was strung up had been left out in overnight rain, so that when Looey was hung, the swollen noose didn't slip and he was left suspended by the neck, kicking and cursing until someone had the decency to cut him down and set him free.

'The palm-grove's droned lament, before Levuka's Trade,' was how Kipling described the trade-winds leading the coconut fronds of Levuka in their timeless rustling dance.[48] Many an hour I've been a spectator at that dance, and sorry Rudyard, I've never heard them make a droned lament. When the trade-winds are in flow they are constant, and the flickering they set in the fronds of the tossing palms sounds like the rush of white-water rapids, or heavy rain on a tin roof, comforting in the fullness of a clement force of Nature.

The town faces the full brunt of the trades, for the only shelter its harbour provides is that of the coral barrier-reef, upon which the cobalt swell of the Koro Sea is forever pounding. The aquamarine lagoon laps at the base of a stone seawall built long ago by Britain's Royal Engineers. Dappling fig trees and coconut palms shade the grassy swathe behind the wall, facing which is Beach Street, with its the colourful row of clapboard stores fronting the lagoon. Behind the row of shops are the flowering hedges of the back-lanes, the old churches, the pavilioned park, and steep, verdant slopes climbing up to basalt peaks. Down these forested slopes the Lovoni tribe came from time to time, trekking over from the island's interior, often intent on burning the town to the ground.

In Brewster's Levuka, big sailing canoes just in from the outer islands were hauled up on the beach; next to which Fijian sailors bivouacked for the night under their matted sails, drinking and singing until the small hours. Warships from the navies of the great powers would be riding at anchor in the harbour, for there were rumours of a French protectorate in the offing, and of the USA exercising its territorial ambitions. German traders, buoyed by the results of the Franco-Prussian War, flew their flags bravely along the town façade; while the British came and went, umming and ahhing over Fijian offers of cession to the Empire.

The Fiji Times had just opened its doors on the Levuka waterfront and an editorial described the frontier mood,

> We have had rows enough during the last week to satisfy everyone for two fortnights, and if broken heads, black eyes and narrow escapes from a Japanese disembowelling with the broadsword, or a few gentle prickings with a fourteen-inch ham-slicer are not

sufficient to make us all go about with revolvers on our belts, as many of the cautious do, yet they make us all wish either for a magistrate that would be a terror of evildoers, or for a beacon to sweep the beach of the drink-maddened ruffian.

One hundred years later and Levuka was about as tranquil as a seaside town could be. Many an evening we strolled the seawall with loved ones, keeping the moon company as it slunk among the loom of mountains. The gunboats, the flag-hoisting proclamations and the stern magistrates had all come and gone, leaving a place rich with little else but its history. There is a beguilement lingering in that place and even after all these years, I find myself back in Levuka every now and then, dog-legging to it in the course of travels to somewhere else.

Whilst over-nighting in the old town, it has been my habit, for many a decade, to stay at the Royal Hotel, for the old pub still stands. I take the same upstairs corner room, and sit on its narrow sloping verandah, with the wooden shutters propped up so I can look out over the reef towards the volcanic silhouettes of Lomaiviti. The sound of the tumbling creek below soothes the soul. The creek curves around the old building, flowing from the waterfall above the town, down to the choppy lagoon.

I feel a tenuous tie to the place, for though my family has not lived there since the 1880s, Levuka memories still trickle through the generations. Because we are essentially a Suva family, our family names do not appear on the sides of the war memorial on Levuka's waterfront in commemoration of those who went from there to fight for the British Empire in the battlefields of the First World War.

When you read the memorial's names, you see some of those families live on in Fiji; but most have moved away or were cut off by the war itself. I also spare a thought for another group of people, the German traders who were part of Levuka's lifeblood for a good part of its existence, whose names are not on that memorial.

We are given an account of the fate of the German traders by Arthur Griffiths, son of the founder of the Fiji Times, who was born in Levuka in 1871 and spent most of his childhood there. In his unpublished memoirs, Arthur recalls how the Germans dominated the Levuka waterfront, their shops and stores stocked with goods to exchange for the copra of the island planters; and how, whenever anniversary or event afforded opportunity, they decorated their buildings with Teutonic flags. It is pretty much forgotten in the Pacific today, that it was the German traders, in particular Godeffroy & Co. of Hamburg, who introduced the all-important copra trade to the Pacific Islands.

In Levuka's narrow lagoon, for many a pioneering year, reeking copra cargoes were loaded onto square-rigged German sailing ships, that up-anchored to follow the wind to far-off Baltic ports. And then came the Great War. Arthur recalls the changes it bought to a little Fijian town at the other end of the world,

> During the First World War every German resident was deported from Fiji and consigned to concentration camps in Australia. I felt at the time that such drastic policy was unnecessary, for those people were law-abiding old residents who were doing no harm. I had grown up amongst them and felt for them a friendly and neighbourly respect. My kindly feeling was further disturbed when, at the conclusion of the war, some of these German residents decided to return to the land in which they had spent the best part of their lives, but on arrival they were met by a lot of hoodlums who dumped their personal belongings into the sea.[49]

If your heart does not go out to them, it must be hard: first the concentration camps and then a homecoming to turn tears of happiness to bitter sorrow. Where did they go after that? I went to school in Suva with descendants of three of those Teutonic families, but what happened to the rest, the Pfeiffers, the Beckers, the Kraffts, Evers, Swetzers and Hedemanns? There would have been no place for them back in war-ravaged Europe … up the river to Paraguay maybe, or some other quiet corner of the Americas? The world keeps turning, and now for the most part, the Anglo families have gone from Levuka too. But the facades of their trading stores are there to this day, be they Anglo or German, their well-worn wooden counters now stocked by the wares of shopkeepers from Mumbai and Shanghai.

A predecessor of mine as a district officer in Fiji was an Englishman by the name of T R St-Johnston. The days of the dinkum beachcomber were dimming by the time he was posted to Lomaloma in Fiji's remote Lau Islands in the second decade of the twentieth century. By then the Crown's regulations were better established on our main islands and opportunities for castaways, in the manner of Old Hands like Jimmy Housman, were diminishing. And so, like flotsam and jetsam, the remittance men and runaway roamers were pulled by moon and tide out to such leafy sanctuaries as Lomaloma. For a while St-Johnston shared their existence,

> I have known of cashiered army officers, Austrian counts out of favour, Italian doctors who have made 'professional mistakes', escaped French convicts, remittance men (there was quite recently an Oxford 'billiard half-blue' acting as marker in the saloon at Mac's Hotel), and a hundred and one of that vast army of men who have lost their positions in the old world, never descending quite to the depths of the city doss-house or the Salvation Army shelter.

> In addition to these men of a higher class there were also rough old stagers of a different stamp, ex-whalers, deserters from ships, broken-down miners, and riff-raff generally from Australia and the South Seas. These were the real old beachcombers, a genus now nearly extinct. The good old days, when square-face gin was a shilling a bottle and 'the Government' was as yet young in the land, were the halcyon days for them.[50]

There was All Serene Jack, who ended his days as a free patient at the Lomaloma hospital. Long ago he was shipwrecked in the barque All Serene and drifted with his fellow-survivors for countless days until lots were cast as to who should live and who should die. Jack was amongst those who dined on his fellow passengers and survived, and no more was said about it.

Joe Thompson, the mad American, lived with his wife Mary, a Manihiki woman, on the neighbouring island of Vatu Vara. He purchased the island with gold from a seemingly endless source, the origin of which he never disclosed. Word in the Islands was that he was one of three survivors of a wreck that had carried bullion and that the other two survivors had 'died'.

Joe dubbed himself 'The Patriach' and wore a long robe and little round cap on the two days in the week he'd declared holy: Sundays and Wednesdays. The Patriarch also declared the end of the world imminent and refused to receive any letters whether private or official ... a not unreasonable stance methinks for a man at the end of the world. For those of a treasure-conspiracy bent, it will no doubt be tantalising to learn that while Mad Joe lived on Vatu Vara, there was a corner of the island, called Qilabalavu, which The Patriach declared forever tabu for anyone but himself to visit. I fancy I hear the sound of metal-detectors being pulled from dusty cupboards.

Many of the old hands in the Islands were relics of the gold rushes of California and Victoria, and the fever had never quite washed clear of their blood. Late one afternoon an excited copra trader burst into St-Johnstone's office in Lomaloma, in his hand a big lump of yellow-streaked quartz. St-Johnstone took a dig at the quartz with a knife and applied some handy acid to it. Sure enough, the rock was rich in gold.

The trader explained breathlessly what had happened. As everyone knew, it was a trick of some Fijians to put heavy rocks into their copra sacks to tip the payment scales in their favour. On a busy day, the trader wouldn't have time to open every sack to see if he was being cheated; only in turning out the copra at close of business would he spot the offending rocks. Seeing a glint of gold in one of the rocks that day, the trader had run up and down the beach trying to find all the Fijians who'd recently sold him copra. There were many of them in attendance, for there was a sporting celebration at Lomaloma and they'd sailed in from all the surrounding villages and nearby islands. All that the frenzied trader wanted to do was establish where the rock had come from; but suspecting a cunning trap and fearing consequent punishment, none of the Fijians would own up to the rock or its origin.

During the Second World War, my father enjoyed the hospitality of a true gentleman of the beach, one Milton Craig. Milton was often described as the last of the remittance men, though of course the species is far from extinct in the Islands today. Milton and his Fijian wife lived at Lodoni, up the Tailevu coast, where the dusty road ran out and a few shacks were dotted along the muddy foreshore from whence the little ferry to Levuka set off across the sea. With the outbreak of the Second World War and the Japanese war machine descending in Fiji's direction, a company of the Fiji Military Forces was deployed to Lodoni with orders to defend the coast in the event of attack. They set up camp in Milton Craig's field.

My father was then a lieutenant in the Fiji army and was one of the four officers in that Lodoni detachment, led by the acting company commander, Ratu Edward Cakobau, great grandson of the aforementioned King Cakobau. Month after month they readied themselves for combat with the Japanese, scanning the horizon from their lookout post on top of a nearby hill, until the Battle of Midway raged away in the ocean to the north and the immediate threat of a Japanese invasion of Fiji was averted.

In Milton Craig's field, their host was often an amiable presence, and Ratu Edward and my father regularly availed themselves of Milton's invitation to call by in the evenings to listen to the Australian Broadcasting Commission's nine o'clock news. For a description of Milton and his house, I call on a former Fiji district officer, Philip Snow, who knew both well and with whom I've been corresponding of late. Philip knew Milton in the 1930s and describes him as someone who would have been 'an attractive figure in any setting – it didn't matter that it was under the popping petrol lantern of a tin hut in Lodoni.' He dressed in a singlet riddled with holes, dirty shorts hung to his knees and he meandered about barefoot. His white hair tousled and his silver mustache droopy, Milton exuded benevolence and a gentle humanity.

A tumbledown shack would not be an unkind description of the abode the remittance man happily shared with a menagerie of birds, insects and mammals, all of who regarded the place as much their home as his. An owl blinked from the cobwebbed rafters of the unlined tin-roof, occasionally swooping through the room to alight on a better perch. The bird was a boon, said Milton, because it drove the mosquitoes from the house with the flapping of its wings.

The first time Ratu Edward and my father sat on Milton's moth-eaten couch to listen to the much-prized radio, their combined weight on the sagging settee caused a great racket when the chickens nesting under it departed in panic. Milton approved of the chickens nesting habits as it made the collection of eggs that much easier. Raggedy cats and dogs slept on the shack's wonky chairs, from which with indignant looks on their faces they would be gently tipped, to allow human guests to be seated. Philip Snow said that if you took a meal there, you were in heavy competition with clouds of flies and the over-domesticated dogs. The tongues of the latter met under your chin as you forked a pile of tinned meat into your mouth, the animals as ever remaining unrebuked by Milton.

Milton Craig came to Fiji in 1889 with his twin brother Willie. They were well-educated men from an upstanding family of Staffordshire, their father a member of parliament, another brother becoming a baronet. There was money in the family from coalmining it was said, but for some reason the twins made a break from it and washed up in Levuka. The quarterly arrival of remittances from Staffordshire was the signal for good times amongst the town's drinking fraternity and it is remembered that if one of the twins was away from Levuka when the joint remittance arrived, the other brother spent it all anyway. Apparently this never led to recrimination, for they were true-to-each-other twins and money was just there for the spending.

Willie died in 1930 and a special remittance arrived from England to equip his grave with a suitable tombstone. Milton assembled Willie's friends for a wake, spending the funds the way Willie would have liked. With the liquor purchased, they drained each bottle and used the up-turned empties to line the grave. A former principal of Levuka Public School, Len Usher, met Milton shortly after his twin brother died and I quote from a Pacific Islands Monthly story that Len wrote in 1947 when Milton himself passed on.

It was Milton who told me of what happened when a Suva business house sent Willie a series of increasingly threatening letters

109

about his outstanding indebtedness. For a time Willie treated the letters with silent scorn but at last he was moved to reply.

'Gentlemen,' he wrote. 'Recent medical research has shown that one of the most prolific causes of cancer of the rectum is the application of paper on which there is writing in ink. Will you please render your accounts in pencil in future.

We can but guess what rests in the heart of a burnt-out remittance man when his race is nearly run. After he died in 1947, a poem that Milton Craig had penned was found among his papers.

Fear not, there is a love that never dies
But passes hence to ever brightened skies,
To that dear one whom we can ne'er forget
And longing pray that she were with us yet.

He's not pining for a ship out of Lodoni to Staffordshire, or begging redemption from the powers that be for a life spent in careless profligacy; he wrote the poem for Matilda, his faithful Fijian wife, after she had drifted on from mortal shores.[51]

The progression from beachcomber to remittance man in the Islands was supplemented by the passing through of classifiable eccentrics. In the 1950s, when he was a district officer on Fiji's northern island of Vanua Levu, Peter Westwood was acquainted with the quirks of Norman Mackenzie-Hunt. In a letter to me, Peter once described Mackenzie-Hunt as,

One of the oddest people I ever met. Meetings with Norman tended to take place halfway up the long Nabouwalu jetty, where he was hard to avoid. He bore a striking resemblance to the ancient mariner, though he had no beard, long wisps of white hair descended from his sun-hat and not only did he 'stoppeth one in three', but practically everyone else as well. Holding you with 'his skinny hand' and transfixing you with 'his glittering eye', he would demand to know what you were doing in Nabouwalu and why. He would then flash out one of his visiting cards which read:

Norman Mackenzie-Hunt FRGS
Conchologist, Philatelist and Planter
Contacts throughout the World
and at 'The Grange',
Nabouwalu, Bua

I was not invited to 'The Grange' but was told it was a broken-down *bure* with packing-cases for furniture.

One of the handful of other Europeans in the vicinity of Nabouwalu in those days was Father Chêne, the priest in charge of the Catholic mission at Solevu. Apparently Mackenzie-Hunt was an avowed atheist and always called the priest Mr Chêne. In return, Father Chêne would courteously address the stamp-collecting conchologist as Father Hunt.

By my time as a district officer in the 1970s, the eccentrics were still coming through thick and fast. Little yachts would bob up over the horizon, in from Fanning, Futuna or islands further off. Their salt-encrusted crew would turn up on your doorstep in search of a feed and a lie-down, and since you'd been brought up to have an always-open door, they got these rudimentary comforts from you. I used to refer to these visitors as hoverers, because they'd hover around like curious birds, before wheeling off to who knows where.

I was living down on the Viti Levu south coast at Naitonitoni, before the tarmaced highway came through, and there were still families of the Old Hands, the beachcombers, the early wayfarers, settled by the beaches and up the rivers of our district. Many were indistinguishable in appearance from their indigenous relatives, but they still carried the family names: the Danfords of Waiyanitu, the Works and Morrells of Naqara, the Wises of Wainividio, the Rounds of Naisigasigalaca.

A couple of miles up the beach from Naitonitoni was a cemetery where many of the Old Hands found their last resting place back in the nineteenth century.

There was no road to that place, out beyond the rice fields in the scrappy littoral fringe of the Navua delta, just a narrow track through the scrub under a high canopy of coconuts. Occasionally while on fishing trips in my little Seagull-powered punt, I would land at that secluded spot. The sea had eroded the sandy point on which the cemetery lay to such an extent that at high tide most of the graves were submerged, as if the ocean were reclaiming its own.

I'd pull the bow of my punt onto the cemetery's narrow beach, take a seat in the shade and observe the headstones cutting through the wavelets of the shallows. In the sheen of early evening, I thought they looked like a grey flotilla, setting sail for the spirit island of Buretu. There was something about those sailing headstones that affected me deeply: all our incessant loss, the disconnection of place, the inevitable washing away, with the falling of tides, of culture, knowledge and life.

The world turns and turns, and those isolated islands where All Serene Jack and The Patriach ended their days have passed through many an eccentric hand since then. They say the world is now a blander place … but is it? One of those islands was purchased by Hollywood's Mel Gibson, fresh from the success of his violent portrayal of *The Passion of Christ*. Another has been inhabited since 1983 by Da Free John and his tithing followers. Da Free John? Look him up on the Internet: John Franklin, born 1939 in New York; moved to California and had his divine reawakening in Hollywood on 10th September 1970.

Da Free told the Californians that he was 'the conscious light of reality itself – all-in-all surrounding, all-in-all pervading, and standing free at the heart of being.' They heard that the story of his coming was the beginning of a new sacred culture and true religion, and on the basis of that, enough of them were sufficiently impressed to purchase for their avatar the outpost island of Naitauba in Fiji. There on 11th January 1986 his 'yogic establishment of divine self-emergence occurred'. One wonders what the island's Fijian plantation labourers thought of that occurrence.

On the various other websites I've googled Da Free, I see that the all-too-familiar allegations of gross sexual misconduct and coercion of waverers are countered by equally impassioned defenses of the guru by his current followers. Da Free's definitive biography is entitled '*The Promised God-Man is Here*', the title alone being enough to make some people glow with gratitude for impending salvation, even as others tilt from the whiff of hokum.

In 1908 my great-grandfather, Herbert Ambler expired before breakfast on the verandah of his Suva cottage. He was of a Shropshire family whose sons for five hundred years before him were farmers, soldiers and vicars of Norman churches along the Welsh border. After his passing, Shropshire was an ever-fading star in the Fiji family's firmament, so that by my time it was little more than fable.

Years ago at Suva Point, I was browsing the jumble-sale at St Luke's church, drawn to it by sweet wafts of banana cake and guava jelly that had meandered down the shady lane to our verandah. In those days we were domiciled a few coconut trees down from the little stone church. St Luke's is part of our family fabric, for my grandparents lived in the adjacent house and helped build the church. Within its walls my wife and I were married and our children were christened.

What made that particular jumble-sale memorable, was that next to a tottering trestle, heavy with pink-iced sponge and door-stop fruit-cakes, I detected a trunk of old books. Rummaging therein, from deep within the papery piles, an unlikely booklet made its way into my hand. I flipped it open and saw the line, 'Clay lies still, but blood's a rover.'

The booklet was a copy of Housman's *A Shropshire Lad*, a work I'd not heard of until that jumble-sale. I saw it was published in 1896, back in the days when Herbert Ambler was doing his roving. I purchased it and went home to brew some tea, retire to the verandah and read. When I learned how he perceived the Shropshire of his childhood, my tentative hold on an ancestral home retreated further into the fog of forgetting.

> What are those blue remembered hills,
> What spires, what farms are those?

That is the land of lost content,
I see it shining plain,
The happy highways where I went
And cannot come again.

My grandmother, Herbert Ambler's daughter, who retired to that cottage next to St Luke's, related that before the first rough roads were cut down Viti Levu's south coast, her father would sail down to Deuba. He had a small vanilla plantation somewhere along the Deuba foreshore and told her the aroma of vanilla would drift off the beach as you approached it from the sea. My grandmother sometimes shared such daydreams with me, I suppose because she saw I liked to listen. I held onto that one, harbouring never-realised plans to become a fragrant vanilla farmer myself one day.

Much later in my life, I was on a visit to Huahine in the Society Islands. This high island, with its bright lagoons, scalloped beaches and green volcanic peaks, truly fits the romantic view of Polynesia. Huahine was once the producer of the Pacific's best vanilla, but by the time I got to there, vanilla production was minimal at best. I happened to meet a surviving vanilla farmer who showed me over his little plantation and took me for a wander into the forest at the back of his neighbour's land.

'*Regardez!*' He was pointing up into the huge trees above us. There were vanilla vines, way up there, gone feral, their pods dangling from branches fifteen metres above the ground. I asked what was going on, and he told me the Huahine farmers had abandoned their vanilla plots and gone to Tahiti and Mururoa to earn wages in the nuclear bomb industry. After the farmers abandoned their vines, some of the vanilla just refused to give in and had headed for the treetops.

That wild vanilla stuck with me as a kind of totem. It was surviving up there in the rain-forest canopy, an aromatic living relic from a time when men were not blowing up the foundations of our atolls, were not poisoning for all time the only planet known to harbour life. Wild vanilla, fragrant and free, abandoned, resilient, loving of life; when the old structures collapsed and its minders departed, it had transformed itself, made its way to the treetops and was thriving in a land of restored content.

I'm diverted by a brief time-travel from the Polynesian island of Huahine in the early 1990s, into Kenya in the 1920s and a farm at the foot of the Ngong Hills. In *Out of Africa*, Karen Blixen wrote of how she once gave shelter to a man who was way down on his luck. He'd exhausted all other options and was undertaking a dangerous walk through the wild to Tanganyika, hoping to find a change of fortune. The man was a Swede, who claimed he'd lost his way and somehow ended up at her farm. Karen knew him by sight as the unpopular *maître d'hôtel* of a Nairobi establishment that she'd stopped frequenting because of his annoying mannerisms.

At the entrance to her house, the man displayed no faith in her hospitality, nor in his own powers of persuasion, when he asked if he might have a meal and bed for the night. Against the grain, she assented and provided him with both, then drove him at dawn the first ten miles of his perilous journey.

When Karen sets him on the road with sandwiches and a bottle of wine, she waits to watch as he exits through the thorn trees, down the dusty way to all his unknowns. The traveller pauses on the brow of the last hill, turns in her direction, takes hat from head and waves farewell.

Of that moment, Karen wrote something that touches the higher self, words that resonate within like a bell, in the fading tone of which one can detect echoes of the Nazarene,

> I felt my heart filling with the love and gratitude which the people who stay at home are feeling for the wayfarers and wanderers of the world, the sailors, explorers and vagabonds.[52]

Quo vadis? Some are travellers longing for a place to lay down long-carried loads; others have not left yet but see the road-gods beckoning. Either way, we may get to wondering whether we'll ever know home again. There's an oblique sort of route-map to follow, and we'll see some signs along the way: signs of the constancy of change. And like William Cary we will probably encounter the suspicions of the settled ones, for farmers in fenced fields have never liked nomads.

But if we consider Ben Gunn's bond with cheese on the one hand, the vexations of non-attachment on the other, and then again the fundamental connection we have to all things, we have cause for pause. So let's take a little time to rest in the shade of a roadside tree, where we can contemplate again the deeps of John Donne's words. Foxes have their holes, but we homeless ones search on for sufficient answer. We may permit a distortion of Archimedes's principle to allow that in our vagrant absence, we've been displaced by a weight of equal proportion. The clichéd homily tells us no one is indispensable, so maybe we just have to face it: all that we loved has given up waiting and taken up with someone else.

Odd, and yes Fate can indeed be cruel. Odysseus found it so, and took it out on Penelope's suitors with a questionable degree of chagrin. But as Milton Craig is our witness, we can reject the Odyssean approach. Even if lost to some Conradian corner, we still have the choice to lighten up on ourselves, toughen up, cast off regrets and venture further up the river. Taking Karen's lead, we enjoy a last wistful look around, fill our hearts with love and gratitude for all the other wandering vagabonds, pull up our breeches and set off like old Basho on the pilgrim path, summoned on by the stars.

GILBERT & ELLICE ISLANDS

GILBERT & ELLICE ISLANDS

POST OFFICE · GILBERT AND ELLICE ISLANDS COLONY
25. APR. 44

POST OFFICE · FANNING ISLAND
25. APR. 44

PASSED BY CENSOR No. 1

GILBERT AND ELLICE ISLANDS COLONY

Mrs E. L. Smyth,
41 Mt Albert Rd,
Mt Albert. S. W. 2
Auckland.
New Zealand.

tarawa

Follow Me

Full moon pulls from nocturnal sea, to reveal a luminescent water-path quivering from shoreline to dark horizon. Pale light shines through aqua arcs under the crests of waves that are curling up the reef's narrow channel, working hard against current's outward flow. Fishing boats jostle at anchor, tugged by the rip running fast from the tight lagoon; the sea is being sucked to the bulge under that swollen moon.

A warm breeze has crossed the ocean. It wraps around me, fluttering my flimsy cotton collar. Here in Avarua the wind is pure, for in the direction from whence it comes, out beyond the Tropic of Capricorn, four thousand empty miles of ocean must be crossed before you sight the coast of Chile.

Along the shore the shuttered town has retired, dozy from the day's trade-wind buffet and the squint of sea-fractured light. I'm suspended above the tide, leaning on the rail of Trader Jack's deck. Behind me, moonbeams light the crazy spires of volcanic plugs that vault from gardens at the back of the little town ... Rarotonga by moonlight, another provocative night in the Cook Islands.

A big man shambles in, acknowledges respectful greetings and takes a seat at the bar. I'd met Sir Tom some twenty years before, when I was Fiji's protocol officer back in the late Seventies and he the visiting prime minister of the Cook Islands. As a medical doctor he'd worked on NASA's space programme until, turning his hand to politics, he'd become the elected leader of his island country. Since those political days, Papa Tom as he was known in the Cooks, had been sailing the ocean, following the ancient star-maps of his Polynesian ancestors. He'd crossed a lot of open water in a double-hulled canoe, *Te Au O Tonga*, the Mist of the South, sailing north to Hawaii and the Marquesas, eastwards to Tahiti, westwards to Tonga, and to Aotearoa in the south.

At Trader Jack's our sailing talk finds its way to the big news of the time, namely the America's Cup regatta to be held the following year in Auckland. Others join us, and the chat is good, as is the rum. We talk about how the regatta will be held in Polynesian waters for the first time, and on one matter the bar is agreed: it would be an outright shame if the America's Cup, the world's premier sailing event, missed the opportunity to pay homage to one of man's greatest sailing traditions, the oceanic voyaging of Polynesian canoes. My sixth rum downed, and Papa Tom and I shake hands on a deal … if I can arrange a prominent place for *Te Au O Tonga* in the opening ceremonies of the regatta, he will have the canoe sailed to Auckland in time to participate.

Our Avarua words proved true, for *Te Au O Tonga* made it to Auckland in 2000 and with conch-shells blowing she came before the America's Cup opening ceremony. There was much that followed from that undertaking, but now that I think of those days, there are three personal indelibles that come to mind.

The first is from a work-boat at dawn, out at the edges of Auckland's Hauraki Gulf, where I went to greet the canoe as it sailed in from the northeast, having crossed thousands of miles of rolling ocean swells. As if on the breath of antiquity, *Te Au O Tonga* slipped in silently from horizon's lip, following the course of its ancestors out of ocean's maw.

The second was walking onto the *marae* above the canoe's landing place on Orakei beach, in the company of the water-logged Rarotongan mariners. The *marae* is the tribal meeting ground of the Ngati Whatua, Auckland's Maori founders, and there we witnessed the same ceremonies of arrival performed in essence across the islands of the Pacific, down through the millennia, as Polynesian voyagers crossed and recrossed the ocean for love and war, for trade, discovery and wild wanderlust.

The third occurred after the regatta's opening ceremonies, when the leaders of the America's Cup syndicates and their captains were invited to a waterfront lunch to hobnob with New Zealand's finest. Papa Tom and I were invited as representatives of *Te Au O Tonga*, and in the usual mêlée of such events we found ourselves at the edge of the scrum. I offered to dive in to retrieve wine, and when I eventually emerged with the glasses, I found myself in the company of not one, but three worthy knights. Sir Tom had been joined by the conqueror of Everest, Sir Edmund Hilary, and by New Zealand's more recent hero, the round-the-world yachtsman Sir Peter Blake.

Over the next half hour while they chatted, I kept their glasses filled and listened to what was said by those three tall adventurers. What stays with me most of that very special experience, was their extreme modesty in each other's company, and the respect and deference with which they asked questions of each other: questions of technique, of exceptional circumstance, and on the glory of Nature.

That tenuous Rarotongan adventure is germane to this story, because the same interests and energies that were propelling me at that time of my life, also led to my involvement in the establishment of a Pacific Islands display at the America's Cup village in Auckland. The display was fitted out with thatch-roofed booths in which various island countries showed their wares, while cultural groups from the Islands performed dance, song and craftings, promoting tourism and the products of the Islands to the well-heeled followers of the regatta.

One day at the village display, I happened to be standing near a wall pasted with material from the Republic of Kiribati, including a map of that country's main atoll, Tarawa. A group of American yachties wandered up in Bermuda shorts and boat-shoes. Having sailed through some of them, they were interested in the Islands and stopped by for a closer look. I saw one of their number stiffen, a grizzled old codger, ivory-bearded, with bandy legs. He was rooted to the spot before the Tarawa map, gawping in silence. Then he took a step back, lifted a shaky hand to forehead and held it there in salute.

There were younger people in the group, and as the Americans moved away, I waylaid one of them long enough to learn the old trooper was his uncle and that he'd been a Marine in the Pacific War. The old fellow went to Tarawa, just for a few days, back in 1943 and he said it was as close to the gates of Hell as you could come in the living world.

The Americans departed. I went over to the island map and ran my finger over the beaches, over the lagoon that I knew from my father's stories had once run red with American blood. Absently I rearranged the pile of tourist brochures beneath the map: come to beautiful Kiribati, come to Tarawa and see for yourself, they told me. So I did.

What ever happened to Grimble's pattern of islands, the venerable Colony of the Gilbert and Ellice Islands? Like Bechuanaland, Ceylon and Siam, they've disappeared from our maps. We know that place-names change with the ebb and flow of history's tide, and now we talk of global warming condemning atoll countries to the fate of Atlantis and Lemuria.

But for the time being, the Gilbert and Ellice Islands do still exist, only by different names. In 1979, on regaining independence, the colony amicably split into a couple of sovereign nations: the Ellice Islands, populated by Polynesians, became Tuvalu, and the Micronesian Gilbert Islands morphed into the Republic of Kiribati.

From birth, the Republic of Kiribati was a precocious child. If you measured the distance between its western and eastern extremities, when it first stepped into the light of day the atoll republic was already one of the world's largest countries. At the same time, it hit the statistics books as the country with the largest disproportion of sea area to land resources, the former vast, the latter minimal.

Take a look at an atlas and the chain of atolls that was the Gilbert Islands can be seen sitting astride the equator at about 173 degrees east. And then, thousands of miles off in the direction of the Americas, the previously uninhabited Line and Phoenix Islands can be found. In colonial times the latter were British territories, although America laid claim to a few of the islands in question.

The Line and Phoenix Islands were known in those times for their tin-can mail deliveries, as trans-Pacific flying boat depots, and for the mushroom clouds of atomic bomb tests. Then, thanks largely to the efforts of a handful of enthusiastic British colonial administrators, at the time of the colony's independence these geographically Polynesian islands were rather generously lumped into the Republic of Kiribati's boundaries. As it had been prior to the independence and division of the Colony of the Gilbert and Ellice Islands, the capital of Kiribati remained on the atoll of Tarawa, as far off from the Line Islands as Washington DC is from California.

While still a youth growing up in Fiji, I was very aware of those islands, their names carrying enduring thoughts, poetically peripheral. Down at the Princes Wharf, sitting on oily hessian sacks by the reeking copra sheds, we'd see scruffy trading ships come butting into Suva harbour, in from the Gilberts loaded to the gills with deck-passengers. During school holidays, we spearfished with a small sling-shot spear we called a *kilipati* or Gilbertese sling. In our museum in Suva there were pieces of Gilbertese fighting armour, including a helmet made from a spiky puffer-fish skin and swords with blades of sharks' teeth. In the Tamavua garden of a friend's house, were two giant clamshells, their ceramic smoothness a delight to touch. They'd been lugged all the way from the Gilberts; shells so big you could curl up in their cool white contours, as snug as a human oyster.

In my father's time as *aide de camp* to the Governor of Fiji and High Commissioner for the Western Pacific, he'd had responsibilities in relation to the Gilbert and Ellice Islands. Later, with eight children to get to bed, he sometimes read us *A Pattern of Islands*, Grimble's tall tales from a lifetime of work in the Gilberts. The opening lines are submerged somewhere deep in my memory,

> I was nominated to a cadetship in the Gilbert and Ellice Islands Protectorate at the end of 1913. The cult of the great god Jingo was as yet far from dead.[53]

Yes, Gilbert and Ellice was a place at the edge of imagination. Thanks to Grimble, you swam towards sleep pursued by hungry tiger sharks, or found yourself wrenching an octopus from where it had fastened to your face. There were other Gilbertian readings: of Becke's stories of the wild American freebooter Bully Hayes marauding through Micronesia, and of Robert Louis Stevenson sailing to the northern Gilberts to meet the corpulent King

Tembinok' of Apemama. RLS's imagery of this king's Lilliputian domain, forged an impression of islands fraught with reasons to avoid them,

> There is one great personage in the Gilberts: Tembinok' of Apemama: solely conspicuous, the hero of song, the butt of gossip. Through the rest of the group the kings are slain or fallen in tutelage: Tembinok' alone remains, the last tyrant, the last erect visage of a dead society. The white man is everywhere else, building his houses, drinking his gin, getting in and out of trouble with weak native governments. There is only one white in Apemama, and he is on sufferance, living far from court, and hearkening and watching his conduct like a mouse in a cat's ear.[54]

Our Suva life was scattered with many a Gilbert and Ellice tit-bit: friends with Gilbertese grandmothers and a stamp-collecting classmate with most of the Gilbert and Ellice stamps. I remember one of those in particular, a red stamp, a one and ha'penny I believe, upon which two islanders calmly surfed an outrigger canoe across a coral reef. I remember Gilbertese students, dressed in white cotton, coming to our little wooden church in Gordon Street. At school we learnt about the sorrow of the slave trade, how Peruvians stole the people of the Ellice Islands in pre-colonial days, to work and perish in the guano mines of South America.

Down on the Suva waterfront, when our school put on Gilbert and Sullivan concerts, I fancied there was some connection with the Islands. I was wrong; the Gilberts were named for a not-especially distinguished captain of the Royal Navy, the Ellice Islands for a not-especially distinguished British parliamentarian.

The names may have changed with independence, but while the Ellice Islands nomenclature no longer figures on our maps, the Gilberts Islands live on; for Kiribati is the indigenous pronunciation of Gilbert. Thus, Captain Gilbert remains one of the few of Nature's creatures to have a country bearing his moniker, joining the eponym company of Captains Cook and Marshall, King Solomon, King Philip II, Columbus, Bolivar, and all those saints for whom the island nations of the Caribbean are named.

In summary, we Suva youngsters knew the Gilbert Islands, but for some reason they seemed always a place that people came from, with precious few ever seeming to go to them. There was, however, a time when that was not so. There was a time when it was the fate of tens of thousands of young Americans to go to the Gilberts, in November 1943, two years after the bitter shock of Pearl Harbour's destruction.

And yes, from that time there would always be a heavy import that accompanied the name Tarawa, the sound of it making some people decline their heads in sadness. For like Normandy, the name can never quite be quit of the shrouds of the Second World War.

Our fathers fought that war, the Pacific War, the ultimate oxymoron; and we were born in its aftermath, touched by its tragedy, sustained by the sacrifice of so many. Apart from our continued existence in the Islands, there were some smaller benefits that accrued to us from the war. In my case, like many people from the South Pacific, because of the Pacific War and my mother's beautiful sisters, I have cousins spread across America.

And then in recompense for our women, there was all the stuff the Americans left behind: airstrips, wrecks to dive on, left-hand-drive trucks, cargo cults. Then there was Marston matting, honey-combed sheets of iron about ten feet long and two feet wide, abandoned by American army engineers after the matting's use on military airstrips and roads. These rusting sheets ran though my Suva childhood. We used them for cubby houses, to make bridges across streams, to fence vegetable gardens, and surround our chicken-runs as first lines of defense against mongoose attacks.

Remnants of the war were underground too, and for as long as a packet of matches would last, we explored the air-raid caves cut deep into the soap-stone hills of Suva. People said there was a whole American field hospital tunneled somewhere under Suva. Above ground, after a hard day at primary school, one that had often been spent reading war comics at the back of class, we would go up through the breadfruit trees to the abandoned shore batteries at Veiuto. There, amongst the grotesque graffiti of the crumbling cement walls, we'd lounge in the gun-housings like AWOL Marines, studying the finer points of cigarette smoking.

The day came when I set off on my journey to the Republic of Kiribati. In preparation for my journey I read a book called *The History of the United States Marine Corps*, and until that time, the full horror of the Battle of Tarawa had not registered with me. It had always been a loaded name, yes, but the reality of those few days of battle had not been revealed. Amphibious landings under enemy fire in the Solomon Islands campaign were part of family lore: when the US army landed on New Georgia's beaches, my Uncle Pony Scherrer was severely wounded by enemy fire and was lain on the beach with the other wounded, one of whom was a Fijian commando companion who died in his arms. But it is in the Battle of Tarawa, that war's essence of horror is distilled in full measure.

Very early in the Pacific War, the Japanese Imperial Forces occupied the Gilbert Islands. With Britain, France and Holland on their knees in Europe, the Japanese War Cabinet had seized the opportunity for a resource grab and struck out to extend the imperial boundaries from Burma in the west, to the Gilberts in the east.

As a demonstration of the empire's progressive new order, upon arriving in Tarawa, the Japanese forces had rounded up twenty-four British subjects and shot, garroted or beheaded them all. Those severed heads lying in the Tarawa sand were a macabre harbinger of things to come.

But on the same day they had struck south into Malaya, the Japanese made a historical miscalculation on the scale of Napoleon's Russian campaign. They snuck up on the American Pacific Fleet in Pearl Harbour and turned the place into a colossal crematorium. What a blunder, what a turning point in world history, one that saved us in Fiji and other places to the south from unavoidable capitulation to the Japanese navy. Washington was thereby given no option but war, and at that stage of its illustrious history, the USA had never lost one of those. Soon Kansas farm-boys, Pittsburgh steelworkers and drawling brawlers from all over America would be rolling up our island beaches.

In the meantime, the Japanese command stationed over four thousand troops on Betio, one of the many tiny islets that make up the extended string of Tarawa atoll. The task of this force was to defend Betio's all-important fighter airstrip.

With fifteen months to prepare, the invaders made a job of it, turning the island into a near impregnable fortress. They laced the surrounding reefs with mines, strung curtains of barbed wire across the coral and positioned rows of reinforced concrete pillars to channel invaders into the cross-fire of well-prepared killing grounds. A perimeter-wall of coconut logs, four feet high, topped the beach; behind which over one hundred machine-gun posts were set up with inter-locking fields of fire across the lagoon. Big gun emplacements, sunken pillboxes and defensive bunkers with reinforced concrete walls six feet thick, were connected by a network of tunnels and trenches. Over the bunkers and pillboxes, the Japanese piled sand in deep layers; for born of the ocean's pounding, sand can absorb huge punishment.

In the eleventh month of 1943, punishment came. For days on end, B-24 Liberators flew up from Allied airstrips in the Ellice Islands to bomb the crap out of Betio. Carrier-based dive-bombers joined the attack, while three American battleships hurled thousands of tons of explosives onto the tiny island. In terms of concentration of fire, it was one of mankind's heaviest-ever bombardments, involving environmental despoliation on the grandest of scales.

Then came the moment of truth, when American landing craft were lowered into the ocean slop and sent off towards the atoll. A great fog of smoke and blasted atmosphere had enveloped Tarawa, so that from out there on the water you could be forgiven for thinking the only task for the Marines was to go ashore and bury the enemy dead.

How wrong you would have been. Not only can sand take a lot of punishment, but if the tide is not high, the coral reefs that created the sand will snag anything trying to cross them. The Americans thought there would be enough clearance over the coral for their landing crafts to pass. There wasn't, and they were soon grounded on Tarawa's adamant reef, sitting ducks for machinegun fire and the Japanese artillery.

At bombardment's end, the Japanese had emerged from their underground hideouts to see the lagoon full of stranded landing crafts. Across the watery flats, they opened fire on their hapless foe.

Those Marines that weren't killed in the boats, jumped into the water to face a suicidal wade ashore. The air scythed with invisible metal, slashing up anything in its way. Out there in the table-flat lagoon, the only things above water were the flesh and bones of US Marines. The nearest cover for these exposed bodies was the island's log-wall perimeter, still half a mile away across the water. It was the only place to go; but over that log-wall, the weapons of their undoing were chattering without pause.

What signals must a brain give a leg to take such terrible steps? None that I can imagine. Wading the stark void of Betio's lagoon, stumbling across its maze of jagged coral, young men pushed on through the Tarawa tide directly towards the source of all that searing death-metal. Guided by what will? Devotion to duty, tenacious courage, bludgeoned discipline or blind-eyed terror? It was a bitter draught they'd been served, truly a devil's cocktail with only the tiniest drop of hope, a splash of side-kick's blood, icy fear stirred into residues of desperate valour.

Loaded with battle gear, drunk with that cocktail, some stepped into holes in the reef, gurgled down and drowned. Most kept their heads above water, most were lacerated lifeless by machine-gun fire. Battalions of men were butchered, so that the Marines coming in with succeeding waves had to push through the fresh bobbing flotsam, the litter of spent humanity, the water pink with the essence of dead comrades.

The targets of the landings were the northern beaches of Betio, code-named with prescience as Red Beaches One, Two and Three, but only the landing on Red Beach Three achieved any degree of success. Those that made it to the beach, shattered by the ungodly experience of getting there, huddled under the coconut-trunk wall. Stunned faces trembling on the narrow shore, looked back in disbelief from whence they'd come, the lagoon awash with the bodies of their buddies.

Most of the survivors were leaderless, their officers left out there face down in the water. A few inches above the wall, the air was blurred by the barrage streaming from enemy guns. No way forward, no way back, no way up but down to death. Who would willingly stand and go over such a wall? Even with a mind muddled by the Devil's cocktail, not me, and dare I suggest, not most of you.

A wounded Marine colonel rallied his survivors under the coconut wall. He grabbed a cowering corporal, who said his squad was all blown away. Pointing along the precarious slither of beach-shelter, the colonel told him to work his way amongst the men, pick any he wanted and say the words, 'Follow me!'

They went over the wall and for every man that died, another survived. Yard after eternal yard, they established a beachhead. A bloody page of the tragedy turned and it became the defenders time to die. Pillbox by pillbox, bunker by bunker, the Marines edged forward. Grenades into the firing slits of pillboxes, explosive charges down the air-vents of bunkers, flame-throwers filling underground fortifications with fire; for three days the killing proceeded, night and day.

On the second day, the Navy got the tide right and landing craft crossed the reef to pick up wounded and drop supplies. American tanks made it ashore. Now reports were coming in of Japanese soldiers committing suicide in their bunkers; rifles in mouths they were pulling triggers with their toes. That night, the Japanese troops at Betio's eastern end charged the American line. One Marine company was nearly over-run in a savage hand-to-hand struggle, but they held the line and in the morning around their position counted the corpses of three hundred enemy soldiers.

Admiral Shibasaki commanded the Tarawa garrison from a two-storey bombproof blockhouse, behind massive walls of concrete and steel, the whole structure buried under a hill of sand and protected by rings of machine-gun pillboxes. On the third day, the structure's defensive ring was breached and US assault engineers clambered up the sandy slopes of the admiral's lair. A fierce firefight sacrificed many on that man-made hill, until a bulldozer made it through and bladed sand across the openings of the bunker. The admiral and two hundred exhausted men were entombed inside. The bunker's air vents were still open and into these the engineers poured drum after drum of gasoline. In went charges of TNT followed by the whump of subterranean explosion. From underground came muffled screams of men on fire.

At the end of the third day's fighting, the guns fell silent. An American Hellcat fighter landed on the airstrip; Betio had been secured. The extraordinary cost of a series of equally extraordinary miscalculations and sacrifices was totted up: over a thousand US Marines perished in the onslaught, along with all but a handful of Admiral Shibasaki's four and half thousand fighting men.

Forty-five years later, I approached the admiral's bunker, its grey pockmarked walls still looming by the Betio beach. For all the bulk of its reinforced concrete, with rusted iron-rebar mangled in every aperture, the walls of the graffitied bunker now seemed vulnerable. No longer could they have sustained the ultimate punishments of war, for the great intercessor was gone, their covering of sand long blown back to the lagoon from whence it came.

The day was oven-hot, I was sun-burnt, bitten crazy by Tarawa sand-flies, ill from food-poisoning. Through the flicker of coconut frond and saw-toothed pandanus, I came up to the dark entranceway. The light of day was harsh, the inner shadows of the bunker deep and rank. I stumbled in, my feet catching in the waste of the ruins, a neglected clutter laid down over all the decades of my life.

Nostrils affronted, eyes adjusting, it became evident the bunker was now a place for illicit drinking, scrawling of obscenities and random defecation. Pushing on down a dim corridor, until in a back corner of the structure I stepped into a shaft of sunlight. Insects whirred up in the beam of brightness to a hole in the cement roof and my eyes followed the flickering wings to that patch of sun-filled sky. Vision blurred in the white ray, time distorted, and the horror of where I stood gripped me. In one monstrous moment among three days of monstrous events, gasoline had come flooding down through that opening, lapping through the bunker about the feet of stricken men, waiting in the oven-crush for the spark that would incinerate them all. I gasped my way from the horror-shadows, out into the burning light of beach and lagoon. To make the sacrificial wade through the naked water and the scything air, or be buried alive and await the flames? Either way, Tarawa's name was forever writ in the book of dread.

I'd flown to Tarawa on Air Nauru's Boeing 737. Leaving Fiji, bound for Micronesia, you can't help but notice the baggage-holds being loaded with cooler-boxes. In fact there were more taped styrofoam containers, chilly-bins, eskies and food-cartons going into the aircraft's hold than travel bags. It seemed a potent sign of atoll conditions today, that Micronesians jet home with food as their luggage.

From Fiji we flew to Nauru, where the aircraft filled with Gilbertese con-tract-labourers returning to Kiribati. There were no seat allocations and the jet was stormed like a department-store sale. Beaming usurpers had to be prised from business class seats, to take their place further down the fuselage. It was equatorially hot in there as we waited for the engines to start, but they would not start, for we had a stowaway amongst us.

The Nauruan ground-staff stood at the front of the plane admonishing us all; someone should not be on board. The Gilbertese passengers were in high spirits, wild laughter and fecund body odour cloyed through the confined space. There was a standoff, further admonishment, further stand-off, for the culprit was not giving in easily. Admonishment turned to official anger, more laughter from the Gilbertese, more official anger, more laughter. Eventually the ground-staff advanced down the aisle, checking our tickets one-by-one. Not until they reached the very back-row of the plane did they find the stowaway, an overweight young man with a ghetto-blaster on his shoulder. He deplaned with a dopey grin and wandered off along the airport road.

The shrill laughter continued all the way to Tarawa. I had a mother and lap-child in the seat next to me. While the mother shrieked at her friends' hilarious stories from several rows back down the aisle, the baby screamed out loud for the duration of the flight. The cause of the writhing infant's discomfort was plain to see. Large impetigo sores, weeping thick yellow pus, covered the child's feet and hands. Due to the punishing economy of modern airline seats, by the time I disembarked at Tarawa, much of this discharge had found its way onto my adjacent arm and leg.

The jet circled the atoll, and we picked out the airstrip transecting one of the long islets. From the air, well-worn paths could be seen crossing the runway and along these paths, pigs, dogs and people were promenading. The jet swung around on final approach and one presumed the promenaders would be making way for us. Touchdown, and half-way down the runway a glimpse of clusters of people at holes in the runway fence, waiting for us to pass before resuming their roaming. Along the runway verge, dogs and pigs scampered in all directions.

Welcome to the Republic of Kiribati. A front-end loader advanced on the jet and our bags and leaking chilly-bins were soon being chucked into the jaws of its bucket. The loader trundled back to the open-sided arrival shed and tipped its load onto the ground. After several of these dump-runs, the loader created an impressive luggage-mountain, over which Micronesian mountaineers began climbing to pluck forth their seeping eskies and dribbling food-cartons. My soft-leather carry-all was eventually unearthed from the base of the pile, soaked through with the mountain's effluent, a stinking combination of defrosting meat and fish juice.

I was in Kiribati at the behest of the Pacific Forum's secretariat, to report on possibilities for enhancement of exports from the atoll republic. Booked into Tarawa's only hotel of note, prime property of the government of Kiribati, a week's residence lay ahead.

It proved to be a long week, for the hotel had issues, management issues. A new manager had just been appointed, a civil servant whose paper-shuffling perseverance, tided through years of bureaucratic tedium, had been rewarded with this, the heady management eyrie of the government hotel.

It transpired that his managerial installation demanded ceremony. Not one but many, continuing day and night for most of the time I resided at the hotel. The staff, their relatives, close and distant, guests from the ministries, former office colleagues, all took time to engage in the ceremonies, which took place in an open-walled, thatched structure out on the hotel's waterfront. This attractive building was presumably meant as a recreation area for paying guests, but the latter, not wishing to intrude on the portent of ceremony, kept a glum distance. A skeleton staff provided us with sullen service, their intemperate attitude understandable considering all the speech-making, feasting and dancing they were missing out on.

At cocktail hour on the first night, I befriended a fellow guest, a large agricultural bureaucrat from the Kingdom of Tonga who'd been attending a phytosanitary symposium in Tarawa. The symposium was over and he was desperately waiting for a plane to get him the hell home. Unusually for a Tongan, he advised me against eating … stick to imported beer and packets of potato crisps, he told me. He'd been at the hotel for a week now and every other guest he'd met had some form or other of food poisoning.

Without much success, I looked for alternate eating-places on the atoll. The Bairiki hut serving what the menu described as 'Ham Bugger' and 'Stuff Steak' looked the most salubrious, but when you feel under the weather, and ghetto-blasters and waitresses are in shrieking disaccord, a concrete hot-box is no place to be. So it was back to the gauntlet of hotel dining, each swallow a gamble, Tarawa roulette. On my side was a gut of Fiji iron that had held true in all my wanderings through the dodgy eateries of the Indian subcontinent, so I figured I was up to the challenge. Within a day or so, I was down and out, passing blood in the toilet.

The menu had been promising enough, Lobster Mornay featured daily, but like ninety-nine per cent of the menu, the lobster was pure fantasy. The only menu items that could be counted on actually appearing were Australian corn flakes and canned Australian orange juice. In the kitchen they put ice-blocks in my orange juice. Big mistake; the smell of the water emitting from the shower in my bathroom was repellent, I should have known better than to abide that ice.

I contracted shigella, a notifiable disease in most countries. How is it spread? By people not washing their hands before preparing food, and from the faeces of those so infected. What are its symptoms? Stomach cramps, fever, vomiting and bloody diarrhoea. I could see the hotel kitchen from my room. How I longed to lob a hand-grenade gently through one of its open windows.

Each day I engaged in a trembling trek from sweaty bed to fetid bathroom. The toilet was broken. I procured a bucket and wore a rut between shower and toilet running the flushing detail. Each day I left a note at the front desk asking for a change of room, or for a plumber to fix my toilet. Neither eventuality materialized. Finally heeding my Tongan companion's advice, I gave up eating.

Out on the hotel waterfront, the ceremonies of welcome continued. Great solemnity, relieved by bouts of wild hilarity, emanated from the thatched gathering. A new order was being inaugurated out there, alliances were being forged, loyalties dedicated, promises of a beautiful future were being made.

Dawn broke on the longed-for day of departure; with any luck Air Nauru would lift me away before sunset. I found the hotel manager in his office, preparing for the day's ceremonies. Sinking weakly into the chair before his desk, I summoned all my powers of deference. I summarised the state of my room: the sulking fridge with mildew levels suggesting at least two months since last it worked, the lampshade shattered into exactly thirteen pieces, the carpet more rotten than not, a cupboard drawer stinking of something so severe that hotel staff had obviously judged it unwise to ever open again.

But it was the toilet that presented us with the real problem. As politely as possible, I calculated that in all the time the manager was being fêted out front, I'd been carrying a bucket around my room for so long that I was effectively an employee of his. I tried and failed to lighten the moment, suggesting I might even qualify for the employee-of-the-week award. His eyes narrowed and I moved on to my purpose. I wished to inform him, with deepest regret, that before I settled my bill I required a twenty per cent discount on my room tariff, in lieu of water-carrier wages.

He was, as I have said, a seasoned civil servant and his first reaction did his profession proud. From way above the coconut trees, he acquainted me with the hotel's regulations, the acts of parliament they were governed by, and all the other laws and licenses pertaining to the functioning of the flagship hotel of Tarawa. I was welcome to peruse them, he would be happy to make them available to me, but he could assure me that nowhere therein would I find provision for a manager to grant a discount to a guest.

Too weak to argue, too tired to move, I just sat where I was and lamely repeated my demand. Short of throwing me out, he had a problem: he had ceremonies to go to, there were still people out there waiting to fête him, deeply desiring his wise leadership, ready to listen all day to his prayers for unity and progress. A crease of consternation furrowed his brow, the beginnings perhaps of executive stress.

To cut to the chase, he launched an appeal to my sense of compassion. He'd been in the job for less than a fortnight, dedicating himself to service of his government, of his people. I should realize his hands were tied for he was bound to obey the laws of the land, and he carried a heavy burden of high management responsibilities on behalf of the Republic of Kiribati. I was unmoved.

He briefly tried annoyance, muttering veiled threats at the wall behind his desk, before saying his presence was urgently needed elsewhere, whereupon he left the room. I felt bad for him, I knew I was spoiling the dream-run the last fortnight had afforded him, but something had to give. I craned around and saw the manager pacing back and forth on the path that twisted through the undergrowth behind the accommodation block. He came back towards the office, saw I was still there and returned to the path.

Next I spotted him behind the accommodation block in deep discussion with the front-desk clerk. The manager was listening intently. A few minutes later, he was back at the office doorway. He seemed to be restored to the majesty of his office. He took his executive seat, straightened the pen on his desk, and donning the purple mantle of bureaucracy announced, 'I got authority to give you ten per cent discount. That is the limit of my authority.'

Perhaps the front-desk clerk was aware of a wily loop-hole in the law; more likely he just had managerial potential. I got to my feet and we consummated the deal with plastic.

From the hotel you drive west along the string of islets that make up southern Tarawa, the densest single-storied concentration of humanity in the Pacific. The islets are now joined by causeways running across the lagoon. And what a dazzle of a lagoon it is, in fact there is nowhere to go to escape its beauty. Blue shades overlap: the calm of duck-egg shallows, ripples of turquoise kingfisher, streaks of peacock-breast out yonder. Snow-white fairy terns flicker above silver sprat-shoals, as black men o'war glide up high with forked tails and crimson bandanas. And skimming across the blue at breakneck speed, you will see the white of fluttering sails, for the Gilbertese still love to race their outrigger canoes, free of sand-bound cares.

In the canoes and the remnants of traditional architecture you see the wonder of what the people of the atolls achieved. Complex cultures, intricate artifacts, robust legends and beliefs, hardy people descended from adventurous ancestors and a way of life super-refined by the narrow limits of the atoll environment. You can but marvel at their resourcefulness, when you consider the days before packaged foods and medicines, before the arrival of internal combustion engines, navigational aids and chilly bins.

But now there was another glint along the edge of Tarawa lagoon … that of aluminium beer cans … the predominant brand, Victoria Bitter. Well might Victoria be bitter at the litter of them all, for they were everywhere, dominating the display of plastic and tin that spread along the beaches, roadsides and public places of southern Tarawa.

Tarawa is what academics used to call a development pole. Most developing countries have one, the national centre towards which previously rural people flock to pick at the scraps of the new order. As a late entrant to all the seductions of the consumer age, out on the edge of human story, it was plain that the atoll Republic of Kiribati was mixing itself a potent brew. Too many people were congregating in a fragile place too small for all the hungry demands, lacking the escape of a nearby mainland or mother country, population exploding, groundwater polluted by sewerage, feared diseases rife, sea levels inexorably rising; Tarawa's problems were compounding.

I wished to broach some of these problems with one of the republic's high civil servants. I was told he was too busy to see me. I persevered. When I made it to the inner sanctum, an air-conditioned office in the Ministry of Tourism, the too-busy official pretended to be engrossed with reading a weighty tome. Avoiding my enquiries with dexterity, not long into our meeting he excused himself for a lengthy visit to the bathroom. My eyes ran over the title of the book he had been purporting to read, 'Mine and Metallurgical Industries in Iran'.

I had time to kill. I flipped the book open. It was published in Tehran in 1992 by ESCAP, a UN economic and social commission. So this was the way of the world: a United Nations agency pays for the publication of a book of limited interest to a select band of metal-heads. Flush with funds, the commission finds itself burdened with unreadable copies of an obtuse metallurgical book and ships the tome to any country that will accept anything from the United Nations without asking why. As to the mechanics of the unblemished book making its way from the container stack of Tarawa's jetty, to its current use as a footrest at the Ministry of Tourism, I was unable to formulate a definitive answer.

When you cross the causeways of Kiribati for the first time, across the reefs to the little islands of Bairiki and Betio, it is difficult to suppress the idyllic view of Tarawa. For these were the romantically remote islands of canoe-racing aesthetes, where professional wizards worked the magic of kindness, where tribal dreamers inherited powers of porpoise-calling, where giant *maneaba* filled with the elaborate discourse of proud gentlefolk[55], the islands Grimble told us,

> ... were peopled by a race who, despite the old savagery of their wars and the grimness of their endless battle with the sea, were princes in laughter and friendship, poetry and love ...

Arriving at Betio, you are at the terminus of the atoll's long line-up of islets. Romance exits stage left, pursued by a tiger shark; for unavoidably ahead are the big guns the Japanese purchased from the British in Singapore, before the commencement of their un-pacific war. The ironic testimony of the guns endures, for their great grey barrels still point uselessly south.

Venture to the north side of Betio and you have fetched up in the marginally bustling hub of a vast swathe of the Central Pacific. Here is the republic's entrepôt and administrative centre. It was here too that the American fleet disgorged its sacrificial Marines in 1943, on this islet's beach that those ineffaceable words 'follow me' were uttered.

Now the only ships I could see off Betio's shore were Japanese. They were freighters from Yokohama and Kobe, lying at anchor, awaiting their turn to offload containers of canned fish, instant noodles and beer.

I could not leave Betio without paying respect to the fallen. I pulled *The History of the United States Marine Corps* from my bag and followed its maps past the port complex, the latter under construction courtesy of a Japanese government grant. Without much difficulty, I found Red Beaches One and Two, the site of the war's watery slaughter.

But I could not bow my head in silence upon the hallowed beaches; instead I stood in shock. What I had come to at the end of my pilgrimage was a great reeking mass of rubbish piling high along the Red Beach foreshore, a sagging, stinking peninsula of refuse creeping steadily out towards deeper water.

If there was ever a statement by the Gilbertese that this had not been their war, then this rubbish dump was it. So be it. But what troubles me still, as a man who loves his Pacific world as much as any, is recalling my walk out to the edge of the Betio rubbish dump and seeing how in the lapping of the tide, the rejected rot, the seeping poisons, the impervious materials of dubious progress, were staining their way out into the lagoon.

All through the surrounding waters the oily substances, the festering filth and floating muck were spreading away across the calm lagoon, and amongst it all were little dark heads, groups of children swimming amongst the mire. For a while, the sight of them and their poisonous surroundings sank my heart to the bottom of Betio's bombarded lagoon.

It was late afternoon, that time when calm water takes on the sheen of light blue metal and floating blobs turn to chocolate shadow. The children pushed the bobbing rot aside, they moved towards me through the tide, like little Marines progressing through lifeless forms. They hit on the battered shore, bright souls shining up through limpid dark eyes, expecting, deserving all the best possibilities and rewards of lives to come, just like those Kansas farm boys, in fullness of health and knowing all the joys of creation. They clambered on up through the detritus, ascending towards uncertainty.

Guam Survivor

It's a long way, my friend, to the Republic of Palau, sitting out there in that far-western corner of the Pacific. When you get down to it, Palau's not really on the way to anywhere. Back in the 1990's, I was requested to visit this Micronesian apogee, to prepare a report on how the island republic might increase its exports. Palau was calling.

To get there it was necessary to book a clutch of island-hopping flights that zig-zagged around the Western Pacific. En route I discovered that all these flights were at off-peak times when airports have only skeleton night-staff and you must find benches on which to cat-nap while you await pre-dawn departures. Somewhere along the way, I sleepwalked into a bus that took me to a hotel where I died on a bed.

Eventually I resurrected from the void to the dim shadows of a humming room. Pulling heavy curtains aside, full-frontal-mid-morning glare assailing, the aluminum slider stuck then jerked aside, permitting my egress onto a narrow balcony slimy with an air-conditioner's dribble. Oven-hot air crinkled my tee-shirt. The aerial view of an empty amusement park lay below, and beyond that a vista of cement buildings set against a background of scrubby hills randomly strung with power poles. Something about it all sapped my soul.

Where was I? It was a lot like a lot of other places, but this was somewhere I'd never been. Coffee was required.

In the elevator the bride's half of a Japanese wedding party jostled in. Amongst that tittering crush of smooth limbs and smoother chiffon, before we reached the ground floor, most of my fellow descenders managed to have their photographs taken brandishing the two-fingered peace salute. The lobby was teeming with more Japanese and the thought crossed my mind that I'd caught the wrong flight and ended up in Okinawa.

The concierge was dressed up like a New York bell-hop. He looked vaguely Filipino and I figured he'd sort it out for me. The bell-hop bowed and said, '*Håfa Adai*.'

In my ignorance I thought he'd just mangled, 'Have a good day'.

'Thank you, and the same to you. Excuse me, what ... country ... is this?'

Trick question? Very tentatively he suggested, 'Guam?'

Yes, that was it. I was transiting the Micronesian island of Guam, in that case still on track to my Palauan destination. Lifting a brochure from the please-take-one-pile, I studied it while absorbing caffeine in the hotel lobby. 'Guam's unique Chamorro culture and language is a blend of Spanish, Micronesian, Asian and Western influences,' explained the Guam Visitors Bureau.

It said *håfa adai* was the Chamorro equivalent of Hawaii's *aloha*. I also learned from the GVB brochure that Guam was an unincorporated US territory and that it was clearly modeling its tourist industry on Hawaii's. I wondered what an unincorporated territory might be and who'd thought that one up.

Brunch seemed like the next best step. The dazzling concrete strip of Pale San Vitores Road ran by the hotel, so offering out *håfas adais* to all and sundry, I footed my way up the pavement. Casting around for a suitable cafe, through the palms running down the centre of the boulevard I spied the sign of the Håfa Adai Gun Club. The enigmatic signage demanded closer inspection.

The ballistics club was upstairs from a concrete-cubed collection of Asian shops - sushi-ya, adult video store, escort service, massage parlour, acupuncture clinic. The gun club had no windows, the heavy front door opening onto a carpeted reception area, where a girl sat behind a velvet-fronted desk. Judging by the sounds of muffled shots coming from beyond another heavy door, that was the place where club members were making *håfa adai* with their guns.

It was then I recalled that even if it was unincorporated, this was US territory and America was gun-lobby-land. This thought gave me pause. From all I'd read, the second amendment was fast on the draw and the receptionist's expression was losing its welcome expression. I doffed my fedora and made for the door.

When it comes to brunch, you're spoilt for choice in Guam's Tumon Bay. There's Planet Hollywood, Starbucks, McDonalds, Subway, Hard Rock Café, Baskin Robbins and Thank God It's Friday - what happens to the latter's trade on the other six days, one just has to wonder.

I dined in one of the trans-global fast-fooderies. Which one? Does it matter? The food dissolves as it hits one's tongue, transforming into sweetly over-refined slurry, before heading on down for a chemically-rich, hormonally-endowed transition. I saw the brilliant plan: eradicate the desire for food, thereby combating the over-exploitation of our planet's limited resources.

As you step along Pale San Vitores Road, you see more of that brilliant global future. You are on a remote Pacific Island, but you could be in a precinct of Los Angeles, with a touch of Taipei or Tokyo Disneyland. Wandering through the Tuscan columns of the Galleria entrance, one glides over marble floors, mid the silken flutter of Hermès scarves. The perfumed manicure of international retail engulfs you: Dior, Chanel, Dunhill, Tiffany, Cartier, Dolce & Gabbana, 'etcetera, etcetera, etcetera'.

When did the mind-numbing sameness of globalised, aspirational consumerism assume its place as the ultimate leisure activity, the glossy path to personal fulfillment? How was it that humanity succumbed to that horseshit?

Down here on Pale San Vitores, even the Visitors Bureau's gloss on Chamorro culture doesn't get a look in. In the transnational bazaar it is local character and local industry that is the loser, and when you look at the brands and the customers, you see it's every bit as much an Asian cop-out as it is American and European.

Fleeing the retail strip, I found a gap through the great barrier of foreshore hotels and stepped onto a long sandy beach. Joyous day! Out there in the blue and white dazzle of Tumon Bay was an impressive lagoon with gentle surf rolling onto a reef about a quarter of a mile out. I stripped off and swam out for a better look. While dense groups of tourists frolicked in the warm shallows directly in front of their relevant hotels, further out the water was crystal clear, cool and free of other swimmers.

Lolling about out there I took in the sweep of all the beachfront hotels, their names emblazoned high on the sides of room-towers serrating the sky. Excuse another brand-list, but here goes: Westin, Holiday Inn, Nikko, Pacific Islands Club, Marriott, Hotel Okura, Hilton and Outrigger. For a little island in the Pacific, Guam was exceptionally well-hung with hotels, but it was hard to shake the sneaky feeling it was a poor man's Waikiki and that something distinctively Guamanian was missing.

Floating in that Tumon waterbed, I gazed up at a giant, ice-white cumulus boiling into the blue-on-blue sky. The cloud lumped restlessly on, lumbering out across the Philippine Sea like a lost polar bear. It was soon replaced by several more looming off the island, passing overhead, ephemeral, bound for recycling in rains and rivers.

Eyes closed now, I lazily aqua-warbled the cloud song, 'Rows and flows of angel hair, and ice cream castles in the air.' I was slipping into a gentle state of marine meditation, when into water-filled ears came a deeply sustained rumble.[56]

Looking up, I saw that through the turbulent clouds a long silver shape was advancing. Moving slowly, wide wings out-stretched, bouncing in buffets of tropical updrafts, a giant B52 Stratofortress was coming in low, with wheels exposed for landing, wing-flaps down and shuddering hard, the bomber's great silver underbelly pregnant with nuclear weapons.

Guam is a military outpost. After the Spanish-American war of 1898, the Americans purchased the island from Spain and the US Navy was given the responsibility of governing Guam for over half a century. Even during the war years when Japan occupied the island, it was run by the Japanese Navy, who renamed it Omiya Jima and went about the island intent on instilling a fervent spirit of respect for the Emperor of Japan.

When the war began going badly for Nippon, the occupying forces took things out cruelly on the hapless Chamorros. As a result, to this day Guam's annual festival hangs around 21st July, Liberation Day, when the US Marines reclaimed the island from the Japanese Navy at great cost to human life. Despite the bacchanalian noise generated by these annual victory festivals over the next three decades, a Japanese corporal, thinking his country's surrender unlikely, hid in the Guamanian bush until he was discovered in 1972.

But it is not the survival of the determined corporal that this narrative is advancing upon, it is that of a woman. Our female survivor wasn't born in Guam, but lived there as a teenager after the war when her father was in charge of the medical services of the island. She was there when her mother died of cancer and was buried in one of the island's cemeteries. She was there when she met and married her first husband and had her first child. For reasons I will shortly explain, she is the survivor that mattered to me.

What made me think of her that day was something I found on the beach of Tumon Bay. I'd emerged from my swim and was taking a stroll down the beach, marveling at all the proto-Christian wedding chapels constructed along the beachfront for Japanese post-nuptial photo-ceremonies.

Towards the top of the beach in front of one of the hotels, I spotted what could only have been the partially-buried remains of a wartime pillbox, emerging a few feet above the sand. To most visitors I guess the pillbox would have looked like part of a storm drainage system, but if you've seen these structures elsewhere in the Islands you know what they are.

On closer inspection, I found the structure's firing-slit was just above the level of the beach-sand, through which a couple of wary Japanese gunners would once have scoured the bay. I got down on my belly and slithered in under the flat cement roof, so that I was inside looking through the slit at what was once the gunner's field of vision. I tried to imagine what it was like to be one of those men, doing their bit in the defense of Omiya Jima, ready to deal out multiple metallic deaths, facing almost certain death themselves.

Now as you peered through the slit towards the horizon from which the invaders came, you were confronted by a view that captured the futility of war, *in extremis*. Blue sky, sapphire sea, white sand, and all along the waterline, playing in the shallows with bright pink balls and yellow plastic boats, a thousand Japanese tourists were frolicking. The time-worn concrete framing the view begged an explanation for this happy scene. The millions of corpses of the Pacific War, the gruesome suffering of tens of thousands of prisoners, of the wounded, of the raped, of the tortured and the mutilated, all these demanded an answer.

I lay there trying to figure a way through the quagmire of history, through the irony of it all. It was then that the memory of what my Guam survivor was made to endure imposed itself, for her life was branded by that bitter irony, and I felt compelled to put down in writing a little of her story.

Before I do that, I should record that I lived in Japan with my wife and children for four years in the early 1980s. They were four of the happiest years of our lives, amongst considerate people living in a regimented but vibrant society. I can think of no other metropolitan location on this earth where, surrounded by millions of people, it would have been safer to bring up our young children.

I was in Japan serving as a diplomat from Fiji, and when I was introduced to Emperor Hirohito, I crossed the long throne room at the Imperial Palace to bow deeply before a man once considered to be a god. The Japanese economy was booming, Tokyo was flowering, and with our Japanese friends we worked and played like there was no tomorrow. When I left Japan, I kept up my Tokyo associations and in the 1990s, by then running my own company in New Zealand, my biggest client was a Japanese bank. Japan has been good to me.

I say for every benign heart in your society, you'll find one in Japan; likewise for every miserable bastard you've got, Japan's got one too. In the context of this story, I also say it is militarism that gives the ruthless xenophobe and heartless hoodlum the opportunity to indulge their ugly appetites, and when war breaks over us, for them it is feasting time.

Allow me, one more precursor. After Neville Chamberlain's death in 1940, Churchill rose in the House of Commons and said,

> History with its flickering lamp stumbles along the trail of the past, trying to reconstruct its scenes, to revive its echoes, and kindle with pale gleams the passions of former days. What is the worth of all this? The only guide to man is his conscience; the only shield to his memory is the rectitude and sincerity of his actions. It is very imprudent to walk through life without this shield, because we are so often mocked by the failure of our hopes and the upsetting of our calculations; but with this shield, however the fates may play, we march always in the ranks of honour.[57]

Universal honour and its dark twin, malevolent injustice, are not the preserve of any one people. Please remember these words, my friend, as the story of the Guam survivor is told.

Her father was a gregarious doctor in the Royal Dutch Indonesian Army, her mother from a Rotterdam family with a colourful past in jet mining, phrenology and vaudeville trouping. On the Indonesian island of Flores, the young Dutch couple adopted the first of their children, a boy whose mother had died in childbirth. From Flores they were posted to Surabaya in Java, and there the subject of our story, a baby girl named Loelie, was born in 1934. By the time the Japanese army invaded Singapore in 1941, the young family was living in Bali and another daughter and baby boy had been born to them.

The day came when as a seven year old, Loelie saw silver planes fall from the clouds to dive-bomb their home town of Denpassar. Come March 1942, and the Japanese were in control of Indonesia, rounding up the European population and interring them behind wire. The little family of our story made up just six of the eighty thousand Dutch civilians incarcerated by the Imperial Japanese Army in the infamous prisoner-of-war camps of the East Indies.

The IJA commenced separating the Dutch men from their families, holding them for the rest of the war in all-male POW camps, in her father's case on the island of Sumatra. Meanwhile, along with her mother and three siblings, little Loelie was to spend the next three and a half years in three different camps around eastern Java; taken from one camp to the other in over-crowded cattle trucks, like Hitler's victims in Europe, shielded from the eyes of the outside world.

Later in life, Loelie wrote a memoir about those years and it makes harrowing reading. Early on, the Kempei Tai, the Japanese equivalent of the Gestapo[58], took her young mother away to 'a very bad hotel' where she was starved, beaten and subjected to acts that she was never able to relate to her daughter.

Such were the conditions of scarce medical supplies, crammed sleeping racks and starvation rations, that sickness and disease were soon rife. Then, on top of vermin infestation and rudimentary outdoor ablutions in the equatorial mud, they had to learn to contend with the peculiarly cruel punishments the IJA favoured.[59]

She contracted beriberi, her infant brother was ravaged by malaria and her younger sister plagued by kidney disease. Dysentery, epidemics of whooping cough and all the other ailments of malnutrition were commonplace, so that by war's end a fifth of all prisoners had died in the camps. One records a statistic like that with such ease. And if it gives you pause, if it brings a stumble to your day, the Stalins of this world will only scoff. But when you ponder that each one of those unjust deaths was an ultimate personal tragedy, it is hard to let go of the IJA's crimes.

In the listlessness that comes with beriberi's bloating, she would have to force herself to get up to queue for the daily ration of a teacup of boiled rice slurry. She watched her playmates die, she watched her playmates' mothers die. She watched when the camp gates opened for the bullock-cart to haul out the daily dead. She watched when her mother was stripped to the waist and beaten with a bamboo cane. She was just nine years old then, but she and her younger siblings were taken by an IJA guard to the camp commandant's office and made to watch their mother's beating. As the flaying continued, blood streaming down the maternal back, her mother's crime was contemplated: the procurement of the scraps of smuggled Javanese food without which her children could not have survived.

Too many movies may have made us immune to these scenes. We may even find them clichéd, as if we've actually experienced the emotions involved from the fatuous padding of our theatre seats. But the endless parades in the searing sun, the barking of Japanese officers, rifle-butt beatings, the lashing of racial hatred, and far, far worse, it all happened over and over again, repeated throughout the camps of the blithely-named Greater East Asia Co-Prosperity Sphere. Like it or not, forgive or forget, we continue to live with the consequences of those deeds.

In our family's camp there was a Dutch doctor, a small woman, who worked night and day for the welfare of the prisoners. Dr Engels was her name and she delivered the only baby born in the camp. On a day of particular heat, when the prisoners had been standing on parade under a blistering sun for many hours, the pram containing the tiny baby was placed by its carer in the shade of a tree at the edge of the parade ground.

A Japanese officer marched over to the pram and Dr Engels walked over with him. The officer removed his sword and used it to edge the pram back into the sunlight. In protest at the officer's action, Dr Engels placed her hand on his sword where it pushed against the pram. That was all it took. They beat Dr Engels savagely on the spot, with the whole camp looking on, then dragged her off to a holding cell for further brutal punishments. In this way one presumes the honour of the officer in question was being restored.

Around this point if one felt like taking the whole ethos of *bushido* and assigning it to the sordid memory of that officer, I'd say you'd be justified.

Three days later it was Emperor Hirohito's birthday, Tenno-Haika as he was referred to in the camps, the divinity who presided over the Cabinet that was running Japan's war. He was not then the distant constitutional figurehead I was to meet on a number of occasions in Tokyo some forty years later. Tenno-Haika was the man who when his forces conquered Singapore in 1942, mounted a white charger and rode out to acknowledge the jubilant Tokyo crowds gathered at his palace gates.

At the emperor's birthday parade in that festering Javanese prison, the camp commandant was in a celebratory mood and decided upon a gesture in the mode of Pontius Pilate. To celebrate the happy day, short of letting them all go, he would grant the prisoners one special birthday request. No doubt he envisaged dolling out extra rations of rice-balls to his starving charges. But the response from the camp was unanimous, 'Release Dr Engels.'

The wish of the prisoners was granted. Now strip yourself of that blasé immunity and stand with those emaciated prisoners on the parade ground. Come to attention with everyone else. Hear the absolute silence of all those women and children, as they pay Dr Engels her last respects. She carries terrible internal injuries, meted out by the honorable ones; but she walks unaided before them all, making her way back to the prisoner's medical station to die before the night is out.

At Ambarawa camp, all the boys who'd reached the age of ten were separated from their mothers and marched out of the camp to uncertain fates. When Loelie's adopted brother Peter came of age he was made to join the marchers.

With no idea where their sons were being taken, mothers were reduced to the futile misery of looking on as their boys filed away from the wretched camp. Well did they fear, for when post-war accounts were told of the perversions to which the boys were subjected, it did not leave a pretty picture of humanity.

Peter's private descriptions of his experiences are grueling in the extreme. Towards the end he was put on a list of boys who were too weak for heavy work, since their imminent demise was predicted. In spite of his being on that infirm list, the death of his bed-wetting friend resulted in Peter being ordered to take his friend's body out of the camp for burial. The corpse was thrust into an empty rice bag and Peter dragged it out through the prison gates. To his subsequent advantage, before Peter re-entered the wire, he came to some high ground, where he spotted another larger POW camp off in the distance.

Stars Over Ambarawa was what Loelie called her wartime memoir, the title reflecting the one happy recollection she had from those Javanese camps, a vignette that gives a glimmer of what the stolen golden years of her child-hood might have been. She writes that some nights when the hunger pangs were so bad they couldn't sleep, and the noise of whimpering children and complaining women got too much to bear, her mother would sneak her children out of the barracks into the camp's dark yard. They all knew that if caught, their punishment would have been dire.

> Our mother would take us three, now Peter was gone to wherever, and we would lie in a ditch and look at all the stars, about which she would tell us stories. She would point out that we couldn't see the fence around the camp from our place in the ditch, and if we just looked up at the night-sky we were free. She told us father was probably looking at those same stars and Peter too. How I loved those evenings.[60]

Month followed month, with the prisoners knowing naught of the doings of the wider world. Beyond their ken, the end of war was approaching, so that signs of uncertainty were creeping in. The behavior of their captors was becoming erratic, but whether this bode well or foul for the impris-oned was unclear, thus adding to their anxiety. Rations were curtailed further and now our young survivor's mother became so ill she seemed to be dying. Just in time, they were issued corn on the cob with their rice, and this somehow helped the skeletal mother to turn her back on death's door.

Finally the camp commandant summoned his last parade and informed those he'd tortured for the last three years that Tenno-Haika had 'graciously consented to finish this war.' The ensuing silence of disbelief was broken by the sight of what looked like a herd of monkeys approaching the camp. Skinny boys were climbing through the wires, pushing open the camp gates - the surviving sons had returned.

The camp Peter had noticed in the distance after burying his little friend, was what the boys had headed for as soon as the prison gates were opened, scavenging for food as they moved across the countryside. Peter found his family, but he could not speak; for what he found was a huddle of sallow spectres, shivering with fever, his mother too weak to stand and greet him. He gave bananas to his siblings and gently placed into his mother's lap a chicken whose neck he'd snapped along the way.

Their trials weren't over. They looked on with envy when Dutch men straggled into the camp to be reunited with their families. Their father was not amongst them and they were told he was dead.

The outside world filled them with fear, it had been so long and it looked so big out there. And now they were advised to remain in their camps, for their own safety they were told, as Indonesian nationalists had begun a campaign of violence against the Dutch. But the young mother, sick as she was, insisted her family get out of the camp to make their way back to Surabaya. Two days after their departure, the nationalists arrived at the camp, herded the remaining survivors together and threw hand-grenades into their midst, killing and wounding hundreds.

In Surabaya, their chances weren't much better. The Javanese were seizing their moment to end three hundred years of Dutch colonialism and while negotiations between representatives of the Dutch and the nationalists were underway, a campaign of terror was waged by the provocateurs. Our desolate little family had stepped from the frying pan of prison repression into a new fire, for of all of the new theatres of violence in Indonesia, Surabaya was amongst the worst.

With daily killings in surrounding streets, they hid in the pantry of their old house as goon-gangs moved through the dark yards outside, muttering murderous catch-cries. On one of these terrifying nights, the youngest of the family, now five years old, was wracked by the malaria he'd contracted in the camps. This was the worst attack of delirium and fever he'd ever had, and they had somehow to subdue him or they'd draw attention to themselves. As they huddled in fear over the delirious child,

> We had not even a candle and when he went into convulsions, I saw my brave wonderful mother break down for the first time, she was sobbing unable to do much but sponge him down.[61]

Skinny Peter rose to the challenge. Dodging the wandering death squads, he scuttled around the alleys of Surabaya to find a Chinese doctor who gave him quinine and aspirin to save his little brother. He returned with the medicine, his feet badly lacerated by the glass embedded along the walls he'd had to scale.

The British Army sent Ghurkas to Surabaya in an attempt to quell the killing; but the fighting got worse and a decision was made to evacuate the Dutch families on the limited British shipping available. The plan was to relay these malnourished women and children to nearby Australia, as a safe staging-post. But the enlightened Australian waterfront workers union had other ideas. They were in sympathy with the Indonesian nationalists and didn't want any remnants of Dutch colonialism on their sanctimonious soil. This, at a time when the labour movement of Australia was the core entrenchment of the White Australia Policy, was admirably arcane.

While the philosophers of the Australian waterfront pontificated their political sentiments, women and children were dying in Java. The Ghurkas too were taking a heavy toll, and it is to these Himalayan men that our young survivor owes her life. Her mother heard the British were planning a marine evacuation, so on the appointed day, tracked through Surabaya's backstreets by nationalist gunmen, the family made a dash for a nearby Ghurka sanctuary. The children held hands as they ran, the mother carrying the baby and their only luggage, a small suitcase with a few clothes and family photo albums therein. With bullets zinging by their heads, they made it through a hole in the perimeter as Ghurka riflemen returned the fire of their pursuers.

Truckloads of evacuees were heading off from the Ghurkha camp to the waterfront, but the risks were high. The first convoy of trucks to leave for the port had been ambushed, doused in gasoline and ignited. Few of those inside the burning trucks survived. A Dutch lady friend of Loelie's family was in that convoy; she witnessed the eldest of her six children jumping to safety from a truck, but could do nothing for the rest of her little ones. They screamed to her for help, but they were trapped and incinerated. What would it do to a human heart I wonder, having shepherded one's infants through every scourge of a Japanese prison camp, to see them now fried alive by a terrorist's torch? What ideal, high and mighty or ever so humble, could be used to salve that woman's soul?

The convoy our family boarded made it to the waterfront, but here too the gunmen were waiting. Again the Ghurkas' fire held off the gangs, as the women and children crammed aboard a landing craft. Buffeting their way out across the Surabaya harbour, they listened to bullets pinging against the craft's metal flanks. A ship loomed overhead and British sailors threw down rope-ladders. The women and children clambered up and setting foot on the ship's crowded deck, our young survivor told herself, 'I'm not going to die today.'

The ship MV *Bulolo* took them to Singapore[62], where the Changi military base, lately the IJA's prison camp for fifty thousand Allied servicemen, became their new home. Here they spent the next four months living on army rations - corned beef, crackers, tinned and powdered this and that. She remembers their still suffering from lice and scabies at Changi, but life was looking up.

Half way through their stay at Changi, four years after they were forcibly separated, her father walked back into their lives. There was little time to dwell on the happiness of their reunion, for epidemics of polio and measles promptly broke out in the camp, and her father's medical services were required. He quarantined his own children in their room and stayed well away for fear of infecting them.

Finally the first batch of frail survivors from the Indonesian camps was shipped from Singapore to Holland on the *Niew Amsterdam* ocean liner. Measles broke out on board and when the ship docked in Rotterdam, some sixty little coffins were carried down the gangplank. As a result of this tragic disembarkment, more shipping was provided and eventually it was our family's turn to sail. They passed through the Suez Canal, where Loelie's memoir recalls they were issued by the Red Cross with woolly clothing, the first they had ever possessed, in preparation for the chill of a Europe the children had never known.

After a brief recovery spell in Rotterdam, her father was posted to Curaçao in the Dutch West Indies, where the family lived in their first real home since the bombing of Denpassar. Although all seemed well to the children, the effects of the Indonesian camps were taking their toll on her parents. All who knew them say her mother and father were deeply in love, but their marriage was lodged in the damaged goods department.

And so her mother returned with the younger children to Holland, while her father and Peter remained in Curaçao. He took up with a nurse, was divorced by his wife and married the other woman. Some years later our Loelie's mother became critically sick in Holland, so her father returned from Curaçao to look after her and the children. The diagnosis was cancer with life expectancy of only another year. On learning this, he divorced his second wife and remarried his first wife, with the double-Dutch undertaking that he would remarry his second wife when his first wife died.

In search of a warm island climate for the year left to a dying mother, the patched-up family moved to Guam, where the father took up the post of Guam's director of public health. Though the island was American, it was so war-damaged that senior American doctors were apparently uninterested in going there; thus the Dutch doctor was able to assume the post without passing the American medical qualifications that would normally have been required. War damage was a condition with which he was familiar.

Our subject was now sixteen years old, and on the flight from Manila to Guam, she met a handsome young man with a pair of racquets under his arm, one for squash and one for tennis. A year later she would marry this young man, two months after they buried her mother in Guamanian soil and shortly before her father kept his bargain and remarried. Her father was thus of the rare breed who have been married four times, but only to two women.

Now our Guam survivor became a mother herself, giving birth to the first of her seven children. With a husband and a baby daughter, she moved to Hong Kong, and then to the sunny isles of Fiji. There she lived a life less ordinary. Her adventures were many, her friendships rich and intellectual. But she was to enter bad years of dependency on alcohol and painkillers, along with the slow, painful dissolution of her first marriage.

The truth is she was never quit of the IJA camps of Java, nor the streets of Surabaya. Whenever the Ghurka regiment would come to Fiji for jungle training exercises, she'd go and see them, drink rum with them, and repeat the story of the escape from Surabaya. The Ghurkas presented her with one of their *kukri* machetes in remembrance of hardships shared.

In the last decades of her life, she was able to voyage back to Indonesia, to look for a childhood lost to Japan's war. Happily she found vestiges of pre-war happiness in her old Balinese home, a discovery that occasioned many subsequent visits. And wherever she went on her travels, a trail of cloves followed her; for in another demonstration of survival of the darndest kind, she chain-smoked high-tar Indonesian *kretek* cigarettes. They say the most enduring memories come from our sense of smell, with just one idiosyncratic whiff cartwheeling us back through time. It was thus that the happy times of her Balinese childhood became almost tangible to her in the smoky haze of those aromatic *kreteks*. The first one each day, she said, was like the breath of an angel.

I confess I used to buy that clove-laced contraband for her whenever her supplies ran out, for they didn't sell *kreteks* when she lived her last years in clean, green New Zealand. I'd procure them from a Russian tobacco shop in the bowels of Sydney's King's Cross and despatch them to her with the next courier crossing the Tasman. Why did I do that? Because she was my mother-in-law and she deserved anything that would give her solace, along with anything I could to meet the eternal debt I owed for what had been given me.

I speak in the past tense because she died a few years ago now. When the news came of her death, we converged in Auckland from around the world to farewell a very special spirit. Her daughters, son, grandchildren, her younger brother, her sons-in-law, husbands and friends were all there. We watched as her offspring talked her from the shore, fashioning from the sorrow of the moment a singular funeral so true to her. For several nights she lay in an open coffin in the house of one of her daughters while we gathered around to tell stories, to laugh and cry, drink wine and whisky, play guitars and sing the sad and joyous songs she loved. A Maori funeral celebrant entered the fray like one of the family, with a *hongi* for all, including the deceased.[63] The party went on for days, all the while, we non-smokers lighting up her ample stock of *kretek* to blow angel's breath about her.

So there I was, flat down on the Guamanian sand, under the battered cement roof of the pillbox in Tumon Bay. Prostrated before the passage of time, I was caught up in a moment of awe, not for the flitting present manifested by the hordes of incoming tourists beyond the machine-gun slit, nor for the tortures of a war long past, but for our Guam survivor. Sands of testimony were running through my fingers and as I said earlier in this story, I determined then to write something of her days, before mine joined hers in the forgetfulness of this mortal life.

She is the necessary cause of my happiness, I understood that as I lay in the sands of Tumon Bay, giving thanks for her survival. Within the womb of she who marveled at the stars of Ambarawa, a spark of life began a wondrous journey into this world. Her baby became a child, became a woman, became my abiding lover, the mother of my children, the completion and bewildering fulfillment of my happy life.

Some live a life that is blessed; for reasons unknown to them, conjunctions conjunct, thesis and antithesis synthesize, and things just keep on turning out right. They are confronted by no blitzkriegs, no pandemics, or savage turns of fortune. But for others, sometimes for a whole generation of others, there is an overload of suffering. Childhood passes in a shiver of fever, guts pang with incessant hunger, death palls fearfully all around. What is the reason for this inequity?

I cannot say, but may it be that we only know our happiness through the suffering of those others? If that is so, then it is fit we should judge ourselves by how well we live our happiness in the context of their expense. And how can happiness be anything but empty myopia if it does not hold to charity of thought and deed? How can it be anything but solipsistic if it does not love mercy, if it does not seek to ease the suffering of others, and keep faith with the universality that has been promised? Until you too pass on from this material world, live well my friend.

If I could have risen at question time in Westminster back in 1940, I might have asked Winston, with all his great grasp of history, 'Would the Prime Minister please explain in whose ranks he regards rectitude and sincerity as having marched? And by what code will we be deemed fit to join those ranks of honour?'

With his own long and at times deeply compromised war record to consider, how he would have answered my queries is not immediately clear to me. So I would have put an easier supplementary question, 'Is the scourge of war not the ultimate proof that race, religion, and the nationhoods they spawn, are what make such misguided fools of us all?'

Let me here cease my gentle interrogation, and under the same stars that once shone down on Ambarawa, conclude this homage to my mother-in-law, Loelie Wijnberg.

NA SALOQU E DRUKA E DRUKA
E DRUKA VEI SUVA

SUVA

My Home Town

And so, dear companion, I hear you're off to see Suva. To satisfy your admirable curiosity, you say you want to poke around my old home town. It's good to see you're going in winter, Fiji's most pleasant time of year, yes, 'cos summer can be a sauna. You've asked for a helpful comment or two, to take you through our balmy metropolis, so I've prepared this parochial traveller's guide for your amusement.

Let me suggest you start from the beginning. To do so, you must go down to the Suva waterfront and stand on the seawall facing Government House, the grand colonial edifice in which the President of the Republic resides today. To the right of where a soldier in crimson tunic and scalloped white *sulu* will be standing at the gates on stoic guard duty, if you look carefully you will be able to pick out vestiges of the village of the original inhabitants of Suva. On the flat foreground lawns of the Government House compound, before the emerald carpet rises to higher ground, you can spot here and there a series of vaguely rectangular knolls emerging from the land. Those knolls are the *yavu*, the house foundations, of the original Fijian settlement, the *koro makawa* of Suva.[64]

The reason the clipped lawns no longer support a Fijian village goes back to the provisions of a contract between the directors of a speculative Victorian company and the purported King of Fiji, Ratu Seru Cakobau. It was in 1868 that a property deal was signed between King Cakobau and the Melbourne-based Polynesia Company, to cover a rather dubious Cakobau debt. The word 'dubious' is used because the debt was essentially fabricated from the 1849 misfortune of an avaricious trader based on nearby Nukulau Island, who also happened to be the American Vice-Consul in Fiji. What followed the 1849 misfortune was an extended period of international extortion, including bombardment threats visited upon Cakobau and his people by the US Navy, all of which drove Cakobau to the financial remedy offered by the Polynesia Company.

The arrangement was never fully consummated. The Polynesia Company went bust, and in time the American government magnanimously forgave the so-called debt. The relevance of this sorry tale is that before the company became defunct, under the deal's auspices some bona fide settlement of land did occur in and around Suva.

So it was that in early September 1870, the SS *Alhambra* sailed in through Suva's main passage to disembark one hundred and seventy migrants onto the shores of the ample harbour. The white settlers came from Melbourne, women and children amongst them, seduced hence by the Polynesia Company's promises.

This landing had a rather contingent air to it, for the vessel's skipper was unsure whether the anchorage he'd made was Suva or not. Its identity eventually confirmed, the Melbournians were off-loaded into a whaleboat that took them as far as it could across the foreshore's tidal mudflats. Up to their knees in mud, the settlers watched the *Alhambra* depart, leaving them to discover the many pitfalls of tropical pioneering.

About that time, the Fijian villagers resident on the land that was to become the front lawns of Government House, were induced by King Cakobau to move across the harbour to the promontory on which their descendants have lived ever since. The name they gave to their new village was Suvavou, literally 'New Suva'; and if you turn from your place on the seawall, you can pick out the houses of Suvavou across the shimmer of the harbour. From such inauspicious beginnings, the future capital of Fiji was spawned.

Next I ask you to stroll into town for about a quarter of a mile, staying on the harbour side of the road. You will pass our once Grand Pacific Hotel on your left and the staid grey spread of Government Buildings on your right, until you come to the front of the Fiji Development Bank. You are now in the area known to Suva people as Naiqaqi.

The last verse of a favourite old Suva song has the following lyrics, and you might notice their reference to Naiqaqi. In the notes to this story, I've translated their meaning for you.

> *Mai raica na loma ni koro*
> *Sai divi e veigauna taucoko*
> *Turaki, Baniwai kei Naiqaqi*
> *Na yaloqu e druka e druka*
> *E druka vei Suva.*[65]

The name Naiqaqi means the crusher, and it was so named for the milling efforts of the early settlers William Brewer and Paul Joske.[66] The latter was the same man for whom the volcanic plug across the harbour is named Joske's Thumb. From where you are now standing, if you look past the development bank, out across the harbour, you can't miss the up-turned thumb on the far shore, gesturing its approval towards Suva.

Joske's son was the accomplished administrator and author, Adolphe Brewster, who'd changed his surname to his mother's maiden name in order to avoid the anti-German sentiments of the time.[67] Adolphe had been one of the young men who came ashore from the *Alhambra* that day in 1870, and he described early Suva in this way,

> Fiji in those days was the 'back-of-beyond, a never-never country',
> and Suva a peaceful backwater into which news from the outside
> seldom filtered.[68]

Brewer and Joske built Suva's foreshore sugar mill in 1873 and it was situated on the opposite side of Victoria Parade from where you are standing.[69] In those days, the beach was where Victoria Parade now lies and a jetty stretched out over the water that then lapped where the Fiji Development Bank towers today.[70] Imagine the clatter from the mill, the racket of its three sets of rollers and the sweet smell of boiling cane juice. Imagine too the aroma of rum wafting in the sultry air and a rustic board advertising the sale of Joske's Three Star Pineapple Rum.

Tragically for Brewer and Joske, the fields of Suva's hinterland were to prove unsuitable for sugar production, so that by the end of 1875 the enterprise was abandoned. Brewer committed suicide, Joske was ruined and their milling enterprise would probably have been quite forgotten, were it not for the Naiqaqi name and the thumbs-up from across the harbour.

Naiqaqi resonates for anyone like me who attended Suva Boys Grammar School, for the edifice of the Development Bank, rising at your back, squats on our old playing fields, and the ill-kempt two-storey cement building next to the bank is the old Grammar School hostel and assembly hall. Today this part of Suva is fast being crowded out by the inevitable ferro-cement towers of questionable aesthetic and commercial merit, so I ask you to continue with your leisurely promenade into town.

Soon you'll pass the old town hall, the venerable Cable & Wireless building and the Sukuna Park reclamation. You'll know the latter from its leafy expanse and because coming from it will be the amplified fervour of one or other of the Pentecostal churches in full proselytizing flight.

Carry on past the park, until you see on the opposite side of the road a two-storey building called Victoria Arcade. Cross the road and you'll find yourself being badgered at the arcade's entrance by young exponents of the art of shoe-shine. You are not one crass enough to refuse, so while your nether leather's being brushed and buffed, you will have time to take in the happy diversity of Suva's passing parade.

Proceeding thereafter to the atrium of the shady arcade, your shoes cleaner than they've been for some time, you'll find a café at which you may reward yourself by sipping a refreshing cup of tea. In the 1960s, this café was where Suva's smart set rendezvoused, gossiping among the potted palms and purple bougainvillea.

Idling with some friends at the café in 1968, we spotted the bulk of Raymond Burr, the Hollywood film-star striding purposefully into the arcade. We knew who he was because he'd recently purchased Naitauba, a remote Fijian island,

and was spending up large around Suva equipping his hideaway. Next to the café was a fancy frock-shop, serviced by a statuesque *fa'afafine*. Burr made a bee-line for the shop, swept the Polynesian vamp into his arms, and planted a sustained lip-clincher worthy of *From Here to Eternity*. This momentary vignette made quite an impression on the youthful idlers at my table.

The arcade was built on the site of McDonald's Hotel, once Suva's haven of choice for travellers. For the first half of the twentieth century, the creaking boards of its dim corridors undulated out to a latticed verandah overlooking the centre of Suva. Rupert Brooke languished here during his 1913 visit to Fiji and from the hotel's verandah watched the fiery ends of days for which Suva Harbour is famous,

> The sunsets here! the colour of the water over the reef! the gloom and terror of those twisted mountains! and the extraordinary contrasts in the streets and the near country.[71]

When the poet comes to write about Suva's inhabitants, the 'extraordinary contrasts' Brooke is struck by are: etiquette-obsessed English people, mournful Indian indentured labourers, weedy Australian clerks, and gay Fijian natives. Thankfully for their sensibilities, the local Chinese and resident New Zealanders are spared the strokes of his pen.

A step across the road from Victoria Arcade is Suva's hub, The Triangle, on the corner of Thomson Street and Renwick Road. While lingering at The Triangle take care not to fall prey to a sword-seller, for he will sweet-talk you into paying an exorbitant price for a piece of stained wood which any fool can see is good for nothing but firewood. In the initial stages of his con, the sword-seller will extract your name, which he then hurriedly etches into the soft wood of his spurious artefact. Working the fraudulent ties of friendship supposedly established, he'll then force the sword upon you and demand a royal ransom.

There's a certain irony to the chicanery of these sword-sellers, for these artistes come from the very village I mentioned earlier, Suvavou. *Plus ca change* ... it's not difficult to view the devious logic of their commerce as little different from that which deprived them of their ancestral lands.

As long as a tropical deluge isn't in progress, which it is most every summer afternoon, The Triangle is a pleasant place to sit and watch the town go by. I hear with a touch of trepidation that they're planning to 'beautify' The Triangle, but one must hope for the best. It has a venerable *ivi* tree at its apex and some scattered benches to rest on in the shade of coconut palms that one prays will not be beautified from existence.[72]

Over the years, these shaded benches have afforded a good place to contemplate change, for in the days of the early settlers, the Suva foreshore was where Thomson Street now lies, and the benches sit on land reclaimed from what was once the mouth of a tidal creek. Brewster wrote with affection of that *ivi* tree. His little party squatted under it after they were delivered to Suva in 1870, and he recalled boiling many a billy of tea under its sheltering branches.

In the middle of The Triangle is a plinth with four great pieces of Suva's history engraved upon the four sides of the stone. I dearly hope the beautifiers don't mess with this historic marker, because according to Professor Schütz, three of the four inscriptions on it are mistaken, and every town needs a folly.[73]

On the first side of the plinth is the statement 'British Crown Colony 10th October 1874.' This much is true. On the second side is a tiny mistake wherein it says the first Christian missionaries, Reverends Cross and Cargill, arrived on 14th October 1835. In fact they arrived on October 12th. The third side tells us public land sales were held on this spot in 1880. Wrong again; according to Brewster who attended the sales, they were held in 1878, further down Thomson St under another *ivi* tree next to Nubukalou Creek. The fourth side proudly tells us, 'Suva Proclaimed Capital in 1882.' Pity about the word 'proclaimed' because 1882 was indeed the year of the capital's physical move from Levuka to Suva. But the proclamation of Suva as capital, approved by Queen Victoria herself, was made in 1877.

My Fiji forbears were amongst those who followed the capital from Levuka to Suva. 'A heartless desertion,' the Levuka-based Fiji Times called the government's move, with the social consequences likely to have the effect of making Levuka 'rather dull for some time to come.'

As a mariner, I doubt my great-great grandfather, Captain Petrie, would have had much to gain from leaving Levuka; but his wife was not a fan of the old capital from the time a Lovoni warrior broke into her house wielding a war-club. Had she lived a hundred years later, she probably would have stayed in Levuka, for in recent decades such occurrences became so widespread in the 'new' capital, that the windows and doors of most Suva residences have been fitted with security bars.

School lists for 1887 show my great-great grandfather Captain Petrie's daughters still attending Levuka Public School in April, and then by December attending Suva Public School. Thus I take 1887 to be the year we became a Suva family. It was exactly one hundred years later, that Marijcke and I decided to quit our home town, but I'll get to the reason for that later.

Once the colonial capital arrived in Suva, there were government institutions to be built, officials to be housed and infrastructure constructed for their support. A detachment of Royal Engineers went to work surveying and road-building, so that the bones of a foreshore town, one square mile in size, soon fell into place. Settlers and merchants steadily gravitated to the law and order of the new capital, and with trans-Pacific shipping adopting the spacious harbour as a favoured port-of-call, Suva soon lost it's status as a peaceful backwater.

I want to take you now in the direction of the port, so rise up from your shaded bench by the *ivi* tree and keep walking down Thomson Street until you get to the bridge over Nubukalou Creek. If you pause on the bridge, you'll catch sight of Princes Wharf at the creek's mouth and along the banks of the estuary, salty fishermen selling their colourful catches from jostling *faipa*.[74] Hopefully as you stand there, the tide will be very high, for if it is not, you'll note that the aroma is.

167

From your vantage point above the creek you'll be able to see where Cumming Street begins its short but fascinating progress. But before you lose yourself in the shops of that much-described alley, I'd like you to continue along Thomson Street, on the harbour side of the street, some forty paces. If you stop now and turn in the direction of the harbour, and if seventy years could be lightly pared away, you would be standing at the entrance of an old wooden store. Imagine a typical tin-roofed, clapboard, South Pacific store, trading everything from knick-knacks to sly-grog dispensed at the back of the shop to clients in the know. The shop's proprietor was once well-liked around town, an affable young Japanese by the name of Shima.

The store is no more and Shima is long gone from the scene. In fact, Shima left Suva just before the attack on Pearl Harbour. He is a forgotten name in Fiji today, but in World War Two he was notorious amongst the soldiers of the Fiji Infantry Regiment. When they were fighting the Imperial Japanese Army in the jungles of Bougainville, they reported a voice that came to them in the lulls between the fire-fights. Fijian words were called through the shattered trees from the Japanese lines, from someone who knew their language, enticing them to lay down their arms.

Some of the regiment's officers had patronised the back of Shima's shop in Suva and they knew he spoke fluent Fijian. As they could think of no other Japanese who did, the supposition spread that it was Shima who was calling to them beyond the bullet-ridden tree-trunks of Bougainville. Though the Shima rumour was widespread amongst the Fijian soldiers, and thereby was known to many back in Suva, it was never verified, and Shima did not return to Suva after the war. The popular conclusion was his pre-war presence in Suva had been as a fifth columnist and that he'd probably perished in the war.

In the early 1980s I was in the Fiji diplomatic service, based in Tokyo. One day my secretary came in to tell me that there was an old Japanese man at the embassy's reception requesting assistance. She said he spoke Fijian. I asked him into my office and after exchanging a few pleasantries, got down to the details of his request of me to put him in contact with a Fijian daughter he'd sired before the war. The affable gentleman smiling at me across my desk was Shima.

Push on now behind where Shima's store once stood, past the fishermen on the banks of the creek, past the briny tang of gutted fish and the fumes of outboard engines, and cut across the road to the fecund bustle of the civic market. Navigate on through great piles of hairy root-crops, the acerbic tang of kava stalls and the emerald spread of bundled fern-heads, past baskets of seaweed, glistening *bele* and broad taro leaves. I'm taking you through to the bus-stand, and I apologise in advance that, as a result of the rich market experience, your shoes will no longer be the shiny paragons they were when you left Victoria Arcade.

At the bus-stand you must seek out the Nasese bus, for you will shortly be boarding it for a ride around the southwest flank of the peninsula. The bus-stand has all the bustle of a Bombay railway station, with its blaring bus-horns, choking spumes of diesel smoke and the stench of over-flowing rubbish-drums. High-spirited jibes are tossed from bus window to bus window as passengers prepare to be quit of the city's clutter.

Board the bus and reach down to curbside vendors to purchase the snacks we once purchased for a few pennies before our bus-rides. Surely they sell them to this day: rock-hard boiled corn, packets of freshly roasted peanuts, and so-called 'hard bean' - salty, chili-hot, fried peas. The detritus from the mass-snacking is no doubt still being ejected through the myriad of open bus windows. Consider for a moment the lot of the stoic City Council *broomsala* as he goes about his Sisyphean task below you.[75]

There used to be a regular Indian driver of the Nasese bus who fancied himself above all the squalor of that Suva bus-stand. You could not help but note his exacting standards of personal hygiene, even if they could only be considered as such within the narrow cleanliness of his personal world. Before setting off on the Nasese run, our driver would invariably put his head out of his side-window, wait for a gap in the crowd, then commence his toiletries. Placing the finger of his left hand on his left nostril, he would take in a deep breath and hoink out, with impressive velocity, a ropy stream of yellow snot. The left finger would then accomplish a deft wipe of said nostril and flick the results into the street. Another deep inhalation, left finger now on right nostril, and a second gelatinous jet would hit Suva's civic cement. The left finger would now wipe the right nostril and follow in the manner of the first flick. After the withdrawal of head from window, our fastidious driver never failed to properly complete his toilet routine; for he kept a handkerchief in his top pocket solely for the task of carefully wiping clean the operative finger.

Once your bus lurches off, it will wind through the city's congested innards for a little while, then break free along Queen Elizabeth Drive, motoring breezily along the foreshore, with the bright harbour slapping the seawall to your right and the dreamy profile of Beqa, the fire-walkers' island, brooding out there on the horizon.

In the excellent company of Suva's less well-heeled citizens, you'll be bouncing by the botanical gardens named for Sir John Bates Thurston - one of Fiji's most enlightened early leaders; the Suva Bowling Club - its restaurant the home of a truly excellent Meaty Bone Soup; past the Government House gates once more, and the foreshore buildings of Draiba. Now you are approaching Nasese.

My grandmother was born down here in Nasese, a waterfront locale emotively ingrained in the Suva soul. The acclaimed photographer, Rob Wright, lived most of his life a few yards from its seawall. Rob gives this description of the place,

> Nasese is a romantic Fijian name which describes the sound of waves lapping at the shore. The locality was well named for our home faced the beach of those days, and beyond it lay large tracts of grey muddy sand, coral patches with blue channels running in between and, in the distance, the white curling foam of combers on the fringing reef.[76]

Now you turn into Ratu Sukuna Road, so that the sea is behind you as the bus rumbles along the edge of Nasese, with Chinese stores at your right and the Nasova police-barracks on your left. You will cross Leveti Creek, where as children we launched our homemade tin-boats to venture down through the Nasese mangroves to where the creek entered the harbour at Turner's Bridge. As the bus climbs up Ratu Sukuna Road, you'll see Draiba School on your left, and the school's sloping playing field on which mid-week training sessions were held in the days I played for the Gaunavou rugby club.

The bus will take you up through the now-posh precinct of Muanikau and it will probably stop at the bus-stop opposite Marou Road, with the official residence of the American ambassador on the road's corner. It was down that road that Loelie, my jaunty mother-in-law, raised her six beautiful daughters and infant son. You could catch her most days taking that corner, decked out in dark glasses and a cowboy hat, at the wheel of a cream sports car.

Service Street is next, so named because it was created in the wake of World War Two and along much of its length, lots were made available to ex-servicemen. Careering around the bend, the bus will climb up to Duncan Road, where you will be entering the part of Suva which once went under the prosaic name of Extension. Extension by name, extension by function, it was the first residential precinct to be added to the original plan for Suva. The first two generations of my Suva family lived in Extension and the sixth generation, in the form of my daughter, recently resided there too. Most of its streets were dubbed by the self-important governor at the time of the precinct's creation, in honour of himself and his family, from which are derived the names of Des Voeux Road, Pender Street, Marion Street and Denison Road.

I ask you to get off the bus at the corner of Denison and Duncan Roads and walk about fifty paces back along Duncan Road. On your left hand-side is the site of Don Dunstan's old house. 'Don who?' most non-Australians would say. But in the great southern land he's remembered as a favourite son.

The thing is, he wasn't an Australian son; he was a son of Fiji. Before he became the premier of South Australia, a position he held throughout the 1970s, he had a past, and that past was in our islands.

Don was born in Suva in 1926, while his father was managing the Morris Hedstrom store on the banks of the mighty Rewa River at Nausori. He attended the Boys Grammar School in Suva, where he was a friend of my uncle, Peter Kearsley, the latter serving as his playground protector in view of Don's rather effete nature at the time. He went to university in Adelaide, qualified as a lawyer and married there, but returned to practice law in Suva in 1949.[77] It was as a young lawyer that Dunstan lived in that Duncan Road dwelling.

Finding his way back to Adelaide, he was elected to state parliament and went on to become a significant figure in Australian political history. Don was at the forefront of legal changes in favour of aboriginal land ownership and the working conditions of women, and they describe the decade of his South Australian premiership as witnessing a legislation programme aimed at a just, artistically sophisticated, multi-cultural community. Interestingly Don reportedly insisted that he wasn't going to be the standard bearer for gay rights in Australia, even though his sexuality in the latter part of his life made it clear he batted that way.

At a national level he championed the abolition of the White Australia Policy, his impassioned calls on the subject at the annual conferences of the Australian Labor Party eventually being nick-named 'Don's motion'. In this endeavour I see clear inheritance from his Fijian experience.

Towards the end of 'Don's Decade', he decided to make a sentimental return to his old home town under the guise of an official visit. At the time I was the young buck running the protocol section of Fiji Ministry of Foreign Affairs, so it was to my Suva office that the Australian diplomats came to ask if we might receive the premier in an official capacity.

Our standing rule was that we only turned on the public tap for visiting heads of national governments, thus premiers of Australian states didn't qualify. But when I minuted my minister, Ratu Sir Kamisese Mara, he directed that in Don's case we should make an exception and bestow on his visit a semi-official status.

Accordingly I arranged for a chauffeur and a government car to drive him around, a hosted dinner in his honour, and a gratis holiday villa at Pacific Harbour suitable for the accommodation of a premier and his private secretary. For the day of his arrival I set up a little welcoming party on the tarmac at Nausori airport.

A visiting head of government would normally be received on the tarmac by the prime minister and all the ministers of the Cabinet, but since this visit was in the semi-official category, I'd arranged for Adi Lady Lala Mara, the prime minister's wife, and a clutch of junior ministers to be present. The stately lady in question was one of the three traditional paramount chiefs of Fiji, so the premier was in fact being highly honoured; but more pertinent was that Adi Lala was a friend of Don's from back in his Suva days.

As soon as the premier's aeroplane came taxiing to a halt, and steps had been wheeled over to its front door, I led the official welcoming party out onto the tarmac. The plane's door swung open and out stepped Don, closely followed by his private secretary. I was standing next to Adi Lala and she muttered an inadvertent, 'Gosh!'

Don and his Ray-Banned private secretary had been working out, there was no denying they'd been working out a lot. Sculptured biceps, tanned and terrific, bulged under the short-sleeves of their white shirts. The private secretary had been pumping those barbells so much it looked like his sleeves might burst before we got him to Pacific Harbour and into the relief of a bathing suit.

I met Don at the bottom of the stairs and took him over to Adi Lala. They kissed and she then took him down the short line of assembled ministers with whom the visiting premier exchanged pleasantries.

Adi Lala was a close friend of my mother's and she was aware my mother and Don knew each other while growing up in Suva; so at this point she turned to me and said, 'And this is Peter.'

'Hello,' said Don shaking my hand.

'He's one of Nancy's boys.'

The premier, pretended to mishear Adi Lala. Still holding my hand, he cocked an eyebrow and cooed, 'Oh, a Nancy boy!'

It's a downhill stroll for you now, into Denison and along MacGregor Road until it becomes Gordon St. Halfway down Gordon and you'll see the sign for Goodenough Street. I've always approved of the nomenclature of that street, for it's nothing spectacular, but suffices for its purpose. The leafy thoroughfare was in fact named for Commodore Goodenough, one of the commissioners appointed by Gladstone to advise on Fiji's second offer of cession to the British Crown. Not long after his Fiji visit, the Commodore died of tetanus as a result of an arrow wound received in the Santa Cruz Islands.

St Andrews Presbyterian Church dominates the high ground of the street and I bring the church to your attention because it is one of Suva's oldest surviving buildings. It was built in 1883 by the Scots who settled Suva, men with names like MacGregor, Duncan, Robertson, McHaig and Thomson, and some of its early timbers were salvaged from ships wrecked on Suva's reef. The devasting hurricane of 1895 decimated the church, but it was quickly rebuilt and has fulfilled its purpose ever since.

My family has long-worshipped at this church, going back to the days when my great-great grandmother Emma Petrie sat on its pews and the sound coming from the road outside was of horses hooves and carriage wheels.

At the *bogi drau* memorial service held for my father at St Andrews in 2008, it was agreed a stained-glass window should be installed in recognition of my parents' many years of service to the church and to Fiji. It is now in place, to the left of the front door as you face St Andrews. Made in Nadi under the supervision of Charlie Singh, the window was installed by John Morgan, the very same who survived at sea in an eskie for two nights and two days.

St Andrews has become a church whose multi-cultural congregation is made up mostly of people from Kiribati, Vanuatu, Tahiti and the Cook Islands, Protestant Christians whose mother-tongue is not Fijian. Thus our design for the window chose as its theme the blending of the church's Scottish roots with the flourishing of its present-day congregation of Pacific Islanders. Up the centre of the window, a coconut palm rises straight and tall from the edge of a moonlit lagoon. The deep blue bar of the ocean, out beyond the reef, forms the arms of a cross behind the palm trunk, while behind this crux, a rising moon reflects on the lagoon to create a circle. The moon transforms the scene into a Celtic coconut cross.

Regretfully I'm not going to take you up Cakobau Hill to our old home. A few years ago they put a bulldozer through most of our picturesque Berkeley Crescent neighbourhood, including our old Raicakau home, so St Andrews is my Suva *yavu* now. I can't help but be puzzled by the bunker mentality of planners, be they bureaucrats or politicians, and their determination to destroy any remnants of the elegant aesthetic of old Suva; can't help but wonder why they don't take such development projects elsewhere. There are huge areas of vacant land around Fiji, where rural people badly in need of jobs would be so grateful to have close-by developments. I know we must all embrace change as being the one constant in our lives; but change can be for the better, it does not inevitably mean destruction of heritage.

When extremists amongst the Fijian ethno-nationalists took to arson in 1987, burning down many of the old shops of Marks Street, it was time to reflect on the earlier words of a Fijian political leader who said, 'If Suva were to be burnt down, the Fijians would lose nothing but the record of their debts.'[78] But the wheel is turning, and with the rapid burgeoning of the middle class, indigenous Fijians are fast becoming the property owners of Suva's buildings. Arson may thus now prove a less frivolous option.

Suva became a fully-fledged city in 1952, and by the 1980s you could no longer call it a pretty little port town. The urban sprawl had ventured over the Nasinu hinterlands to encroach on the alluvial plains of Tebara and it was working its way gradually along the narrow littoral strip of the Rewa-Namosi coast. By the time the colonial period came to an end in 1970, Suva had ceased to be a town dominated by the Europeans who'd built and run it for a hundred years. For about thirty years around that time, with the exception of the rump of government properties and the accommoda-tion of diplomatic and regional bodies, ascendancy over the city's fortunes was gained by Indian merchants and an increasingly urbanised Indian population.

The winds of change swept through Suva after the Second World War, with the old order fading away and new freedoms becoming the norm. Expectations rode higher with the epochal moments of independence in 1970 and the indigenous boil-over of 1987; and with each new surge of its expansion, Suva incrementally accrued all the stressful symptoms of under-funded urban development. The capital took on the burdens of squatter settlements, uncollected trash, pot-holed roads, corrupt building inspectors and mushrooming crime.

These days the streets of Suva seethe with a new demographic: milling crowds of young Fijians migrated in from the countryside and the outer islands. Some of these young Fijians have jobs, but many are just wandering about looking for a slice of the urban action, and where houses and gardens were once delineated by hibiscus hedges or frangipani trees, Suva now sports high security fences and razor-wire. Some would say they are bringing the place full-circle, from its indigenous origin, to European development, to Indian ownership, back to indigenous dominance. But the picture is more universal than that, for though its Fijian future is secure, Suva teems with people of all colours and creeds, and more than any other place can be considered the capital of the Pacific Islands.

Last time I was in St Andrews, I looked down at the worn boards and said a prayer for Suva. I prayed that one day this town would be freed of crime and fear, and that the day would come when the strong would see it was for the protection of the weak their strength was given, and that the bars in the windows and the barbed-wire on the walls would be taken down and hibiscus hedges bloom again. I prayed for the inheritors of my home town, hoped they knew how well the success of their exertions was wished for, and prayed that in their lives they would learn to love the ground from which the city grew, so they too would protect it and see as degrading the littering of the land and the decimation of Suva's vestigial corners of charm. In the company of the shades of those who created it, I prayed for loving guidance of all citizens of our harbour city, on behalf of all of us in this living world whose spirits still fall to Suva.

This Suva tour is not yet over, my friend, but we shall take a break from it for a little while. I will come back to it and we will complete your scenic circuit. But fair warning: it won't be very scenic, more in the nature of a political tour. It will take you to places where you may see the tortuous stepping-stones along which a quartet of *coups d'état* made their way. But before we undergo that sternly necessary Fiji excursus, I'd like to present you with an interlude on an easier subject - leprosy.

Makogai

I see Makogai every day. It greets me at the start of my working hours when the computer blinks on to commence its hypnosis. And then when evening falls, Makogai is there again to farewell me as the lights of my study are dimmed. I see that distant island because it's picturesquely present, plum in the middle of my screen-saver. The latter is composed of a photograph I took a few years ago while holidaying on the island of Wakaya, in Fiji's Lomaiviti Group. Since that photograph encapsulates for me the loving fullness of life, I'm going to flick it onto my screen right now and tell you what I see.[79]

The bottom half of the scene is filled with a rope-hammock strung between two coconut palms. The hammock entwines the chestnut hair and languid limbs of my wife, those limbs that gave life to our children. She wears a black, one-piece bathing suit, dark glasses and a broad pandanus hat with bright red Fiji hibiscus flashing at its brim. In her elegant hand is a novel, the engrossed reading of which has caused her head to tilt away lagoon-wards. The stealthy photographer has captured the path of a shaft from an afternoon sun that has pierced a canopy of palms and curved the hat's shadow across the contours of her face. A gentle ray of sunlight caresses the allure of her upper lip.

This vision of my happiness is framed by the droop of deep-shadowed palm-fronds, except in the space below the hammock, where footsteps in the crunch of coral sand show the route taken from a recent swim in Homestead Bay. Some six paces from the hammock, the waters of the bay flop and sigh away. A wavelet purls to the right, as soft as light blue milk.

Only further out, beyond the lee of a rocky point, can you see the effect of a breeze rippling across the sea, out where the reefs of the Koro Passage stipple the sapphire surface. Eventually your gaze rises to that ever-deceiving demarcation, the cobalt band of a pitch-perfect horizon. Out on that line your vision lands on the island of Makogai, its four green mountains reassuring in their symmetry, forever sedentary. White cloud-puffs wander off to the west.

> There was another island! Bali-ha'i was an island of the sea, a jewel of the vast ocean. It was small. Like a jewel, it could be perceived in one loving glance …like most lovely things, one had to seek it out and even know what one was seeking before it could be found.[80]

Makogai is a special island, with special hopes and special dreams, for it once had a defining quality that made the words 'Come to me, Makogai!' turn generations of Pacific Islanders' hearts to stone. Within a triangle extending from Tarawa to Rarotonga to Honiara, just the idea of Makogai induced a shudder of dread, for this was an island whose inhabitants knew no more the embracing limbs of their families, a place where light did not fall on the faces of their loved ones.

In South Pacific parlance, the inhabitants of Makogai were thought to be living a half-life. They were out of sight and to most people they were out of mind. When they were thought of at all, it was with a mixture of compassion and revulsion, with an obduracy driven by notions of tough love, proper obligations to public health, and what today can seem like ignorant prejudice. For fifty-seven years of the twentieth century, Makogai repelled all but those required by law to be on the island for the treatment of leprosy.[81]

To understand the dread of leprosy, one must understand the disease, so let us get closer up to it. Even today there are things we don't understand about this malady and the unknown has ever been adept at fostering fear and loathing.

One bug left in our communal ointment is the fact that the bacterium responsible for leprosy has yet to be cultivated in a laboratory, so that a vaccine to combat it remains undeveloped. Another is that we still haven't identified how the bacillus enters our bodies, through broken skin or through the mouth? They say that transmission by nasal droplets is the best bet, in situations of prolonged close contact, though leprosy bacilli in sloughed skin could be another source.

At highest risk of catching the disease are people who live in endemic areas in deprived conditions. An insufficient diet, contaminated water supply, inadequate bedding, and the presence of other diseases that compromise immune function, such as HIV, are all thought to be contributing causes, so that leprosy is often described as a disease of the poor. About ninety-five per cent of us are at no risk of catching leprosy, because we are naturally immune to it, and therein lingers the cruel irony of the banishment imposed over the centuries on the victims of the disease.

Leprosy is believed to have originated from a single clone of the leprosy bacillus, probably in East Africa or the Middle East, with successive human migrations carrying the pandemic around the world. In one of the early books of the Old Testament, God lays down the law to Moses and Aaron on leprosy. He is reported as being very specific on how leprosy should be dealt with.

> And the leper in whom the plague is, his clothes shall be rent, and his head bare, and he shall put a covering upon his upper lip, and shall cry, Unclean, unclean.

> All the days wherein the plague shall be in him he shall be defiled; he is unclean: he shall dwell alone; without the camp shall his habitation be.[82]

Myth has the returning armies of Alexander carrying leprosy home to Greece and the survivors of the Crusades doing the same for the rest of Europe. As a result thousands of leprosaria, hospices for the confinement of sufferers, existed across Europe in the Middle Ages, and those confined within these monastic retreats were seen to be existing between life and death in an earthbound purgatory. If they ever ventured forth, they might only do so with clapper and bell to warn of their diseased approach.

By the fourteenth century, leprosy had peaked in Europe, and its prolonged flourish was over by the eighteenth. Gradually improving standards of hygiene had put the bacillus to flight, as had the progression of immunity and natural selection evolving from the other great European pandemics of smallpox, cholera and plague.

And then in the Norwegian leprosy outbreak of the nineteenth century, persuasive evidence arose to demonstrate that enforced isolation of the infected was a valid community response. With no known cure for leprosy, the Norwegians effectively used quarantined leprosaria as their main control against the disease's spread amongst a wider susceptible population. Thus it was that isolation hospitals for the treatment of leprosy became the norm in the nineteenth and twentieth century, as leprosy continued its slow march around the planet.

The Pacific Islands were one of the last areas to be reached by the bacillus, culminating in the crisis on Nauru between 1920 and 1929 when thirty-five per cent of the island's population were afflicted with the disease. Today, leprosy infection rates are falling in the world, but there are many places where the disease prevails: in Brazil, Burma, India, Nepal, East Africa and the Western Pacific.

Meanwhile the World Health Organisation statistics for 2006 showed an increase in reported cases of leprosy in the Western Pacific, so it cannot yet be called a disease of the past. In fact, leprosy afflicts half a million new people each year and there are still nearly three million people in the world suffering its debilitating effects.

But that which sets us apart today from humans who lived for thousands of years with no real remedy against this great scourge, is that we now have a cure. In the 1940s the dapsone drug was developed and was put to general use in leprosy hospitals like Makogai in the 1950s. When the bacillus evolved antibiotic resistance to dapsone, so that the drug became broadly ineffective by the 1960s, two other anti-leprosy drugs, rifampicin and clofazimine, were administered to patients, with increasing improvement in cures. Since 1981 the World Health Organisation has endorsed a multi-drug therapy that incorporates all three of these drugs in order to circumvent dangers of resistance to any single drug. This multi-pronged offensive defeats the bacillus to such an extent that domestic administration of the drugs is now the norm.

'Count your blessings, son, count your blessings,' I hear my departed father say. Two that I will number up today are that my family does not live in poor conditions in a leprosy-endemic area, and secondly, they're most probably in the ninety-five per cent pool of humanity that is immune to the bacillus.

If I was not in that immunity pool and had contracted leprosy in the years before effective drug treatment, say in Fiji during my grandfather's time as a young married man, how would I have been rearranged when that germ set to work within me? The answer would largely depend upon whether I had contracted tuberculoid leprosy or the lepromatous variety, the latter occurring if I had little or no resistance to the infection. There are many variants and combinations between these two forms, but they may be thought of as the two extremities in the disease's spectrum.

If it was tuberculoid leprosy I had contracted, I would mainly be afflicted by nerve damage, leading to loss of feeling in my hands and feet, in turn leading to damage and contraction of my fingers and toes. The chances of my cure would be high and I would not be particularly infectious.

If I had contracted the lepromatous form of the disease, I would be in for a rougher run. My skin would thicken, with unsightly nodules and ulcers bursting upon it. I would be contemplating a future of increasing deformity, it would be very difficult to cure me, and I would most definitely be infectious. Left untreated, my affliction would be progressive and result in permanent damage to my nerves, skin, limbs and eyes. My nose would probably collapse and my eyes could well lose the power of sight.

As the first symptoms became manifest, I would have wavered between doubt, depression and panic. I might conceal them as long as I could, that I might stay with my family to fulfil my purpose and care for their welfare, and more selfishly, that I might be sustained by the warmth of their love. But at the same time a more altruistic voice would be whispering in my ear, telling me to do what was best for them, telling me to go away in order to protect them from the bacillus harboured within.

I could not have borne the torture of that separation, so when the effects of the disease became apparent to all, I would have hidden out in the nearby hills, with my family close enough to bring me victuals and scraps of human company. They would have had to be furtive, for if discovered, the authorities were bound to deport me to a far-away place of exclusion. And when someone from my village did report me, it would not be long before I was rolling across the Koro Sea in a wooden ketch, bound for the dreaded island of Makogai. As the island of isolation arose from the seas ahead, I would have settled on the conviction that I was going there to die.

Statistically my conviction would have been about half right back then, but as the years passed by Makogai's death rate declined, so that when the hospital closed in 1969 only a quarter of the hospital's total patient-count lay buried in the hillside behind the hospital. Of the four thousand odd patients the hospital treated during the fifty-seven years of its existence, the greater balance favoured the living, most of who returned cured to the island homes from which they'd been so cruelly sundered.

At first sight of Makogai, I might have wondered why this particular island had been selected for the segregation of my fellow sufferers. Back then, I would probably have known that Fiji's leprosarium was previously located on the island in Beqa, at that island's closest point to Suva. The Beqa leprosarium had been established in 1900, but its facilities were inadequate and some sensitive Suva souls were offended by the sight of a leprosy colony on their horizon.

The colonial administration thus decided to establish a better facility on an island wholly devoted to the treatment of leprosy. Their choice of location came down to two adjacent islands out in the Koro Sea: Makogai and Wakaya. They were about the same size, both were freehold plantation islands and both could be easily accessed from the provincial headquarters of Levuka. The die was cast; the government picked Makogai, and Wakaya went on to an ironically different future. While one island was to isolate the wretched victims of leprosy, the other's destiny lay in pandering to the whims of the world's rich and famous, applying luxurious salves to the precious sensibilities of privileged lives.

The Makogai leprosy hospital was a publicly-funded operation, ruled by a government ordinance and overseen by a resident medical superintendent who was responsible for law and order as well as the medical care of patients. A settlement was built on the eastern side of the island, out-of-bounds to patients, where the medical superintendent and the government workers lived. On that side of the island a dairy farm and bakery were established to service the hospital's kitchens.

A road ran around the southern coast to the west and north side of the island, where the leprosarium was spread along the scallops of three leeward bays. Dalice Bay was the central of these and on its shoreline was the main hospital compound, including the women's wards and the convent for the Roman Catholic nuns who served as the hospital's nurses. A school and two churches were erected further up Dalice's shore.

On the north coast were five men's villages of sturdy timber cottages populated respectively by Fijians, Tongans, Gilbertese, Cook Islanders and Samoans, for shortly after its opening the Makogai hospital began receiving patients from around the Pacific Islands. To the south of the hospital were another four villages for Chinese, Europeans, Solomon Islanders and Indians.

As an arriving patient, sailing through the passage into Dalice Bay, I would have seen the nuns moving along the shore amongst the other patients, the nuns' identity clear from their snow-white ankle-length habits and pleated wimples. Not even the sight of these strange creatures would have lifted my spirit, for in the long transportation from my home, at every turn my eviction from society would have been confirmed to me. I was now an outcast.

And as I made my way further and further from my home, the stigma of my uncleanliness was now preceding my approach. Every quarantined truck and deck that carried me hence, was swabbed and sterilised the moment I stepped from it. The plague was in me, and I plainly saw that I was defiled.

As soon as the longboat offloaded me onto the island's shore, I was given the rules and regulations. I saw Makogai had policemen to enforce those laws and watched them searching incomers, confiscating any opium found amongst their effects. Later I would see how they patrolled at night, ensuring no contraband was smuggled ashore from passing fishing-boats.

I learnt of the hospital's medication, painful injections of chaulmoogra oil that many believed had no curative effects at all. Everywhere I looked I found debility, for now I was surrounded by patients in every stage of leprosy's ravages, the limping and the lame, the scarred and disfigured. I saw the stubs of amputated and stunted limbs, the smashed faces, and on smelling the nauseating whiff of leprous ulcers, I visualised the debasement of my future narrowing ahead.

Most distressing for me was the pathos I observed in family visits, visits that happened twice a year, visits that because of limited boat space and the hardened circumstance at home, touched only a small portion of Makogai's patients. The murder of these brief reunions lay in the strained formalities, in the vigilant eyes of the supervisors, in the tentative touches and lack of embracing, in the bans on gift-giving lest the disease be spread.

Within me came a conviction which nearly slew me: I did not wish my family subjected to all this humiliation and I might never see them again. But they were ever on my mind, and day by rotting day came doubts about their welfare, their whereabouts, their survival, even their fidelity.

My outrage hardened, until anger's run was done, and within my heart, the desire to live began withering. My defilement and the journey out to this diseased extremity proved my continued existence could only arouse disgust and fear, with perhaps an ounce of distant pity here and there. I was unclean, unclean, the Good Book told them so; and there was now no use to which my life could be put, no place for love. I was an outcast in this world, without dignity, and without hope.

And yet there was a miracle rising from the ground on which I stood. For Makogai became the island of hope. In time I discovered there were trusty allies on the island who would help me battle my demons, mighty allies dedicating their lives to the defeat of a Biblical bacillus.

In my village were men who spoke my mother tongue and who'd been through all the fears that were plaguing me. I learnt many things from them as we weeded, planted and harvested together in the plantations maintained around the island's coast. We built little boats and fished together in the lagoon between Makogai and its outlier Makodraga. We sang in choirs, played sports, entertained each other, and in their good company, slowly I returned to the precious boon, the mysterious wonder of life.

Moving among us were people whose daily vocation was the transformation of despair to aspiration, of fear into hope. It is in love of their memories, of their own sacrifices, that I describe some of them here.

First there were the nuns, without whom the hospital would simply not have functioned. They were a multinational group of women in the congregation of the Missionary Sisters of the Society of Mary, who in the passage of time were joined in their nursing work by the Fijian Sisters of Our Lady of Nazareth. In addition to their general nursing duties in the hospital, the nuns made daily visits to the men's villages to change the dressings on leprous ulcers and check on the general health of patients. They also issued rations and ran the dispensary, the patient's cooperative store, the hospital kitchen and the laundry. In support of Makogai's medical superintendent, the sisters gave anaesthetics, assisted at surgical operations, undertook physiotherapy, occupational therapy and X-ray duties, and carefully maintained the island's medical records.

Those nuns were not all immune from leprosy and one of their number, Sister Maria Filomena, became afflicted, struggled on in service and then died on Makogai. The nuns desired a priest to serve as their chaplain and the first one appointed, Father Schneider, was drowned when his boat capsized while making the crossing from Levuka. The second priest, Father Nicouleau, gave nine years of devoted service before contracting the disease. He worked on amongst the patients for another five years before taking his place in the cemetery that was growing up the hill beyond the hospital.

Service was everything for those Makogai nuns, and after fifty-seven years of daily devotion to it, may we leave them thus, with due adjustment for gender,

> Greater love hath no man than this, that a man lay down his life for his friends.[83]

The nuns were led on Makogai by the Reverend Mother Mary Agnes, a native of Brittany in France, who came to Fiji as a teaching and nursing nun in 1893. She arrived on Makogai in 1916 and served the leprosarium continuously until her death in 1955. Mother Mary Agnes was the leprosarium's backbone; her yes was yes, her no was no; she rewarded self-sufficiency, took pride in her surroundings, loved discipline and instilled the same in her sisters and in the lives of the patients. To borrow Ratu Sukuna's description of her, the Reverend Mother was Makogai's spiritual architect; and then there were the words of the governor of the colony, Sir Arthur Richards, when he awarded her the MBE in 1937,

> Without her marvelous devotion it is difficult to see how Makogai could ever have existed.

She was Fiji's Mother Theresa, but if sainthood is going to elude this daughter of Brittany, then let it be conferred instead on the leprosy patient Ernest Wolfgramm, for he was the island's other great agent of hope. When we consider Ernest, we recognize it was in the patients themselves that the crowning inspiration of Makogai lies. Men, women and children who had been sent to Makogai in conditions of great despair, worked through suffering and pain to discover qualities of courage the disease could not quell.

There was Semisi Maya, the self-effacing Fijian who blossomed on Makogai and at its sister institution in Suva, St Elizabeth's Home, into Fiji's leading artist of the 1960s. Because his hands and arms were weak and deformed by leprosy and polio, Semisi used his mouth to hold paintbrushes and discovered delicate painting tools in the shape of his knuckles, elbows and the hairs of his arms. His lyrical water colours were exhibited around the world, the proceeds directed at his request to the welfare of his rural village in Tailevu.

Then there was Tokoriri, a patient from the Gilbert Islands, who made himself an outrigger canoe not much longer than himself and went fishing in it early one morning in the open sea beyond Makodraga. With a hand-line and sardines tied as bait to his hook, he snared a great fish that dragged him and his canoe around the ocean. His fellow patients saw him out there and wondered at what might be happening. They knew him to be a master fisherman, but they had never seen a canoe behave in such erratic fashion. All day long he battled that fish under an unforgiving tropic sun, never flagging in his determination to land the catch of a lifetime.

Late in the afternoon, Tokoriri's efforts were rewarded by the sight of his quarry, hauled up exhausted under his narrow hull. Down there in its watery element was a 426 pound black marlin, dwarfing the outrigger canoe even as it rested below. Before his quarry had time to regather its energy, the fisherman slipped overboard to plunge a knife deep inside the vitals of the mighty fish. With the marlin's struggles over, Tokoriri wrestled it to the surface and secured it with his line to the canoe's side.

By now on the verge of collapse, the Gilbertese patient paddled back through the rollers of the passage and across the broad lagoon to where his gaping friends stood on Makogai's shore, witness to Tokoriri's enduring feat.[84] They say Ernest Hemingway took inspiration from that Makogai story before writing The Old Man and the Sea, the book that won him the Nobel Prize for literature.

But it was Ernest Wolfgramm who hoisted the banners that led the patients' battles of will, and it was he who stood foremost in the restoration of their dignity. He came from Vavau in Tonga, the descendant of a nineteenth century German trader. In 1923 he was sent from Tonga to a boarding school in

New Zealand, on the outskirts of Hastings, and three years later was found to have leprosy. At that time, New Zealand had an isolation hospital for leprosy on Quail Island nearby Christchurch, and thence Ernest was shipped at the tender age of seventeen. Not long after, he was in the first group of patients from Quail Island to be dispatched to Makogai, an island outpost he was never to leave. He died of his disease in 1948 at the age of forty.

This was a man who was cut adrift from the joy of family and boyhood friends. Feeling the weight of that deprivation he once wrote,

> Mother died the year after I got here. I think she and I were the best pals that ever lived.[85]

His small earnings on Makogai were devoted to the upkeep of his aged father in Tonga and two little sisters. Ernest was a man who pined for his homeland, but was doomed to see it no more; a man who longed for every adventure in a wide open world, but was sentenced to a life of confinement and pain; a man who was ever denied the loving embrace of a woman, who was denied the right to raise a family of his own. This is a man who might well have stood on that island shore, raised his scarred face and bandaged hands to the sky and cursed the heavens.

But Ernest Wolfgramm was not such a man. On arrival in Makogai he was asked to take charge of the schoolboys and in his spare time applied himself to helping with furniture-making, house-building and engineering jobs. He was apt at these tasks and in time was put in charge of the workshop where furniture and boats were made and repaired, where the island's engines were overhauled, and where, under his charge, many a hesitant man found new purpose in life. Ernest studied music and organised an island band, putting on concerts, even produced Shakespearean plays that were performed by his schoolboys for the entertainment of the hospital staff and patients.

During World War Two, Ernest was instrumental in arranging a Makogai contribution towards the allied war effort. And then, even though towards the end he could use his hands for nothing but the clumsiest work, with funds supplied by the kind-hearted people of the New Zealand Lepers' Trust

Board, he built a movie theatre at Dalice Bay. Through such high-minded initiatives, this dynamic Tongan force reached in to what is good in all of us, he lifted people from all the island's diverse communities to transcend their lonely pain, to reclaim their self-respect.

Ernest Wolfgramm was at one with the spirit of Makogai. Of him it can be said there was compassion and altruism enough for an army of the rest of us. In words all the more moving for their simplicity, another patient said this of the big Tongan,

> This man Ernest, he was our leader in the leper station. All of us in Makogai left somebody behind when we went there. I left my wife and three children and went to live out of the world. At first I wanted to die, but this man Ernest made me want to live. He was also a leper, but he was a man among men – tall, powerful and strong, with something that came from inside him … he made me live by teaching me what he knew.[86]

I would also like to record something of the dauntless medical superintendents who administered Makogai from its start to finish, all the way from Dr Hall to Dr Dovi, men who with their wives and in some cases families, took up residence on the island to share the isolation of the inmates out in the Koro Sea. In the early days, they and their stoic wives were shunned by some on the mainland who considered them tainted by association with leprosy. But that was small meat to these people; for they were engaged in a greater fight against ignorance and disease, one that bore responsibility for the lives of the hundreds of patients in their charge.

Dr Austin served as the medical superintendent of Makogai for twenty-three years, his reign on the island described as firm, just and kind. And when I think of Dr Austin, I think of his wife sharing that time with him; caring not only for the good doctor, but for the welfare of his staff and patients as well. It was a life-style deprived of so much we take for granted, but there were great rewards to be had from the toil. One of those Makogai superintendents, Dr Beckett,[87] expressed as much in these two sentences,

> Hope returned to those who had lost it is an unusually touching sight. Had Makogai done no more, it would have justified its existence.

Even though the resolution of the right drug treatment for the cure of leprosy had yet to be finalised, by the mid 1960s the case for segregation of leprosy patients was losing its steam. Dr Beckett, had this to say at a meeting of The Fiji Society in Suva in 1966, three years before the island's leprosy hospital was closed,

> Although leprosy is a contagious disease it is not highly infectious like measles or smallpox. Indeed, some types of the disease are not infective at all and even the most severe lepromatous case is only a slight danger to those about him. The disease is nowadays curable. We do not worry about the spread of tuberculosis nor do we insist that sufferers from the disease be locked up in hospitals. Why then do we insist that all patients who suffer from leprosy be segregated for years in a place as isolated as possible? I suppose it is because the ravages of leprosy are on the outside of the body: we can see the nodules and ulcers of the disease on the skin. But we cannot see the more destructive inroads of tuberculosis on the tissue of the lungs so we do not fear it in the same way. Were it not for this irrational fear of leprosy, Makogai would never have been instituted.[88]

Desmond Beckett's comparison with tuberculosis is telling, for the leprosy bacillus is closely related to that of tuberculosis. It is also relevant in that because of their geographical isolation and lack of historical exposure to both the leprosy and tuberculosis bacilli, Pacific Islanders possessed no natural immunity to either of them.

During World War Two, when my father was adjutant of the Fiji Infantry Regiment's 3rd Battalion, he was dismayed by the prevalence of tuberculosis amongst the battalion's Fijian soldiers.

I hardly gave tuberculosis a thought, until routine medical checks in May 1945 established that some of these Fijian soldiers were afflicted with TB. The medical authorities ordered immediate chest x-ray examinations of all personnel in our 3rd Battalion and the results were quite shattering. Eight per cent of the battalion was suffering from active TB, requiring immediate hospitalisation and treatment. Another twenty per cent showed TB symptoms and required outpatient treatment.[89]

That alarming discovery, especially considering the fitness of the men concerned, prompted the colonial authorities in Fiji to mount an anti-tuberculosis campaign. And when the time came to memorialise those who died on active service in WW2, the government and returning service-men agreed that instead of constructing stone memorials, a fund would be established to eradicate the scourge of TB. A wartime hospital at Tamavua, on the outskirts of Suva was converted into a TB sanatorium and medical teams dedicated specifically to the task, so that over the next two decades tuberculosis was largely defeated in Fiji.

Suva's main hospital is the CWM, the Colonial War Memorial Hospital. It is often incorrectly thought to commemorate the servicemen of the Pacific War; but was in fact built in memory of those who served in World War One. Meanwhile the TB hospital still functions in Tamavua, its legacy from the soldiers of World War Two enduring, and since 1969 it has had a suitable neighbour - the PJ Twomey Memorial Hospital for the treatment of leprosy. With the spurious benefit of hindsight, we can see now that this is where the leprosy hospital should have always been, within the wider community, not sequestered on an island beyond the horizon. And as I write those words, I am reminded that my two children were born but a stone's throw from those two Tamavua hospitals.

We were all touched in some way by Makogai in twentieth century Fiji. I didn't know it at the time, though my parents did, that the father of one of my close school-friends was a patient at Makogai. My friend boarded at the Boys Grammar School hostel in Suva and would sometimes come up to our

Raicakau home for weekends. Looking back on that now, I feel so keenly his need to conceal his father's status from his peers. Part of the pathos is that we wouldn't have cared tuppence had we known, as evidenced by my parents' example.

As it happened, my father had been to Makogai in 1942, in the dark years before a cure for leprosy was in sight. He was then ADC to the governor of Fiji, Sir Harry Luke, who was making a farewell visit to the hospital in which he'd taken a special interest during his four-year tour in Fiji. Progressing through the wards, out of instinct of manners, my father stepped forward to open a door when the Reverend Mother and the Sisters approached it. With his hand still on the door knob, he recalled the Reverend Mother giving curt orders. He was whisked away by one of the nuns to have his hands washed and sterilised, and receive the admonishment, 'Please do not touch anything in these wards.'

There is an extract from Sir Harry's diary for the day in question and I quote it now as an adieu to those years.

> 11th July: Sailed early for Makogai, where we arrived at 8 a.m. In between the farewell address to me from the patients and their usual happy little performances of songs and dances, I presented his OBE to Dr Austin. Despite my protests the reverend mother, who interpreted for me, would insist on leaving out all the bits I said about herself and the sisters, so when she finished interpreting I asked McGusty to say a special piece about her so she should not get away with it ... After half a century of service in Fiji she is as vigorous as ever. Then went around the wards and houses and talked a little to all the patients ... We lunched with the reverend mother in the convent and then left. As we steamed out Ernest, the half-Tongan patient who has made himself the unpaid engineer and handyman of the settlement, steamed round the ship in the launch he built, towing a boat-load of other patients who sang the Fijian song of farewell Isa Lei to us. More than ever does Makogai epitomize the words 'self-help'.[90]

During our last stay on Wakaya, Marijcke and I decided to pay a visit to Makogai. The island had been calling me for a long time and though I'd sailed by or flown over it a hundred times or more, I'd never set foot ashore.

That call to Makogai has a place in Fijian myth, for as I have touched on, there is an idyllic island within its lagoon called Makodraga. This island was the home of the god Ramacake, the same for whom my old friend Meli Ramacake had been named.[91] The god had a unique way of calling people to Makodraga, more specifically of luring beautiful women to the island. He would lie down upon his sleeping mat and emit a mesmerising melody through a bamboo nose-flute, the Fijian wind instrument of old. The flute's magical nature took its notes across the waves as far off as the mainland, and when they fell upon the ears of the woman for whom the bewitchment was intended, she was soon in a canoe bound for Makodraga.

In our case, we crossed the Koro Sea in a fibreglass fishing boat in the company of two Fijian boatmen. The sea was bright blue and kicking. All around flocks of brown boobies and black-capped terns dive-bombed boiling shoals of sprats. Skipjack tuna were leaping from the shoals in a frenzy of chasing and feeding. We zig-zagged our way north to Makogai through all this flashing fish-flesh, playing our bit-part in the logic of the food-chain with lures set deep to snare the yellow-fins preying on the skipjack from below. We were soon sufficiently rewarded. Two big tuna lay on our deck, silver-skinned slabs of taught muscle, slapping canary-yellow tails, with scarlet blood oozing from the cruel of a steel gaff's puncture. We pulled in our lines and motored on to Makogai.

A passage through the island's broad barrier reef opened to us at the island's northwest corner and we turned towards it. Breakers were curling over coral barricades to left and right as we rolled on through to enter the calm sanctuary of Dalice Bay. Makodraga was there on the north side of the bay, and in spite of all that had passed since, its white sand beaches and waving palms still hinted of Ramacake's charms. To the south side of the bay sat an islet, the rocky pyramid of Tabaka, and dead ahead under the lee of the high green hills of Makogai, lay the ruins of the leprosy hospital.

One of our boatmen pointed at the bay's northern headland and told me, with grave Fijian authority, that the hospital's terminal patients were taken out onto that promontory and shot. The rewriting of history is so prevalent one doesn't always react, but I couldn't let this one pass. I told my companion I knew for a fact no patient's were shot by the island's authorities. He countered by saying they were given lethal injections out there. No, I said, that was not true either. The island was run by the colonial administration's medical department and was staffed by Roman Catholic nuns, all of whom were sworn to the preservation of life and bound to the laws of the country. He nodded at what I said, but held his gaze on the headland with the look of one who knows better.

There were once two long wooden jetties protruding into the bay, one for hospital visitors and one for patients, but now only the stub of one of these structures remained. We moored our boat to a remnant concrete post and set off to find what the island held.

Even before reaching the end of the jetty it was clear Makogai's many years as a model leprosarium were but a fading memory. The picturesque fore-shore lanes, lawns and gardens, so evident in photographs of the hospital's hey-day, are all abandoned now and over-run by the littoral bush. The only immediate reminder of the neat rows of wooden hospital buildings once fronting the bay, is a topsy-turvy cement staircase. Evidently it had climbed to a second-floor ward, but now leads only into heaven's clear air.

The houses that remain in Dalice Bay have the air of a squatter settlement. As we approached, people emerged uncertainly: uncertain of our purpose, uncertain it seemed of their own place on the island. They were a mixture of government employees and former employees, joined by an aglomeration of dependents and hangers-on.

For most of the forty years that have passed since the hospital closed, the island has been run by the Ministry of Agriculture, in that body's various guises under the variety of ruling governments of the day. In the 1980s and 1990s, the ministry used Makogai as a quarantine island for a sheep-breeding programme and has of late purported to be using it as a centre for aquaculture. At a cursory glance, absolute under-funding of the latter and of everything else on the island was evident.

I explained to those who came forward that we were on Makogai principally because we wished to pay our respects in the island's cemetery. A cluster of polite Fijian children offered to show us the way; so off we all went, down a narrow track overhung with four-score years of vegetal growth, in the company of a pack of smiling, long-tongued dogs. Some fifty paces on our way, clouds of hungry mosquitoes fell in with our procession through the tall trees.

Amongst the shrubbery, moss-covered concrete could be seen at every turn of the muddy path: steps to where once there had been a building of some sort, the base of a wall, a mechanic's sump, a house foundation - all in the python grip of curling tree roots. Makogai's forest was very evidently in the final stages of reclaiming its own.

We came upon the former prison of the island, a small building to the right that housed a handful of women prisoners, and one to the left for the men. Here walls still stood, though roofs were long departed. The detritus of storms-past littered the interiors with branches and rotting leaves from which young coconut trees were shooting. Heavily rusted grill-doors still hung in the openings of four cement cells. I found the prison toilet, its throne gone, but a cast-iron cistern still hanging on the wall at a crazy angle.

To one side of the men's gaol was a single cell: what looked like a sweat-box for solitary confinement. It stopped me in my tracks, made me wonder at how low life can take you. To contract leprosy and be sundered from friends and family would be a lot to bear; but then to run foul of the hospital's regulations, be committed to this island prison and then somehow become so enraged that confinement in a mosquito-filled sweat-box was imposed … it was the seed of nightmares.

We continued on toward the cemetery, until through the trees an Ankor Wat ruin loomed ahead. From the crumbling side of a high cement structure I saw a pawpaw tree growing, its roots straggling down the side of the wall. That wall faced another dilapidated facade and the remains of a concrete floor stretched between them. The building's other two walls and the roof were long departed. We climbed up a solid stairway onto the floor and it was clear we were standing amongst the good works of Ernest Wolfgramm, for six small windows were set in one of the facing walls - the movie projection apertures of the Makogai theatre.

There was a door in the projection wall and we looked through it to the rubble of a small ante-room where a pair of nuns had once operated whirring projectors. I turned to the wall upon which the projectors beams were thrown and pictured myself amongst the mesmerised audience, enthralled by fantasies of the silver screen, freed for a while from the press of our adversities.

From that monument to one man and many, we walked on towards the cemetery, which we came across where the mosquitoed littoral land began its climb up the Makogai hillside. Evidence of sporadic weeding around the graves of the lower part of the cemetery could be seen and a rustic sign erected at the cemetery's entrance announced,

> The upkeep of this cemetery is sponsored by the French Government.
> This is in memory of the French Catholic Missionaries buried here.

It was a disappointing sign, for the nuns were not missionaries in the normal sense of the word. They were not there to proselytise or convert. They lived on Makogai as nurses in selfless service to the amelioration of suffering. A French taxpayer standing before the sign might well be a little disappointed as well. A little bit of money goes a long way in Fiji when it comes to weeding, but only a small portion of the cemetery showed any evidence of upkeep.

Nevertheless, we had the French Government's sponsorship to thank for the rudimentary weeding of the ground in the vicinity of the grave of Reverend Mother Mary Agnes, and I was pleased to find Ernest Wolfgramm's resting place amongst this dappled clearing.

I had brought a copy of Sister Mary Stella's book on Makogai with us, and as there was now a curious gathering of islanders standing about us in the overgrown cemetery, I read them passages from the book describing the good works of the reverend mother and the Tongan altruist. After that one of our boatmen said a Fijian prayer and then we left the forlorn hillside in silence.

Down the forest track the chatter resumed, up and down our human and canine procession through the bush, but it was a melancholy walk for me. An inner short-coming of mine sometimes transforms compassionate thoughts into completely useless tears, and the hillside cemetery's consumption by the forest, the rot of the lepers' prison, the *tristesse* of the theatre's demise, and the general vegetal throttle of the place had conspired to get me quite downcast. Arriving at the foot of the jetty, I imagined those many moments of departure, when after years of separation, a few brief hours of closely-supervised reunion came to an end, when once more loved ones were torn apart, the utterly sundered left to cope with the dreadful uncertainties of their lives, and I despaired.

But then I lifted up my eyes and my wife was there with me, in fullness of health, and beyond her was the lagoon, reflecting the afternoon light. And along the shore I saw the relic of the old stairway climbing to the sky, a clear blue sky. Children splashed along the waterfront, running with the loping, flop-eared mongrels. The bacillus had departed this place.

Our boat was tugging impatiently at its mooring, ready to resume the journey. Great joy of joys, leprosy's curse had been lifted from the island forever, and any sufferer of the disease today who has the basic human right of access to curative drugs, can be rid of the bacillus for good. The inequity of human experience persists, but at least for the great majority, the scourge of this ancient liability is erased from the ledger of our lives.

With these extremes of feeling we departed Dalice Bay. And as we returned to the bright blue wash of the Koro Sea, I recalled the sentiment of something Desmond Beckett had penned for the opening of the leprosy hospital in Suva in 1969. We sailed off south, but that sentiment stuck in mind as Makogai receded in our wake, the four green mountains of the island eventually taking the place I now have reserved for them upon the horizon of my screensaver.

I've since fossicked around amongst my papers and have found the programme for the Suva hospital's opening ceremony. This is what Dr Beckett wrote for that happy day,

> The lovely island of Makogai is deserted now. It slumbers in the Koro Sea. No matter what use it may be put to in the future, it will never again see so much human suffering or so much love, kindness and simple happiness. Let us remember it then, not as an island of isolation and affliction, but as a place of healing, both of body and of mind, a source of hope and a repository of tender loving care in inexhaustible supply.

For the doctors, the workers, the families, the sisters and all the patients, for Mother Mary Agnes and Tokoriri and Semisi, and Ernest Wolfgramm, may I say for them all, amen to that.

Is it possible that man's heart can harbour amid such ravishing natural beauty, feelings of hatred, vengeance or the desire to destroy his fellows? ~L.T.

The Coup Tour

A man was crouching, writing with his finger in the dust at his feet. He was on holy ground. A posse of policemen, priests and lawyers stood about him. They were gathered by the man with one intent - his entrapment.

As bait for the mind of the crouching man, the self-righteous had produced a woman who'd been caught in the act of adultery. Strict interpretation of the law demanded her death by stoning for this offense. Death by stoning! Even though this all happened some time ago, dear friend, it's hard to imagine such barbarity ever existed in law. But exist it did, and does so to this day in certain benighted corners of the world.

Those assembled around the sand-scribbler knew of his strong views on public morality and how he spoke freely on justice to any who cared to listen. It was thus that his words had come to the ears of the men who ran the town, and the reported words worried them, for they had a subversive, sacrilegious edge.

So the high-hats had sent out their agents, tasking them to snare the irritant philosopher before his thoughts caused them trouble. The men stood over the fallen woman. With much pummeling of hands and pointing of fingers they demanded the scribbler give his views on the unholy punishment the holy law demanded.

But that crouching man just continued to write with his forefinger in the dirt, calmly, as if he heard not a word of their barrage. He knew their purpose and that just one word against the law would allow them the arrest they sought.

Mocked and shamed by the mob, the distraught woman trembled at what lay ahead. There was a stone wall nearby, and against this she'd soon be cowering, while these agents of probity lifted up their chosen rocks and threw them at her, again and again, 'til the last gasp of sweet life was bludgeoned from her body.

At the sight of her distress, the man stood up and an apprehensive hush fell around the place. Still in silence, he looked at each of the woman's accusers, peering deep, in mute deliberation, addressing character and conscience.

Then in measured tone he uttered these words, 'He among you who is without sin, let him cast the first stone.'

The communal hush continued as these words were pondered. Next, a strange thing happened. One by one, the priests and the lawyers and the policemen all drifted away. The mob did the same, slinking off in shame. For the man's words had entered and aroused the decency lurking deep within all hearts, and the accusers found themselves convicted by their own judgements.

Soon only the man and the woman remained. He turned to her and said, 'Where are your accusers? Has no man condemned you?'

When she answered that none had done so, her saviour counseled her thus, 'Neither do I condemn you. Go home, and sin no more.'[92]

I wish to begin this *coup* tour of Suva on Ratu Cakobau Road. For this road was named in honour of Ratu Seru Cakobau, the paramount Fijian chief who led the cession of Fiji to the British Crown in 1874. That deed signed by Ratu Cakobau and his fellow high chiefs, was to bring Fiji over a century of the Queen's Peace; an era in which the law was sacrosanct and oaths of loyalty meant what they said.

If we stand now on this leafy avenue and look back at what has since passed, we can see that era as coming to end not with Fiji's independence in 1970, but with the series of illegal events in 1987 that led to the advent of Fiji's republic.

Ratu Cakobau Road starts down by the harbour and runs inland straight as a die. To one side of its avenue are the royal palms of Thurston Gardens, to the other a row of *baka* trees. The latter are the local variant of the banyan tree, large handsome trees with fibrous arterial roots hanging from wide-spread branches. Sadly they make a diminished line-up today, their number thinned by hurricanes and civic neglect. The *baka* trees delineate the southern edge of Albert Park, the expanse of rugby, cricket and hockey fields that stretch from Ratu Cakobau Road across to the Government Buildings precinct of Naiqaqi.

Allow me, dear friend, a brief personal digression from this *coup* tour. I'd like to tell you that in my life, I ran out onto the fields of Albert Park many hundreds of times, usually for a game of rugby. That sporting obsession started when I was about nine years old, as a member of the inglorious Boys Grammar midgets team, which succumbed to repeated thrashings from the likes of Nabua and Draiba Fijian schools. I was still playing the game at the hoary age of thirty, for the Gaunavou B team in the weekly Suva competition, sometimes in the company of one of my six brothers, for they too were keen on rugby. Yes, Albert Park is fertilised by a century of sweat, spit and blood, and there's a bit of that grass out there that's still ours. Seven blades will suffice.

Those regrets I've expressed about the *baka* trees are only partly based on aesthetic or ecological sentiment. I have a more prosaic feeling of grateful attachment to them as well, for they were our changing rooms before and after games. We hung our clothes on their branches, sat on their bench-like roots to lace our boots, and when no one was looking, used nooks in their trunks as urinals.

From Albert Park, Ratu Cakobau Road climbs up from the park to end at the entrance to The Domain, which in my youth was the residential area for senior civil servants such as my father. Whenever I'm in Suva, every step taken up the road's gradient leads me deeper into memories of my salad days.

The steep part of the road ascending from Albert Park used to be known locally as Cakobau Hill, and down this we raced in our rickety box-cars, without sissy helmets, during the soap-box derbies of the Hibiscus Festivals of the 1950's. At the top of the hill you will note the British high commissioner's residence on the right, which was our family home in the late 1960s; and just past it are the white gates marking the entrance to Berkeley Crescent, at the far end of which we lived in the late 1950s and early 1960s.

Before the road begins its climb up from Albert Park, you may still find there a set of mouldy concrete steps leading down from the curbside to the rugby field below. There are just half a dozen steps and most young people would rather jump from the wall than use them. They've been there since 1953 when a decorated stairway was built to convey Queen Elizabeth to the *veiqaravi vakaturaga* held in her honour in this southeast quadrant of the park.

Queen Elizabeth was, and some say still is, the Tui Viti, the great unifying chief of the thirteen kingdoms of pre-cession Fiji. This was a role that descended to her from the day in 1874 when the sovereignty of these islands was ceded by the leading chiefs of Fiji to Queen Victoria and her successors.[93]

Back in 1953, the young monarch was on her first visit to Fiji, as part of a Commonwealth tour in consequence of her coronation earlier in the year.[94] On arrival in Suva, The Queen was driven to the top of the humble steps of which I write, to be met by the pre-eminent Fijian of the time, Ratu Sir Lala Sukuna, who escorted her down the steps onto the park. They passed one of the towering *baka* trees, festooned with presentations of tapa cloth, fine mats and a long display of butchered pigs, and proceeded down mat-pathways through a silent, seated throng of Fijians to a covered dais where Queen Elizabeth took her ceremonial seat.

Once she was seated, the silence was broken by the assembled Fijian women intoning the *tama*, a drawn-out cry of respect. After further silence the menfolk boomed out another deep *tama*, thereby signifying the commencement of high ceremony.

A sailing canoe had been positioned by the dais and now a long file of Fijian women approached for the *Qalowaqa* ritual, performed only for women of highest rank, splashing seawater onto the canoe's bow and leaving a whale's tooth upon it before retiring. Next came the *Qaloqalovi* ceremony in which Ratu George Cakobau, the direct descendant of Ratu Seru Cakobau, presented a second whale's tooth with the request that The Queen accept it and with it the loyalty of all Fijian people. This she did and thenceforth the full ceremonies proceeded according to the custom of the land, including The Queen's quaffing of ceremonial kava from the same coconut-shell dish her grandfather and father had drunk from when as young men they visited Fiji.[95]

Let us jump forward now by thirty-three years, to when on this same patch of ground, Pope John Paul was accorded similar *veiqaravi vakaturaga* ceremonies of welcome. Yes this man, high in the pantheon of world leaders credited with bringing the Cold War to an end, also graced the green fields of Albert Park, accepting our whales' teeth and mystic kava.

On the day in question, I was seated cross-legged on the ground close to where His Holiness received Fiji's welcome and heard him say the words of response that were so gratifying, but certainly not surprising to hear. He said that Fiji was 'a symbol of hope in the world.' I say 'not surprising' because most committed Fiji citizens of the day really believed this was the way it was. The old adage has it that pride comes before a fall; but I should cut us some slack, for on reflection it really was quite remarkable how far Fiji had come as a multicultural, multiracial nation on that happy papal day in November 1986.[96]

It's time now, my friend, to venture across the park to ground zero. Our destination is easy to find: just walk directly across the playing fields of Albert Park towards the high clock-tower rising from the grey monolith of Government Buildings. Ground zero lies directly under the clock-tower.

Once across the park you will be on Southern Cross Road, named for the landing of Kingsford-Smith's kite on Albert Park during his epic trans-Pacific flight of 1930.[97] Crossing the road, you'll notice it diverges into a high-ceilinged portico, from which a broad cement staircase leads up into the shadowed interior of Government Buildings.

Ascend this stairway and you're in an octagonal atrium over which the clock-tower stands. In the fulcrum of the atrium, there used to be a fine bronze bust of a Fijian head mounted on a plinth. At the time of writing this account, the plinth still stands but the bust has gone, leaving a ragged cavity from whence it was wrenched.

If you stand beside the plinth, you will see there are four entrances converging on the atrium. You must explore each of these, for this is where on 14th May 1987, Fiji's history changed for ever.

The last time I visited it, the atrium had a rather degraded air. One of the large marble tableaux listing the names of governors who presided over one hundred years of Fiji's progress was chipped and cob-webbed, while the other was partially covered by peeling stickers and notices. If it is still so, it will be hard for you to comprehend that this was once one of Fiji's most hallowed spaces.

When you stand by the broken plinth, with the steps to the park at your back, you are facing a set of varnished swing-doors, a modest portal to national sanctum. As I write these words, the High Court of Fiji now sits in those chambers; but up until that era-ending day in 1987, the structure ahead housed Fiji's Parliament.

On a rainy mid-May day in 1987, the House of Representatives was in session. A leftist government, dominated by representatives of Fiji's Indian community, had been elected to govern the country a month earlier. Ever since, the capital has been awash with a cocktail of jubilant elation, sullen anger, cocky reformism and ugly rumours of impending violence.

A few minutes before ten o'clock on the Day of Lost Oaths, a burly Fijian strode past the plinth and took a seat in the public gallery of the parliamentary chambers. His handsome Melanesian face sported the vanity of a handle-bar mustache and he moved like the athlete he was. The man was

208

wearing a light grey suit, the bottom-half of which was a tailored Fijian kilt. On his feet were military brown sandals, on his chest the red and green diagonally-banded tie of the Royal Fiji Military Forces.

Some of those within the parliamentary chambers noticed the man seating himself in the public gallery. Amongst them was his uncle, the newly-elected speaker of the House of Representatives, Milton Leweniqila, who was presiding over the chambers from his high seat, looking much like a bullfrog in a horse-hair wig. Milton briefly wondered why his nephew, Lieutenant Colonel Sitiveni Rabuka, third-in-charge of the country's army, was taking time off to listen to a parliamentary debate.[98]

From the Opposition benches, one of the newly-elected indigenous members of parliament, a verbose bruiser of the 'Fiji for the Fijians, India for the Indians' ilk, was giving his maiden speech and lambasting the Government members for their rejection of chiefly Fijian leadership. He paused as from the clock-tower above the familiar Naiqaqi carillon resounded, followed by the slow tolling of the hour. Each stroke echoed down the corridors of governance, like footfalls to the years of disappointment lying ahead. Then on the tenth toll, Fiji's *coup d'état* era was underway.

Ten men dressed in a motley collection of jackets and floral shirts crossed the octagonal atrium to enter the parliamentary chambers. Their heads were hooded by gas-masks, each man carrying a pistol as they trespassed through the chambers.

Onlookers were transfixed, stunned by the incongruity of what they were seeing, as the weird interlopers stomped to positions covering the Government benches. Observers recall a chorus of collective suckings of breath through fogged-up gas-masks and the thumping steps of the intruders' heavy boots. In retrospect, these were the sounds of democracy's coffin having its lid hammered on.

One of the men was not wearing a gas-mask, his identity hidden instead under a black balaclava of heavy wool. He stepped forward into the space dividing the Government and Opposition benches and uttered words that stun-gunned Fiji's legislature, shocking words that proclaimed a military take-over of the State.

Outside in the atrium, a dozen soldiers armed with M16 assault rifles were ready to extinguish any resistance to the *coup*. Inside everyone was sitting tight; everyone except Colonel Rabuka, who now rose from the public gallery and strode across to the speaker's podium.

From this vantage point he spoke firmly, with bizarrely self-assured authority, telling everyone to remain calm and stay seated. Then he turned to the Government benches, and indicating the exit leading to the atrium, said, 'Mr Prime Minister, please lead your team down to the right'.

The astonished prime minister, Dr Timoci Bavadra, looked for guidance to the speaker. From under his grey wig, an equally astonished Milton gave a nod that urged compliance. Rabuka repeated his command to the prime minister and now Bavadra was standing, his colleagues with him, filing out of those chambers for ever. It was meekly done.

Through the atrium the soldiers herded the Government members, twenty-seven in all, down the steps to the portico on Southern Cross Road where two army trucks were sheltered from the rain. One of the absconded ministers, Dr Tupeni Baba, recoiled at the sight of the trucks and refused to enter them. Rabuka took a gun from a soldier, made a show of cocking it, and pointed it directly at the minister, ordering him into the truck. Minister Baba complied.

Loaded up with their human cargo, the trucks growled into motion. A grim gathering of onlookers watched as Rabuka returned up the steps to the atrium and the infamous path awaiting him, while the deposed government faded away into grey veils of Suva rain.

Next on this tour, I'd like to direct you to where I was during the events just described. If you return to the plinth in the atrium and stand again with your back to the park, you'll notice a verandah stretching away to your right. It was along this access-way that some of the soldiers came in their approach to the parliamentary chambers moments before the *coup*. I know that because I saw them moving along it.

As you depart the atrium and walk along that verandah, you will see below a quadrangle of parked cars, and on the other side of the quadrangle, the guarded entrance to a four-story building. When I worked in that structure, it was prosaically known as 'New Government Building' and perhaps still is. The Prime Minister's Office was on its top floor, as was the Ministry of Foreign Affairs, wherein I worked in the late 1970s. The Ministry of Information took up most of the building's ground floor and this was my base in 1986 and 1987 when I was running that organ of government.

On the *coup* morning of 14th May, we had a bevy of overseas journalists in the ministry's media room and were serving them kava as we responded to their enquiries. This room had windows open to the front of New Government Building, so that as our kava was being supped, we had no view of the goings-on in the quadrangle at the building's rear.

In the busy media room I was in the process of pouring cold water on suggestions that Fiji was embroiled in a dangerous political crisis. In the middle of my extolling of deeply embedded Commonwealth values, one of my ministry colleagues put his head through the door and beckoned me. I went over and he told me there was something funny going on outside in the quadrangle. I decided to check it out.

Going out through the guarded doorway to the quadrangle and looking up at the verandah opposite, I spotted servicemen in bulky raincoats moving towards the parliamentary chambers. Nobody nearby had any idea what was going on. It was a little unusual, but these were unusual days and I concluded a security exercise must be underway.

I was about to return to my duties in the media room, when I saw a familiar face among the people milling about in the quadrangle - the *roko vakacegu* from the island of Taveuni, Ratu Kitione Kubuabola.[99] Few in the streets of

Suva would have recognised him, but if you were from the northern islands of Fiji, you knew he was a very powerful chief indeed.

Ratu Kitione was standing as still as a statue on the far side of the quadrangle, like a resolute coach on the sidelines of a vital game, concentrating his gaze on the parliamentary chambers. It was ten years since I'd last seen the old chief and I wondered what he was doing here, so far from his home island. On the point of going over to greet him, I remembered my responsibility to the restive journalists inside, so I returned to ply them with more kava and consultation.

I've written about what happened next in my book *Kava in the Blood*, thus I'll only repeat hereunder an abridged account of what was given in those pages, written when the memory of the day still burned like a brand on my temporal lobe.

As we were quaffing our kava in the media room, the overseas journalists were quite rightly outlining a host of harbingers of social and political unrest manifest in Fiji since the recent change in government. One of them had even heard that officials of our ministry were receiving anonymous death threats, thanks to our role as the mouthpiece of the new government.

We were countering with more rounds of kava and explanations of cross-cultural tolerance, respect for governmental authority and the peaceful nature of Pacific Island problem-solving, when the door was kicked open and gas-masked soldiers burst into the room. They formed a half circle around the open door and trained their guns on our suddenly mute gathering.

> Through the doorway and into the protective half circle formed by the soldiers, stepped Lieutenant Colonel Sitiveni Rabuka. He lifted a hand-gun and said, 'Where is Peter Thomson?'
>
> The open-mouthed faces of journalists and ministry staffers turned as one from the scene at the doorway to where I stood. I stepped forward and Rabuka motioned me down the corridor past a line

of rigid typists to my office. Once in my office he said, 'Take this down.' As I sat at my desk I noticed he turned his revolver away from me towards the floor.

Right away he dictated while my fingers flew across the paper, 'The Royal Fiji Military Forces have taken control of the Fiji Government to prevent further disturbance and bloodshed in the country. I am on my way to Government House to seek recognition. I ask that the public remain calm and continue with their daily work. In particular I ask that the Fijian community do not take advantage of the situation.'

He told me to get this message broadcast on Radio Fiji and released to the media. Then he was gone.

Rabuka went to Government House to seek support from the governor-general for his actions, but he got no comfort there. The next I heard from him was a phone-call from the Queen Elizabeth Barracks from whence he rang to dictate another news release informing the public that 'ex-government members' were safe in army custody and would be released as soon as a 'caretaker government' was formed.

In the afternoon he was back in our building, explaining his actions to the diplomatic corps in a hastily arranged meeting in the Ministry of Foreign Affairs. I attended that meeting and the next across the corridor in the Cabinet's meeting room, where local journalists and a growing contingent of foreign media crew were assembled.

Tragic as it was for Fiji's future, from the moment Rabuka fronted the cameras, it was apparent the media had themselves a champ. He answered their questions with candour and authority, he had charisma, was photogenic and he clearly enjoyed the attention. Within days, as a result of this and subsequent press conferences, the Fijian colonel's mustachioed face, not to mention his Rambo-like name, had more exposure around the world than any citizen of Fiji before him. [100]

Next morning Rabuka's 'caretaker government', the so-called Council of Ministers, had its first meeting and resolved to immediately work on the governor-general with a view to obtaining his recognition of the military's *fait accompli*. Meanwhile the country's judges had gathered and were standing firm on the over-ruling tenets of the Laws of Fiji.

Up at Government House, the governor-general, Ratu Sir Penaia Ganilau, was teetering on the very edge of our constitutional fundament. The full weight of the State of Fiji, the covenant of welfare of its people and property, had fallen upon his broad back, and a great battle of wills was underway.

Grappling with him at the lip were the military forces in effective control of the country, the judiciary's uncompromising legal advice, the bitterly divisive ambitions of the thwarted parliamentary parties, and most dire of all, beckoning from the abyss, the ghastly spectre of violent ethno-nationalist revolution. His position appeared untenable, but there was still cause for hope, for as a leader, Ratu Sir Penaia was tested and true.

I am a personal witness to the fact that all the while, Ratu Sir Penaia held dear to one tenant: that in the end, his actions must be acceptable to Her Majesty The Queen in all her many roles. It should be remembered that as well as being Tui Viti and Head of State of Fiji, Queen Elizabeth was the leader of the Commonwealth of Nations. Thus in those tumultuous May days, I took strong moral comfort from Ratu Sir Penaia's vice-regal stand, especially when I answered the governor-general's call for me to join him at Government House to become his permanent secretary.[101]

Over the next few days, the Fiji judiciary formulated a lawful plan for the governor-general, where-under he dissolved Parliament, proclaimed himself the executive authority of government, called for fresh elections, and established a Council of Advisers to advise him on running the country in the interim. He would not recognise Rabuka's Council of Ministers, but in practice would include many of its members in the Council of Advisers. It was a ragged compromise, but it allowed the country a way forward under the wise leadership of an honorable man.

Our *coup* tour will shortly take you back to the plinth in the atrium; but before it does, you will need to hail a cab for a two-minute ride into town for the enjoyment of a short sojourn under the flamboyant trees of Sukuna Park. This green swathe in central Suva is of course named for the afore-mentioned Fijian leader, he who greeted Queen Elizabeth at Albert Park in 1953.[102] I take you now to Sukuna Park because, if the atrium at Government Buildings was ground zero on 14th May, this park was the hot zone.

Walking over to the southwestern corner of Sukuna Park, you'll notice the concrete façade of the Suva Civic Centre, an ugly duckling of the 1960's sort. Six days after the May *coup*, the Great Council of Chiefs assembled in this building's auditorium to deliberate on an indigenous response to the national emergency. Since independence, many citizens had come to think of the chiefly council as a colonial relic, wherein Fijian chiefs and indigenous officials had long gathered to advise the colony's governor on the views of indigenous Fijians. But when the state fell apart in 1987, the majority of indigenous Fijians looked to the chiefly council for guidance, for its deliberations were closed to others and they saw in the council's membership all their traditional leaders assembled.

My boss the governor-general was the most powerful traditional chief of northern Fiji, but this did not guarantee him an easy ride at the Great Council of Chiefs. Ratu Sir Penaia had been making it clear through public broadcasts and press releases that Colonel Rabuka's regime had to be dismantled, and that its political prisoners were to be released and press freedoms restored. He'd emphasised that the laws of Fiji were in place and operative, and in these broadcasts made directly to the people of Fiji, counseled them to be patient, to be calm and to keep the faith.

There were many in the council who resented Ratu Sir Penaia's steadfast position and when he addressed the gathering of chiefs and reiterated his position, saying that as The Queen's representative he stood by his oath of loyalty and would only act within the law, he was rebuked. It was plain the chiefs wanted to finish the job Rabuka had begun. At that juncture, their desired outcome was one that would entrench political power in the hands of indigenous Fijians, most likely through defying the governor-general and endorsing Rabuka's Council of Ministers.

As the council met inside the auditorium, a restless crowd milled around Sukuna Park, largely made up of supporters of the ethno-nationalist Taukei Movement and Colonel Rabuka. It was clear that with one feisty word from their leaders, this mob was ready to storm the Bastille.

When a group of Indo-Fijians gathered that day near Government Buildings, for what they described as a public prayer meeting, the indigenous mob swirled down Victoria Parade from Sukuna Park and laid into the gathering with punches and kicks. The Indians fled, but the mob had smelt blood and returned to the park in riot mode, smashing cars, shop-fronts and any unfortunate non-indigenes they came across. In *Kava in the Blood* I wrote,

> The clammy spectre of inter-ethnic violence which had hung hauntingly over us for some weeks now, had briefly but unmistakably exhaled its foulness into the streets of Suva. Now spontaneous street violence was spreading to Nausori and Suva's suburbs where Fijian mobs were looting, assaulting and stoning people and property. That day's rioting was another confirmation we were at the edge of a precipice of awful consequence.

The next day the governor-general again went to address the Great Council of Chiefs, this time with a more conciliatory speech. I have another quote from *Kava in the Blood* for it emphasizes how far out on a limb Ratu Sir Penaia was taken by his commitment to his oath of office,

> The large crowd of Fijians assembled outside the Civic Centre booed as the governor-general's car bore him to the council meeting. In Fijian cultural history this sign of disrespect for one of the highest chiefs of the land was unprecedented, graphically demonstrating the extent to which dogs of anarchy were let loose in our midst.

In his speech that day, the governor-general stood firm on his legal position, but said he would not undermine the best interests of the Fijian people as expressed by the council's deliberations. Ratu Sir Penaia won the chiefs over in support of his position, but in the process had to accept a knot of Taukei Movement stalwarts into his Council of Advisers, a body which up until that time had been shaping as a politically-balanced selection of elected leaders and technocrats.

As a result of the compromise at the Great Council of Chiefs, executive authority for the country was now conferred by all but the deposed government onto the ample shoulders of Ratu Sir Penaia, and the formerly ceremonial establishment at Government House, became the executive office of Fiji. Ahead of Ratu Sir Penaia now lay months of sustained struggle to restore the nation's integrity, a battle he ultimately lost; for amongst those appointed to advise him were many who covertly worked against the governor-general's will.

Before our tour departs Sukuna Park, there is one more moment to contemplate. This came at the end of the Great Council of Chiefs meeting, after the compromise between the council's hard-liners and the governor-general had been hammered out. Even though the army brass-band had been summoned to soothe the crowds which for the last two days had occupied Sukuna Park and its surrounding streets, the mob still ruled the city. They were waiting for one man to give them the signal, and until he did, they would stay where they were.

That man was Colonel Rabuka, the hero of the hour. In little over a week he had achieved iconic status among the indigenous Fijians, and whatever individuals may say today, back in the middle of 1987 the great majority of them adored him.

Fiji's long-serving prime minister, the paramount chief of eastern Fiji, Ratu Sir Kamisese Mara, and the council's chairman, Ratu William Toganivalu, came out onto the Civic Centre's balcony to face the Fijian throng assembled in the park below. A microphone and public address system had been installed on the balcony for speeches to be made to the crowd, but as they spoke, it was apparent Ratu Sir Kamisese and the chairman were like the warm-up acts at a concert. Five thousand restless Fijians were spilling over the perimeters of Sukuna Park, waiting for the main performance.

Then the man of the hour stepped up to microphone and the crowd cheered him as one. The governor-general's compromise at the Great Council of Chiefs was never an endorsement of the *coup d'état*, but Rabuka had got rid of the elected Labour government, was now head of the military, and he would stay in the political frame by right of membership of the governor-general's Council of Advisors. He was way ahead of the game, and when he lifted his arms like a prize-fighter and cheese-caked at the baying mob, people like me feared for the future of our country.

Here was a new kind of Fijian political leader. One who lifted his arms in self-congratulation in the presence of high chiefs, itself a culturally disrespectful act; a man who was not of chiefly heritage, but was now the champion of the Great Council of Chiefs; a man who as head of the army was supposed to be the guarantor of public order, yet at the same time publicly played to the mob.

At Government House he had us duped, good and proper. In the months ahead Rabuka played the role of adviser on home affairs to the governor-general, which gave him oversight of the police and army portfolios. The governor-general took all of his security reports and advice at face value, and in Ratu Sir Penaia's presence, the colonel made great shows of level-headed loyalty. We wanted to believe him. The alternative was hardly palatable.

We took at face value the charismatic colonel's explanation that he'd only done what he did to save the country from bloodshed. Hidden from us then, was the evidence that all along he'd been in cahoots with the Taukei Movement's campaign of violence and intimidation. Little did we know the extent of his ambitions and how he would betray the governor-general's position with a second *coup* in September, a *coup* which for me resulted in four days behind bars, sleeping on the floor of a stinking, mosquito-filled military cell as punishment for my bit-part in upholding the law of the land. Had we been more prescient, had we not lived in hope for the better, perhaps we would have foreseen all that was to come in that moment when a victorious young colonel strode out onto the Civic Centre balcony and threw his arms in the air.

So back we go to ground zero, my friend, to the atrium of Government Buildings. I mentioned there were four entranceways to the atrium and we have yet to go down the last of those. If you stand again by the plinth with your back to the steps, you will see the fourth way, a long verandah heading off to your left. Proceeding down this verandah and turning right near its end, you will then notice ahead another flight of steps leading down to the front of Government Buildings. Go down these steps, past the bust of Ratu Cakobau in its lily-filled water-feature, to stand in the shadow of the bronze statue of a striding Fijian, clad in morning suit and hung with many medals.

At the foot of this statue, in September 1987, supporters of the rebellious Taukei Movement dug a hole in the lawn and lit the fire for a *lovo*. A *lovo* is a Fijian ground-oven that operates by way of heating stones in a fire-pit, upon which layers of leaves and food are placed, before more layers of leaves and soil seal off the heat for the cooking process. There are two important points to understand about this piece of Taukei Movement street-theatre.

The first is that *lovo* were used to cook human bodies during the days when cannibalism was rife in Fiji. Anthropophagy ceased with the advent of Christianity in Fiji in the nineteenth century, but its memory lingers. Ratu Cakobau for example, the great chief who led the cession of Fiji to the British Crown, had consumed the prime cuts of countless human bodies prior to his conversion to Christianity. Even to this day, it's very common to hear people utter the word *bokola*, usually spoken in jest but as often as an insult, describing a human corpse that will shortly be consumed by the living.

The second point is that by September 1987, the governor-general's ceaseless efforts to heal the nation were bearing fruit. He was by then only days away from sealing agreement on a caretaker government made up of the elected leaders of both sides of the dissolved House of Representatives, to serve in effect as a government of national unity.

Of course the big losers from this much-desired outcome were going to be the provocateurs of the Taukei Movement, whose talents for intimidation and disruption were not going to be required in the healing process ahead.

It was thus time for them to play their last cards and these turned out to be the widespread acts of arson, looting and violence that spread through Suva in mid-September. The *lovo* by the statue was just one more of these cards, and down at the fire-pit Taukei Movement extremists Veisamasama, Vesikula and Raikivi stalked about, letting it be known that if their leaders were further insulted, the perpetrators would end up in the *lovo*.

At this time, the deposed prime minister Dr Bavadra, had as his spokesman a bright young journalist, Richard Naidu, who happened to be driving by Government Buildings while the *lovo* was being prepared. Below the bronze statue he saw smoke and a group of Fijians carrying spears and wooden clubs dressed as warriors of old. So he stopped his car and went over for a closer look. But the Fijian 'warriors' recognised Naidu and set on him, chasing Bavadra's man across the road to the lobby of what is now the Suva Holiday Inn, where they laid into him with their weapons. Shocked hotel guests witnessed the intervention of the hotel's duty manager, whose fighting off of the attackers ensured Naidu lived to nurse his wounds in hospital later that morning.

Before we leave this sorry scene, it is meet that we turn and pay our respects to the man for whom the bronze statue is shaped. Who was this much-decorated figure? The answer has been touched upon twice already in this story - Ratu Sir Lala Sukuna, the same Fijian chief who escorted Queen Elizabeth onto Albert Park in 1953. The statue of the greatest Fijian leader of the twentieth century was unveiled by The Queen on a subsequent visit to Fiji after Ratu Sukuna's death in 1958.

Ratu Sukuna was descended from the great chiefly families, but leadership was not his by right; he had to earn it through his many high achievements and the quality of his character. Intelligence, bravery, breadth of outlook, foresight and dedicated service to the betterment of his people are all qualities well-described in Deryck Scarr's two books on Ratu Sukuna; suffice to say here that more than any man before or since, Ratu Sir Lala Sukuna had shaped the response of indigenous Fijians to the modern world.

It is relevant to the wider context of these chronicles to know that Ratu Sukuna was very influential on the course of my father's life. Amongst his many duties, the Fijian chief was an honorary *aide de camp* to the governor of Fiji when in 1942 my twenty-two year old father arrived in Fiji to take up duties as the substantive ADC at Government House.

Though thirty-two years separated the ages of the two men, they got along very well, and in 1943 Ratu Sukuna was instrumental in having my father placed in the Fiji Infantry Regiment's Third Battalion, as second-in-charge of a company led by Ratu Edward Cakobau.[103] Then in 1956, Ratu Sukuna chose my father as his successor in the culturally sensitive role of chairman of the Native Lands and Fisheries Commission. Of Ratu Sukuna's time at the head of the commission, his biography states,

> No Europeans were appointed under Ratu Sukuna's regime until near the end of his life, when he was succeeded by JS Thomson who thought as he did.[104]

'Til the day he died, my father regarded it as one of the great compliments paid him in his life, that he could be described as a man who thought as one with Ratu Sir Lala Sukuna. I know this because he wrote as much, more than once in his correspondence with me.

Over the decades that seas separated us, my father and I indulged in a regular exchange of letters that lasted from when I first went off to boarding school in 1962, until the letter he wrote me on the day of his death in 2008. Many of his aerogrammes are fixed into the back-covers of my voluminous collection of Fiji books and I quote from one now, dated 4th January, 1999,

> In the year before his death I had several one-to-one discussions with Ratu Sir Lala Sukuna. At that time the likelihood of the Pacific Island territories becoming totally independent seemed unlikely, and the 'old man' constantly told me that insofar as Fiji was concerned, it should not even be contemplated for at least a hundred years!

Both men have gone to their graves with unassailable reputations for integrity and dedication to the best interests of Fijians regardless of race, so I place the above interchange in the public domain without trepidation.

We are all creatures of the times in which we live, and times change. In Ratu Sukuna's biography, his views on democracy's relevance to Fiji are clearly stated in an official memo written in 1949 on the subject of constitutional change,

> The truth is, the democratic elective system has no place in a country where racial questions loom large.[105]

But a modern State demands a democratic elective system, and that is the challenge ahead for our nation: to establish an inclusive formula embracing Fiji's special qualities of race, culture, class, religion and vanua into a citizenry bound by the principle of equity for all. In 2009 people are still asking how long it'll take for the effects of the 1987 coups to be erased from Fiji's consciousness and many find themselves scratching their heads for an answer. We all pray that by Ratu Sukuna's count there is not another half century's scratching ahead.

But in 2009 a new road is emerging, admittedly under a temporarily authoritarian government, but with the distinct commendation that it will be to a homegrown design. From what I have read, it offers a route that aspires to a national future of sustainable democracy and de-racialised governance.

The Fiji Roadmap that has recently been laid down provides a time-frame that gives ample time for the country to settle down and work out a new model of polity. What is being forecasted is that racially-segregated general elections and parliaments will finally become a thing of the past, and that citizens will share a common name and common national purpose. That is a road I am willing to travel with renewed hope in my heart for the body politic of Fiji.

From Ratu Sukuna's statue, our tour will now take you to the waterfront, along picturesque Queen Elizabeth Drive to where the shadows of *baka* trees dapple the waters of Suva Harbour, to where, out across the bay, you can spy ranges of cockscomb mountains marching away to Colo.

Half a mile along the waterfront drive, you must turn again into Ratu Sukuna Road where it cuts inland and runs for another half a mile up to Veiuto. Here on the recumbent knob of Suva's peninsula, the tour will arrive at the gates of the new Fiji Parliament Buildings. We have come here because beyond those gates on 19th May 2000, a third *coup d'état* took place that cut even deeper into the guts of Fiji.[106]

Before we contemplate Fiji's second ruinous May day, standing here at the gates of Parliament allow me to give you a fast-forward summary of what passed in Fiji's body politic during the intervening years. After his second *coup*, in September 1987, Colonel Rabuka did away with the office of governor-general by declaring Fiji a republic. Rabuka then tried and failed to run a government largely made up of hard-core Taukei Movers. Next he asked Ratu Sir Kamisese Mara to return as prime minister and Ratu Sir Penaia Ganilau to serve as president, handing executive power over to them at the beginning of 1988.

In 1990 at the behest of the Great Council of Chiefs, a new constitution was promulgated that was heavily skewed in favour of indigenous Fijians. In 1991 Rabuka resigned from the army to concentrate on a political career and in 1992 the SVT, the political party endorsed by the chiefs, was elected to govern with Rabuka as prime minister. In 1994 Ratu Sir Penaia died and was succeeded as president by Ratu Sir Kamisese.

General elections in 1994 reconfirmed power in the hands of Rabuka's SVT. But then in 1996, Rabuka saw the light and began working with Jai Ram Reddy, the leader of the Indian NFP party, on a fairer constitution for the country which was eventually adopted by Parliament in 1997.

Elections under this new constitution were held in 1999, with both Rabuka and Reddy's parties rejected by their respective electorates, seemingly for daring to take the country to a syncretic centre. Confrontational democracy was once again mauling Fiji's racially-divided populace, and as a result of the fragmentation of the Fijian vote, Mahendra Chaudhry's Labour party now had the most seats in Parliament. Chaudhry became Fiji's first Indian prime minister in May 1999. In the wake of Labour taking office, the Taukei Movement was revived and familiar sounds of rabble-rousing began to be heard.

And so to the year 2000 and the ground-hog day of 19th May, the onset of two months of national degradation. That morning the attention of the media, and that of those tasked with the nation's security, was on an indigenous protest march moving through central Suva. Some two thousand strong, the march was being led by disaffected Taukei provocateurs.

At 10.45 am, a van turned off Ratu Sukuna Road into Veiuto, passing unchallenged through the gates of Parliament.[107] Out of the van climbed seven casually-dressed men who made their way directly to the parliamentary chambers, to where the House of Representatives was in session.

Arriving in the chambers, it transpired the intruders were heavily armed and that four of the seven were Fijian members of the CRW, the army's Counter Revolutionary Warfare squadron, with Uzi submachine-guns at their sides. Two of the others were *kailoma*, the Speight brothers from a family of Tailevu dairy farmers.[108]

Entering Parliament, George Speight announced, 'This is a civil coup. Hold tight, nobody move!'

Prime Minister Chaudhry and his fellow parliamentarians kept to their seats, but Speaker Dr Apenisa Kuruisaqila[109] was made of stern stuff and he stood up saying, 'What is this?'

'This is a civil coup by the people, the *taukei* people,' announced Speight, 'And we ask you to please retire to your chamber right now, Mr Speaker. Please cooperate so nobody will get hurt.'

Dr Kuruisaqila stood his ground and repeated, '*Na cava*? What is this?

'This is a civil *coup*, with arms and ammunition, by the people for the people,' came Speight's reply. 'Please just tell them not to get up!'

As the sinister seven waved their guns about, the speaker remonstrated, 'It is an illegal act, you know that!'

Speight said if he made things difficult for them, they'd be forced to use their guns and promptly ordered the parliamentarians of the Opposition benches to vacate the House of Representatives with the speaker.

Pointing directly at Speight, Dr Kuruisaqila told him, 'If you have to shoot anyone in this House, you shoot me first!'

Speight discharged his gun twice, not at the speaker but into the parliament's ceiling. With the shock of these explosions slamming around the chamber, it was clear the next bullets would hit human flesh, so the parliamentarians capitulated. As the speaker and the Opposition benches filed out of the chambers, those on the Government benches succumbed to the indignity of being handcuffed by their captors.

For forty minutes, Speight paced around Parliament with his mobile phone at his ear. He told the captured parliamentarians they'd be filled with surprise when they saw who the real coup leader was and that he'd be turning up any time now. But the phantom leader never arrived and Fiji still speculates as to who he might have been.

Who did turn up were hundreds of young Fijian men who jogged up Ratu Sukuna Road from the protest march in central Suva to join the invasion of Parliament. These wild reinforcements were the first of the thousands of Fijians who would fill the grounds of Parliament to serve as human shields for the hostage-takers.

Apart from the men of the CRW squadron, it was soon clear that factions of the army were supporting the *coup* as well, for more soldiers arrived to aid the seven intruders and further arms were delivered to the outlaw soldiers.

It has been publicly reported that the army's third-in-command, supervised the delivery of these arms and New Zealand's minister of foreign affairs went public in accusing the officer concerned of complicity.

Inside the Veiuto parliamentary complex, George Speight was assuming the role of *coup* leader by default, though the Fiji Times would not take long to decide the correct description for him was '*coup* spokesman'. He spoke for an indigenous agenda referred to as 'the Cause', but exactly what this was, and which particular Jacobites it stood for, were never fully spelled out. It was quite obvious his strings were being pulled by powers beyond the public eye, powers that have never been completely revealed.

Speight spoke little Fijian, having been schooled at my *alma mater* the English-speaking Suva Grammar School on the Veiuto foreshore, and for a decade or more had resided in Australia and the United States. But he did have Fijian forbears and many of the indigenous people of the provinces of Tailevu and Naitasiri seemed to develop an overnight love for the man. With his copper dome shaved to a shine, his executive suits, white shirts, flash ties, mobile phone and shoot-from-the-hip lines, the international media lapped Speight up.

Yes, for the foreign media it was Rabuka-time all over again. Here was another photogenic iconoclast in an exotic island country, a man of the moment with a penchant for press conferences, prepared to speak his mind however misguided it might be. In leadership qualification and articulacy, Speight was no Rabuka; but the media's demand for pithy sound-bytes and the ability of their editors to create them, made this *coup*-boy look better than he was.

Once the army's initially confused disposition towards the 'civil *coup*' began settling against it, military roadblocks were set up around Veiuto and the Speight Gang found itself in a classic hostage stand-off. With the members of the nation's elected government as their hostages and a human shield provided by their rag-tag throng of reveling supporters, the kidnappers dug in as the weeks dragged by.

Speight's sense of his own importance rose and darkened like the cumulous clouds that daily build over Suva Harbour. Precipitation fell on the press corps gathered for his increasingly irrelevant news conferences. Those who were really driving this crime against the nation were beyond the parliamentary complex, conferring behind tapa screens. *Kunekune na yaloka ni dilio*.[110] Many have been named and some have even had their day in court. Some have threatened legal action if their names are ever again associated. But many have stayed behind the concealing screens, their shadowy outlines merely glimpsed or guessed at, so that the full story of 2000 has yet to be told.

The civil *coup* immediately revealed itself as being uncivil in the extreme. The prime minister, cabinet ministers and government parliamentarians would be held hostage for fifty-six days, and be deprived of all but Red Cross intermediary contact with their families during those desperate days. From day one, the Indian parliamentarians were separated from their colleagues and confined to an office building in the complex, while the Fijians and *kailoma* remained for the duration in the parliamentary chambers.

For refusing to sign a letter of resignation, Prime Minister Chaudhry was given a life-threatening beating by his captors. As the days ground by, two months of national humiliation passed, while the living conditions for the hostages became increasingly tedious and squalid.

Outside the hostages' two makeshift prisons, the parliamentary complex turned into a heart of darkness festival. This was a carnival for the disaffected, as Suva's slum-dwellers and nothing-to-lose Tailevu-Naitasiri villagers mingled with outlaw soldiers, evangelical churchmen, out-of-favour politicians, hardened criminals, opportunistic businessmen and hymn-singing Fijians bussed in from the countryside.

With caches of weapons purloined from the army camp, while their camouflaged snipers kept guard in the surrounding bush, the CRW soldiers drilled a rag-tag paramilitary force to defend the parliamentary complex against the regular army. At all hours trucks drove in and out of the place, transporting droves of high-spirited coup-supporters, along with carcasses of slaughtered pigs and cattle, and piles of looted root-crops to feed the hordes who'd set up camp throughout the complex.

Day and night the thud and clank of kava being pounded echoed through the buildings, accompanied by shrieks of wild laughter, fright and anger. Shattered glass lay all around where offices had been turned into dormitories. Wanton besiegers vandalised wherever they went.

Great slabs of fly-covered meat hung from trees in the compound as previously-manicured lawns turned to muddy bogs. Laundry lines were strung about the place, smoke drifting through as ground-ovens burned, the acrid smoke mingling with that of marijuana and tobacco.

Toilets blocked and Suva rain descended, so Speight's supporters, in their hundreds, took to defecating on the buildings' floors. Mangy stray dogs and tethered pigs sorted amongst the rubbish, where blowflies filled the air, attracted to growing piles of rotting refuse and fresh from the stench where primitive toilet grounds were spreading about the Veiuto grounds.

From their parliamentary stronghold, the Speight Gang's armed foot-soldiers made forays into the city, spreading a fog of fear and frustration across the peninsula and the countryside beyond. They robbed at will, trashed the national television studio, set selected buildings on fire, and killed police and army personnel.

Hampered by compromised leadership, the police fought off Fijian looters smashing their way through the shopfronts of Suva. But there was only so much the security forces could do, as was evident the day Speight was shot at by the army. His vehicle had failed to stop at a military roadblock and when Speight was recognised, soldiers opened fire on him. Speight sped back to the safety of the parliamentary complex, let it be known he'd survived an army assassination attempt and that the lives of the parliamentary hostages were now at grave risk. The spooked outlaws of Veiuto took to their barricades, firing warning shots of impending violence.

Insurrection spread quickly through areas of Fiji where support was strongest for the Cause. In Speight's Tailevu province, Korovou town's police station was seized and twenty-five soldiers, policemen and civil servants were taken hostage. In historic Levuka, heritage buildings were burnt and the town's tuna cannery occupied. The tourist industry, normally a sacred cow, was not spared, when several exclusive island resorts were invaded. Schools closed indefinitely as parents feared for the security of their children.

Prison riots broke out in Naboro, the country's main prison complex, and then Fiji's main electricity source, the Monosavu hydroelectric dam, was taken over and shut down by disaffected Naitasiri landowners. Power was now rationed and a curfew declared in Suva as illegal roadblocks manned by angry Fijians sprang up around the nation.

Just when it seemed things couldn't get much worse, the people of Fiji were stunned to learn the soldiers of the northern division's army barracks had mutinied and declared their support for Speight's cause. The dogs of national anarchy were baying at the leash, and the leash was strained to breaking point.

On 9th July, the army regained the upper hand when its commander, Commodore Bainimarama, shook hands with the Speight Gang on a deal known as the Muanikau Accord. Under this settlement, the supporters of the Cause were given everything they wanted: the overthrow of the Chaudhry government, the removal of Ratu Sir Kamisese Mara from the presidency, the abrogation of the 1997 Constitution, a commitment from the army's interim regime to review ways of strengthening indigenous rule, and an amnesty for all of the Speight Gang's actions. In return they were to release the hostages and return the army's weapons.

Such was the national shame, some hoped the parliamentary complex would be swallowed up forever. It would not have taken long for the Veiuto bush to reclaim the land and obscure the vandalised structures. *Wa butako* vines, mile-a-minute creepers and *wa kabo* ferns would have crept over the buildings; just as prickly sensitive-grass and *vaivai* bushes would have made short work of the parliamentary grounds. Soon the trunks and leafy branches of *baka* and breadfruit trees would have concealed the defiled ruins from Ratu

Sukuna Road, and like a *koro makawa* beyond recall, the whole catastrophe could have been eventually wiped from our consciousness.[111]

But braver hearts prevailed, and the parliamentary complex was refurbished and reopened for business when an elected government returned to office in 2001 under the leadership of Laisenia Qarase, a dour Fijian banker arbitrarily appointed to the job by the army's commander. In what looked decidedly like premeditated strategy, once the parliamentary hostages were released, like so many of Fiji's political compacts, the provisions of the Muanikau Accord were scrapped. The army explained this was not because the accord had been made under duress, but because the outlaws did not stick to it by returning the army's purloined weapons.

Thus the civil *coup* may have achieved its short-term aims, but within weeks of the accord Speight and many of his accomplices were under army arrest. By February 2002, the *coup* spokesman had been convicted of treason, with a subsequent death sentence commuted to life imprisonment. George Speight was expendable. Having over-played his role as spokesman for the Cause, the snappy front-man was hung out to dry in a primal Fiji prison cell. All along he'd been swinging from a rotten tree.

There was a very dangerous branch yet to drop from that tree, but to see where it fell, you will have to take another taxi-ride across town, my friend. Ask the driver of your dilapidated tenth-hand Suva taxi to take you back through the city to where Edinburgh Drive carries you up to the soapstone ridge of Tamavua. The rattling jalopy will proceed along Princes Road, past all the swank properties where the diplomats live: the Hedstrom's old residence now the Fort Kangaroo walled-community of the Australian high commission, the Crompton's place now the residence of the Indian high commissioner, and the new American embassy rising close by the Mormon temple where golden Moroni floats high in the Suva sky.

When you see Mead Road on your right, get your driver to turn into it and descend the slopes of Samabula until you come to Maddocks Road.[112]

Arriving at the end of Maddocks Road, you'll discover you have been transported to the back-gate of QEB, the army's Queen Elizabeth Barracks. You won't be able to enter therein, so have the taxi drop you at the Maddocks Road turning-circle, ask the nervous driver to wait for you, then stroll slowly across to the QEB boom-gate.

Standing outside the gate, you'll be able to glimpse ahead into the army's inner sanctum, where about fifty yards along the barracks road, you should be able to see the edge of the parade ground to the right of the road. Beyond the parade ground, the land rises to a red-roofed, single-storied colonial building. That modest structure is the officer's mess, the heart of the heartland.

Right next to where you are standing, on the left-hand-side directly behind the gates, is the guardhouse. Within the thick white walls of that low building, are two rows of bare cement cells. If I recall right, the cell in which I was detained for four formative days in September 1987, was the second on your left just past the front room of the guardhouse. Since you won't be allowed inside for a closer look, I'll summarise a description of it as written in *Kava in the Blood*.

My cell was seven foot by five foot, a plastered cement box. Its exterior wall had two tiny windows set high up, without mosquito gauze and crossed with iron bars. The miniature windows were to prove quite ineffectual in the ventilation of the cell's hot, dank air. The interior wall had a narrow door of iron bars set to one side, bolted and secured with a heavy lock and chain. The only other opening was a drainage hole at the floor level of the exterior wall, presumably for those times when the cell's rough cement floor was hosed down. A previous occupant had scrawled his name on the wall, 'Kabekoro, 1982'. There was a stench in there. I thought it might be from the human excrement smeared up the side of the wall, but that was well-dried. There was no doubt about it, the smell came from a mattress that was rolled up in the corner of the cell. Studying its qualities, I deduced the sour smell was a combination of the effects of mildew on damp, coconut-fibre innards, together with an accumulation of many years of sweat, vomit and urine from a long line of inebriated soldiers. I was to find that going down on the limp lumps of that mattress was like lying on a dead toad.

Ahhh, sweet nostalgia! I have but to close my eyes to rekindle those barrack-room fragrances and the dainty cadence of my four days in the military: bugle-calls and marching men, the curt commands of superior beings, the smoke and growl of army trucks stopping and starting at the boom-gate as they checked in and out of our *coup*-maker's den, permanently grumpy duty sergeants barking over the stomp-stomp-stomp of heavy boots syncopated with fine salutes and drills.

And how could you forget the throbbing pulse of those barmy tropic nights? The guardhouse rocked with nocturnal din, and not a minute of fun was missed, for the needles of a thousand ravenous mosquitoes ensured wakefulness 'til dawn. The entertainment was anything but mundane: from the retching moans of the drunken soldier in the cell next to mine, to overheard remarks of returning truck-drivers with their snatches of news from the curfewed city; from the clatter of loaded weapons falling on the cement floor by my ear, to the guardhouse bashing of an errant soldier or two. This was, after all, the gateway to Coupcoupland, the exact location of which was not quite clear to me in September 1987. Was it out there beyond the gates where Maddocks Road curved off to a wider world, or within QEB up amongst the polished silver of the officer's mess?

But my purpose in bringing you to this boom-gate is not to convince you of the joys of army life. Sadly, it is to mark another dark day in the annals of Fiji that should not be forgotten – 2nd November 2000, the mutinous day four innocents were slain at the barracks and four mutineers were subsequently beaten to death in revenge. Had you been standing at the QEB gate that day, you would have been well-advised to beat a hasty retreat up Maddocks Road without looking back, for there were bullets flying everywhere and the sanctity of human life was in abeyance.

Incredibly, the mutineers were made up of some forty members of the Counter Revolutionary Warfare unit, the same 'elite' mob who had been instrumental in carrying out the parliamentary putsch six months earlier.

Some say the CRW was established during Rabuka's post-1987 time as head of the army, to act as his palace guard. That the troublesome unit was still in existence in November 2000, six months after the Speight coup, and in a position to execute a mutiny against its own command structure, demonstrates just how divided and ruthless some sections of the army had become since Rabuka's national abrogations of 1987.

On that November 2000 morning, the CRW rebels first took control of the barrack's armory. Having secured the army's weaponry, they equipped their fellow rebels and set off up the slope towards the officers' mess, their mission to secure the entire camp and capture the head of the military, Commodore Frank Bainimarama. But the Commodore and his bodyguards were alerted to the attack and a fierce firefight ensued between the advancing mutineers and the desperate defenders of the officers' mess. In the heat of this battle, the Commodore made a narrow escape from the camp, descending a bushy gully at the back of the mess with bullets zinging by his ears.

By mid-afternoon the rebels had secured the camp, at which point presumably the next stage of the plot was meant to swing into action, namely the seizure of the reins of government. But that stage never eventuated, for the army's Third Battalion came storming back from its countryside training exercise and laid siege to QEB. With confusion now reigning amongst the CRW, before the day was done the army had snuffed out the mutiny.

In the midst of the conflagrations of that wretched day, Ratu Inoke Takiveikata, a senator and former cabinet minister, entered the camp and distributed mobile phones to the rebels. As the paramount chief of the populous Naitasiri Province, Ratu Inoke's traditional title is the Qaranivalu, which translates literally as 'the pit of war'. Once again it was clear the CRW was acting on understandings given from places of influence, beyond the wire of the army camp.

Also appearing amongst the mayhem was the former prime minister Rabuka, the *coup*-maker of old, driving up in a vehicle with his old Major-General's uniform inside. Rabuka had been absent from army ranks since 1991 when he retired in order to legally enter a political career, so his presence at the camp in the middle of a mutiny raised serious questions of complicity.

It is worthy of note that in 2004, the Naitasiri paramount chief was convicted and sentenced to life imprisonment for his part in the uprising. Then, in 2006, it was Rabuka who was in the dock, accused of inciting the mutiny of 2000. The High Court's panel of assessors was split on a verdict of his guilt, with the judge delivering a casting vote of not guilty.

It is well known in the Islands that elements of Fijian society have a propensity for enough devious plots and *liu muri* double-talk to make Lady Macbeth blush and look away.[113] At the completion of the army's 2005 proceedings against the mutineers of 2000, forty-two soldiers were convicted and sentenced to gaol terms. In his summary, the head of the court martial panel admitted there were niggling doubts whether all the key-players behind the mutiny had been or would ever be exposed. The military's commanding officer had very nearly been assassinated, but the court martial process showed a level of restraint that was attributed by many as a desire not to further aggravate those within the country, and indeed within the military, who were still in sympathy with the elusive Cause of the *coup*-boys of 2000.

That millennial year was a bad one for Fiji. It was the year that shattered the belief that groups of Fijians would never again take up arms against other groups of Fijians. It marked the year when Fiji's bogeyman changed from over a century of indigene confronting non-indigene, to a new era of indigene versus indigene. This was the year when the ghoul of violent separatism showed its ugly face in Fiji and nobody liked the look of it. Its contorted expression was all too familiar to modern Melanesia. We'd seen it in Bougainville's bloody conflict, in the emergency of New Caledonia, in Vanuatu's Coconut War, and the insurrection that very nearly wrecked the Solomon Islands.

Commodore Bainimarama summed it up when he told a group of chiefs who supported the Cause that if democratic government wasn't restored, Fiji was on its way back to the 1800s. The point he was making was that prior to Fiji becoming a British crown colony in 1874, the indigenous populace was in a constant state of tribal warfare, attendant to which were tyrannical warlords, human sacrifices and cannibalism. 'Is that where you people want to take us back to?' asked the Commodore. 'We will be shooting each other looking for food.'[114]

There is one last stop-off on our *coup* tour of Suva. So please resume your seat in that rattling taxi, my friend, and head for the great green expanses of the National Stadium. Have your driver take you down through dense housing of Nabua to where the Fiji Golf Club spreads its sodden fairways along the shores of Laucala Bay.

Push on down Fletcher Road, over the Vatuwaqa River to beachside Muanivatu, where on the northern corner of Statham Street's turn-off is some rising land with a jumble of concrete residences built upon it. There was a time when that land was a broad and shady lawn on which stood a modest colonial bungalow. I tip my fedora whenever I pass the ghost of that residence, for in 1921 my mother was born within its clapboard walls.

On to the intersection with Laucala Bay Road, where jutting into the sea to your left, you can spot the stone breakwater of the old seaplane base where my mother worked as a young woman during the Pacific War. But our goal is not that far in the past, we are heading to the right and to recent history at the gates of the National Stadium.

Through the stadium gates and you'll see the playing field, still known to older hands like me as Buckhurst Park. It is hallowed ground for the national rugby team, on account of Fiji defeating the British Lions at this ground in 1977. Yes, my friend, 25 to 21 was the triumphant scoreline. Ha! I just had to squeeze that day of glory in here somewhere.

Now take a wander out along the field's halfway line and imagine a rugby ball planted out in the centre of the field. The time is very close to four o'clock on the afternoon of 1st December 2006, when the whistle will blow for the kick-off of a rugby game that will be reported around the world.

The game is the annual rugby clash between the police and army teams of Fiji; hardly a newsworthy event you might say. Five thousand members of the disciplined service community, family and friends are gathered to cheer their teams, for there are bragging rights at stake. The annual competition between the two sides had been drawn five times, won twenty-one times by the army team and twenty-one times by police.

And there is a revered prize at stake, the Sukuna Bowl, a broad kava-bowl trophy presented back in 1951 by the father of the nation, Ratu Sir Lala Sukuna, to foster brotherly love between the disciplined forces. I'm sure this is all riveting information for Vitiphiles and rugby addicts, and for the sake of the latter I should record that the 2006 game was won 17-15 by the police team, after they scored a last-minute penalty. But again, a domestic sporting contest was hardly copy-fodder for hard-bitten global news-hounds.

What was newsworthy and why they all sat around with twiddling pens and dangling cameras, was that sitting in the grandstand, next to the country's vice-president, Ratu Sukuna's nephew, Ratu Joni Madraiwiwi, was the commander of the army, Commodore Frank Bainimarama. What made him newsworthy was that he'd been making it very clear he was going to execute a *coup d'état* any day now.

He'd given the elected government certain deadlines to do certain things or be deposed, and the government had not done them to the military's satisfaction. Everyone therefore knew a *coup* was coming and it would have already happened but for the match to decide the Sukuna Bowl. The Commodore had made it clear nothing would stand in the way of the rugby game, and it was not 'til the following week that the government was overthrown.

If you control all the guns in the country and have a steely resolve forged by dodging the bullets of your appointed assassins, there's no particular need to have a dramatic *coup*. You watch the rugby and then next Tuesday as commander of the military, you get the Fiji Gazette to publish a declaration of a state of emergency saying,

> At approximately 1800 hours tonight, Tuesday 5 December 2006, I have with much reluctance assumed executive authority of the country, etc, etc. Thank you and God Bless Fiji.

There were three curious things about this last *coup*. The first was that Bainimarama was overthrowing Qarase, the very man he'd installed as interim prime minister when the Speight Gang overthrew Chaudhry's elected government in 2000. True, Qarase had subsequently taken office in a constitutionally legal manner after general elections that his SDL party clearly won, but still he owed his ordination to the army commander. Over the intervening six years, Qarase and the Commodore had fallen deeply foul of each other's affections, with the prime minister trying and failing at some high-stakes plays to depose Bainimarama from his leadership of the military. This was all no secret to the Fiji public, who were free to study the Byzantine plots and subplots on the front pages of the local newspapers.

The second curious occurrence was that former prime minister Chaudhry, victim of both the 1987 and 2000 *coups*, joined Bainimarama's post-*coup* government as its minister of finance. *Coup*-beneficiaries had become *coup*-victims, and now *coup*-victims were becoming *coup*-beneficiaries. Many more fingers scratched many more heads in consternation, trying to work out exactly who Fiji's defenders of democracy truly were, which was a more practical use for the digits in question than pointing them in opinionated directions of blame. An unblushing Chaudhry justified his move by saying,

Last year's *coup* was warranted. One cannot forget that the current constitutional crisis had its roots in a growing discontent and frustration with six years of bad governance …[115]

The third curious occurrence was that Fiji's 'coup culture' was set on its head by the 2006 *coup*. The earlier *coups* had been all about restoring the indigenous Fijian establishment and shoring up the supremacy of indigenous Fijians, with the overwhelmingly indigenous Fijian army working closely with the Great Council of Chiefs and Fiji's Methodist Church hierarchy. But the 2006 coup was quite the opposite, initially leaving many Fijians and most foreigners, in some perplexity about what all this meant. The army was setting out to turn back the ethno-nationalist tide let loose in 1987, and to free the people of Fiji, non-indigenes included, from the prejudices of the past.

Around the kava bowls of the Islands, indigenous Fijians pondered what all this meant for them, and initially they were confused. They saw how the army was discarding the old certainties like dregs of kava, and it seemed the institution they had always believed to be *their* army, was adopting the agenda of the Fiji Labour Party, a party they'd overwhelmingly voted against at every general election. Though most realised the agenda of the ethno-nationalists had once again lead the country into deep trouble, it was in their nature to hold firm to old cultural loyalties.

But by 2009, to the consternation of many a foreign observer, it was becoming obvious that the government of the day was earning the support of Fiji's pragmatic populace. The *matanitu* is the *matanitu* and it shall be respected by the people. In Fiji it seems, if the leader of the day is firm and even-handed, so much the better.

The public mood I garnered on my most recent visit to Suva was one of ambivalence about politics, with prudent approval for the government's commitment to development and reform. Even in conversations with former opponents of the government, I was told there was general acceptance of the status quo while the country pursued the roadmap laid out for Fiji's progress back to parliamentary democracy in 2014.

Well, until next time, that's the end of our *coup* tour, my friend. So let me shout you a sun-downer at the varnished bar of the Royal Suva Yacht Club and we'll wrap up your Suva sojourn, sipping on Bounty rum while the sky turns twenty shades of fuchsia out beyond the palm fronds, the tinkling yacht masts and the abandoned fishing boats under the harbour hills.

You know, all through our tour I couldn't help but be dogged by the thought that we'd got ourselves lost in the mangroves since 1987, tangled up among all those roots with no apparent path out of the quagmire. I read that the United Nations decreed special measures we all should observe to safeguard the rights of indigenous peoples of the world, but really, the indigenes of Fiji are way beyond those concerns. It's true they must face the challenges that confront most developing countries: accelerating rural-urban migration coupled with all the usual suspects of squatter settlements, criminal activities, domestic violence and reassessment of community values. But the indigenous

Fijians make up a growing proportion, now over sixty per cent, of the nation's population. They own well over eighty per cent of the land of Fiji and as their rugby players attest, they are members of a vibrant, healthy race.

To get out of that tangled swamp, my humble counsel is that it is time for the people of Fiji, of all shades and creeds, to ditch divisive leaders. We need men and women at the national helm who stand for the broader and higher good, not those who spread discord through narrow or populist orientations. And I also counsel that the time has come in our nation's development when we should do away with the racial politics that led us astray in the first place. Politicians who provoke race-based fears should be named and shamed, for the reality of recent Fiji demographics demonstrates there's no justification for that brand of vote-mongering. The world has changed so radically in our lifetimes, making the prejudices of old just no longer valid. How wonderful it is that America now has a *kailoma* president!

If you know Fijians, you must wish them well. If you were raised by Fijian carers, if your family stood side-by-side with them in defense of nation, if you played in their rugby teams and sang with their string bands, you cannot but be ever thankful for the experience. If your children were delivered by Fijian hands and the same hands helped you bury your forbears, if you have benefited so much and so often from their hospitality, and have shared in the bountiful *yalo vakaloloma* of their humanity, you cannot help but love them. And if all that is so, I believe you will stand with me right here and now, my friend, to thank God there is on this planet a place as gloriously beautiful as the islands of Fiji, and a natural composition of people as fine as the Fijians. And it is inconceivable to the two of us, you must agree, that anyone should do other than wish them well on the rigours of the journey.

Pious Princes

Imagine this, dear companion. I was reclining under a palm tree that was declining over a beach, upon which in intermittent laps, the South Pacific Ocean was inclining. In my hand was a 1954 cookbook, *The Tenth Muse* by Sir Harry Luke, within which I was reading of a place about as romantically distant from a Pacific Island beach as it was possible to be. Thus do words transport us.

Sir Harry wrote,

> It was my fortune in 1920, when I was British Chief Commissioner in the three Trans-Caucasian Republics of Georgia, Armenia and Azerbaijan, to be entertained at many typical Caucasian banquets, a process that required on the part of the stranger some training and a certain corporal elasticity if it was to be undergone without disaster. How the Georgian officers of those days retained their greyhound figures despite the quantities they ate and drank is a mystery I never solved, unless it was by means of the vigorous *pas seuls* which they would execute between courses.

> These banquets, which never got under way until at least two hours after the time for which one had been bidden, began with cold *zakuski* (hors d'oeuvres), eaten standing and washed down with small glasses of vodka. The *zakuski* were always so appetizing that the uninitiated were apt to leave insufficient accommodation for what was to follow. Fresh caviare straight from Baku, bears' hams, mushrooms steeped in wine, smoked river trout, salmon and tongues, and every conceivable savoury dish were an irresistible temptation to the unwary, largely thanks to the fact that good vodka (for there are many grades, ranging from wheat vodka to that made of wood pulp) is the world's perfect apéritif.

At this stage it was the amiable custom of one's Georgian hosts to drink – to the accompaniment of cries of *Allah verdi*, the Turkish and Tatar for 'God has given' – the health of the visitors in a pony-glass of wine, which had to be lowered without heel-taps by both toaster and toastee and demanded quite definite powers of endurance on the part of the visitors if the hosts, as in the case of a military mess, were many. For each host claimed, and exercised, his privilege. My friend Prince Napoleon Murat, great-grandson of Joachim Murat, Napoleon's Marshal and subsequently King of Naples, and grandson on his mother's side of the last Queen of Mingrelia, told me in Tiflis - he was then a General in the Georgian army - that when he left the French army to go to Russia as an officer of the Imperial *gardes à cheval*, his new Russian brother-officers welcomed him at a banquet which lasted uninterruptedly for two nights and the intervening day.[116]

I found this then, and find it still, to be impossibly exotic material. Hot and cold *zakuski* in a Georgian military mess with vigorous *pas seuls* between courses, in the company of his friend Prince Napoleon Murat and grandson of the last Queen of Mingrelia! Mingrelia?

I went to a library and dug around for traces of the Mingrelians, where I learned that a Dadian dynasty ruled Mingrelia for eight hundred years. The Dadian sovereigns were known as Their Splendours The Pious Princes of High Rank, Duke of Dukes of Mingrelia. Orthodox Christians, they ruled from their capitals Zugdidi and Sukhum Kaleh, spawning splendid chess players, lordly chamberlains, generals of the highest rank, and marrying off their young princes of piety to Their Highnesses The Most Brilliant Princesses of Imerati.

Even though the Dadians have been trampled beneath time's indifferent tread, in a very ephemeral sense I detect a gossamer thread of connection to those missing Mingrelians. I have in my papers the Christmas cards sent by Sir Harry Luke to my then youthful parents, and in those cards he invariably asks after the infant progress of my brothers and me. Thus has Sir Harry, by generous application of the rule of six-degrees-of-separation, strung that tenuous thread.

Much as I'd like to delve further into the arcane affairs of the Dadian dynasty, I'm conscious of the fact that we must hoist our packs my friend, and move on. Pacific destinations await us, and history's rolling mists have long-enveloped Their Splendours The Pious Princes. They rule the Mingrelians no more; the Bolsheviks saw to that. But before bidding farewell to their noble shades, let us briefly call on Ozymandias, 'Look on my works, ye Mighty, and despair!' For look now, the Bolsheviks have gone the way of the Dadians.

From Caucasian distractions we may return to the Pacific Islands and the Kingdom of Tonga where pious princes rule to this day, their kingly line of descent stretching back a thousand years to Ahoeitu, the first Tui Tonga. Tonga is the last of the great Polynesian kingdoms, the imperial ambitions of the American and French republics having destroyed the Hawaiian and Tahitian kingdoms back in the nineteenth century.

I pause here, dear friend, to make an intervention on behalf of others who are reading this chronicle of island affairs. You and I are deeply interested in variations in political systems and governance; and we've agreed that like religions, their value should be understood not by what they purport to be, but rather by the demonstrated effect they have on their followers. However not everyone shares our anthropological passion for such matters, so in complete contravention of literary norms, this intervention respectfully advises readers not interested in the clash between traditional and imported systems of government in the Pacific Islands, to just skip on through to the next chapter.

'Long may Tonga be suffered to remain an oasis of happiness in this distracted world,' Sir Harry Luke once wrote.[117] The world may have remained a distracted place, but much as one would concur with Sir Harry's sentiment, an oasis of happiness might not be the way most people might describe Tonga today. Like all developing countries it has a plethora of problems, and like all Pacific Island nations, limited natural resources and oceanic isolation constrain their solution.

Uniquely in the Pacific Islands, never in its history has Tonga surrendered sovereignty to another nation. The maintenance of this national freedom, upheld throughout the big power gamesmanship of the late nineteenth century, was largely due to the existence of Tonga's stalwart monarchy. Only in 1900, with both Germany and France breathing down Tonga's neck, did young King George Tupou II sign a treaty of friendship with Britain as a protective measure for his islands.

From that time until very recently, the British maintained a consulate or high commission at a modestly elegant residency under the sighing *toa* trees on the foreshore of Tonga's capital, Nuku'alofa, a short walk along the seawall from the quaint buildings of the royal palace. Like the latter, the residency speaks of another era, a broad single-storied colonial bungalow in which Queen Elizabeth dined on her coronation tour of 1953.

My father first stayed in the residency when he was Sir Harry's ADC, having flown over from Suva with the governor in a Shorts Singapore seaplane. That was 1941, but he came back to reside there longer in 1965, accompanied by my mother and sister, when he was acting as the British Commissioner. During that time my mother and the reigning monarch, Queen Salote, became friends, and I'm told my mother was the last non-Tongan to have a palace audience with the much-loved Queen before she passed away.

I remember the Nuku'alofa residency well, for I went across to Tonga on business in 1988. Stepping into the bungalow's cool interior, signing the visitor's book and taking tea with the high commissioner, was like entering a sun-dappled time-warp. He showed me the old hard-back, jumbo-sized, navy-blue British passports that he still dispensed, for though British consulates around the world had long been issuing the maroon European soft-covers, these had yet to find their way to Tonga.

In 2006, London's Foreign and Commonwealth Office closed the British High Commission in Nuku'alofa. It seems the distracted world was in need of the meagre funds required to run the office in Tonga, for the FCO said it would be diverting the resultant savings towards counter-terrorism activities and the fight against international crime and nuclear weapons proliferation. What can you say to that?

'Obviously it's a matter of sadness, but we understand the pressures the Foreign Office are under,' the then Crown Prince Tupou'toa intoned diplomatically to a journalist's question in Nuku'alofa. But from my writer's desk in Sydney, I say to no one in particular, 'Horseshit!' A doorway to an 'oasis of happiness' was closing, and the pittance of coinage needed to maintain a benign office among people of goodwill was being tossed into a political slush-fund full of the aforementioned.

Truth be known, the Tongan monarchy had long and lasting influence over Fiji, so much so that Fijians up until recently looked eastwards to the mana of the Polynesian hierarchies, rather than to their sundered Melanesian cousins in the archipelagos to the west. If you take a good look, there are few of the chiefly families of Fiji whose bloodlines are not heavily laced with Tongan genes, sufficiently infused over time that they inculcated Fijian culture with an element of deference towards those royal lines across the water.

Had the European powers not shown up in the Pacific in the nineteenth century, there's a good chance Fiji would have become a vassal state of Tonga. In 1855, Ratu Seru Cakobau and his Bauan forces were facing ignominious defeat at the hands of rival Fiji armies, when the Tongan monarch answered Cakobau's plea for help. Commanding a fleet of thirty double-hulled canoes transporting two thousand burly Tongan warriors, the King of Tonga sailed across the Pacific, bringing with him guns, spears and Christianity. His timely arrival in Fiji saved Bau's bacon, turning the Battle of Kaba into a rout in Cakobau's favour and sending his enemies fleeing through the land with reports that a man had to be mad to fight against Tongans.

As a result of that campaign and many earlier incursions, an expatriate Tongan prince by the name of Ma'afu gained political control over eastern and much of northern Fiji. When you couple the Tongans' military prowess with the geopolitical opportunities presented by endless in-fighting between the various Fijian states, together with the web of consanguinity they'd inwrought within the great families of Fiji, it is clear the Tongan star was rising high and bright over the islands of Fiji.

But in those turbulent mid-nineteenth century years, there were other stars burning in Fiji's firmament; notably the battleship diplomats of the US Navy, who were putting the Fijian leadership under the pump over an imaginary unpaid debt. As a result of these pressures, the Fijian chiefs, led by Ratu Cakobau, turned to Britain, collectively asking Queen Victoria to take on the sovereignty of their islands. After initially demurring in 1867, she accepted and a Deed of Cession was drawn up and presented in Levuka in 1874. Ma'afu signed the deed, indeed his was an essential signature, but one senses the begrudging reluctance of the Tongan aristocrat as he put pen to paper.

In his letters to me over the departed decades, my father ever loved to work in a quote from Burns, for the poems of Scotland's immortal bard were his literary touchstones.

> O wad some Pow'r the giftie gie us
> To see oursels as others see us![118]

Such lines would then be lightly extrapolated into a paternal homily designed to help one through some testing situation. The homily might for example be that however hard done by you might be feeling, you could be sure there were many who'd happily trade their lot for yours.

I suppose if you were a Dadian holed up in the depths of a Georgian winter, with the wind knifing down from snow-choked passes of the Caucasus mountains, the notion of reading a cookery book while reclining with twiddling toes on a sunny Fijian beach would have been impossibly exotic material. For I suspect there were only so many vodka shots, bears' hams, and hot and cold *zakuski* you could swallow, before a certain *ennui* set in. Damnably bored by chess games, chinless Imerati girls and the worm-tongue blandishments of the lordly chamberlains of Mingrelia, you might well have traded all the splendours of Sukhum Kaleh for a humble hut on a South Seas beach with access to a half-decent pile of books, a fishing line and a simple kitchen garden.

Some say that in the end, this is all that romance amounts to: the desire for the unattainable, the different, the unexamined, denied us for reasons of time, space or a sorry lot in life. But there's more to it than that, dear companion, we know that in our bones. As we live and breathe, romance is alive!

In the end, the romantic view might be all that distinguishes human intelligence from that of the machines. Our poetry and songs, our holding to the truth of love and beauty, the special place we reserve for ritual and pageantry, for the continuity of culture and mystical interpretation, all these are as much a part of our future as they have been our past. The night-sky makes it so, for the greatest romance of all is the majesty of space and our spinning existence within it.

For all the triumphs of scientific determinism, when set against the unnumbered awe of the universe, there comes a point when the strident proclamations of a Cambridge don can seem as intransigent and arrogant as those of a jihadi mullah. Thankfully we can take refuge from such absolutism, for many of our greatest scientists believe the world is never that arbitrary, that the fundament is in essence grainy, and that as Einstein concluded, beyond the discernible there will always be something subtle, intangible and inexplicable.

We have all been touched by romance. All have known the magic of place and circumstance, of a particular person, collections of creatures, moments of luminance, times suffused in love, beauty, even ecstasy. But within our skulls the running dogs of revisionism, let's call them the lemon-lipped censors of our thought processes, have been hard at work. The mind's bean-counters have been running the numbers, they've been doing it clinically on logic's behalf, trying to erase romance from the books. Fat chance! Why? Because in the end, the ultimate reality is mystery.

When I look back to the years I worked in the Namosi hill country of Fiji, in the first half of the 1970s, lemon-lips have suggested my recall of the place is overly romantic, that I hold the time, the circumstance, and the people too fondly to be true. But I remember it all. I remember the daily mountain rain, how your sweat-soaked clothes were ever in the process of becoming sodden in tropical showers or river-crossings, and how they never quite dried out, steaming on weary bodies plodding up hills into the next rain-cloud, or dangling damply from a reed by a smoking village fire.

I cannot forget the repetitious fevers that came with lack of immunity to bacteria living in the hill villages, fevers that split my head, wracked bones and took body temperature to delirious heights before drenching bedding with swamps of sweat. I remember the open-pit toilets at the edge of the village, balancing on a log above the shit-pit, being enveloped by flies and mosquitoes and sticky mud, and the sour, smoky acridity of communal body odor. And no one who ever walked them could forget the arduous slopes of the hill tracks, kept viscous by tropical downpours, two steps forward, one slipped back into knee-deep puddles of wet red mud.

In those days there were no roads in Namosi beyond the coastal stretch, so to get to the hill villages you took outboard-powered punts up the flood-scarred gorges of the Navua River for some twenty miles or more. Disembarking at Namuamua village, you shouldered your pack and took to shankless pony, heading north up a long climb through kava and taro gardens until you were enveloped by the rain forest. Upon cresting the forest ridge, the track continued northwards, skirting ravines, ascending and descending many a hillside with multiple crossings of the rushing rivers of the hill province. And in all those days of traversing the district tracks connecting the various hill villages, you were totally free of the sound of an internal combustion engine.

The passage of pack-ponies along the tracks set up corrugations and water-filled foot-holes, into which prudent animals stepped to avert a stumble that might send them tumbling to their deaths in a rocky river-bed far below. Meanwhile, human traffic did its best to avoid these muddy water-traps, for to slip into one was only fun for those trudging along behind the victim. In the 2008 version of my book *Kava in the Blood,* there's a photo of me crossing such corrugations on the Nakavika track, in which I am gallantly mounted on a pony. This was in truth my one and only horse-ride along those tracks.

On that occasion, I'd hired the pack-pony at the mouth of the Wainikoroiluva River, thinking to save myself the effort of the day's long trek to Namosi. Leather riding-kit was a luxury well beyond the pale, so a hessian sack was thrown over the horse's back and a bridle fashioned from a twist or two of rope. I set off up the hill-track that day on my willing little mount, while wiser travelling companions followed on foot.

At the end of the day's trek, we emerged from the rain-forest, to see the Shangri-La valley of Namosi winding away below us. Wood-smoke rose in the still evening air from the kitchen hearths of thatched villages dotted along the river's run, the smoke wisping up towering cliff-faces that soared on both sides of the narrow vale. And as we descended into the valley, villagers from the outlying hamlets fell in with our plodding procession, all bound for our nocturnal meeting in the chiefly village below. Romance reigned.

A thick river mist had settled in by the time we reached our Namosi destination. My rump was completely numb from the day's ride and I stank of a low blend of horse and human reek. Thus, prior to the commencement of the village meeting at which I was required to officiate, I staggered bandy-legged to a river pool to take a cleansing dip.

The moment the cold water of the Waidina River came into contact with my bare arse, the raw pain was so intense I discovered I could walk on water. In this manner, yelping like my nether-end was being attacked by a school of piranhas, I made it to the far bank where I began a demented dance. Those of my travelling companions who witnessed my leaping pirouettes, judged it a rare performance. The dance petered out, their mirth subsided, and I allowed them to inspect the damage. It was discovered that courtesy of the tortuous track, the rough sack-saddle and my rain-soaked shorts, two skinless circles the size of bread and butter plates had been carved into my previously numb bum.

Our hosts sent for the district nurse, who I'm ashamed to say resided several villages down-river. She eventually materialised from the night-mist carrying a kerosene lamp, at which stage my guilt was mitigated by finding she was a childhood friend who'd lived in my parent's household at Natabua when she was training to be a nurse. She lost no time in having me drop my *sulu* in order to apply soothing unctions to my weeping rump.

Thereafter that night, rather than observing the *de rigueur* Fijian custom of sitting cross-legged on the village mats at formal meetings, my attendance, my address and my consumption of the evening's long supply of kava, were conducted from a position of gingery recline, with a crocheted pillow jammed under my ribs as support.

My friend, now that you've been to Fiji, you want to know more. You've asked about the continuance of the Fijian chiefly system and whether the *ratu* are really still relevant.[119] I know you suspect the system is anachronistic and think the time has come for it to dissolve away in the global mash. Let me give you my answer by way of a tale or two.

Pride of place in my library of some six hundred annotated books on Fiji, goes to *Mission to Viti* by Berthold Seemann, a German botanist who worked out of Kew Gardens in London.[120] In 1860 he spent nearly a month in the Namosi district collecting botanical specimens, during which time he was primarily based in the same village in which I received those soothing unctions a century and a dozen years later.

During his visit, Seemann was privileged to enjoy the patronage of Kuruduadua, the Tui Namosi, king of what-was-then the independent state of Namosi. Kuruduadua was a great leader of his people in war and what passed in those parts for peace. By all accounts he led from the front, listened to the counsel of his people, and possessed a mind constructively open to interaction with the outside world. All who knew him, said the king's word was his honour.

Seemann was eloquent in describing Kuruduadua's considerate hospitality, his intelligent statesmanship, subtle etiquette and intellectual curiosity, making the observation that while,

Kuruduadua was still a heathen. He said that our religion was good, but there were few true Christians in the group, and he hated hypocrisy, and did not profess to be better or anything else than he really was.

It is in the universality of such lines that I honour the German botanist, for it is clear he in turn honoured the integrity of his host. I labour this point because Kuruduadua was a man-eater and his dynasty was one of the world's most notorious of cannibal kingdoms.

The various tribes of Fiji were ever at odds with each other and the custom of the land demanded cannibal feasting at the conclusion of overt hostilities. As mementos of such feasts, the trees of Kuruduadua's Namosi capital were hung with the skulls, pelvises and thigh-bones of the victims, while elaborately carved cannibal forks, used exclusively for dining on human flesh, were treasured as family heirlooms.

The first European visitors to Namosi reported scenes that greatly coloured the Victorian imagination on the subject of anthropophagy, and the cartoonist's vision of victims being trussed and boiled alive in big iron pots, belonged very much to the reportage of *bêche-de-mer* cauldrons being used for this purpose in Fiji. Kuruduadua had such a pot, in which a man had lately been plunged head-first into boiling water, and Seemann engaged the king in prolonged discussions on reasons for desisting from such culinary practice.

In Fiji today there is a delicacy attached to the subject of cannibalism, diplomatically put along the lines of 'one does not talk of rope in the house of the hanged man'. But to deny Fiji's man-eating past, be it for reasons of delicate contrition or spurious retro-anthropology, is akin to holding that Scandinavian forbears were averse to forays south intent on pillage and rape. Or for that matter, that Parisians were not amused by the public guillotining of their fellow citizens, or that the English never indulged in hanging, drawing and emasculating troublesome northern neighbours before piking their heads above London Bridge.

Fiji was widely known around the world, for much of the first half of the nineteenth century, as the Cannibal Islands. Nautical doggerel attached itself accordingly,

> Hikey, pikey, wankey, fum,
> How do you like your 'taters done?
> I like 'em done with their jackets on,
> Says the King of the Cannibal Islands.[121]

That cannibalism was common throughout Melanesia and Polynesia is well known, but it seems to have had an orgiastic zenith in the chiefly capitals of pre-Christian Fiji, when people recount that not scores but hundreds of bodies were served up at great post-war feasts.

Being at the top of the food chain, the chiefs and priests were able to enjoy the choice-cuts of the victims' bodies, these being the heart and tongue, the latter sometimes forcibly procured, barbequed and consumed before the horrified eyes of the donor. This method alone demonstrates cannibalism was more than an excess of Epicureanism, more than mere acquisition of protein. For masticating the body parts of a person and succumbing to all the ensuing digestive gripes, even as the victim looked on, could only have been for the purpose of utterly belittling a serf, slave or shipwrecked sailor, or was indeed the ultimate punishment of a hated enemy. Thus, while a chief's bodily appetites might be the beneficiary of these victuals, it appears that what was really important for the diner was the fostering of his notoriety.

The King of the Cannibal Isles was Ratu Seru Cakobau, he who in 1874 led the cession of Fiji to the British Crown. Ratu Cakobau abandoned man-eating, widow-strangling, human sacrifices, polygamy and other revered customs of the land in 1854 when he converted to Christianity. Thereafter his subjects followed their leader's steps to the Methodist's baptismal fonts, *en masse*, and Christianity was known for a long time after as *na lotu nei Ratu Cakobau*, Ratu Cakobau's religion.

But cannibalism held out longer in the hill country of Viti Levu, beyond the domains of Cakobau and the other coastal kingdoms. The last Fijian clubbing, cooking and consuming of a missionary took place up there, as late as 1867, in the valleys of the Vatusila tribe. The missionary, Reverend Baker, was not cooked in his jacket, but local legend has it his boots were not removed and as the diners were unacquainted with leather footwear, a long time was spent chewing the oven-roasted boots.

No doubt there were many others subsequent to Reverend Baker, whose travails were concluded courtesy of a thorough roasting in a Fijian ground-oven, but their names are not recorded. With the cession of Fiji to the British Crown, the old cuisine became effectively *passé* and a proliferation of tea and cakes spread to even the most remote villages of the Fiji Group.

Nevertheless, anthropophagous terminology remains in the Fijian language, sometimes used in a threatening way, but usually in jest. Ratu Cakobau's descendants used to play on the notoriety of their famous ancestor, and were known to enjoy the repartee of a cannibal quip or two. One such, well known to Suva residents, arose when an urbane scion of the Cakobau family was traveling out of Fiji on an ocean liner.

At dinner on the first night out, the Fijian chief was invited to sit at the captain's table in formal evening dress. After appropriate introductions, he picked up that his fellow diners had been all a-twitter at the prospect of dining with a descendant of the famed King Cakobau. When be-gloved waiters stepped up to take orders, after long inspection of the evening's menu the Fijian chief seemed unable to make a selection. Waiting until the table's full attention was upon him, he advised there was nothing on the menu that took his fancy, but he would be obliged if the waiter might bring him the ship's passenger list.

A thought occurs to me here that just as all of us have killers amongst our ancestors, if we go back far enough, we must also all have cannibal forbears.

Those who were killed were statistically less likely to leave progeny behind and the same goes for those who were eaten. It follows that the killers' bloodlines, extrapolating over the generations in combination with others of their ilk, are alive and well. We are thus the progeny of the killers not the killed, the descendants of the consumers not the consumed.

Now I have a confession to make. No, I have not knowingly partaken in the consumption of human flesh, and putting aside the occasional nibble of a fingernail, I am not inclined to ever do so. My confession is that I don't share the innate revulsion most people have for the subject. I'm certainly not advocating dining on the dead, and I'm one hundred per cent opposed to murder and vivisection, but I can't help feeling that a deceased mammal is a deceased mammal, and as the guarded testimonies of ship-wrecked sailors and Andean plane-crash survivors attest, anthropophagy is preferable to death by starvation.

But dear friend, you may think me guilty of sensationalising Fiji's cannibal past, of succumbing to the sort of prurient enthusiasm so prevalent in Victorian times. That is not so; all I'm doing here is pushing aside the many obfuscations on the subject I've had to listen to over the years. To demonstrate my true feelings on the subject, I'll say goodbye to it with this extract from that favourite scientist of mine, Dr Berthold Seemann.

This account arises from the good doctor's sojourn in Namosi in 1860, when he was in conversation with a Namosi villager of his acquaintance. For the purposes of debate, Dr Seemann had put it to the villager, that with the many tales of cruelty and cannibalism emanating from Fiji, there was a widely held perception overseas that Fijians were lacking in natural affection.

> He replied, there might be amongst his countrymen, as well as the whites, people who had not much feeling; but those who denied the Fijians natural affection, either understood them very little, or else represented them in such black colours for some purpose of their own. 'When leaving home,' he continued, 'all my thoughts are with my family, and I am never so happy as when I am under my own roof, and have my wife and children around me. When a few days ago my youngest boy was ill, I sat up with him three

nights, and it would have broken my heart had he died.' The man was a savage, a heathen, yet could any Christian parent have spoken more warmly or naturally?

Fortunately, affection is wisely placed by Providence beyond the reach or influence of any system, right or wrong. Like a beautiful flower, it springs up freely in any soil congenial to its growth. If the Fijians were only half as black as they have been painted, they would long ere this have been numbered amongst the extinct races; for no society, however primitive, can possibly exist, if the evil passions - the destructive elements - preponderate over the good. The best vindication of their national character is their national existence; the best proof of their living a life as free from vice and corrupting practices as any heathen can be expected to live, is a physical development on an average far above that of which our own race, with all its advantages of civilisation, can ever hope to boast.

Such were the people Kuruduadua commanded and he had to be wise in statecraft and consultative in leadership to hold their respect. That he held their respect is clear from the written accounts of the time, to which may be added the report that his family remain the benevolent leaders of the people of Namosi to this day.

Throughout the three years in the early 1970s that I worked in the Namosi Province, I had a great companion in Ratu Leone Matanitobua. He was the assistant *roko* for the province, this hands-on administrative position giving him a perfect grounding for his future role of leadership. For he was the great, great, great grandson of Kuruduadua, that last majestic cannibal lord of the Namosi people, and this bloodline meant Ratu Leone would one day have to lead his people as the Tui Namosi.

As well as working together on rural development projects, dispute resolution, disaster relief and the various administrative tasks required of us by the government and the people, Ratu Leone and I spent our leisure time together at our home in the little town of Navua. This fine metropolis, lining the eastern bank of the mighty Navua River, had at that time yet to receive the benefits of electricity. Our club was the Navua Farmers Club, a wooden shed on the riverbank just big enough to contain a small pool table and a rudimentary bar. Next door was the front verandah of SS Khan's store where we'd drink kava, smoke Pall Mall, and play draughts with anyone who figured they were good enough to take on SS Khan's clever young son, our resident champion.

On Saturdays we played for the Veivatuloa village team in the Navua rugby competition. By rights I should have been in the Service team, made up of the local policemen and other civil servants; but Ratu Leone insisted on my playing for his village team. The village of Veivatuloa was along the coast from Navua and was only accessible by a long walking track or by boat, so there was no such thing as mid-week team practice or strategy sessions for our Veivatuloa side. We just turned up on Saturday at the allotted time and place, and played our hearts out.

After the game, bruised and bloodied as much from the state of the gravelly ground as from collisions with the opposing players, those of the team that didn't have to set off to their homes along the coast, would retire to my house at Naitonitoni with a carton or two of cold beer. As I had no fridge, we'd have to drink the beer quickly if we wanted it cold, at least that was our excuse.

Ratu Leone's childhood friends, the sons of Esava Duasuva, were stalwarts of the team and were usually amongst those who'd join us at Naitonitoni. Their family string-band Caucau ni Qaributa had recorded Fijian songs that were regularly played on the radio, so once the beer was *ekdum khalas*, we'd mix up the kava, light the kerosene lanterns, pull out the guitars and spend the rest of the night alternately singing up a storm and telling tall stories.[122]

I'm just not sure why those days kick up such romantic dust for me. Maybe it was the vibrancy of being in my twenties, or that I found work so fulfilling back then, straight out of university immersed in a daily effort for the communal good, in the excellent company of people doing the same. Our income was a fraction of that earned by a Sydney street-sweeper, but we had the incalculable reward of the good regard of the villagers and farmers we served, and we got to live our lives in the grandeur of Namosi's natural setting.

To bask in that grandeur, all you had to do was your job. You had but to lift your eyes as you trudged the muddy Wainikoroiluva tracks to see the jagged peaks of the Korobasabasaga Range marching alongside you, those same volcanic peaks that Rupert Brooke called 'the terror of the twisted mountains' as he fantasised about them being an entry point to Hades.

You had only to step out of the thatched meeting house in which you were deliberating with the people of Saliadrau, Navunikaba or any other of those Liga ni Bai villages, to relieve yourself of the bucket-loads of kava you were consuming therein, to appreciate the privilege of your position. The villages were usually located on the banks of rushing mountain rivers, so that peeing in the moonlight at the perimeter of the village, the only sounds capable of rising over the river's roar would be an occasional roll of laughter from the meeting house, or the dull thud of more kava being pounded for the hours ahead.

All around lay the dark hills through which you had come, and into which you would foray on the morrow; but for now you were embraced in the communal hospitality of this village, this settlement built entirely from the reeds, poles and vines of the surrounding forest, lit by kitchen hearths and hand-held lanterns, an ancient human commune in the twilight years before the advent of roads and electricity and telephones that would change all this forever.

Someone once described traditional Fijian houses as disemboweled haystacks - an apt image from an exterior point of view, but not so from the inside. Seated within a well-constructed *vale vakaviti*, rustic artistry was evident in the intricate construct of patterned reed walls and soaring house-posts twisting and gnarled, with beam and rafter joints elaborately bound by coconut sinnet.[123] The pounded-earth floors were covered with springy vegetation and plaited bamboo, overlaid again by layers of pandanus mats;

so that sitting cross-legged upon such floors for hours on end, and later stretching out on them to sleep, was never an ordeal.

There were no hot *zakuski*, dollops of fresh Baku caviare or shots of vodka to be had, but we ate with gusto whatever the ladies of the villages served: steaming piles of root-crops and forest yams, boiled eels as thick as your arm, river prawns steamed in bamboo, and boiled *bele* leaves, with the green *bele* water our accompanying wine. There were no toasts 'without heel-taps', but every meal was proceeded by *masu*, a softly spoken Christian grace. Food was laid out in a long line upon the floor with diners sitting cross-legged on either side, eating from plates without utensils, but ever-observant of tidy manners and considerate etiquette.

Inescapably, before and after those meals, there was hour upon hour of kava consumption, often the strong 'green' variety drunk in the highlands. Our 'corporal elasticity' was saved only by the arduous march of egress to the next village.

The presence of Ratu Leone coloured everything we did in Namosi. His Naibukebuke clan, carried in it all the history of the Namosi people, with all the great tragedies and victories of their days irrevocably entwined within his chiefly bloodline. Thus, much as they loved Ratu Leone's playful company, they gave him all the respect due to the future Tui Namosi.

I say 'playful company' for a reason. Such was his sense of humour and desire to bring entertainment to the people of those isolated villages, that he would ever be setting traps for us as we travelled. Even before we left Navua, he would have put in motion all sorts of plots and subplots to ensnare the government team in arcane cultural transgressions of which we coastal dwellers were quite innocent.

With Ratu Leone and me in the vanguard, our team would be made up of various combinations of an agricultural officer, women's issues officer, forester and doctor, or if circumstances required, a policeman, rural development engineer or education officer. Being Fijians from other parts of the Islands, the Government officials were always fair game for the hill people.

To strengthen our side, we'd pretty much always be accompanied by a certain assistant health inspector from Suva, at my request, a Rewan who had a prodigious capacity for kava consumption. This man was engaged in a running war of practical jokes with the Namosi villagers, the latter referring to him as *na i vuniwai ni valevou* or the latrine doctor.

At times you felt you were part of a troupe of travelling entertainers making its way through the highland villages. For instance, Ratu Leone would often lead us into making unwitting mention of a plant or animal that was an ancient totem of a certain clan or village. As such totems were taboo to mention, the members of the offended party were accordingly free to impose *ore* on us. These traditional punishments usually involving the consumption of punishingly large quantities of green kava, or being willfully harassed in sight of all, by the most aggressive women of the supposedly offended clan or village. The government team invariably left certain villages, Nakavika springs to mind, in a kava-induced state of dishevelment, much to the mirth of Ratu Leone and his accomplices amongst the village plotters.

Ratu Leone Matanitobua personified for me the robust validity of the Fijian chiefly system, the embodiment of the interactive, consultative process whereby the communal good was hammered out in the presence of the unifying chief. He was a chief bound by consanguinity and history to his people, his genetic code along with those he led, forged up there in the hills of Namosi for as long as oral history recorded. It was taken on trust that his judgement and motivation were for the communal good and it was plain from his lifestyle that his reward lay not in land, money or high national office, but in fulfilling his destiny to see to the betterment of his people. I know this because we worked together on a daily basis for three years and in that time he never faltered in that commitment.

The full story of what happened in Fiji's year of shame, the millennium dawn of 2000, has not and probably cannot be told. There have been confidential lists of coup-collaborators drawn up in high offices, names whispered around the kava bowls, insinuations and speculations bandied about, defamation cases threatened, sideways movements, overseas postings, and threats of worse to come if pushed too far. There is talk that there were many lean and hungry Cassius types in the civil and disciplined services, of deep-pocketed, pot-bellied merchants 'as false as dicers' oaths', of shadowy bands of defeated politicians and convocations of fundamentalist traditionalists. Lips behind upheld hands muttered the names of some of the highest chiefs of the land.

There are many who believe the root of the rot was not in the ambition of the puffed-up front-men, nor in the commercial greed of those who greased the wheels and hoped to benefit, nor with the opportunist thugs who took to the streets at the first whiff of violence and thievery. They say Fiji's year of torment was only able to occur because of an unresolved family feud within the most chiefly of Fiji's clans. If that is true, then the drama has more pathos than the darkest of Shakespeare's tragedies.

By way of background to that drama, in 1995 at the invitation of the Great Council of Chiefs, my father, Sir Ian Thomson, came from retirement in Scotland to address the council on the subject of leadership. After his address, he was interviewed by the Fiji Times and the following day the paper ran the interview, backing it with a supporting editorial. The thrust of the newspaper's story was my father's call for Fijian chiefs to receive formal training, so that they could better cope with the leadership challenges of changing times. But he also took the opportunity to warn of the dangers of not appointing successors to fill the chiefly seats left vacant by death. Without captains, he pointed out, ships were placed at great risk and there were at that time too many vessels without captains in Fiji.

In particular he warned of the danger to the nation if a successor to the title of the Vunivalu of Bau was not installed. Understanding the import of that warning is a lesson in the workings of Fijian society, and seen in the context of the year 2000, they were proved to be prophetic words. He was later to write,

> It would appear that without the Bauan representative in their number, the *Turaga Bale* have lacked their clout that was so apparent in yesteryear.[124]

The Vunivalu of Bau for much of the nineteenth century was Ratu Seru Cakobau, called by some the King of Fiji, though his dominions never extended beyond a third of the archipelago's territory. Nevertheless, the Vunivalu is the pre-eminent of the three paramount chiefly titles of Fiji, presiding as it does over the most senior of the country's three geopolitical confederacies, Kubuna, the geographical centre of the Fijian archipelago.

Fiji in the nineteenth century was fertile ground for warfare and it is historically instructive to know that the direct translation of the Vunivalu title is 'the root of war'. It is also useful background to know that during pre-colonial times when the little island of Bau was rising to prominence, it was not merely might of arms that allowed the Bauans to rule. Their greatest asset was the wily and at times fearsome skill of the Bauan chiefs in the realpolitik arts of diplomacy. The island was a master-den of plotters, of enough spinners of webs of espionage, conspiracy and double-cross to hopelessly entangle their enemies. The expression *na vere vaka-Bau*, the intricate plotting of the Bauans, comes from those turbulent times, and remains very much alive in the Fijian psyche to this day.

The last Vunivalu of Bau, Ratu Sir George Cakobau, the great, great grandson of Ratu Seru, died in 1989 after a long and able public service that had culminated in his role as the nation's governor-general. After his passing, it fell to the Vunivalu's clan, the Tui Kaba, to decide amongst themselves who the most appropriate of their number was to be anointed as the new paramount chief. But the clan was divided, finding themselves unable to make that far-reaching decision, and as of writing these words in 2009, the Tui Kaba have still not done so.

Some of the chiefly clan insisted on the successor being one of the off-spring of the late Vunivalu's first marriage, while others promoted the children of his second marriage. Others supported the sons of Ratu Sir Edward Cakobau, and there were yet other bloodlines within the clan whose claim had to be considered. Thus the title remains vacant, and people are getting used to it being that way.

Shakespeare told us the head that wears the crown is an uneasy one. The same can be said for the clan and the confederacy, and thereby the nation, that has marched on all this time without having in its vanguard an annointed bearer of Bau's high mantle. And it that long absence, the acts and the scenes of history's dense plot have been changing.

Some may recall that when the *coup d'état* of 2000 was unleashed on Fiji, George Speight, a conveniently articulate frontman was in place to give the international media their daily jollies. With his white shirt and tie, clean-shaven head, mobile-phone forever at ear, not forgetting his authoritative Suva Grammar School accent, this man was a very twenty-first century *coup*-maker. It may also be remembered, that between the glib insults he directed at foreign prime ministers, Fiji's Indian population, and most of the treasured principles of democracy, he talked often, but always rather elusively, of 'the Cause'.

So much did he talk to the assembled journalists, that one day he called for the overthrow of the 'Sukuna-Mara dynasty'. If you were from Fiji, your jaw dropped at the beguiling poison of that barb. It was partly a nonsense line, since no such dynasty exists in the sense of it being extricable from the consanguineous matrix of Fiji's chiefly bloodlines. Nevertheless, his comment gave us pause … and we thought, was that it? Is that what the Cause amounted to?

We all knew the history of how the great Fijian leader, Ratu Sukuna, had chosen and appropriately groomed the young Lauan chief, Ratu Mara, for national leadership. We knew that the success of that process had given Fiji wise national leadership for most, I repeat most, of the twentieth century. But some, I repeat some, of the Bauans and those of the Kubuna confederacy they lead, felt their position of pre-eminence had been side-lined by the chosen ones who prevailed in the transition from the Ratu Sukuna decades to those of Ratu Mara.

While the late Vunivalu was alive, such disaffected ambitions stayed on the sideline, for that great chief was true to Fiji's higher interests. But some say that disaffection and thwarted expectations simmered on; so that after his passing, the pot came to the boil, not just for Bau, but for the province and confederacy it leads.

Then with the ongoing failure of the Tui Kaba to appoint their leader, they say the pot boiled over, spreading a mess of confusion across the land. Some would say that unless the clan settles its differences, making themselves subject not to their ambitions but to the obligations of their birth, the relevance of the traditional Fijian chiefly system faces inevitable decline.

The hands of factions of disaffected Bauans and their liegemen were all over the *coup d'état* of 2000. That was clear from many of the public appearances of those shameful fifty-six days when Parliament was held hostage. The names of certain of the chiefs involved can be garnered from local news reportage at the time, along with reserved conversations with those in the know. It is no coincidence that the vice-president of Fiji appointed in 2000, who was later sentenced to four years in prison for what Fiji's High Court judged to be treasonous assistance to the *coup*-makers, was a high Bauan chief. And it remains a moot point whether the disaffected ones who strode the stage of the 2000 *coup,* were but ambitious actors mouthing the overt and subliminal script of that dark play, while the scripts were being prepared in the plotting corridors of *na vere vaka-Bau.*

The Elizabethan bard demonstrated how in European states of old, when the firm hand of leadership faltered, turmoil and trouble advanced the cause of thwarted ambition. If it was strong and just leadership that brought balance to the affairs of state, then its lack was clearly destructive. We saw how the murderers who did Macbeth's dirty work were men who'd persuaded themselves they were sufficiently incensed by 'the vile blows and buffets of the world' that they'd do any deed 'to spite the world.' Sound familiar? Yes, we see their spawn today in the caves above Kandahar.

Ratu Sukuna was a Bauan chief, as were Fiji's other great post-independence leaders Ratu Edward Cakobau and Ratu George Cakobau; men who spent themselves in service of nation. We look still to Bau for such men, chiefs who would lead wisely, of whom we might say it was done well and was fitting of those descended from Fiji's trusted bloodlines. For those of us who have had to stand upon the sidelines, watching mutely on, it has been none of our business who the Tui Kaba choose as their leader. But I break the silence of taboo because many are now muttering that the Fijian chiefly system has become redundant, and I don't believe it to be so.

And I break my silence because until my dying day, I hold the memory of the late Vunivalu with deepest affection. Thus are my gratuitous words written, that the Tui Kaba will not give us cause to turn our heads away; that we will not be forced to echo the Danish prince and say the late Bauan chiefs were truly men upon whose like we shall never look again.

Fiji's abiding sense of connection with the British Crown is hinted at in the face of the former head of state, Queen Elizabeth II, still in 2009 looking out from Fiji bank notes two decades after the declaration of the republic. And lest we forget, Fiji's coat of arms still carries the national motto of 'Fear God and honour the King.'

The people of Fiji claim many generations of connected destiny with the British royal family, the connection going back to the critical period in the history of indigenous Fijians when the paramount chiefs of Viti ceded the sovereignty, land and governance of their islands to Queen Victoria, her heirs and successors. Their chiefly trust was not misplaced, for in return, one of Queen Victoria's first acts as Queen of Fiji was to give the land back to the Fijian people. She made it the task of her representatives, Sir Arthur Gordon and his vice-regal successors, to see that the land was properly divided amongst the traditional Fijian owners with their proprietary rights recorded for all time.

It can be confidently conjectured that if land ownership had been left to the commercial ambitions of Fiji's non-indigenous settlers, the Europeans, Indians and Chinese, indigenous communal title would have long been a thing of the past. There are many today who believe that would not have been a bad thing and that Fiji's economic development remains hampered to this day by the fact that some eighty-seven per cent of the nation's land resources fall under inalienable communal title. But the great majority of indigenous Fijians remain grateful that their *vanua* was secured for their people for all time by Queen Victoria's command.

With the colonial fixing and subsequent recording of communal land titles, came the necessary corollary of codification of clan membership and of the chiefly hierarchies. A birth register for indigenous Fijians, the *vola ni kawa bula*, establishing the on-going membership of the clans, was put in place and has been maintained to this day. In theory and largely in practice, every indigenous Fijian knows what clan they belong to and over which lands their clan has perpetual ownership.

Because they were an integral part of the land ownership system, the chiefly titles were also codified, from the base of lower-ranked chiefs up the social pyramid to the paramount chiefs of the land. At the top of this pyramid were the three great chiefly titles heading up the three traditional confederacies of Fiji, and above them, sitting at the apex of that monolithic social structure, was the monarch to whom Fiji was ceded in 1874, who happened to live in a castle on the other side of the world. This is the way it was, until a military *coup d'état* in 1987 led to the arbitrary declaration of a republic and the consequent toppling of the pyramid's apex.

In an ideal Fiji, the traditional chiefs represent not just the interests of the confederacy, province or tribe they lead, but the well-being of all people who live within those boundaries, whatever their ethnic origins. In practice this has not always been the case, but there have been many such Fijian chiefs in the past, and their words and deeds have been held in the highest national respect, by all people of Fiji, regardless of tribe or race. In this regard, Ratu Sir Edward Cakobau springs to mind, a leader for every citizen of Fiji, described as having an elegant genius for friendship.

There is a vibrant joy to living in an ethnically diverse country like Fiji; but as we have witnessed, given the right combination of belligerent politicians and ambitious provocateurs, latent ethnic tensions can be made to boil over into communal conflict. In the past, the great chiefs of the land came forward to stem such conflict and defend the rule of law. We look for them today.

My friend, we have agreed there are two political lessons we have received along the way. The first is that no system of governance is perfect. The second is, whether we like it or not, family dynasties are an important part of our story.

Most of us are now democrats and accept we must live with democracy's inherent shortcomings, mainly because we've yet to devise a better system of being governed. The monarchies are usually family dynasties we've put up there to perform a necessary function on our behalf, namely, in the spirit of the Arbroath Declaration, to defend our laws and freedoms. And where we've learnt by trial and error that some monarchies have not provided good governance, we have replaced them through evolution and revolution with presidents and other such potentates of state.

And so to your question about the Fijian chiefs, dear companion, who or what will replace them you ask? Not so fast, I say, for they have a moral authority grown from the land; their ancestors led and the people followed them.

Even in this Internet Age, it is to be confidently expected that the intricate ancient culture of Fiji will evolve at its own pace and volition, meeting the challenges of the twenty-first century in its own way, bringing with it the ingrained Fijian values of hospitality, mutual respect, humour and reciprocity, to weave a usefully different strand in humanity's fabric. In this evolution the chiefs will organically play their part.

So I answer you by saying that if those indigenous Fijian values, including the chiefly system, are respected, even cherished, by all citizens of Fiji, then the future for Fiji will be sound, and the people of Fiji can as one confront the pressing issues not just of their islands, but of this tormented planet.

But I will leave off answering your question by deferring to the words of Ratu Sukuna's nephew, Ratu Joni Madraiwiwi. As the Roko Tui Bau, he holds a chiefly title that is high in the echelons of Fijian social structure and his powers of interlocution hold many an echo of his prodigious uncle.

For indigenous Fijians there is a struggle between embracing other communities and maintaining a distinct and separate identity. There is ambivalence about compromise. It is feared something might be indelibly lost in the process. Unity of indigenous Fijians is thus extolled as an ideal because it is perceived as the only way they can protect their 'Fijian-ness'. The reality is far more complex and in truth it is difficult to imagine such a strong and vital people ever losing their identity.[125]

As to where the chiefs sit in this complex and at times loose grip on unity, Ratu Joni is clear that their role is subject to the many transitions occurring in Fijian society today. The chiefs share leadership with senior Fijian politicians, bureaucrats and the clergy, and of course the military. Ratu Joni says it is inaccurate to portray Fijians today as obedient to their chiefs, for the chiefly system and the relationships between the chiefs and their people are more consensual and organic than that.

The system as it exists today is not feudal, in that people do not have to do what they are told by their chiefs. It is a symbiotic relationship reflected in the saying *Tamata na tamata ni turaga, Turaga na turaga ni tamata* - the people belong to the chiefs and the chiefs belong to the people - neither can exist without the other.

Where decisions have to be made, a chief will consult his *matanivanua*, or spokesman, and his or her elders and close family. He or she may even decide to consult a wider circle. As traditional ties weaken with the times, it is a bold chief who will unilaterally impose a decision. The reason is simple. In today's society, those who are relied on to implement the decision have choices. Thus the Fijian chiefly system exists at the pleasure of the people.

In the Fijian language there are many pretty and witty idioms.[126] *Turaga vakasenitoa* is one. This refers to a chief who has the character of a hibiscus flower - nice to look at, but with no scent at all. Though hibiscus chiefs may cut dashing figures in society, if they serve no people and as such have no followers, they're not of much use to anyone and might as well drop their titles. Let's face it, my friend, in our travels about this spinning globe we've spied many a pious prince strutting the fancy boulevards, their elaborate perfumes failing to mask the realities of redundancy.

Fiji is not England, and it's not the Republic of India or the one-of-these-days Republic of Australia. And as long as the *lewe ni vanua* find confirmation of identity and social comfort in their *vanua* with its inherent chiefly system, and are prepared to extend that stability in a positive spirit to all citizens of Fiji;[127] and as long as chiefs reciprocally serve their people and through the authority thereby gained, take it upon their shoulders to safeguard the interests of all the people of their provinces, whatever their race or religion; then my stand is and will always be, 'Long live the Ratu!' But if that responsibility of reciprocity is abandoned and if repeated realities demonstrate vacuums or failures of leadership on the part of the chiefs, then as inevitably as night follows day, the future of Their Splendours the Pious Princes will gradually become as dim as that of the Dukes of Mingrelia.

The Money Bird

On 14th January 1981, Lote Buinimasi and I raised the Fiji flag in Tokyo. As the *chargé d'affaires*, I made a short speech to the small gathering of Japanese officials and Pacific diplomats present on the roof of the Tokyo Prince Hotel, and thus was the Fiji Embassy in Tokyo declared open.

Later that year, our ambassador arrived from Fiji with his letters of credence for presentation to Japan's head of state, Emperor Hirohito. But before the ambassador-designate left Fiji for Japan, it fell to me to make our side's arrangements for the presentation of those letters. So down Sakurada-dori I went to the Gaimusho, Japan's ministry of foreign affairs, to set in motion the delicate process of scheduling an audience with the venerable Emperor.

In the course of the first Gaimusho meeting, a zealous official from the protocol office let slip that while arrival at the Imperial Palace should normally be by way of official limousines, there was provision for arrival by horse-drawn coach. My ears pricked up and I said we would like to give consideration to the option of equine propulsion. There followed much side-muttering, changing of subject and a bowed exit by the protocol official.

At my next Gaimusho meeting, the appointment process nudged forward a step or two, and the matter of horses and coaches was delicately touched upon. Was I serious about this? I replied that in the Pacific Islands we were quite bound up in traditional ceremony, so I thought it would be appropriate for our ambassador to arrive in the most traditionally respectful manner. This response gave rise to deep intakes of breath through clenched teeth and much scribbling in the note-pads of the ministry.

A few days later, a small delegation from the Gaimusho came to our embassy in Mamiyana to let me know that the imperial horses were stabled far off in the countryside, half the way up to Hokkaido in fact, and that the imperial coaches would have to be staffed by all manner of coachmen, footmen and

271

mounted police. I said that if the equine option was not actually available to us, we would of course be happy to drive to the palace in our cars.

'No, no, no, it is available, Thomson-san, just that, frankly speaking, it is not common practice to choose it.'

'Well if the option is available, Fiji would like to choose it.'

'*A so deska,*' the officials of the delegation fell into a huddle, then their leader asked, 'Are you sure, Thomson-san?'

'Yes, horse and coach, please.'

After many more meetings, on the appointed day we dressed up in rented top hats and morning suits and went with our newly-arrived ambassador to a downtown hotel where our little party was met by the palace's master of ceremonies. In the hotel driveway two elegantly lacquered carriages awaited us, each emblazoned with a gold chrysanthemum, the emperor's crest. The ambassador's coach was draped with red and gold velvet and its driver and footman wore gold-braided uniforms. The former sported a be-feathered tricorn, the second a rather nautical bicorn worthy of the very model of a modern major-general. Lote and I were transported in the second coach, our driver and footman more understated in their top hats with red and gold hat-bands. All around, horses were snorting and clopping their hooves.

We set off into the maelstrom of modern Tokyo, a cavalcade from golden antiquity, three Fijians disporting through Marunouchi with an escort of ten mounted-police riding fore and aft. A small army of whistle-blowing policemen shut off the intersections of central Tokyo to allow for dignified passage of our fourteen-horse-powered procession.

I have to admit the considerable inconvenience we caused to the motorists of the metropolis weighed on my mind; but vestiges of guilt were erased by the site of Tokyo's spontaneous thousands, cameras snapping, happily lining our route, waving as if we were princes of an exotic realm.

272

Some years later, while relaxing over rounds of *mizowari* with a Japanese friend in an Azabu bar, I related this vignette.

'How many people in your country?' he asked.

'About eight hundred and fifty thousand.'

'Less than my home town; just a small Japanese city,' he shook his head. 'They shut down central Tokyo for you!' A long suck on his teeth, 'Only the size of a small Japanese city, eh!'

'It's nothing to do with size, Yamazaki-san. Your home city's just an over-sized town. Fiji's not a city, it's a sovereign nation.'

'I don't think that's it, Thomson-San,' he said with a sly grin. 'In this world, size does matter.'

If you pull out your atlas, my friend, you'll see Tokelau sitting out there in the central Pacific about eight degrees south. The nearest landfall of any consequence is Samoa, two day's boat-journey south. Tokelau is populated by some one thousand five hundred people living on three atolls that are sufficiently far over the horizon from each other for inter-atoll travel to be limited at best. Total land area is ten square kilometres, none of which is arable. There is no airport, for there's no room for one; no roads, for there's nowhere to drive; no bridges, for there are no streams to cross - rain-water being sponged up by all the coral and sand. For some hard-to-understand reason, flies, day-mosquitoes and rats flourish in this isolated oceanic environment.

In 2006 and 2007 Tokelau was slated to be taking its final steps towards self-government and it was expected that it would shortly make its humble entry into the community of nations as probably the smallest country of all. Politically correct citizens of the world were presiding over not one, but two Tokelau referendums, to rubber-stamp this bold progression.

273

But like many of the Pacific Islands before it, Tokelau approached the glories of national sovereignty cautiously, rather bewildered as to the referendum's origins, the impetus in this case coming from the government of Aotearoa-New Zealand, under the eagle-eye of the UN's committee on decolonisation. Not surprisingly, neither the 2006 nor the 2007 referendum got the votes necessary for constitutional change, and Tokelau remains a non-self-governing territory under the administration of Aotearoa. As such it remains on a UN scrutiny list that includes such doing-nicely-thank-you islands as Bermuda and the British Virgin Islands.

My tutor in Pacific Anthropology at Auckland University, Professor Tony Hooper, spent time living on the atolls of Tokelau and co-wrote an ethnographic history of the place. I repeat here his description of the lay of the land,

> Atolls are special kinds of places. Unlike other islands, whose shores and headlands cut off and oppose the surrounding seas, they are more a growth from the sea itself, built of structures more marine than geological, and subject to the winds and weathers of the ocean which both surrounds and washes over the enclosing reef to form a lake within. The patterns of the land and water are all horizontals: seawards, the rank grey-brown reef rising to a slight crest at its outer margin with its silver-white line of breaking water; beyond, the long mid-ocean swells rising and falling almost at eye level, their course barely deflected by the slight bulk of the island; within, the more gentle lake of the lagoon meeting with the far islets, which rise, at their highest points only five metres or so, above the level of the reefs on which they rest. Their bulk is sand and coral rubble thrown up by the sea, whose storm-driven surges from time to time claim a bit of them back.[128]

Tokelau is on the way to nowhere, so that until recently it had no regular shipping service. It has no harbours and there are no reef passages to allow entry to the three lagoons.

When the longboats go out to meet the boat from Samoa, the movement of cargo is disproportionately one way, for there's only a pittance to be earned from the country's exports of copra and handicrafts. Meanwhile there is an expectation when you live in the world today, that you must have the basics of imported foods, medicine, fuel and machinery to be participants in human progress. On top of the wide imbalance in trade, Tokelau must now grapple with all the new national costs of bureaucracy and development, so that for the foreseeable future the great bulk of Tokelau's budgetary resources must be provided for by the tax-payers of Aotearoa.

Meanwhile, the great majority of Tokelauans have voted with their feet, migrating to Aotearoa while they can, to become full and valued citizens there. The last estimate I saw, figured that about six thousand Tokelauans lived down in the bustling cities of temperate Polynesia.

When I lived in Auckland, Polynesia's de facto capital, I spent a lot of time listening to the band Te Vaka, still my favourite interpreters of contemporary Pacific Island music. The band was made up essentially of descendants of Tokelauan immigrants, supported on one track by the massed voices of the Auckland Tokelauan Choir. Te Vaka's songs tell of humanity living out there in oceanic isolation, subsisting on the most meagre of natural resources, and of the sadness of the departing migrants as they see their atoll homes sink away from view, possibly forever. *Ki te la!*[129]

Had Tokelau put on the mantle of self-government, it would have had to behave like all the other nations, sending people to that never-closing caravanserai of talk-fests, the international conferences, assemblies, symposiums and commissions. It may seem ludicrous for a country of fifteen hundred people to assume such onerous obligations, but the same is true for many other small Pacific Island nations which have through diverse means shouldered the cost of these activities for over three decades now. To put it bluntly, had Tokelauans delivered the referendum results its overseas sponsors hoped for, the islanders would have been drawn into an unsustainable vortex of responsibilities. Thankfully for them, they did not.

The atoll-dwellers have a history more inspiring than most, and there must be more imaginative ways to sail with their faces to the wind in these uncertain days, even if the dreaded day arrives when rising sea levels force the abandonment of the atolls. Theirs is a story of chartless navigators pulling up dots of land from the midst of perilous voyaging, of the establishment of enduring human settlement within the barest of natural parameters, and of the spawning of cultures harmonious with the natural laws of Oceania. And most inspiring of all, when we look into the delicate culture of the atolls, we find that all the best of human feelings were able to flourish there: nourishing care for fellow beings, aspirations of excellence in craft and profession, celebration of spirituality in music, and the filling of hearts with faith and love.

Compared with Tokelau, Niue is a giant, for it has a land area twenty-five times that of Tokelau and is supposedly the world's largest example of a raised coral island. And yet when last I looked, it supported a population of only seventeen hundred, just two hundred more souls than those resident on the tiny Tokelauan islets.

You might wish to consider Niue more advanced than Tokelau in a political sense, for it has been self-governing now for over thirty years; but you might choose to reconsider when you look at the harvest of those three decades. Upon purportedly entering the community of nations in 1974, in synchronicity with all the other emerging sovereign states of the time, Niue set itself a goal of self-reliance. But that goal has proved to be beyond the island's capability and in the interim, most Niueans have taken advantage of their New Zealand passports and migrated south.

The rump that remains to run the island is proudly Niuean, but overwhelmingly dependent on annual hand-outs from the government of Aotearoa. If the last sentence provokes outrage in the breasts of Niueans and all those who, like me, hope only the best for them, all I can say is, *fakamolemole*, please read on.

I went to Niue in 1998, alighting on the rock at night, courtesy of Royal Tongan in the good old days before the airline went bust. 'The Rock' is how Niueans refer to their island because that's basically what it is, a great big knob of coral sitting on the summit of a lonely underwater mountain. There are no creative island embellishments of long sandy beaches, turquoise lagoons or outlying islets to soften the outlook from the knob; for the Rock stands alone.

I'd booked to stay at Niue's new hotel, as I'd heard it was one of the swankiest new resorts in all the Islands, with two glittering pools and a cocktail bar perched on a cliff hanging out over the ocean. I was into swanky resort hotels in those days, as my business partners and I were building one in Fiji at the time, with a thirty million dollar bank-loan hanging over our heads like a B52 with engine trouble. Since the Niue resort's construction had been paid for in the main by the taxpayers of Aotearoa, and as I happened to be one-such in those days, I was doubly keen to see how the resort was faring.

Palangi, or variations thereof, is how people of European extraction are referred to in Polynesia. As I emerged from the little terminal building, a *palangi* emerged from the Niuean night, saying he was from my destination hotel. He took my bag and put it into the hotel van, then drove me down a very dark road to the even darker resort. The driver left me in the van and I sat there for a while listening to his receding footsteps and the brooding silence of the surrounding foliage. A light flicked on and I saw that the driver now stood behind the check-in desk of the hotel lobby. I walked in and gave him the usual details, after which he switched from duty manager to porter and carried my bag through the gardens to my room. As he went he flicked switches on to light our way, for which I was grateful as I could hear the movement of the ocean far below us and knew a cliff-edge must be somewhere nearby.

On the way to the room he advised that since there was only one other guest staying in the selection of twenty-four ocean-view rooms, it would be best if I took a ten-minute taxi-ride into Alofi, the island's capital, to get my meals.

Having established by then that this Jack-of-all-trades was also the resort's general manager, I posed a few questions as to how the resort was running. His answers were couched entirely around his diligence in the field of cost-cutting. Thanks to a dearth of clientele, the finances of the hotel were in deep trouble, and he'd been sent up from Kiwiland to stop the hemorrhage. In summary, it seemed that under his prudent reign all the expendable running expenses of the resort had been cut away, such as staff, entertainment, food and beverage. All he needed to do now was make himself redundant and the cliff-top undergrowth would be able to reclaim the resort. We said goodnight, and as the undertaker returned to his no-doubt spartan quarters, one-by-one he turned off all the resort's lights.

I sat out on the verandah of my room in the dark, listening to the seductive rush and suck of the swell on the rocks below. There was no moon, but the Pleiades were sparkling like tipped jewels just above the black rim of the ocean.

The place was lonely, but it was beautiful, and I thought how defeatist it would be to mothball the resort. 'If-you-build-it-they will-come,' a graduate from the Kevin Costner school of economics must have been droning over the resort plans, as Aotearoan aid funds fluttered about the room.

Over a breakfast of coffee and banana-bread in a charming Alofi café, a local lady gave me her version of the empty hotel's conception. According to this lady, a few years ago it was Niue's turn to host a big regional meeting to which heads of government would be descending. People of prescience pointed out that Niue was unable to provide suitable accommodation for all these very important people, for there was but a motley collection of hotel rooms in Alofi.

There were, of course, plenty of vacant village houses on the island, since most of the population had abandoned the Rock to pursue their fortunes in Aotearoa. But nobody had ever heard of politicians and bureaucrats being hosted in such humble circumstance, so the plans for the new resort found themselves on fast track. To be fair, in the great history of foreign-aid-funded white elephants, many have been born for lesser reasons.

The next day I was sitting on the verandah of Sir Robert Rex's store in Alofi. Though it has no direct relevance to this story, bear with me while I pass on a yarn I've heard told in beach-bars as far apart as Honolulu and Honiara. It concerns the origin of the Rex moniker in Niue. George III, Hanoverian king of England back in the eighteenth century, married the Germanic royal, Queen Charlotte. But before doing so, George is held by some to have procreated three children by a pretty Quaker lady named Hannah

Lightfoot, out of Middlesex. There is even a claim, discounted derisively by the supporters of the bloodline pumping through subsequent British royals, that George married Hannah, thereby making the three children in question quasi-legitimate heirs.

The eldest of the three children, who bore the name George Rex, moved to South Africa where he eventually died; but one of his offspring made it around to the South Pacific, finding sanctuary in Niue, where the Rex family lives to this day. The late proprietor of the store, upon whose verandah I was sitting, was the first and longest serving premier of Niue, Sir Robert Rex, the father of the nation, who was knighted in 1984 by a representative of The Queen. As I say, as far as I know it's just a bar tale, but I'm sure there are many Hanoverian descendants who would be delighted to know they may have relatives in Niue.

So anyway, there I was sitting on the Rex verandah, passing the time of day, when I witnessed what I thought was a fantastic display of Niue's warp. The verandah was a fine old one of the South Seas variety, affording a view out over the ocean; and it was out there on the briny waves, way off in the distance, that I caught sight of a large ocean-liner heading directly our way.

On a busy day, Alofi has a pleasantly soporific air, with gentle people addressing their greetings to the occasional passer-by. However, on this day there was no-one at large in the streets of Alofi but me, for there was a critical parliamentary debate underway and it was an all-consuming one for the citizens of Niue. I'd given up trying to make appointments for meetings that morning, because everyone was either in parliament or had their ears jammed to transistor radios, listening to every word of the debate.

From what I could gather at the periphery, the debate was around the unconstitutionality of a pay-rise the cabinet ministers had recently allocated themselves. The rapt attention the debate was receiving from the populace related to the fact that the aid-cake from which these pay-rises came, was the Rock's only cake. If the ministers took more than their fair share, there'd be less for everyone else to divide.

Relaxing on the Rex's verandah, I added up the number of Niuean parliamentarians and government bureaucrats, and multiplied that total by the average number of dependents each had, coming up with a number quite close to the island's resident population. After further pondering, I realised this was a remarkable new model for a country; one where there was a vibrant parliament and attendant bureaucracy, where the only local taxpayers of note came from within the ranks of these two bodies. It was very tidy, and all credit was due to the political philosophers of Alofi and Wellington for their enlightened vision. For here was a model of democracy that demonstrably could make the citizenry pay attention during long and otherwise boring budgetary debates, surely a recipe for diligent fiscal responsibility in a nation.

As the ocean liner drew closer, a graceful figure came swaying down the centre of Alofi's main road. Seeing me, she flashed a winning smile, which I returned with a casual wave. She was far more interested in the sight of the approaching liner than she was in me, so although we were the only loiterers in the street that morning, we neglected to engage in conversation.

The Samoan word *fa'afafine*, meaning 'like a woman', is the descriptor for a woman housed inside a male body. My fellow loiterer in Alofi that day was clearly *fa'afafine*.

The ocean cruiser hove to, lowered its launches and ferried some four hundred well-heeled tourists ashore. From the warbling sound of their passing, I deduced they came from a range of Scandinavian and Germanic countries and I later learnt that the ship's homeport was Copenhagen.

They were a bemused crowd, for they were ready to swipe their credit cards at any South Pacific cliché the Niueans cared to foist on them. But there was no garlanding party on the dock to greet them, no sellers of hastily-carved souvenirs, no postcards of dusky maidens, no tours of the reef, the beach, or rustic village.

In short, the tourists were totally unmolested as they puffed their way up from the foreshore to alight on the Rock's circuminsular road and wander away up the tarmac muttering. Half an hour later, looking even more bemused now, the sweating visitors puffed back. It was apparent they had concluded that apart from the enigma of the *fa'afafine* and me, the Rock was pretty much abandoned.

I don't know how much foreign exchange four hundred prosperous Northern European tourists could dump on Niue in a day, but I fancy it would be a healthy sum if you did it right. Alas, the populace of Niue was otherwise engaged, lost in that gripping debate on the ministerial pay-rise.

Meanwhile, the elegant figure of the *fa'afafine* took up station in Alofi's open-air market by a roadside stall. She'd placed two ripe pawpaws on the counter of her stall and was purporting to sell them, but really she was holding up her end for Niuean tourism. And as I was her witness, virtually every one of those visitors stopped as they passed by, to photograph the lovely lady with the pawpaws. I thought she deserved a medal for tourism services to the island of Niue, for she obliged every photographer with a flash of her winning smile.

In 1979, when I was working the overseas aid desk at Fiji's ministry of foreign affairs, I went to Manila to attend the annual general meeting of ESCAP. Unless you've spent time in the business of international talk-fests, it's unlikely you'll have heard of this acronym, so I'll spell it out. ESCAP stands for the Economic and Social Commission for Asia and the Pacific, one of five such commissions the United Nations has set up around the globe. With ESCAP, we're talking gigantic meetings, with great webs of working groups, symposiums, standing committees, technical committees, expert advisory committees and regional seminars committed to tasks like managing globalisation, eliminating poverty and understanding all the emerging major social issues of our times. Any self-respecting Asia-Pacific government has to be there to have its say at ESCAP, and so it was that I found myself at the grand Manila conference amongst the ranks of the many Pacific Island delegations present.

Those were the Marcos years, when the new elites were treating themselves to a good time, the days of ASEAN ascending, the Japanese economy rampant, Ferdinand and Imelda glittering at the trough. Lavish would be a hopelessly inadequate word to describe the gala events we attended at the great ESCAP gathering. Delegates sat around conference halls by day, listening to accounts of north-south exploitation and mass starvation, simultaneously dealing with the bilious and soporific effects of the night before. Country bumpkins like us from the South Pacific had never seen anything like it; hypocrisy we were familiar with, but the lavish scale in Manila had us gawping.

From our tower-hotel on Roxas Boulevard you could see the slums of Manila on fire, a great fire that burnt for days. Each country delegation at ESCAP had been allocated a chauffeur-driven Mercedes by the Marcos government and I persuaded the driver of our limousine to take me to see the fire's smoking aftermath. He double-checked the gun under his seat as we made our way deeper into the poorer quarters, and when we got out to walk, he followed several paces behind me with his hand inside his jacket.

The aftermath of the fire presented a desolate scene: acres and acres of smouldering ruins, blackened tin, smoking stumps, desperate faces. As I made my way amongst them, I met sooty families collecting scraps from the ashes of their former homes, bits of twisted metal, handles and nails, which they were loading into little wooden-crate wheelbarrows. They told me the firemen could have saved their houses, but the fire-trucks came only as far as the retail streets where fat bribes could be taken to halt the flames.

Earlier in the week when we went for drinks at the Manila Hotel, the fire was already burning. A great pall of smoke hung there in the dirty sunset as we sipped on our premium whiskies, gazing out from the vantage of the deluxe hotel's MacArthur Suite. The rooms carried the name of the American field marshal, for the great self-promoter had once occupied them, back when he'd famously returned and was marshaling forces to go north and conquer Japan. Our host in the suite that evening was His Excellency Hammer DeRoburt, GCMG, OBE, the president of what was then one of the world's richest countries, the Republic of Nauru. With a population of around seven thousand people at the time, Nauru was second only to the oil-soaked Kingdom of Saudi Arabia in the world's per capita income stakes.

282

We were there because Hammer had invited all the Pacific Island ESCAP delegates up to his hotel suite, and the bar was open. As was customary, we over-stayed our welcome until the point was reached when our host decided to make a night of it. I recall at some stage in the party, discussing with the president his grand plan to ship top-soil to Nauru to fill in the canyons left by the island's phosphate mining. He said the soil could be irrigated with desalinated seawater and we discussed at length the tropical orchards, the livestock and the golf course that would flourish on this verdant island groundcover. I don't know whether it was the premium whisky or the president's charisma, but at the time it all seemed like a fine idea to me.

Sitting virtually astride the equator, Nauru is a raised coral island, like Niue, with no adjacent islands, no surrounding lagoons, no harbours or running streams. Only twenty-one square kilometres in size, the island is the shape of a narrow-brimmed hat, with all the houses, the road and the jet air-port, squeezed along the seaside brim. The populated brim is referred to as Downside, while the bulk of the island, the raised coral reef lifted fifty metres into the sky, is called Topside.

It is in Topside that the saga of Nauru lies, the worked-out mine of one of the world's richest deposits of marine phosphate. Now that the high-grade phosphate has been extracted, Topside is a broad, grey, dusty quarry, eerily punctuated by thousands of coral pillars. Not much moves in the moonscape quarry today. The old mine-road winds through the pinnacles, the vines are working in from the rim, and it would appear Topside has a secure future as an ecological disaster zone. He'd been to the mountaintop, he'd had a dream, but Hammer didn't get around to filling the quarry with topsoil before he passed on.

Gone too is the era of phosphate largesse, gone are the days when the Nauruans would turn up at regional meetings like a happy troop of oil-sheiks. When it had been Nauru's turn to host the annual Pacific Islands heads of government meeting, the 1976 Pacific Forum meeting, I recall their munificence. Instead of putting on the usual Pacific Islands cultural shows of dance troupes and handicraft displays for the amusement of the visiting delegates, the Air Nauru Boeing was laid on to fly the wives to Manila, thousands of kilometres over the ocean, for a therapeutic day of shopping in the Makati department stores.

The good old multi-million dollar payouts are history now. Long-swilled is the heady Nauruan cocktail of dubious financial schemes, smarmy consultants and voracious lawyers. The bar has emptied out. Nauru's investments in trophy real estate have made spectacular losses around the Pacific, and the national airline's been running on empty for longer than I can remember.

It is history now that when the phosphate cheques stopped arriving, the Nauruan economy began falling in on itself; the billions of phosphate dollars in the national treasury evaporating to a point of virtual national bankruptcy by 2002. Desperate measures were being taken and hundreds of fly-by-night shell banks established under Nauru's suspect tax haven laws became favoured conduits for Russian moneylaundering, causing the US government to declare Nauru a rogue country. In 2003 the Nauruan government couldn't pay its public servants, so the tab was passed to Australia. Around that time, the US also registered a formal complaint about Nauru's indiscriminate sale of passports. This they said, was sovereignty for sale.

In 1998 I was being driven around Downside by a young Nauruan civil servant. He was a bright young man who had his heart in the right place, but like many an islander was considering emigrating to somewhere bigger.

He took me to see a netted enclosure of frigate birds and we sat talking on the rocky foreshore while waves played with discarded plastic bottles and empty food-cans at our feet. In the course of our conversation, the late Hammer DeRoburt's name came up and I let slip that I'd met him on several occasions back in the 1970s.

"Now, there was a leader!" my companion exclaimed, with a level of naïve enthusiasm only the young can muster.

After driving around the island a couple of times, for a bit of variation I suggested we take the side-road that climbed to Topside. I knew that Nauru's Government House and a collection of official bungalows were at the summit of the road, overlooking the Topside plateau. So we made the short climb and stopped by one of the bungalows where there was a low stone-wall under some shade trees. I got out of the car and went to stand by the wall, from where there was a view over part of the phosphate quarry.

A paper-trail led my eyes to a rather large refuse pile in the scrappy undergrowth beyond the wall. Occasionally a breeze would puff by and lift pages from the pile, butterflying them out into the quarry's maze of coral pinnacles. I went over and squatted by the source of the paper-trail, seeing from its weathered appearance that the dumping must've occurred a few weeks earlier. I pictured the course of a lazy office-cleaner, or a sly junior clerk disposing of onerous filing duties by taking the short walk to the wall and tipping away the offending paper.

Then I saw that the papers carried the letterhead of the Nauruan presidency and that most of the correspondence was initialed by grand old Hammer himself. I picked up a selection to read, feeling distinctly illicit as I did so. They contained all the usual pleasantries and threats, legal undertakings and excuses, banalities and secrets that the correspondence of heads of government is heir to. Another breeze flipped open a file marked 'Treaties' and fluttered more presidential pages out amongst the pinnacles.

A tense moment passed in my breast at the thought of the archives of a nation disappearing like this: Hammer's legacy, the letters of the father of the nation being blown to oblivion, littering Topside's desolation with the country's history until the next decent spell of rain turned it all to pulp.

My companion came over to where I was standing and I showed him what I'd found. He said it made him feel very depressed, so we drove on down to Downside.

Niue is not alone in coming up with a model of democratic government that should inspire even the dullest students of political science. In the far west of the Pacific Ocean, the Republic of Palau has a constitution which allows all citizens to aspire, with a high degree of certainty, to exalted political office. This system has banished from the republic forever the ogres of alienation and marginalisation, firmly establishing Palau at the forefront of participatory democracy.

In brief, the population of the republic is about twenty thousand, from which one must subtract three thousand guest workers from the Philippines and China. Of the remaining seventeen thousand, about forty per cent are not yet of voting age, so we are left with about ten thousand citizens to fill the political offices of the land.

Where the Palauan system becomes interesting, is that on top of national offices of the President, the Vice-President, the Senate and House of Delegates, not forgetting the erstwhile Council of Chiefs; each of Palau's self-governing states has an elected governor, a capital, a bureaucracy and an elected legislature of its own. When you consider that the tiny republic staggers under the weight of sixteen of these flag-bearing states, with an average population of around six hundred voters but most with much less, you begin to see that it's pretty well inevitable you'll get your turn to be a big knob. And these mini-states aren't just glorified neighbourhood-watch schemes, they perform all sorts of mighty functions, such as issuing their own motor vehicle license plates.

Of course, all of these officers of state must have a posse of bureaucrats to do their bidding, so you see at once a recipe for full employment of the populace. If one imagines there might be a problem of no-one being left to do any work outside the field of government, *a la* Niue, one is mistaken. The Palauan model has found an efficacious solution in the importation of 'guest' labour, and all you require for that cool arrangement to work well is a relatively poor, over-populated country nearby. As for funding the model, one must merely find one or more foreign governments which, for reasons of their own, will dump cash into your ideal democracy's treasury.

When Palau became independent in 1984, it was expected to join its relatives in what used to be called the Caroline Islands, to form with them the Federated States of Micronesia. But with Washington ready to fork out the necessary, for as far ahead as anyone chose to look, the Palauans saw no sense in diluting the new democracy and decided to go it 'alone'. This fiscal forethought was not restricted to visions of endless American moola, for coming with fully-fledged nationhood was the right to vote in international organisations and there were bound to be pay-offs from places that needed your vote.

'We have limited ability to absorb all the international assistance available to Palau,' a bureaucrat told me in his boss's office when I visited Palau. His boss was 'off-island' attending an important international meeting. Most of the politicians were 'off-island' and a sizeable proportion of the general populace seemed to be too.

One heard people in Palauan shops saying, 'Where's Joe, is he off-island?' as casually as if Joe was boozing in the bar across the road. The closest 'off-island' destination is Yap, hundreds of kilometres flight across the Pacific, but that wasn't where Joe'd gone. He was on a shopping trip to Manila or maybe Guam, or just as likely conferencing in Hawaii or Washington. Nobody was really sure.

Of Palau's population of seventeen thousand, over twelve thousand are resident in the causeway-connected islets of Koror, the republic's capital. To counter this imbalance, entrenched within Palau's independence constitution was an undertaking for the capital to be relocated to the adjacent lump of land known as Babeldaob. In case, in your preoccupation with other pursuits, my friend, you've never heard of Babeldaob, I should point out that it is the second largest island in Micronesia. The Palauans have kept faith with their constitution and have built the new capital, high on a green hill in Babeldaob.

When I was being escorted through Palau by an affable employee of the government, he allowed himself to be persuaded to drive from the comforts of Koror out into the brave new world of the capital-to-be, for its buildings were then still under construction.

First we drove over the suspension bridge that soars across the straits between Koror and Babeldaob. According to my proud driving companion it was the largest bridge in the Pacific Islands; paid for in full, he said, by the government of Japan. Next came the highway scything through the empty lands of Babeldaob's high country, the sort of broad highway that brings joy to fans of heavy earth-moving machines the world over. The highway was nearing completion, and with a happy wink and red-toothed grin, my companion told me every inch of it was being paid for by the American government.

I should explain the red teeth. Palau lies on the betel-nut side of the drug-divide running erratically through Melanesia and Micronesia. To the east of the divide are kava drinkers; to the west, the chewers of betel-nut. Kava is derived from a type of pepper plant containing a mild central nervous system relaxant and is usually consumed communally with a degree of ritual. Betel-nut is also derived from a type of pepper plant, but contains a mild central nervous system stimulant and is usually consumed privately without ceremony.

If you are in the habit of chewing a lot of betel-nut you will develop red teeth and will tend to expectorate large wads of maroon spit. Next time you're passing through a betel-nut metropolis like Port Moresby or Honiara, you may take note that the pavements, stairwells and public spaces are liberally brightened with this oral graffiti.

As we drove towards the new Palauan capital, my companion delivered many of these colourful spurts from his car-window in the direction of the passing undergrowth. There was no danger of his liquid missiles hitting pedestrians, for there were none on Babeldaob.

We stopped for a while, to allow him to prepare a fresh mouthful of stimulant from the tin of essentials he carried in his glovebox. He broke open a cigarette and stuffed the tobacco into his mouth, followed by a dash of coral lime and some betel-nut, all the while keeping up an amiable chatter through his mastications.

I asked if I might try some of the good stuff, but he declined, saying it would make me dizzy. Whether he was concerned he might be introducing me to a lifetime addiction, or that I might disparage the taste once I got the various ingredients into my mouth, I found it very un-Pacific of him not to share. There were a couple of decades in my life when I was a big-time imbiber of kava, in fact for two years I owned a kava farm in Taveuni, and the thought of not sharing would just never occur to a kava drinker. My companion's reply had an under-lying element of 'Get your own bloody betel-nut.'

We chatted on. He was down on the Filipino guest workers, whom he said were untrustworthy and forever trying to overstay their welcome. He was down on the Chinese because of their people-smuggling, drug-running and brothels. I don't want to give a negative impression of my Palauan pal, for he was generous with his opinions and saw himself as a go-getter person in line with the straight-up characters filling the American sit-coms he'd been reared on. He'd been to America, received training there, had family living there, and he was big on American cuisine.

When we saw a golden rooster scuttle across the road, he sent a spout of betel juice in its direction, scowling at the chook as it disappeared into the long grass. I asked what was wrong and he replied that he couldn't stand chickens. He'd seen what they ate - beetles and worms - they were dirty animals and there's no way he'd eat one. I wondered if he was a vegetarian, but after further conversation found his favoured meat was frozen supermarket chicken, imported from America, rich in growth hormones, antibiotics and other tasty additives. Strange days indeed, in the South Sea Islands.

Back in Koror I'd heard about the new capital buildings of Babeldaob. They were being built by a foreign construction company, using entirely foreign labour and were being paid for by the government of Taiwan. No one I spoke to in Palau had any intention of moving out to the wilds of Babeldaob and a sense of dread seemed to hang over the prospect of a daily commute from the comforts of Koror.

None of this information prepared me for my first gob-smacking view of the new capital. We came upon a high point in the road and saw, rising from the forest ahead, a huge Greco-Roman complex of columns and pediments, surmounted by a great white dome in the style of Washington's capitol building.

On closer inspection it was even more stunning. Three-storied, air-conditioned buildings, one for the legislators, another for the executive, another for the judiciary, another for the bureaucracy, each fronted by a massive row of Tuscan columns supporting triangular pediments. I did a quick calculation and figured that at a pinch the entire Palauan population could be accommodated amongst these apses and porticos, these colonnaded basilicas. That thought gave me hope there might be method to this madness. Maybe the buildings would serve as a refugee centre in times of national peril; maybe they weren't what they otherwise appeared to be, another gigantic foreign aid folly.

Half a dozen Filipino workers waved at us from a rooftop upon which they were installing a cornice. Otherwise the site was deserted. I strolled around. It was quiet up on that Babaldoab hill, but for an occasional bird call. A scrubby forest spread over the surrounding highlands, unsullied by human settlement.

As I walked around the building site, I discovered that the giant columns were clip-on fibreglass jobs and realised that most of the Greco-Roman embellishments were of this light-weight material, giving the initial gravity of the national edifice a hint of Disneyland.

To me the pity of it all was that Palauan indigenous architecture has an admirably robust icon in the traditional village meeting houses, called *bai*, some of which still survive. Hand-hewn planks make up the walls and floors of the *bai*, dense story-board carvings adorn beams and external walls, while a sharply pitched roof sweeps up like the bow of a proud canoe. Walking around the new capital I saw not a single echo of the beauty of the *bai*, the pervading 'aesthetic' here being Taiwan-meets-America.

As an architectural after-thought, a Palauan motif had been moulded into the external pilasters. The motif was of a long-legged bird pictured in the act of picking up a coin in its beak while simultaneously ejecting a coin from its anus.

'That's the Money Bird,' my companion told me.

'What's its story?' I was intrigued, for the behaviour of the bird seemed a wicked metaphor for what was going on around here.

An ejection of betel juice splattered the base of the wall and he wiped a maroon dribble from his chin. 'I dunno, s'got something to do with tradition.'

About three weeks out of Palau and I found myself in Vanuatu, having my morning coffee in one of Port Vila's commodious French cafés. The headline of the Vanuatu Daily Post had captured me - BOLD CALL TO LEGALISE SEX. It appeared procreation was finding favour with the republic's enlightened legislators, but further reading revealed the story was something to do with the spread of prostitution, which according to the Post was rife in the capital.

Even more riveting was the inside story arising from the prime minister's recent visit to Taiwan. According to the newspaper he'd personally received US$500,000 while there, and without reference to his fellow cabinet ministers in Port Vila had in return given Vanuatu's diplomatic recognition to Taiwan in preference to the People's Republic of China.

As a result, diplomatic fur was flying and hyperactive ambassadors were coming and going. Vanuatu cabinet ministers were in revolt, they posted a motion of no confidence in their prime minister. The Taiwanese flag was raised in Vila, then hauled down, then raised again. The Chinese Ambassador said he'd been pushed and threatened with the clenched fist of the embattled prime minister when he called on him in protest; he no doubt felt vila-fied. All the while the newspapers were giving reports of the prime minister's relatives turning up in Port Vila banks with great piles of US dollars, attempting to convert them to local currency. According to the Vanuatu Daily Post, all Vila was vexed.

I took another sip at my coffee and thought about how it didn't have to be this way for the smaller Pacific Islands. Thus far Tuvalu has retained self-respect in sovereignty, in spite of its gradual inundation by the rising ocean. Formerly the British colony of the Ellice Islands, Tuvalu has had to stand pretty much on its own water-logged feet since independence, because when Britain quit the Pacific it gave us all the big bye-bye. Today, Britain's only remaining Pacific sphere of influence is lonely, brutalised Pitcairn Island, with its population of some four dozen people and long memories of a nasty mutiny.

Untested by the resource curse, the leaders of Tuvalu have demonstrated wise governance by taking the aid available to them and placing it in a trust fund for Tuvalu's future, reinvesting the trust dividends whenever they become due. But even for the prudent Tuvaluans, a viable national future is tenuous, given those swelling sea levels.

There is still an alternative to hopping onto the express train of development and it can be found in out-of-the-way places where the land and lagoon still allow the old ways of subsistence. In 1978 I visited the French territory of Futuna and I enjoyed what I saw. Futuna is part of Polynesia, with its own language and culture, about three hundred kilometres northeast of Fiji. I flew there with friends in a little Piper Aztec, basically for a weekend jaunt.

I knew the French *chargé d'affaires* in Suva, so before we left for Futuna I rang him and asked if I'd need a visa in my Fiji passport in order to land on the island. He said not to worry and that I'd be given a visitor's permit on arrival.

So off we flew up the north coast of Fiji, until *terra firma* ran out and we tipped our wings to set off across the very broad ocean. Eventually we found Futuna, a couple of small volcanic islands rising from the maritime expanse, and to my considerable relief, the plane was set down on the sandy airstrip.

A French gendarme, *avec kepi*, was waiting for us. He drove us to the residence of the island's administrator, saying that they'd been alerted I was from Fiji's ministry of foreign affairs. The gendarme said the administrator wanted to know the purpose of my mission. In a way I suppose I was some kind of Fiji spy, but I was at pains to explain my purpose in this profession was entirely private and friendly.

292

The administrator of Futuna was at lunch when we arrived at his gate, and we spotted him *a table* out on his spacious verandah, throwing his exasperated hands in the air at the news of our arrival. We also noted the heavily vinaigretted salad-leaf at the side of his mouth when he came down to interrogate us at the gate.

There was not a whiff of hospitality on offer, not even a glass of water after a long flight across the ocean, just the news he wished to impart to me that it was a bad idea to have come to Futuna. He insisted we depart immediately, either on to Wallis Island or back to Fiji.

We had no intention of doing either in a hurry, so I asked if we were being evicted from Futuna. No, no, that was not the case, but there were no accommodation facilities on the island and therefore there would be nowhere for us to sleep, so we should just go away.

Leaving him to his no doubt excellent Gallic lunch, we meandered down the road in the direction of the village we'd just driven through. The first Polynesian we met invited us to stay in his house. Another villager came along and said we should stay in his house. Then they agreed it would be better if we have the use of the newest house in the village, belonging to one of their relatives who was away in New Caledonia. This waterfront house was to be ours for the weekend and it was only when we repeatedly insisted, that they took some money from us for the use of it.

As far as I could gather, the only resident non-Polynesians on the island were the owner of a Chinese trading store, a priest, the gendarme and the cranky administrator. I suppose there must have been a doctor on the island. The people looked healthy and happy, and there was no evidence of over-crowding or over-exploited island resources. I guessed this was so because many of the people of Futuna lived overseas, and as citizens of a French territory, they'd have had all the access they wanted to New Caledonia and France, or for that matter the rest of Europe.

We spent most of our stay picnicking on the stony beaches, surrounded by laughing children and scavenging pigs. It seemed that apart from the churches, the trading store and the very occasional vehicle trundling by, Futunan life was pretty much unaffected by the outside world.

Our house was equipped with the luxury of a transistor radio, which I took out onto the beach, to discover that the only radio signal able to be picked up was the Hindi broadcast from my former home, good old Labasa town in northern Fiji. So there I was, beached on the far outer fringes of Polynesia, relaxing to the tinny sounds of Bollywood musicals.

Pigs roamed free, around the canoes, across the beach, alongside the houses and up and down the road. But there was one place they couldn't go … over the wall. I was enjoying an afternoon stroll when I discovered that circuminsular wall.

Leaving the beach, I'd passed inland through the village, across the road and through the breadfruit groves, when I came upon it. A low wall of rough volcanic stone confronted me, with a rustic stile set into its side. I stepped up the stile and stood astride the wall to look across at beautiful food gardens rising up the mountainside.

From my vantage point, I turned my attention back to the village and then back to the garden slopes, deducing that the wall's purpose was to keep the pigs out of the gardens. The hogs were free to share the village and the foreshore with the people, but there was no way they were allowed beyond this wall.

The gardens were spectacular. They were set in irrigated terraces, much like Balinese rice terraces, with the flow of mountain streams diverted into the top of the terraces and little channels carrying the water down through the gardens of taro, plantain, bananas and vegetables. I'd seen evidence of traditional irrigation terraces like these in Fiji when I lived on island of Taveuni, but they'd long since been abandoned. Here on Futuna, traditional Pacific high-island agriculture was still in action and it was a beautiful sight.

Human endeavor was in harmony with nature, there was a sense of appropriate industry, of sufficient plenitude, of contentment in simplicity. I watched a man and woman descending though the terraces, he with a heavy bunch of green plantain on muscled shoulder, she with great bundles of emerald taro leaves in her arms. The moment made me feel happy to be human. I got off the stile to allow them passage, and there were smiled greetings between us, as man and woman crossed the wall adorned with the bounty of the garden.

Tahitian Turks

In the Swinging Sixties, if you boarded a V-Jet QANTAS Boeing 707 in Nadi and flew across to Tahiti, then up to Acapulco, Mexico City, Nassau and Bermuda before touching down in London, you were promenading an aeronautic avenue known as the Fiesta Route. The temptations of those exotic transit points must have been too much for the V-Jet crews, because every time I flew that way, some technical hitch or other would call for an unscheduled over-night stop.

Whenever such a sleep-over was announced over the 707's intercom, there'd be a cheer from the passengers. We'd then be bussed off to a Tahitian, Mexican or Bahamian beachfront hotel, where the airline would dole out meal-vouchers and pick up the tabs for our rooms. For those of us bound for the dreary confines of British boarding schools, those curfew-free wind-falls were akin to the last meals of condemned men.

One such occasion involved a stop-over in Tahiti. I was in the company of the Crown Prince of Tonga, His Royal Highness Sia'osi Taufa'ahau Manumata'ogo Tuku'aho Tupou, and the daughter of the British Consul in Tonga, Margie Reid. The three of us were on our way to educational institutions in the UK and it was thus a case of seize the day and make a good night of it.

On our grand tour of the clubs and resort hotels of Tahiti, whenever the sound of clattering drums broke out and a *tamure* troupe took to the dance-floor, their leading beauty would make a beeline for the handsome Polynesian prince at my side. A graceful invitation onto the dance-floor would then be smoothly palmed by HRH to his eager accomplice, so that I was able to spend most of the night thrashing my willing thighs among the hip-blurring oscillations of beautiful young Tahitians.

From my earlier visits to Papeete I was already suffering a mild addiction to the essence of Tahiti, and that night of the long *tamure* provided rich sustenance in the English winter ahead. At the time I was finishing off my secondary education at the International Centre of Sevenoaks School in Kent. I was not an attentive scholar. Most of those drawn-out months of 1966 and 1967 were spent acting in the school's dramatic productions, playing rugby for the 1st XV, studying the form-guide of the various Sennockian colleges for young women, and, most bizarrely in retrospect, pursuing campanology in the belfries of the local churches. Work that one out, I can't, except that the nighttime walks to various churches afforded many opportunities for the sharing of No 6 cigarettes with my partners in campanology.

Understandably my academic supervisors were not much impressed by their Fiji recruit, and the senior history master developed a particularly negative fixation. He was only slightly less pudgy than Robert Morley, but had the same moist, pursed lips of the English actor. His quivering mouth was ever poised to pout pearls of witty scorn, usually in my direction.

Back home, my parents would scratch their heads in puzzlement when the school reports turned up from Sevenoaks. I was supposed to be one of their more academically-inclined sons, but the senior history master wrote that my advancement was being impaired by 'muscular philistinism.' He was a classic. Back in class, while he tortured the Tudors, I doodled palm trees and grass-skirts, until the point when old pursy lips would loom up to spray over my head, 'Thomson, you Tahitian Turk!'

The Tahitian bit I got, the Turkish tag I didn't, until my schoolmates explained that Englishmen of my adversary's bent, equated the term with barbarian vulgarity. Other than its onomatopoeic value I still didn't get it, for his hayseed English forbears would have been muck-raking barnyards while Ottoman scholars and sultans, in their marbled palaces, were presiding over a fabulous Mediterranean empire.

My friend, I promised you we would travel much in fertile realms, where flowers flash like lamps and forest waters run fresh and free. So like stout Cortez, let us go. Tahiti is calling. It has been so since first I saw her from the teak decks of the ships bearing me thence as a youth. For it was from such seaboard vantage that the cloud-piercing profiles of the siren island and her sister in provocation, Moorea, were forever fixed in a formative mind. And that image has ever carried subtitles of romance and astounding natural beauty.

When I was eleven, I sailed with my family on the passenger ship *Southern Cross* from Suva to Papeete. At the time, my parents had lately been blessed with a daughter and my mother was pregnant with her seventh son, so we older boys were given the run of the ship. Shortly after leaving Suva, there was great excitement among my brothers when we discovered that Kitione Lave, the South Seas heavyweight boxing champion, was a fellow passenger. He was on his way to a prize-fight in Tahiti. I guess because my brothers and I were junior boxers in Harry Charman's boxing club in Suva, the champ took a shine to us; so that all the way to Papeete, the Thomson boys were able to join the big Tongan in his fitness sessions on the ship's upper decks.

When Moorea and Tahiti's flamboyant peaks were pulled up from the ocean, and the welcoming drums and dancers had done their darndest on the Papeete dock, we naturally assumed the time had come for us to accompany Kitione to the big fight. But here we were hit with a solar-plexus blow that some Thomson boys nurse to this day. We were all under-age and weren't allowed to go to the boxing arena.

That night my brothers and I lingered late on one of the ship's dockside decks. Our friend the bosun pointed out where the fight-venue was and we peered wanly in its direction. Leaning on salty railings, we heard every cheer and every jeer that rolled across the low tin roofs of the waterfront town, as Kitione and the other boxers went about their rugged trade.

They've pulled a prophylactic of tar and cement over Tahiti's sensuality. Where once sandy lanes were sufficient along the island's narrow littoral strip, there are now motorways and flyovers. Condominiums climb higher and higher on jungle-green slopes away above the city, creeping like a tropical rash up the mountain's flanks.

Evermore, O Tahiti! Evermore, the pigments of Monsieur Gauguin, our dreaming stained with the story, evermore the heavy beauty of Polynesians in repose. I have a confession for you, Tahiti. When the master's works come to mind, it's not the perfect patterns of contemplative models I see, but the flow of your landscape behind. The canvases exude your warm-wafted, humid, briny, floral air, infused with leaf and fruit rotting to soil. Speckled chickens scratch orange earth, black pigs snuffle about the undergrowth. A white pony fords a rocky stream, closh-clock, closh-clock, where wax-green fronds flash lagoon-light signals from a restless foreshore. Leaves, dry-yellow, lie brittle under twisted pandanus. Hermit crabs rustle in the leaf-litter. A warning snap sounds before coconut descends, thudding on sand's dull rug, and the pink shore-doves cease to coo. They take flight with wings beating on resonant breasts.

O Tahiti, bruised lover, they say you are Venus gone to fat, a welfare widow. Ever since the second northern ship stowed its dripping anchors, there's been someone defaming you. Drunk on suspect memory, they scoff that you were better in the days they knew you. They let it slip it was they who deflowered you, who had the best of you before your slide. Their carnal mutterings tell of voluptuous volcanic lines, with back-of-hand platitudes about your pleasure-loving kind; yes it was they who were the ones, or so they said, who feasted freely from your lips. I spot the flick of a scaly tail as they turn away, for when they tired of you, those great lovers became your mealy-mouthed detractors.

In 1968, in the vagrancy of my student days, I went to Tahiti and saw for myself the perfidy of the detractors. I was on a boat trip out of Trinidad's Port of Spain, bound for Suva and three years of university studies in Auckland. I picked up two big Gauguin posters at the museum in Mataiea and my student digs were thereafter adorned with Tahitian landscape, at a time when my peers were pinning Jimi Hendrix or Che Guevara to their walls.

Such was my muscular philistinism, I couldn't have cared less about the intentions of the Symbolists and the Post-Impressionists. What kicked right in for me from the posters were the scenes in which the languid models were set, I knew those island landscapes, they had sustained me. And when I learnt that during Gauguin's Montparnasse residency in 1894, he had named his little art school L'Académie Vitti, the Fiji Academy, I embraced the artist.

On that same visit to Tahiti, I saw how Polynesians were progressing with the rest of us, for better or worse, ineluctable change the one constant for all. Yet still Tahiti enchanted, the inheritance as exquisite as ever. As always, the Point of Venus protruded the way its maker intended, the sensual saga of Papeete's waterfront still outweighing all shabby efforts to subdue it, and then and evermore, the pinnacles of Moorea flabbergasted every sunset.

I took the bus from Papeete to Mataiea, to walk the windward coast where the masterpieces of the 1890s were painted, to view Gauguin's palette in the land. It was there in natural abundance, the sap had not been staunched. White-footed yellow dogs still tiptoed down to the hissing beach, down to the land-sea place of uncertainty, and all along the waterfront were all the same conclusive reports of coral being bullied by ocean.

But even as my senses were celebrating, I sat down on a shaded beach and for the first time read Gauguin's journal *Noa Noa*.[130] For that romantic young man, seeds of misgiving began sprouting with the turning of each dappled page, growing to a fruition of betrayal by book's end, for the master proved himself to be sadly lacking in fidelity to you. Europe's artist-in-residence in Polynesia had tired of you too, O Tahiti, he'd joined the literary conga-line of your detractors; and that was hard for a committed Tahitian Turk like me to take.

Later 1 came to see Paul Gauguin, as one of the doyens of disillusionment. When not morosely daubing at his canvases or digging at savage woodcuts, he found time to be a prolific scribe, scribbling many sheaths of Tahitian letters, waspy articles for a Papeete periodical, and of course the penning of *Noa Noa*.

In his letters there are lyrical moments hinting at the eternal power of the paintings, so if you've read them, my friend, you can be forgiven for expecting much from *Noa Noa*. But like *Le Marriage de Loti,* the blockbuster nineteenth century novel that inspired Gauguin's flight to Tahiti, *Noa Noa* is suffused in self-indulgent delusions. Too conveniently naive and patronizing of Tahiti's indigenous culture to be taken seriously, in the end the book reads like one last sorry grope at the noble savage.

In the artist's letters we are given richer access to Gauguin's thoughts on his Tahitian surroundings, before the disenchantment sets in. He says he wishes to suggest in his paintings, 'a luxuriant and wild nature, a tropical sun, which sets aflame everything around it.' He desired for his figures an appropriate setting, believing that,

> It is indeed life in the open air, but at the same time intimate; among the thickets, the shadowy streams, these whispering women in the immense palace decorated by Nature herself ...[131]

Every day before and since, that shadowed palace exists, though many may never perceive its intimacy through the tinted glass of air-conditioned carriages. And from recent visits to Tahiti, it appears many who live there now, like their cousins the world over, are so mesmerised by what is not yet theirs, that they show no love for what nature has provided for all. One would not hold them to account, except that mass indifference has allowed sacred land to be eroded, to be sullied with invasive species, to be paved with mediocrity, and sold off for handfuls of developer's silver.

Nevertheless, Tahiti's glory lives on. Let it ever be so. The majesty of the palace endures among the intimate thickets and shadowy streams, unshaken even by senseless atomic atrocities.

Gauguin had two sojourns in Tahiti: the first from 1891 to 1893, the second from 1895 to 1901. He was a fecund man. Back in Europe he'd pretty much abandoned his Danish wife and their five children when, at the age of forty-three, he set sail for the South Seas. On his first sojourn in Tahiti, living down the coast at Mataiea, he took as his 'wife' the thirteen year old he calls Tehura in *Noa Noa*.

The artist sired no children with his child-bride, but on his second sojourn his next Tahitian wife was Pau'ura, with whom he had a daughter, who died as an infant, and a son, Emile. His Tahitian son went on to have ten children of his own, so there are many great-grandchildren of Gauguin in Tahiti today. Then when the fifty-something artist moved north with his syphilis to the Marquesas Islands in 1901, he acquired the fourteen year old Vaeoho as his mistress, their union resulting in at least a dozen Marquesan great-grandchildren today.

It was with this fecundity in mind, that I was stunned to be told by a Tahitian intellectual that Tehura, Gauguin's first Tahitian 'wife', whose real name was Teha'amana, was in fact *mahu*. The Tahitian term *mahu* refers to an effeminate man who lives as a woman.

This proposition was made while I was enjoying one of the truly great long-lunches of recent times, along the road-less coast of Fenua Aihere at the eastern extremity of Tahiti. It was a festive Sunday and we'd come by boat along Tahiti's weather-coast of waterfalls and coral passages to a friend's waterfront farm. The farmhouse fronted the emerald spread of a dense field of taro and bananas, its verandah facing a tide that lapped not ten paces away, and on that verandah was set a table laden with the produce of land and lagoon.

We feasted, drank, philosophised, drank more, philosophised more, got out the guitars and sang songs from the Australs, from Tahiti and from Fiji. My host's childhood friend from the next-door farm was a man about my age, with a wonderfully big, bare, brown Polynesian belly that forced him to sit far back from our table's edge. He was a king of philosophy, a true Tahitian Turk if ever I met one.

In a jumble of Tahitian, French and English we managed to communicate our audacious ideas. It was the king who said, 'Teha'amana *était un mahu*.'

'No!'

'*Oui* … 'ow you say … she was a he.'

'Impossible! In *Noa Noa* Gauguin writes about her.'

"*La même comme* Loti.' He rubbed his belly with satisfaction. 'Loti, 'ee say 'ees loverrr Rarahu was woman. *Mais* everee-one know, 'ee was *mahu*.'

I had to admit I'd already heard the theory that Loti's lover was a man-woman and agreed there was a ridiculous aspect to Rarahu's voluptuous depiction on the monument at Loti's swimming pool along the littered fringe of Papeete.

"*Pas de théorie*, Pee-terre, *c'est vrai*.'

The king of philosophy came from Mataiea and said little was known about Teha'amana's family in the area. He said it was thought they came from Rarotonga in the Cook Islands, and the word he'd heard was that the reason the mother was so willing to give Teha'amana up to Gauguin, was that the child was *mahu*. On this score they said there had been some church pressures on the family. The king knew about Gauguin's letters boasting of impregnating his 'child-bride', but he was sure a baby was never produced.

Back in Papeete I went to the bookstore and rifled through the Gauguin bibliography. Writ large in the Gauguin legend was the story from *Noa Noa* in which he borrows a horse from a gendarme and goes riding along the coast in search of a wife. The artist claims he found one in the village of Faone, when Teha'amana's mother promptly offered up the 'bride'. The unblushing artist tells us Teha'amana, or Tehura as Gauguin calls her, was 'a large child, slender, strong, of wonderful proportions.'

They return to his Mataiea hut and according to Gauguin, live the life of the Tahitian paradise, '*navé navé fénua* – land of delights!' The last page of *Noa*

Noa features Gauguin's syrupy *a la* Loti abandonment of Teha'amana upon his first return to France in 1893.

Next I opened the picture books to look for the seminal 1892 portrait, *The Spirit of the Dead Watching*, displaying a naked Teha'amana prone upon Gauguin's bed. I found it, but the canvas offered no refutation of the king's pronouncement, for the androgynous Teha'amana lies face down on the bed with legs tightly crossed.

Then I came across a reproduction of the striking 1893 portrait, *Teha'amana Has Many Parents*. In Gauguin's painting of his Mataiea lover, Teha'amana is seated, dressed in a neck-high, striped pinafore, holding a fan, and I saw therein a haunting resemblance that took me a while to place. Anyone familiar with the membership of the All Blacks, the national rugby side of Aotearoa, would see a striking similarity between the face in portrait and the side's granite inside-centre, Ma'a Nonu.

Revisiting *Noa Noa* and collections of the artist's letters, there was sufficient fabrication evident in Gauguin's self-mythologising lines to make it impossible to take Gauguin's love affair with the young girl Tehura seriously. Apart from anything else, the 'love' in the story is patently a sham. He says as much in *Intimate Journals*,

> As you perceive, I do not know love. To say 'I love you' would break my teeth.

In the end I put the pages aside and left the Papeete bookstore firmly of the impression that Gauguin's Tehura was more than one person. There was the Teha'amana some claim to have known later in life as a woman, coupled with the various Mataiea girls and boys of whom the artist writes in *Noa N*oa and in his many letters to his agent.[132] I had noted that it was chiefly of young Tehura that the gammy artist bragged on his return to France in 1893, but this may have been a beat-up for *Noa Noa*. And I had also found more than one heavily homoerotic reference in his work, such that if action followed intention, the eloquent patter of the king of philosophy might have been right in part, that Gauguin's Mataiea princess was *mahu*.[133]

I have a friend in Tahiti by the name of Joël Hart. The first day I met him I was sitting in a Papeete café, sipping a sweet espresso while reading my battered copy of RLS's *In the South Seas*. Joël was sitting at an adjacent table. He looked over the top of his newspaper and said, 'The twelfth chapter of that book is about my grandfather Captain John Hart.'

That's the thing about Tahiti, history has a habit of getting up from the page to take a seat on the banquette next to you, merely to enjoy the harbour view. Sit there long enough and the borders of reality sag. Perhaps it's like that everywhere, it's just that Papeete's lax palpability allows the past more leeway.

Ocean's lap is wide, but the Pacific Islands are her cluster of children, and it took little time for Joël and me to get around to the subject of the Tongan boxer Kitione Lave. Joël has been many things in his time: trade union representative (he met Gorbachev at a 1990 trade union congress in Moscow), farmer, Mormon pastor, official tourist guide, Tahitian language teacher, and boxing commentator for Tahitian radio. As a young man he was ringside with his microphone at the same Kitione Lave fight-night that I was denied attendance of because of my age. Joël's memory is prodigious and he was able to fill me in on much of what I'd missed that night.

It was Joël who introduced me to Paul Gauguin's grandson Marcel, who he'd known since the days Marcel had the catering business at Faa'a airport and Joël ran the airport workers union. Like me, Marcel was born in 1948, one hundred years after his famous forbear. He has his grandfather's hooked Gallic nose and hooding eyelids, but the rest is Polynesian, smooth brown skin, limpid dark eyes and black hair waving down to his shoulders. Any friend of Joël's was welcome in his house, and what a house!

Marcel took us over a roof-top bursting with every brilliant shade of the bougainvilleas he'd planted up there, to an annex created as a shrine to the genius of his grandfather. In a white room the size of a broad billiard hall, with a gallery-wall down its centre, hung a huge collection of the master's works. There was uniformity to the display, for all the paintings were prosaic reproductions by a not particularly talented pair of European artists who'd camped in Tahiti for a spell. The effect was quite gob-smacking, given the impressiveness of the collection and the mediocrity of the reproductions.

Gauguin's grandson commissioned each piece of the collection, and at his behest the reproducers altered some of the compositions of the original works. For instance, in their attempt to recreate the tableau Gauguin regarded as his masterpiece *D'Où Venons Nous? Que Sommes Nous? Où Allons Nous?*, there was a depiction of the artist standing on the rock in the place of the Oriental idol that dominates the background of the original.[134] I imagine Marcel's purpose was to remove idolatry from the painting, but the effect was quite disconcerting.

It was clear to me that in the context of Tahiti, Marcel was being sincere in his dedication to care for the spirit of his dead ancestor. He said it was the responsibility of the living to help the spirits leave this world in peace, and he showed how he had hung paintings in various juxtapositions to pacify his grandfather's turbulent spirit.

The model for the two prone female portraits in the famous canvases: the Tahitian nativity scene *Te Tamari No Atua*, and the haunting *Nevermore*, was Marcel's grandmother Pau'ura. In his gallery, Marcel has hung the portraits one above the other, for a reason. It is particularly powerful to see him standing there explaining the story, when it settles on you that this full-frontal *Nevermore* nude, upon whose limbs multiple millions of eyes have poured, is Marcel's flesh and blood.

Marcel told me the two paintings are related, because Gauguin made a terrible mistake in the nativity canvas when he put a halo around the new-born's head. The baby in the birth scene is Marcel's aunt, who died not long after the original painting, and the faithful grandson holds that Gauguin was profoundly disturbed by the death of his Tahitian daughter, relating it in some way to his depicting her as the Christ-child.

He claims the later depiction of Pau'ura in the *Nevermore* canvas depicted the sadness of the mother at the loss of her first child, and the artist's pledge to never again commit such transgression. By placing the reproduction of the *Te Tamari No Atua* canvas above the nude of *Nevermore*, Marcel is content that he has confronted the mistake and gained atonement for his grandfather. In that hallowed family place, I did not deign to bring up Gauguin's own written explanation of the painting's genesis.

I never met Marcel's late father, Emile, Gauguin's Tahitian son by Pau'ura. But my old friend Dick Smith did back in 1959, when for three magic months *Stardust* tied up on the Papeete waterfront. 112 feet in length, *Stardust* was a wartime patrol vessel Dick personally refitted off Point Piper in Sydney. With little more assistance than a compass, sextant and dead reckoning, he motored her across the ocean to Tahiti, stopping off along the way at the more irresistible of the Islands. His Pacific odyssey would eventually take Dick to Fiji, where he settled and set about founding the first away-from-it-all resorts of the Mamanuca Group, leaving his mark indelibly on Fiji's tourist industry.

Back when *Stardust* turned up in Tahiti, she was loaded down with a cargo of Rarotongan tomatoes that for some reason of bucolic bureaucracy put Dick at odds with Tahiti's administrative authorities. They did not like his attitude and he did not like theirs. Nevertheless *Stardust* was a fine-looking vessel, so they gave her a berth on the Papeete waterfront where she moored for the duration of Dick's stay.

Her stern was connected to the seawall by a gangplank, and up that gangplank and across the esplanade, all the bars of Papeete awaited carousal. Dick caroused, in the process befriending Francis Sanford, a Tahitian with part-American ancestry who was to become the leader of Tahiti's fight for autonomy from France.

One night Francis took his new Australian friend down to the territorial assembly, where a meeting was in progress. Out in the dark street they found some handy rocks and Francis demonstrated his skill at hurling rocks onto the assembly's roof. Dick was just getting the hang of this art, when shrill blasts of gendarmes' whistles broke from the official compound and it became necessary to spend the rest of the evening scarpering after Francis through the back streets of Papeete. But the town was too small for such a fine young pair of Tahitian Turks, so that before too long the French high commissioner issued Dick with a *persona non grata* letter and *Stardust* let Tahiti slip, sailing north to the Marquesas.

During that *Stardust* sojourn on the Papeete waterfront, amongst the harbourside community that Dick mixed with was Emile, the son of Paul Gauguin, and father of Marcel. Emile was by then a sixty year old man with ten children, the youngest being five years old. To support himself and his family, he wove traditional Tahitian fish-traps under the trees of the esplanade, selling them to curious tourists. Dick bought a few of Emile's artefacts, more to help him out than clutter the *Stardust* with woven cane.

But it was a peculiar habit of Emile's that endured strongest in Dick's memory of him. To finish his *oeuvres*, the artisan needed string to bind the fish-traps in strategic places and he was forever running out of the stuff. In the string-borrowing department Emile had exhausted all neighbourhood options, so he evolved a novel alternative observed on numerous occasions by Dick from where he sat on *Stardust's* deck. To acquire a piece of string, Emile would nonchalantly approach the sun-blinds hanging from the fancy shop-fronts along the esplanade, when no-one else was around. With a quick snip-snip of scissors, blinds collapsed on the sill and string was withdrawn from cluttered slats. The sly weaver would then sashay back to the seawall and soon a brand new fish-trap would be ready for sale by the son of Paul Gauguin.

With many a suicidal grumble, Gauguin abandoned Tahiti in 1901 and steamed north on the *Croix du Sud*, a cockroach-riddled steamer that ran the government-subsidised Marquesas route. He was heading for the fabled extremity of Fatu Hiva Island, but it was a step too far for an artist dependent on communication with the art markets of Paris, so he embarked at the provincial centre of Atuona village on the Marquesan island of Hiva Oa.

There he set up his *Maison du Jouir*, the House of Pleasure residence and studio in which he endeavoured to enter his pox-infested body into a new round of what the local priest described as debauchery.

From the House of Pleasure came the great Marquesan canvases: *Horsemen on the Beach*, *The Gold of their Bodies, and Barbaric Tales*, works that hang high in the pantheons of Modern Art. When you consider the obvious sexual menace lurking at the rear of *Barbaric Tales*, you have a dash of hope that Gauguin had begun to see the error of his sexually exploitative ways. But it was not so, for the delicate young Marquesan girls portrayed are real people, models in the mould of those who'd learned to avoid him in Tahiti, and he would take it as his *droit d'artiste* to bed them.

Even as this great art is at work, prodigiously portraying the patterns of nature's palace, there is a hint of gratuitous pillaging; for somewhere in the background, a hedonistic artist is pissing on the flowers of the garden. In the immortality of paint, the Atuona girls enter some kind of high glory; but in life, the hard fact is they were the sexual victims of a syphilitic solipsist who seduced with bags of lollies.

From his Hiva Oa compound, Gauguin inevitably fell to warring with the local officials of the church and the administration, putting as much energy into this ongoing battle as he did his art. Inexorably, the wars of his mind, the disease of his body, and the accumulations of the absinthe and morphine poisons coursing his blood became burdens too many.

The organism which for fifty-five years had carried Gauguin's troubled spirit, gave up the ghost in the month of May 1903. The church claimed the corpse, for Gauguin was a baptised Catholic, and they buried it without ceremony in their Calvary cemetery on a hill high above the Bay of Traitors.

Ninety years after Gauguin's death, the day came when I followed the artist's course to the Marquesas, like a cockle-bearing pilgrim all the way to Hiva Oa, the island where the last strokes of his brush worked canvas. On this, my first visit to the Marquesas, I was a guest of the government of Tahiti Nui and winged my way north over a thousand kilometres of ocean, piercing the cumulus in a silver jet-prop aeroplane.

For all the convenience of civil aviation, the journey was not without its trials. I'd proceeded directly from a Papeete night-club to catch that morning flight, having endured an all-nighter in the bars of the town, attempting to match the disproportionate capacities of my Samoan and Tongan companions.

When the aircraft reached the vicinity of the Marquesas Islands, it dropped in the direction of a pin-cushion of mountain peaks protruding from a boiling blanket of cumulus clouds. I was feeling far from crisp. Flying machine, diligent crew, incredulous passengers, as one we assumed strange and rapidly changing angles in the fog, catching flashing glimpses of rock and vegetation at all points of the compass, before white-knuckling onto a narrow plateau amongst the mountain-tops of Hiva Oa.

Heaving oe'r was then a close-run thing as we tackled the deep-rutted dirt track that served to connect the narrow mountain plateau to the coastal settlement of Atuona. Once again strange, abrupt angles were endured in unison with fellow travellers, as our truck lurched on downwards towards the rocky shore.

We came to a stony beach in the deep grey shadows of mountain-trapped clouds. As if slipped from a Gauguin canvas, bareback riders on small horses slunk by, both ponies and riders bereft of gear but for the floral *pareu* about the riders' hips.

Crunching across beach pebbles, we made our way to a palm-leafed shelter erected for our reception. Speeches were made. Baked fish and pounded breadfruit paste were presented and consumed. Lines of melancholy dancers trooped before the shelter conveying cultural insights.

To be brutally honest, my friend, there was a heavy air about the place. And with or without the ravages of the night before, nothing on Hiva Oa seemed capable of lifting the spirit that day.

311

After the ceremonies, some of us went up into the forest to visit an ancient *marae*, long reclaimed by the roots of giant trees. Standing by lichened stone platforms and rock slabs haunted with countless rituals of human sacrifice, we swatted and cursed as mosquito swarms gorged on our blood.

I wandered off into the trees to find a place to pee. On my way back to our group, I stumbled upon a toothless Marquesan made simple by some accident of birth or life. He was crouching behind the time-ravaged hulk of a *tiki* monolith, peering around its flank of mossy stone, furtively observing my companions. The way he grasped his knees, the lost look on his face, the mystery of his existence, all might have been aptly captured in one of the master's woodcuts.

Before the day ran out, I went to the Calvary cemetery to contemplate Gauguin's grave. It was restful up there among the ordered dead and I sat long in the shade of a frangipani that curled its branches across the artist's earthly end. Surrounded by the scattered ivory of fragrant fallen flowers, I gazed down on the island of Anakee set in the troubled waters of Traitor's Bay, and out over Atuona's red tin roofs blossoming on the thick green canopy of the valley's coconut groves. Every side of the valley but the seafront was fenced in under a gigantic ridge of snaggle-toothed mountains.

The scene below was not always so peaceful. Picking out where the House of Pleasure lay in the lap of the valley, I imagined the artist clinging to his life on the day of the great hurricane,

> At my window, here at Atuona in the Marquesas, everything is growing dark. The dances are ended, the soft melodies have died away. But it is not still. In a crescendo the wind rushes through the branches, the great dance begins, the cyclone is in full swing … the river overflows. The immense breadfruit trees are overthrown, the coconut trees bow their backs and their tops brush the earth. Everything is in flight, rocks, trees, corpses carried down to the sea. What a passionate orgy of the wrathful gods! [135]

For Paul Gauguin that Atuona valley and this green hill were indeed the end of the world, a suitably exotic conclusion to the exile story the artist had so tortuously created. In fact the disgruntled fabulist had wanted it to be otherwise, for he had tired of his barbaric tale and dreamed of returning to Paris to take his paints and brushes on an Iberian adventure. That he wanted out is not surprising, for as in Tahiti, the crux of Gauguin's problems were of his own making. Atuona was full of people whom he'd provoked, *comme d'habitude*, into becoming his bitter enemies.

And for all the valley's soporific calm, I felt an unsettling air above Atuona that day. It was hard to put a finger on, but there was something not quite right about where I sat. The artist had dragged himself to this outpost, a place far removed from the soft South Seas paradise of legend, and in the end it killed him dead.

Up on the crest of the cemetery's hill, I looked at the mound I lingered beside. Scattered with frangipani blossom, it was an impressive grave, obviously embellished over the years as the fame of the artist grew. A metal replica of Gauguin's porcelain figurine Oviri overlooked the plot, a mark in its metal showing it was cast in 1971. Mementos of fans from around the world, shells, flowers, necklaces and notes, decorated the grave's perimeter. The grave itself was made of the great slabs of red volcanic tuff, the rock once sacred to Marquesans, into which a grey river-stone was set. The naturally rounded river-stone was carved with the words 'Paul Gauguin 1903' in an aesthetically rustic script. It was tastefully done, but again, something was out of sync.

In the years that followed, it bothered me that I'd not done the Marquesas justice. I knew from literature they were islands apart, islands demanding a homage I'd not given them in my fleeting earlier visit. So in 2008 I returned, on assignment for Australian Gourmet Traveller magazine, and this time I came by sea, visiting the six main islands of the Marquesas on the vessel *Aranui*, with the gifted photographer Andy Bell as my traveling companion.

Tahiti in our wake, we steamed for two days across the Pacific, with swell rolling in from the southeast, seabirds gliding the lonely troughs and flying fish glittering from wind-blunted crests. Below our hull went the occasional shoal of pelagic fish or a migrating whale suspended in the liquid current; until all the way down, some four thousand metres down, was the land that held up the waters, great oceanic valleys and rutted mountain ranges upon whose peaks the sun never shone.

We raised the lingam peaks of Ua Pou, circled by halo clouds and white-tailed tropicbirds soaring in the thermals. Landfall made, the first member of the remnant Marquesan population I met ashore told me there were thirty-seven varieties of breadfruit on the island. Thirty-seven! Already I was so glad to have come back.

My kindly informant was a lady descended from one of the crew of HMS *Bounty*, and it was her husband who drove us across the mountain to see the *marae* above Hohoi. On the *marae*, before a particularly well-endowed *tiki*, there is a stone slab upon which in times gone by men and women ceremonially consummated their marriages as the tribe looked on. You may run your hand across another of the hoary slabs of the *marae*, on which humans were decapitated, their heads buried in the surrounding house foundations, bones set aside for carvings and needles, skins flayed for tom-toms, and flesh the main course of feasting. Ua Pou was a carnal introduction to the islands ahead.

We steamed on to Tahuata Island to anchor off the village of Omoa and take on cargoes of copra, citrus and noni. A climb up the verdant massif above the village took us in search of the *paepae* house foundations of Pele, the goddess of fire. The ancient platform of stones of the goddess's abode lies there still, among the riotous roots of the dark forest. You may see that each boulder of the platform is moss-wrapped in emerald velvet, and you may listen, just as she did, to the forest's song of birdcalls and rock-dancing waters descending.

Along the craggy coast of Fatu Hiva, we arrived at another valley with another village, Hanavave, echoing to the rush of water over the rock. Here was a jagged caldera rim and a giant Gothic amphitheatre of volcanic escarpments towering into the blue, with feathering waterfalls and eruptions of eroded magma that have created a landscape like no other. The Hanavave caldera is tropic-bird heaven, with invisible up-draught elevators rising to cliff-side

314

nests in their hundreds. Heads craned back, we followed the long-tailed birds turning like fields of ivory crosses against the blue facade of heaven.

But it is Hanavave's stand of giant phalli, erupted and eroded by elemental forces, that make it unforgettable. Giant Gaudiesque stone plugs array along the foreshore and thrust from the hillocks behind. Some are long, some fat, some with a kink here and there, but all are as erect as nature could have hoped for. The early European sailors could think of no more appropriate name for this place than *La Baie des Verges*, the Bay of Cocks.

Off the north coast of Hiva Oa, *Aranui* put down anchor long enough for us to visit the *marae* of Iipona,[136] one of the great archaeological sites of Polynesia. At one end of the *marae* is the Toea Mountain, its cliff-face pockmarked with ledges that until the coming of the Church contained the skulls of the dead and a funerary cave.

Ancient *tiki* up to eight feet tall squat implacably above the broad stone platforms of the Iipona *marae*. Here lies the strange horizontal *tiki*, Makaii Taua Pepe, interpreted by some as being in the act of giving birth.[137] This is indeed a powerful place, so that even for a block of wood like me, standing alone on the Me'ae Iipona, in the shadows of Toea's cliff, there is a strong sense of proximity to spiritual continuums.

Onward to Vaitahu Bay of the island of Tahuata, to share the same anchorage as the bold Spanish navigator, Mendaña, who was to leave his mark and his life in the Solomon Islands. It was 1595 that Mendaña hove by long enough to name the Marquesas Islands for the wife of the viceroy of Peru, the Marquis of Cañete. The locals were unimpressed, blood was shed, and the Christian commander unleashed a cruel cannonade on the villagers as a parting gesture of ill will.

Many a marauding European pirate sailed in on Mendaña's bloody wake; culminating in the all-conquering French admiral Abel Dupetit-Thouars, who chose Tahuata for one of his more sanguinary subjugations of the Marquesans. To this day, there is in Vaitahu village a monument to the Frenchmen who fell in the conquering of Tahuata. There is no such monument for the Marquesan victims; the land speaks for itself.

Of Hapatoni, the other pirogue-fronted village on Tahuata Island, my magazine story reported,

> *Aranui* follows the Tahuata coast, escorted by pods of dolphins, south to the tiny village of Hapatoni. The villagers here are so grateful for the ship's service they insist on presenting a feast of welcome on every visit. Before departure, the drums and guitars are produced, and with post-prandial passengers and crew lounging around under the shade trees, the villagers dance for their guests. This is no slick professional dance troupe; mums and dads and children in everyday work clothes give it their all. A big woman, a boon to the front row of any rugby team, does a graceful *tamure*, and she is joined by one of her relatives who is no more than six years old but knows every hand and foot gesture of the adult dance. The troupe is boosted by other women from the village, one with strong, smooth limbs and a doe-eyed face, stepping straight from a Gauguin canvas.[138]

On the horse-roamed, woodcarver's island of Ua Huka, I went to a little museum to view a modest collection that included two heavily eroded wooden house-post *tiki*, two ornate *ivi po'o*, two whale ivory necklaces, and a funerary box holding an intact human skull.[139] A paved road runs along Ua Huka's inhospitable coast to a windward bay given a degree of shelter by Motu Hane, a giant pyramid rock rising from the sea. On the bay's shore is the village of Hane, and from the breezy beach a lane meanders through the village, past a rusty collection of reeking copra driers.

I took to this lane with joy, threading through cottages garlanded with hedges of hibiscus and bougainvillea, to dine at Chez Céline Fournier and enjoy the finest *poe* the Pacific has to offer.[140] Later I swam between the waves, where fishermen paddled colourful pirogues about the rocky bay, under volcanic cliffs that sang in the steady wind, eery siren songs keening of all things past.

Ua Huka typifies the Marquesas of the twenty-first century. Its population of some five to six hundred souls seems to carry the blood of almost every race known to man and is serviced with more infrastructure - roads, electricity, hospital and modern airport facilities - than any island of comparable population amongst the independent Pacific Island countries. Like the rest of the Marquesas, Ua Huka is largely dependent on the taxpayers of France for the relative comfort of its standard of living.

Idling on the waterfront in conversation with the locals, it appeared they liked things the way they were. Unlike the Protestant Tahitians, the Marquesans are Catholic and when asked, most said if Tahiti voted to become independent from France, they would detach their fate from that of their southern cousins.

And what of that heavy, despondent air, that dolefulness I'd felt on my first visit to Hiva Oa? Now that I knew the Marquesas a little better, did I feel it still? To be true to myself, the answer was yes, even as I spied here and there an uplifting dissipation in my fog.

Geography is the quiddity. The Marquesas sit on the ancient Polynesian canoeway between Hawaii and Tahiti, and are still the first port-of-call for sailors coming south and west from the Americas. This convenience of station was the undoing of Marquesan society, for there are few places in the Pacific where the islanders suffered as much from the familiar depredations of tribal warfare, cannibalism, gun-toting explorers, foreign diseases, fornicating sailors, flag-planting navies, over-zealous missionaries and gin-trading capitalists. When the French seized these islands in 1842, the Marquesans numbered some one hundred thousand souls; that number was culled by disease and lassitude to just two thousand by the year 1920.

The island topography is as daunting as its history. Were it not for the equatorial heat and the coconut trees, a castaway could be pardoned for thinking he was washed up on rocky emanations in the wild South Atlantic. No coral reefs, no sheltered lagoons, no strands of soft white sand, just as Melville put it in his novel Typee,

... bold rockbound coasts, with the surf beating high against the lofty cliffs, and broken here into deep inlets, which open to the view thickly-wooded valleys, separated by the spurs of mountains clothed with tufted grass. [141]

Since Melville's time, the tufted grass has largely gone. The towering flanks of land have been laid bare, thanks to the introduction of scrawny omnivorous goats and feral ponies.

A perceptive young American yachtsman put it this way when in 1934 he dropped anchor in Nuku Hiva's Taiohae Bay. After a visit ashore the crew returned to their yacht, lonely in the bay, and assessed what they had seen, while ...

... smoking East Indian tobacco, occasionally breaking the quiet to talk of the strange disappearance of the proud Marquesan, the fearless Islander. As had many Americans before us, we unhesitatingly blamed the French - blamed them for bringing indentured Chinese, who in turn brought leprosy and plague to wipe out whole villages, as well as the introduction of smallpox and tuberculosis that had left Tai-o-hae a ghost village, inhabited for the most part by people of other islands. A great race had fallen to the acquisitive lust of the North, succumbed to its marshaled commercialism, which is seldom better than it has to be, succumbed particularly to the French - at least, so we thought, ignorant that it was Peruvians, not the popularly criticized French, brought smallpox, that it was an American who marooned a sailor in the last stages of tuberculosis on Fatu Hiva, and another American who was responsible for importing the diseased Chinese labour. And yet it seems that the Marquesas did not fall before the malice of any particular individuals or governments, but rather were dissolved away before a great system that must have power before the reaction of philanthropy can set in, wealth before dignity, heaped warehouses before nobility; a system touching not only here, but penetrating almost every square mile of a once contented tropics.[142]

Before I left the Marquesas, I went back to the Calvary cemetery above Atuona for a last look at Gauguin's grave. It was as I'd seen it fifteen years earlier, only with more pilgrim mementos now strewn about it. The enchantment of the scene remained true, but still there was something about this place that did not fit.

In 1918, the writer Frederick O'Brien had trudged up to the cemetery, in the company of an Atuona acquaintance, to seek out the artist's final resting place. He leaves us this account,

> To find Gauguin's grave we began at the entrance and searched row by row. The graves were those of natives, mounds marked by small stones along the sides, with crosses of rusted iron filigree showing skulls and other symbols of death, and a name painted in white, mildewing away ... Holien and Maui had advertisement of their last mortal residence, but not Gauguin ... the grave of Gauguin, the great painter, was unmarked. If a board had been placed at its head when he was buried, it had rotted away, and nothing was left to indicate where he was lying.[143]

There was veracity in these words, for the church officials could have had no love for a man who'd publicly portrayed the local bishop as a lascivious devil and who'd preyed on the sex of the island's adolescents. Once the church had done what was required of it, depositing Gauguin's Catholic remains in their cemetery, they would have had little or no reason to bother with maintaining his grave. But why, one wondered, would they have allocated a hillcrest plot, in such pride of place, to their rancorous enemy?

When I met Marcel in Tahiti and posed him this question, he answered me with a little story. He once went to Hiva Oa to attend a ceremony honoring his grandfather and took with him a small marble plaque that he'd had made for the grave as a remembrance from Gauguin's Tahitian family. He was able to show me the modest plaque, for he'd brought it back to his house in Tahiti.

He said the mayor of Hiva Oa had not agreed to the plaque being placed on the grave and was given no good reason why. However he was not too concerned about the Atuona rejection, for when he was standing by the grave in Calvary cemetery, an old Marquesan man had approached him and told him his grandfather wasn't buried in that place. The old man said that when Gauguin died he was at war with the priests and was accordingly allocated a plot down in the gully at the edge of the cemetery.

To illustrate the real burial site, Marcel sketched me a diagram with his grandfather's putative grave on the crest of the hill. The sketch showed that if you stand on that crest to face the sea, the place where the old man claimed Gauguin's remains were actually laid, was down the slope to the left.

Marcel shrugged it off philosophically with a '*C'est la vie.*'

The art historians and the moneyed collectors and the museums of the North are looking after Monsieur Gauguin's legacy, even as an honest grandson dedicates himself to Tahitian panaceas for the well-being of his ancestor's spirit. In life the artist suffered much; but all is well now, for art is long and his works are exalted. Evermore the patterns of the landscapes will provoke, so too the shapes of the people moving through them; the dreaming women staring out from the canvas, how they bathe, how they gossip, how they bear fruit and flowers.

And the spirits of the dead are there as well, they too are still watching. I turn to face them, not in fear of the unknown, but in reverence and with thanks, knowing they too suffered for this art we have made our own. To them I lay down this tribute of admiration to their sacrifice, to the poxy dispossessions that came with their reclining to be painted in the boudoir of the beautiful palace. Let Teha'amana, Pohu'ura, Vaiohe, and the other generous princesses, the *vahine no te tiare* who gifted to art the joyousness of their young lives and the glowing gold of their bodies, be revered as long as art survives. Thank you for ever, *maururu roa*. May you live, *ia orana*.

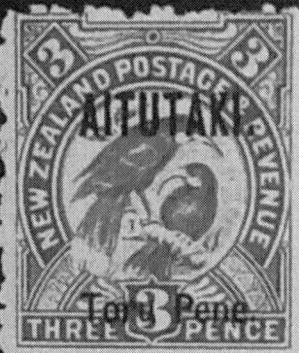

Scribbles in Sand

A writer will do most anything in the cause of literature. Asked by a Hollywood television company to strip to budgie-smugglers and come wading from the Wakaya lagoon, soliloquising on the theme of an up-coming series on the Pacific Islands, I unashamedly complied. As the camera whirred and the director waved me forward through the obliging tide, I gave a performance exuding such enthusiasm and expressions of dubious scholarship as to make David Attenborough crow with delight. No doubt for the betterment of all, it turned out Hollywood was less impressed by what they saw on screen than had been so enthusiastically predicted to me.

During that unrewarded flight of fantasy, I was also persuaded to pen the pitch for a thirteen episode TV series on the Islands. For several months I scratched my beard and scribbled notes, and in the end produced a detailed outline for the series, including the various locations where the episodes would be shot. I named one episode *The View from Bali Hai* for it would tell the story of the American impact on the islands during the Second World War from the perspective of the Pacific Islanders. *Yankee Whalers* would have been fun to film; so too *When Copra was King*, and *Kava in the Blood*.

Then there was an episode dubbed *Scribbles in the Sand*. The plan was to follow the Pacific Island pathways of some famous writers from the North as they fossicked about in hapless search for their version of paradise.

All that effort was not in vain, for recycled below are some of the vignettes that would have appeared on film in that literary episode. If what follows ends up reading like an essay for an English Lit exam, try and imagine it on the small screen, with sufficient exotic footage to entertain your drifting concentration.

On my ankle I carry a tattoo representing a whale-shark fishhook. It was put there by a traditional tattooist in Tahiti on the advice of a Polynesian friend of mine. The same man put the romantic tradition of Tahiti and its surrounding islands up for debate when he told me in heavy Franco-Polynesian accent, 'Pee-terre, the 'ole world 'as come 'ere to ferk us.'

You have to ask why that has been so, how it happened that eating the lotus in Tahiti became the idyll of love-in-the-raw for generations of Europeans and Americans? The answer has its beginnings in the 1771 travel report of the Comte de Bougainville, in which he refers to Tahiti as *La Nouvelle Cythère*, the Mediterranean island of Cythère being the birthplace of the Greek goddess of love. For with the publication of the flowery Bougainvillean account, the Polynesian romance was launched, and consideration of the noble savage's careless promiscuity provoked a sweet torment in the imagination of the North.

That torment of innocent promiscuity in the Islands has been hard to shake, for the fertile furrows of wishful European thinking were ready for the seed. Montaigne had turned the sod, Voltaire and Rousseau scattered on the fertilizer, and an ever-randy public harvested these fields of fantasy, eager for a gratuitous piece of the fructification.

A secondary question may also be considered: was *La Nouvelle Cythère* really the remote temple of free love it was held out to be? From the pages of the nineteenth and twentieth centuries, bevies of philosophising botanists, lusty mariners and highly refined bull-artistes chorus an affirmative response. But in the fading echoes of their words, a suspicion lurks. It suggests that all along, the island was just being exploited as a convenient nautical knock-shop.

To ream the elusive truth, there are libraries of heavy tomes to consult. The ink-slingings of navigators, anthropologists, missionaries, travel writers and novelists, fill the Pacific bibliography with their accounts of Tahiti. The authors are drawn to the island of love by a wide variety of personal compulsions, but for the majority of them, the relatively-free-love-for-all is the be-poxed theme.

It's a rather a limp conclusion to the two questions, but you can at least conclude that a long troupe of horny writers, mainly with an eye to getting by, have been the perpetuators of Tahiti's romantic idyll. Their suggestive scribblings having taken *La Nouvelle Cythère* and spun it for as long as the yearners of the North have maintained their desire. For while romance's flood must always abate, as sure as the tide, it will swell and swell again. Let us have a look at what some of them wrote.

Herman Melville is widely touted as the greatest writer the Pacific Islands have produced. A New Yorker by birth, Melville came to the Pacific on a whaling ship in 1841 and was variously employed as a clerk in Honolulu, a harpooner on a Yankee whaler, and as a beachcomber in Tahiti. Then he returned to America in 1844, never again to set foot in the South Seas. It is thus rather a stretch to say he is a product of the Islands.

In the course of young Melville's Pacific experience, he jumped ship at Nuku Hiva in the Marquesas and was supposedly adopted by a cannibal tribe. An account of this experience is related in the splendid travel narrative *Typee*. For all the writer's muscular morality, *Typee* leans to the popular-fabulous, as displayed in the account of his arrival in the Marquesas.

After six months at sea, Melville's reeking whaler enters a Nuku Hiva anchorage. Still some distance from the beach, the ship approaches a shoal of naked Marquesan girls swimming out to greet the sailors, the long dark hair of each girl trailing behind as they swim, tapa girdles held aloft in elegant hands.[144]

Melville recounts that the whaler sailed 'right into the midst of these swimming nymphs and they boarded us at every quarter.' I don't wish to be too pedantic here, but have you ever tried to get from the water to the deck of a ship without a ladder of some sort, particularly when it is underway? Think nigh on impossible, think Natalie Wood drowning off Catalina.

Physics aside, Melville assures us that,

> all of them at length succeeded in getting up the ship's side, where they clung dripping from the brine and glowing from the bath, their jet-black tresses streaming from their shoulders, and half enveloping their otherwise naked forms.

The girls dry themselves, anoint firm bodies with fragrant oil and string flimsy belts of tapa about their waists, before amorously disporting upon the bowsprit and bulwarks of the whaler. John Murray published *Typee* in London in 1846, more than a century before the likes of Hugh Heffner titillated their way into publishing. Consider now the stretching of starch, the bulging of Victorian imagination, upon reading Melville's ensuing words. For the girls, Melville tells us, were 'easily led into every vice', so that 'the grossest licentiousness and the most shameful inebriety prevailed' for the remainder of the ship's stay in the Marquesas.

> Their appearance perfectly amazed me; their extreme youth, the light clear brown of their complexions, their delicate features, and inexpressibly graceful figures, their softly molded limbs ... wholly given up to every species of riot and debauchery. Not the feeblest barrier was interposed between the unholy passions of the crew and their unlimited gratification.

Rest awhile savage heart! 'Extreme youth?' Back in the parlours of London and Boston, this may have been entertaining stuff, but 'extreme youth'? Today it sounds too like the beginnings of a traffic that continues to this day in countries like Thailand; namely, paedophiles of the northern hemisphere coming south to gratify urges that would be criminal acts at home.

Reading Melville's words bring on thoughts of the vile venereal consequences of rutting with the riff-raff of the Atlantic's waterfront. These thoughts are deflating in the extreme, when you consider the Marquesan race came close to extermination as a result of these and other introduced diseases.

And so to Rupert Brooke, who wrote the lines so loved in the public schools of England,

> If I should die, think this of me:
> That there's some corner of a foreign field
> That is forever England.[145]

How an English corpse provides richer dust than the rest of us, is not quite explained, but a writer must eat and that sort of sentiment sold at the time.

For a rather small body of work on the subject, Rupert has a sure place in any discourse on romantic writers in the South Pacific. And there is indeed enough in Brooke's fray through the Pacific to show that while he was playing to the refined prejudice of an English audience, the young man was beginning to see the world in a different light. He wrote to a friend that he'd acquired 'a rich red-brown for my skin, a knowledge of mixed drinks, an ability to talk or drink with any kind of man.' Welcome to the Islands, Rupert.

He sojourned along the same Mataiea coast that was Gauguin's home two decades before. The American writer, Frederick O'Brien, joined him there. *In Mystic Isles of the South Seas*, O'Brien describes his daily swims with the English poet,

> The water was four or five fathoms deep, dazzling in the vibrance
> of the Southern sun, and Brooke, a brilliant blonde, gleamed in
> the violet radiancy like a dream figure of ivory.[146]

In accord with the romantic idyll, they always swam in the buff; but this fact leads O'Brien to make an observation that rather over-turns all the noble savage voyeurism of earlier writers,

> We remarked that while we plunged into the sea bare, Tahitians
> never went completely nude, and they were more modest in hid-
> ing their nakedness than any white people we had ever met.

Swept up in their dazzling adventure, it never occurs to the northern visitors they should respect local sensibilities and put some clothes on.

The First World War was about to bring darkness to a whole generation of Rupert Brooke's countrymen, but in far-off Tahiti romance was in the air and Rupert was engaged in perhaps the most consummated love affair of his brief life. She was a Polynesian beauty to whom he wrote love-letters as his ship sailed from the Pacific, away to the gathering of European storms and his fatal encounter with a Mediterranean mosquito. It is for her that the eternal love poem *Tiare Tahiti* is penned, for her that hearts are swelled by romance's tide, before the long dry pickings of the ebb ahead,

> Mamua, there waits a land
> Hard for us to understand
> Out of time, beyond the sun,
> All are one in Paradise …

My home town, Suva, the deep-harboured capital of Fiji, was a port of transit for the big-note writers who made their way to the Islands. From our house at the entry to the Government Domain, a box-cart ride down Cakobau Hill brought you under the arched porte-cochère of the Grand Pacific Hotel, a palatial, white waterfront pile with deep verandahs, turbaned waiters, polished brass and silver, and many a creaking cane chair.

In 1953, the GPH hosted a State Ball for Queen Elizabeth, her nocturnal arrival escorted by two hundred Fijian warriors with flaming torches in their hands. American royalty frequented the place as well - Burt Lancaster was filmed there in the title role of *His Majesty O'Keefe*. In later days, local queens were easier to come by, for it seemed the hotel's owner, who was also for a while our country's minister of finance, had a penchant for royal mincers. No visit to the GPH was possible at that time, without one falling under the heavily-manicured eye of one of these elegant floor-gliders.

Earlier in the piece, Somerset Maugham had stayed at the Grand Pacific Hotel. He took tea, smoked a lot of cigarettes and casting a jaundiced eye over the scene is said to have remarked, 'Grand? Perhaps. Pacific? Yes. Hotel? No.'

With the slightly wounded chagrin of hometown boy defending a dearly-held Suva icon, I seek in vain for a peppery retort to Somerset before he buggers off back to Britain. But today one is forced to concur, for the GPH is but a teetering façade, nothing grand about it at all. Someone sold our town's finest to the Nauruans, back in the days when the latter were still up to their necks in phosphate dollars. Under the absentee proprietorship of these Micronesian sheiks, the GPH sadly devolved into a gutted ruin.

Further along Suva's waterfront, a half-mile stroll from the GPH under the now-demolished shade trees of Victoria Parade, was MacDonald's Hotel. A venerably-verandahed pub, MacDonald's sat opposite the art deco façade of the Regal Theatre, and was replaced after the Pacific War by a modern building named the Victoria Arcade. Looking at these names, one is reminded we were a very monarchist Crown Colony, and Rupert Brooke took the micky accordingly. In his letters home, he described Suva as a queer place, much civilised,

> 'full of English people who observe the Rules of Etiquette, and call on third Thursdays.'

Only an Englishman would know what the hell that was all about, so moving right along, we can at least say strongly in Brooke's favour that the poet took the trouble to see far more of the country than Maugham did; even if in doing so, Brooke found Fiji 'macabre'. Rupert trekked up into the same rugged Namosi hill country of which I was the district officer some sixty years later. There he slept in remote Fijian villages where cannibal feasts had been a feature of life in earlier days and he was greatly provoked by accounts of Fijians cutting pieces off live victims, to cook and eat before them. In the dim light of a thatched hut, he put pen to crumpled paper, 'surrounded by dusky faces and gleaming eyes,' to compose a sonnet for Violet Asquith in which he places parts of himself within the pot,

Of the two eyes that were your ruin,
One now observes the other stewing.[147]

Fiji's cannibal past teased the muse of Mark Twain too. In the American satirist's *The Tragedy of Pudd'nhead*, is this homily for America's Thanksgiving Day,

> Let us all give humble, hearty and sincere thanks now, but turkeys. In the island of Fiji they do not use turkeys; they use plumbers. It does not become you and me to sneer at Fiji.[148]

Twain visited Fiji briefly in 1895, in the course of a world cruise. His circuit of the globe is covered in Twain's last book, *Following the Equator*, in which he gives this artistic description of the maritime approach to Suva,

> Yesterday we passed close to an island or so, and recognized the published Fiji characteristics: a broad belt of clean white coral sand around the island; back of it a graceful fringe of leaning palms, with native huts nestling cosily among the shrubbery at their bases; back of these a stretch of level land clothed in tropic vegetation; back of that, rugged and picturesque mountains. A detail of the immediate foreground: a mouldering ship perched high up on a reef-bench. This completes the composition, and makes the picture artistically perfect. In the afternoon we sighted Suva, the capital of the group, and threaded our way into the secluded little harbour – a placid basin of brilliant blue and green water tucked snugly in among sheltering hills.[149]

Twain tours Suva by foot, remarking on the handsome, muscular, clean-limbed, dusky men with faces full of character and intelligence. He writes of young Fijian women, tall and comely, nobly built, sweeping by with chin up and a gait 'incomparable for unconscious stateliness and dignity'.

> We strolled about the streets of the white folks little town, and around and over the hills by paths and roads among European

dwellings and gardens and plantations, and past clumps of hibiscus that made a body blink, the great blossoms were so intensely red …

In Suva Twain dines with local worthies, has his health toasted, makes not one, but two humorous speeches in reply, plays billiards, and pays a call upon the governor.[150] When he is driven up to meet the 'Head of State', the American thinks he's being taken to the governor's 'country residence.' An inebriated tourist can be readily excused such a mistake, for in those early Suva days, Government House did sit at the edge of the clapboard colonial township. At Government House he is mostly preoccupied by the great size, exotic dress and kingly dignity of the governor's Fijian butler; but the writer finds time to avert his gaze and describe Government House's prospect over Suva Harbour.

> There is a noble and beautiful view of ocean and islands and castellated peaks from the governor's high-placed house, and its immediate surroundings lie drowsing in that dreamy repose and serenity which are the charm of life in the Pacific Islands.

Twain takes leave of Suva, writing in his journal, 'we sailed again, much refreshed'. As he crosses the ocean Aotearoa-bound, he writes that the islands in his wake are,

> … the very home of romance and dreams and mystery. The loveliness, the solemnity, the beauty, and the deep repose of this wilderness have a charm which is all their own for the bruised spirit of men who have fought and failed in the struggle for life in the great world …

In 1895, Twain's alter-ego Samuel Clemens was licking his wounds from some bad publishing investments that had led him to bankrupt times. Like Bill Clinton, another bruised, never-say-die Southerner, Clemens was a celebrated public speaker and was making good money from the recycling of past fame and the exercise of a silver tongue. After his Suva refreshment, adoring audiences awaited him around the globe.

In 1909, Jack London sailed into Suva harbour with his gutsy wife Charmian. They were cruising the South Seas, which is always a thousand times harder than it sounds, in their ketch, the *Snark*. The cruise proved the *Snark* to be something of a Boojum.

> But oh, beamish nephew, beware of the day,
> If your Snark be a Boojum! For then
> You will softly and suddenly vanish away,
> And never be met with again.[151]

From Jack's Fiji sojourn comes his short tale, *The Whale Tooth,* a fictionalized account of Reverend Baker's actual experience of being clubbed and cooked in the hinterlands of Viti Levu. The missionary had proselytised a bridge too far, up in the untamed hill country of Fiji's main island.

London's passage to Fiji from Samoa had been confounded by storm and reef, so that while in Suva, Jack is popularly thought to have been much too preoccupied with sacking his worthless captain, upskilling on navigational matters, and refurbishing his awkward ketch, to have given much thought to our charming harbour-town. But allow me to correct history's cursory treatment of the London visit; for Jack had a good time in Suva, he liked the place. I can infer this from some papers in my possession which give a better account - the papers in question being the unpublished memoirs of AG Griffiths, the proprietor of The Fiji Times.

On arrival in Suva, having narrowly missed nocturnal yacht-on-reef-complete-disaster scenarios during the sail from Samoa, Jack went straight to the offices of The Fiji Times looking to purchase Admiralty charts. Arthur Griffiths met him there and wrote afterwards,

> Jack turned with an inquiring look towards me and I was immediately and favorably impressed with his very friendly face. His wavy hair seemed to match his large, open, blue eyes and it did not take long to feel that he was worth meeting. We were soon good friends and with Jentz, my wife, and Charmian we formed a happy foursome.[152]

The Griffiths took the Londons pigeon-shooting in the surrounding Nasinu countryside and they enjoyed meals together. London was a good guy who debated at length with Jentz, a fellow bookworm, on the strength of environment over heredity and other mental teasers. He sent the Griffiths letters on his travels thereafter, writing to them from Sydney about the world heavyweight boxing fight held between Burns and Johnson, saying that Charmian was the only woman present at the contest. Yes, Jack really liked Suva, at least I like to think he did.

When Jack died too young and was laid to rest in the Valley of the Moon, Arthur said he was left with a lump in his throat, 'for Jack was a very lovable man.' Their ships had not passed in the night, they had met and become friends in Suva.

As a marginal post-script to this memorial, I recall that the Burns-Johnson bout was fought at Rushcutters Bay on the southern shores of Sydney harbour, a few hundred metres from where I am now writing these words. If I close my eyes and listen hard enough to the whispering ripples of time, I can almost hear Charmian London's cheers.

It would be mighty fine to be buried in a place like the Valley of the Moon, but if you couldn't get there in time, the Waverley Cemetery on the Sydney cliffs would make an excellent alternative. Sitting high above the surf just south of Bondi Beach, the view from the cemetery out over the Tasman Sea is stupendous. I walked there recently to pay homage at the grave of another Pacific writer, that of Mr Louis Becke.

'Louis who?' most every Australian says. Yet in his day, just a century ago, the dinkum Aussie yarner, Louis Becke, was the man. 'The Rudyard Kipling of the Pacific' the British press knew him as, his work lauded by the likes of Joseph Conrad, Mark Twain and James Michener. No writer of quality stories set in the Pacific Islands was more prolific, and in nineteenth century literary terms, from Valparaiso to far Palau, Becke owned the beach. And that's just it, for the nineteenth century beach is a long way from the sanitized way we see things today.

In Becke's time, island life was as coarse as the sand of the shore-line, so too its language and the characters who prowled it. True to that world he knew so well, were Louis's stories. He was big on Samoan curses, severed heads, gin at five dollars a case, the merits of Manihikian women over other island wives ... let's just say it's mostly material that's not in vogue these days.

For twenty years Becke had hung about the Islands: as a stowaway to Samoa, a supercargo for the notorious freebooter Bully Hayes, a gun-runner, blackbirder and wooer of island women. He was shipwrecked in the Carolines and in the Gilberts, he survived a Queensland trial for piracy, suffered hurricanes, rotting hulks and hard tack, tropical fevers and many a physical attack. He was a trader in the Ellice Islands, New Britain and the Marshalls. He sailed to more Pacific Islands than most of us can name, until the time came when he sailed no more and sat down for the last twenty years of his life to record all those unrefined stories. Louis Becke died in the saddle, in 1913 in a Sydney hotel toiling over his next manuscript. The obituary in Australia's Bulletin magazine read, 'In his strenuous period his favourite recreation was whale fishing.'

It's a pity Louis wasn't buried in Ponape or Apia, or one of the islands where the tourist trade jets us today. Were it so, his grave would have featured in the travel guides, would have become an attraction, and Louis Becke may have been better remembered. Let writers with posthumous aspirations take note - choose one's burial place with careful forethought.

As for Louis's place of birth - Port Macquarie, half way up the coast of New South Wales - it's not surprising there is no monument to him there. Becke wrote of his home town,

> 'It was built by convict hands in the days of the cruel system and nothing but an earthquake or a big fire will ever improve it.'

Becke flashed his quill for the adventure-hungry readership of the greatest empire the world had known. But then just as remarkable as the global breadth of that empire's dominion, was the alacrity with which it unraveled and with which we have all disassociated from its memories. It is in the mists of that denial that Becke's books have been swallowed up - thirty-five of them in all. Yet still, you sometimes come across someone, a grizzled yachtie maybe, a pickled writer perhaps, who you notice carries under his arm a battered copy of *Reef and Palm*.[153]

There is a town in Fiji, Levuka, the old capital, where the ghosts of Louis's days shadow the sleepy waterfront. It was a mariner's town, founded in *beche-de-mer* days, sustained by whalers, pearlers and traders of gin. Long my favourite town in all the Islands, I hesitate to return, for lately opportunist political provocateurs have let loose the dogs of arson, turning to cinder the charms of some of Levuka's finest buildings. Had I a Samoan curse at hand, I would bring it down upon them, but I calm myself by softly recalling a song in its praise,

> *Sai Levuka ga, au nanuma tu*
> *Na kena vei lasa kece.*
> *E na noqu tu, ka raica lesu,*
> *Rui kamica dina vei au.*

Vinaka Rusiate.[154] Since those who loved you left your shore, Levuka, many moons have peeked down from the looming mountain. Among those who wandered your frangipani lanes was Louis Becke, who strewed many stories about you - the tale of *Billy Maclaggan and the Fiji Ram* is one that springs to mind. You haven't heard, or did you just forget? Let me touch on another then, entitled '*Tis in the Blood*, it was the first published story Louis wrote. It begins with the words,

> We were in Manton's Hotel at Levuka – Levuka in her palmy days. There were Robertson, of the barque *Rotumah*; a fat German planter from the Yasawa group; Harry the Canadian, a trader from the Tokelaus – and myself.

Yes, have one for me boys, have one for me in the palmy days of old Levuka.

Melville, Becke, London, Brooke and Maugham, all of these writers had one thing in common; they arrived at their islands by sea - the first three by sail, the latter two by steam. There was another writer whose experience of the Islands was heavily maritime, Robert Louis Stevenson, *Tusitala* to the Samoans, the teller of stories. He sailed so much of the Pacific, including landfalls in Hawaii, the Marquesas, the Tuamotus, Tahiti, the Gilberts and Samoa, that when you read him on the impact of the first South Seas Island being like first love, a memory apart, you may be assured it is because he arrived by sea.

Read Stevenson's opening paragraph to *The Beach of Falesá* and you're with him at dawn on the deck of his schooner,

> I saw that island first when it was neither night nor morning. The moon was to the west, setting but still broad and bright. To the east, and right amidships of the dawn, which was all pink, the daystar sparkled like a diamond. The land breeze blew in our faces, and smelt strong of wild lime and vanilla …[155]

It is the magic of literature that such a moment can forever be enjoyed, first in the writer's recollection and then by successive generations of readers. For such elusive alchemy, many writers find sufficient reason to write. Before the gale blows us away, time allows us to put pen to paper and, like RLS, perpetuate a moment in saying, 'I was there, I saw that.'

The climb from the Stevenson home at Vailima, up the Road of Loving Hearts, to the summit of Mount Vaea is arduous in the heat. At that high place, under the wide and starry sky, lies the shared grave of Robert Louis and Fanny Stevenson. The way up is a steep muddy track, narrow and beset with tree roots, that was cut through the dripping jungle by the strong arms and loving hearts of five hundred Samoans. You too are dripping profusely by the time you reach the summit. When Jack and Charmian London reached it, hand-in-hand, Jack panted, 'I wouldn't have gone out of my way to visit the grave of any other man in the world.'

Somerset Maugham also made the Mount Vaea pilgrimage while in Samoa; let's face it, for a visiting writer not to do so would be inexcusably negligent. As far as I know, what Maugham pronounced on reaching the summit is not recorded. Maybe, preoccupied as he was by the heavy rain he encountered in the Samoas, he said something along the lines of, 'Wide? Perhaps. Sky? Yes. Starry? No.'

On the subject of Somerset Maugham in the Samoas, it is in Pago Pago, in America's Samoan colony, that his most famous short story, *Rain*, is set. The wanton Sadie Thompson of that 'morality sketch' was in real life a fellow-passenger with Maugham on the steamer that carried them south from Honolulu. At sea he did not deign to speak with her, though he noticed her 'long white boots from which her calves, in white stockings, bulged.' When forced by circumstance to put up in a dilapidated Pago Pago boarding house, Maugham invites you, in *A Writer's Notebook*, to imagine his chagrin when he finds Ms Thompson ensconced in the adjoining room.[156] 'You men! You filthy dirty pigs!' he has her say in *Rain*.

Eventually Maugham is able to flee the proximity of Ms Thompson and Pago Pago's incessant downpours by catching the ferry to Apia and a steamer to Suva. In flight from scary white woman, he continues his study of the deleterious effect of the tropical climate on white men and 'the soul-eroding effects of succumbing to the sexual proclivities of native women.' *Au revoir, Monsieur* Maugham.

Like Jack London, Stevenson came to the islands with his wife; not for these two the chasing of nymphs around *La Nouvelle Cythère*. That fact, coupled with Stevenson's pre-established reputation in the literary world and his involvement in Island society, meant he was able to form meaningful bonds with Samoan friends. Considering these friendships and the generally convivial nature of his life at Vailima, there is in his Pacific writing an element which perplexes me. In the manner of Becke, the characters of his island stories speak the hard language of the beach, referring for example to Polynesians as 'Kanakas', a term long since dropped from South Pacific terminology. That is fair enough, if it was true to the times, and the Polynesians no doubt had colourful vernacular of their own to describe the over-dressed pale-skins. But it is the theme of the woeful fate of 'half-castes' that is out of whack for me.

It was an inevitable consequence of the romantic idyll of the Pacific Islands, put bluntly, to lay down with a dusky maiden as soon after landfall as possible, that mixed-race progeny would result. How disingenuous then to extol the former and regret the latter! *The Beach of Falesá* is a good example of this recurring colonial theme and is perhaps indicative of why the literature of RLS and Becke is not much read in the Pacific today.

The story in question is an RLS swashbuckler, but with a charming love story interwoven between a European trader and a Polynesian woman. They marry and live happily ever after, but the last paragraph of the story is a discordant postscript on the pariah status of 'half-castes.'

It is a perplexing bit of hand-wringing for RLS to end with, and I wager he'd greatly regret it today. After all, the progeny of these love-children have been at the heart of Island society ever since, with at least half a dozen Island nations being led by people of mixed descent in post-colonial times. Such language doesn't ring true with Stevenson's own lifestyle in Samoa; and it is only when you read *Vailima Letters* that you come to understand he added the discordant ending to *The Beach of Falesá* to satisfy the prudish demands of his publishers, and what he calls 'that great, hulking, bullering whale, the public.'

In February 1892, he writes to his friend, the art and literary critic Sidney Colvin,

> The Beach of Falesá I still think well of, but it seems it's immoral and there's a to-do, and financially it may prove a heavy disappointment … this is a poison bad world for the romancer, this Anglo-Saxon world …
> I feel despair weigh upon my wrists.[157]

Happily Samoa brings peace and an extension of years beyond what the consumptive writer had been led to expect. His troubled paternal relationship is laid to rest, even as his own emaciated form prepares for its imminent end.

> I have come so far; and the sights and thoughts of my youth pursue me; and I see like a vision the youth of my father, and of his

father, and the whole stream of lives flowing down there far in the north, with the sound of laughter and tears, to cast me out in the end, as by a sudden freshet, on these ultimate islands. And I admire and bow my head before the romance of destiny.

From that same freshet came my family and through its flow the mellow Scots voice of my father reading bedtime stories from the pen of Tusitala, ever his favourite author. Let me hear that voice once more,

Fifteen men on The Dead Man's Chest -
Yo-ho-ho, and a bottle of rum!
Drink and the devil had done for the rest -
Yo-ho-ho, and a bottle of rum!

If in the long journey from Bougainville to RLS, you think *La Nouvelle Cythère* sank beneath the waves, look again, for Bali Hai is calling. James Michener's purple prose won him a Pulitzer Prize for *Tales of the South Pacific*, Rogers and Hammerstein went stratospheric with the musical version, and still the name Bali Hai hangs over more Pacific bars, night-clubs and massage parlours than any other you can think of. The Bali Hai phenomenon was Comte de Bougainville and his horny sailors all over again, only this time the force was with the US Marines.

Michener takes his hero across the waves to Bali Hai, a garden island, populated by eager women, where outriggers gather in welcome and bells ring out at your arrival. In the recycled Cythèrean tradition, most of the inhabitants are adolescent and Michener gets his rocks off repeatedly blathering on about melon-like mammaries of Melanesian maids on the pier. He finds time for conical breasts, firm bosoms, fine and thrusting breasts ... in summary, 'their breasts disturbed him mightily.'[158]

As a brief aside, this reminds me of my first boss in the Fiji civil service, a heavy-set Rotuman with a cigarette-holder ever clamped between his teeth. He was chairing a crowded development committee meeting in Nausori when someone mentioned the possibility of tourism development in our district. My boss slammed the table in a fit of anger, sparks flying from the cigarette-butt wedged into the end of his holder. 'Tourists! Bah! All they want is to see our womens' tits!' A young Fijian colleague caught my eye across the table and winked suggestively.

Inevitably in the South Pacific you hear questions and theories about Michener's prototype for Bali Hai. No doubt the possibility of a hidden Shangri-la lurks on in the male imagination. The way Bali Hai is portrayed of late, you'd think it was Moorea, Borabora or Rarotonga, one of those Polynesian high islands where grass skirts are forever swaying. But you'd be wrong, because Bali Hai was irrefutably Melanesian, overlaid with Anglo-French colonial authority.

At the time of the Pacific War, the New Hebrides was an Anglo-French condominium and as a result indentured labour was able to be imported by French planters from the French Indo-Chinese province of Tonkin-China. Michener's marines call them 'Tonks' and the most memorable of all his characters, Bloody Mary, was a betel-nut-chewing Tonk. Somehow the heresy arose that Aggie Grey in Samoa was the model for Bloody Mary, but there's just no similarity between the two, and anyway Samoa wasn't on Michener's beat, his war being spent on Norfolk Island, New Caledonia and the New Hebrides.

I found myself in the New Hebrides, now called Vanuatu, towards the end of the last century. I was there to talk up trade in vanilla, kava and taro. I went up to the well-endowed northern island, Espiritu Santo, where the Coconut War, pretty much forgotten by all but Melanesia, was fought out in 1980. The island's only town of note, Luganville, showed no scars from the Coconut War, but evoked the ghosts of World War Two at every turn. From the outset it could be seen to be a Seabee job, with a long straight road running along the foreshore, Quonset huts to one side and rusting American war-machines hulked into the tidal flats at the other.

There were two hundred thousand US servicemen living around Luganville during the Pacific War and Michener was one of them. Walking down its foreshore today, you can almost hear the American jibes and Bloody Mary's 'fo'dolla, fo'dolla' from under the banyan trees.

By chance I met a planter out in the glare and heat of the town's long street, and went with him to yarn for a while in a foreshore café under the welcome shade of a mango tree. He said that his house, a few miles out of town, was owned by a French planter during the war and that the Frenchman had let Michener use it for writing jags. He said the house was octagonal, just like Emile de Becque's place, and that during the war there'd been a brothel on the plantation foreshore run by a Tonkinese madam, the model for Bloody Mary. He said that from the house you could see the island of Ambae, sometimes so close you could almost touch it, and sometimes it wasn't there at all, drifting in and out of view depending on the weather and the haze of surrounding volcanoes. The planter said that once on his travels he'd met Michener and the writer confirmed that Ambae was indeed his prototype for Bali Hai.

Now I see that tourism promoters are making the same claim for the island. Yes, tourism has made a small beach-head on Bali Hai. But trouble is brewing on the special island, for Ambae's dormant volcano has recently come to life.

In spite of the tourism industry's desperate efforts to resuscitate the image, it seems *La Nouvelle Cythère's* tide is on the way out. Indigenous writers from the Islands hold the idyll in scorn. The Vaipe stream is dead, Albert Wendt tells us, 'the area smells like a dead horse because of the toilets on the black stream flowing through it.' The struggle is to get by, to get up in the world, and we listen to stories of humanity from its peripheral places, weathering the storm of technological and cultural change broken upon them. Amidst it all, sly island humour kicks in, with Epeli Hau'ofa in *Tales of the Tikongs*, nicely skewering the whole development process.[159] In Tikong, no one is safe from Temptation.

One time-honoured South Seas tradition survives - that of the northern writer swanning south to sigh about the state of the garden since Eve's indiscretion. Like Maugham, Paul Theroux goes moping through, explaining on arrival that he's not always this morose, but his wife just gave him the heave-ho. His best-selling account of the doleful tale is titled *The Happy Isles of Oceania, Paddling the Pacific*, and one presumes there were tongues-in-cheeks-all-round when the publishers decided on this moniker.

Even in the best of health, paddling the Pacific in a kayak isn't much of an idea; after all, Pacific Islanders developed sails and outriggers for a reason. But Paul's not in the best of health. In the opening chapter we're told the other reason for his depression is that he suspects he has cancer, a melanoma in fact. Kayaking between the waves under the Pacific's blazing sun for months on end thus seems an unfortunate choice of activity, and at this stage of the argonaut's circuit, many readers wisely abandon canoe rather than undertake what promises to be a dejected tour.

Paul perseveres. He discovers New Zealanders; they are smug people with old, ill-fitting clothes. He discovers Polynesians; they look as though they all came from Fatland, with swollen cheeks giving them squinty gimlet eyes, so fat he finds it hard to imagine any of them can paddle a canoe as well as he can. He discovers Australians; he fears them because one of them dubs him a wanker, and they are like people who have only recently been domesticated, ever ready to slip into leering familiarity. He meets extortionist Melanesians, who torment and threaten him; they are amongst the scariest people he's seen in his life, he bleats between puffs as he paddles. True to his style, he calls it the way he sees it: for Theroux, *La Nouvelle Cythère* is a Third World rubbish dump populated by reformed cannibals hooked on canned meat.

Just when you think he's going to slit his wrists, Peace Corps Paul rediscovers Paradise, and what do you know, it's in America. The State of Hawaii is where, for Paul, hospitality, smiles and a sense of abundance prevail; here are the truly happy isles of Oceania. Though the Polynesians of Hawaii have been elbowed into relative impotence in their own islands, this is still Polynesia, and Hawaii abounds with rainbows, dolphins, celebrities and a wide choice of fast and frozen food.

I've one more thing to get off my chest about Theroux's book, let's put it in the file of honoring a family story. In *The Happy Isles of Oceania*, there is a five page description of a dinner in Fiji that the writer says was hosted by 'a man I vaguely knew', later described as 'my friend'. He should have stuck with the first description, for the host was one of my brothers and he invited Theroux to the dinner only because a mutual friend in Honolulu asked him to look after the itinerant sad-sack while he was passing through Fiji. The other guest of note at the dinner was the governor-general of New Zealand, Dame Cath Tizard, who actually was a friend of my brother's, their friendship forged when he was building the Regent Hotel in Auckland and Dame Cath was the city's mayor.

Theroux may have been having personal problems, but there's no doubt about his skill as a writer, and his account of the dinner in *The Happy Isles of Oceania* is carefully planned as character assassination. He sets Dame Cath up, leads her playfully on, lets out more rope, then garrotes her. His concluding description of one of the most progressive women of New Zealand of her time is,

> She seemed in the end rather silly and shallow and unimaginative, as well as bossy, vain and cunning, but principled in a smug and meddling way.[160]

Theroux is palpably disgusted by Dame Cath's table manners, but it is her reference to Americans as fat that really throws him. All that solar exposure must have affected the thickness of Paul's skin, for he takes high offence at her quite reasonable assertion that a lot of Americans suffer from obesity. His offence is all the more curious when you take into account the writer's earlier comments about Polynesians all coming from Fatland. The latter are the writer's considered words, passed for print by editor and publisher, as opposed to Dame Cath's light-hearted banter at a holiday dinner table.

Then, from the cat-basket of hind-chat, we are treated to Theroux's counter that it's an unfortunate remark for the governor-general to make because she is 'hefty'. It's a feeble meow, a blunt-clawed swipe that tells you more about the swiper than anything else. But the statement suffers from something that a widely-published author should be shamed for: it is not true. I too met Dame Cath around that time, on several occasions in fact, and she is physically quite a small woman. What he takes for bossiness in her manner, others take for strong leadership qualities; that which he calls vain and silly, others would appreciate as being frank and entertaining at a good friend's informal dinner party.

Unlike the note-taking writer, she was unwinding on a Fiji scuba-diving vacation with her grand-daughter and my daughter, both of whom were also present at the dinner. Theroux's account of the evening is so imbalanced, you feel his credibility crumbling when you think of all those other one-eyed character sketches in his body of work.

So read up, my friend! Read Tusitala's tales, discounting for their time; read Hau'ofa on the seventh and other days, Wendt on flying foxes in freedom trees, Becke on Pitcairn, Palau, Penrhyn, Ponape, Puka Puka, Pago Pago, Papeete, pick any of his islands! Bathe in Rupert's twilight pools, pace the pitching deck with Jack, or do some leaf-trembling with Maugham if that is your preference. Remember it's all just one person's perception, so take it all with a pinch of salt. Lick the mast and you'll find it's salt-encrusted.

All along, *La Nouvelle Cythère* may have been just a chimera. You'll have to form your own view on that, for you are going there now and the essence of the Islands is yours to discover. May you find what you value in the end, and recognise that which devalues. For me the latter is the littering of the land, the depriving of the children, those who have yet to come, of the joys of indigenous forests and clear mountain streams. It saddens me when I see a single generation's gain turn hollow the long guardianship of the land. Humans will squabble on, that is our way; but the land will only take so much from us. It has its own ways of reacting to our greed, and the process is underway the world over.

The land's story will be stirring in its telling and we look for the islander to come who will put it all in words. Meanwhile us grey-hairs, who should be busy at righting our wrongs, are still stomping about the beach. Look at our impatient footsteps in the sand. See how the tide takes them away. There is some hope in that.

The myth-makers of old, the story-tellers of fire-lit villages, pointed to the light on the lagoon, and still it remains as translucent as eternity. Below the island's pinnacled palace, the soaring, cloud-impaling peaks of basalt, we may yet bathe under majestic fountains falling. There is a sense of truth and there is beauty in that. If we search out the tracks, follow the Road of

Loving Hearts, we may find our way back to the generous source. I for one am willing to climb with you.

So under preposterous Pacific moon, I take my inadequate, flowery supplications and lay them at volcano's altar. It has risen in belches of primal red from steaming ocean and lies cooling now in the purple night. The first seeds arrive, buds burst, stems become trunks and bright fruit pigeons are soon in the spreading branches, dropping life upon the land. The waves build beaches in shoreline nooks and I see in the sand that already others have been here before me.

MOTU HANE

The Hermit Cell

At the far rim of Suva harbour, washed up on a bulge in the great coral plateau of the barrier reef, are the islands of Nukulau and Makuluva. They are islets of fine white sand, the sort of reef islands the Polynesians call *motu*. A deep channel swept by swift blue currents separates the two islands, its waters run by tatty cutters and copra boats in from Lomaiviti and the outer islands of the Lau Group.

In days gone by, Makuluva was the site of a government quarantine station, where sailing ships were sent if they arrived flying the flags of yellow fever or measles. Long after the quarantine station closed, its old wooden buildings remained in bare but functional condition, and my parents and their friends used to rent the island for family holidays.

The barrack-like buildings were set among groves of tall coconut palms and in the full face of the trade-winds those streaming palm tops roared like a broad waterfall. The island was a true retreat, for Makuluva offered no anchorage, being entirely surrounded by reef, so that in effect you were bliss-fully marooned on a private island for the duration of your stay.

Description of the old Makuluva is of necessity historic; for after the rifts in the reef occasioned by Suva's mighty 1953 earthquake, with the slow but adamant pace of a sea-snail, the island shifted the length of itself across the reef's fundament. If you walk the storied boards of the Royal Suva Yacht Club, behind its varnished bar you can view a series of aerial photographs portraying this geophysical transformation.

During our vacation days on the island in the 1950s, though the relentless relocation of the island was already underway, the Makaluva lighthouse still sat on a narrow beach midway along the windward coast. I remember stand-ing by the lighthouse at many a day's end, observing its long dark shadow pointing a warning finger towards night's approach, across the surf where evening's ocean rollers burst and boiled on a narrow shore-reef. As those yacht club photos show, the old lighthouse still remains on guard at reef's edge, but it is now far from any shore, for the island has long deserted it.

On Makaluva's leeward shore there was once a peaceful, coral-coralled beach, its white sand marked by turtle tracks at dawn. This was the threshold to a maze of shallow canyons, filled with aqua-filtered sunlight, that day after lazy day was our Makuluva playground. Sharing masks and snorkels between us, we'd go diving down these sandy-bottomed byways, accompanied by shoals of tiny fish, electric blue, shocking pink, flashings of minute silver scales, while black and white sea snakes undulated by and scatterings of bright blue starfish passed under tight brown bellies.

Memorable for me on the edge of Makuluva's reef, was the day a Fijian companion in a dinghy put a restraining hand to my chest, and with a wooden oar in his hand clubbed a mossy rock onto which I'd been about to place my bare foot. The dull rock erupted with brightly coloured fins and the venomous dorsal spines of a stonefish.[161] His awareness and quick action had spared me many days of agony.

It was on the beach at Makuluva that I first saw a hermit crab deprived of the shell at its back. In Fiji we call hermit crabs *kasikasi* and no beach is complete without these humble little crustaceans in their mobile homes. In the splendor of a cream mitre shell tastefully splotched in apricot, or a dapper zebra-striped cone, or more often in the blend-into-the-crowd grey of a periwinkle, they trundle amongst the broken coral and sea-wrack gathered along the high-water mark.

On Makuluva it was commonplace to come across a convocation of *kasikasi* clustered in the shade of a sea-smoothed length of driftwood. They always seemed such a gregarious lot, delighting in *kasikasi* company, with tiny antennae twirling in crab gossip and no discernible purpose for their gatherings but that of shooting the breeze. I imagined these were crustacean cakewalks, with the latest lines of shell on display exciting all the usual fashionista reactions of admiration and envy.

From the dim beginnings of childhood memory, stooping to pick up a *kasikasi* is always one that's there. At the approach of your hand, the little crab, its eyes on startled stalks, scrambles away on stiletto claws, until your fingers grasp it and the *kasikasi* jerks back into its shell like a tight-sprung door. And as that door slams shut, you observe how the shell's aperture is sealed by a pincer-claw as tightly in place as a well-set screw.

Then you would patiently whistle, as if you were the sound of the sea blowing from an empty conch held to your ear, for in this way the alarm of the *kasikasi* was soothed. With a tentative feint or two from confinement, the little crab would emerge to its full extent, stretching from its shell in an attempt to get traction. Fear forgotten, it scratched and nipped at the tips of your fingers until you were persuaded to place it back on the sand and watch it labour off along the beach.

The strength of a particular hermit crab's urge to recommence its peripatetic ways would guide us in the selection of our champions for *kasikasi* derbies. In such ways were our small minds amused in those Makuluva days, and when the going is good, they still are today.

These crab-races were held within a broad circle etched in the sand of the beach. The competitors, tightly withdrawn into their shells, would be gently placed into the very middle of the circle, to the accompaniment of much whistling from the various owners and sponsors.

One-by-one the crabs emerged, lurching back into motion to zig-zag off towards the finishing furrow of the sandy circumference. Worthy champions would be pocketed by their owners to be fattened with crumbs of coconut before the next big race.

It was at the end of one such beach race that one of the bigger boys, to my horror, de-shelled his *kasikasi*. I don't recall it being a case of punishing a lazy steed, showing off, or the sort of casual cruelty to which some boys are prone. He was merely demonstrating a particular property of the species. Seizing the miniature crab by the claws, he gently but steadily began pulling the crab from its shell.

'No! No! Don't!' us younger ones shrieked. It was like watching a tooth being pulled in slow motion and there was something terribly wrong about separating the creature from its abode.

Until that moment, I'd thought of *kasikasi* as being inextricably linked with their shells; thinking they grew together over the years from specks of sand to the big old gnarly ones you sometimes found up among the rustling undergrowth of the littoral trees. It had never occurred to me that their shells were static and dead, while the crustaceans within were still growing creatures.

With a wee plop, the *kasikasi* came free of its shell. Now we had a fascinating and rather icky view of the little crab; for the feisty face that we knew so well was still there glaring back, but he was caught with his trousers down and a panic attack seemed inevitable. Deprived of his splendid shell, the crab revealed a flabby worm of a body, with everything from his shoulders back resembling a pale wrinkly grub exposed to sunlight for the very first time.

The boy threw the shell away and put the shame-faced crustacean down on the sand. Like voyeurs witnessing a naked human accidentally locked out in a public street, we watched the hermit's flustered dash about the beach, his flabby appendage dragging behind.

He scurried across to the nearest shell, but it was too small. Inspecting the next, he found a gaping hole at its rear. Fleeing from empty shell to empty shell, frantically inspecting, hurriedly considering and reluctantly rejecting, until a drab-looking, right-sized cone presented itself. It would do for the while; so with much tugging and squeezing, all the while looking furtively about, the hermit reversed his rear-end into the recesses of his new home.

Right back then, before I could know of all the guises and abodes and countries that would pass through my life like fleeting dreams, I was moved by what I'd witnessed. And many years before I would hear the word being spoken, or get around to understanding its meaning, I thought what I'd seen on the beach that Makuluva day had to be some kind of metaphor.

I've been lucky, my friend, to have lived in an age when women have been able to fulfill aspirations in careers of their own making, rather than only through the proxy of their husbands' endeavours. When the time came that we'd paid off the university loans of our offspring, Marijcke and I took stock. Her career in publishing was forging ahead and my pursuit of mammon had always been a half-hearted affair; so we decided that she would be the sole bread-winner while I kept house and indulged an urge to transform thoughts into words on paper.

This prolonged writing jag has been something of a hermit existence, but I've never undervalued the stay-at-home experience. There was an email doing the global round for a few years that was meant to be a hilarious put-down of American housewives in the 1950s. The gist of the gag was a guide for young wives on how to prepare for husband's return at the end of his working day: the dinner ready and cooked just the way he likes it, the candles lit, mood music playing, martini ingredients at the ready, personal presentation nicely spruced and ready for what that might lead to. I could see how some people would find that funny, in a self-satisfied sort of way, but every time I recall that email I think, 'But that's exactly what I do every evening.'

I mean, why wouldn't you want to? It's logical. My woman comes home, frazzled from a long day at the office, for the sweet relief of a few hours of down-time before sleep and waking to another day of toil. So those few hours are precious. Why wouldn't you do everything you could to make them as pleasing as possible, to embellish them with delight before your days are numbered? I'm sure my mother thought the same way about her evenings with my father.

My Dutch mother-in-law Loelie Wijnberg, used to describe such a candle-lit atmosphere as *gezellig*. In the context in which she used it, the English translation would be something along the lines of cosy, of loving content-ment and well-being. She too liked the considered observances of the domestic table, the role of flowers and light and manners, and the rewards of interested conversation.

Her days were well numbered up last year and we buried her in Auckland with a loving mix of Dutch Indonesian and Pacific Island ritual. But just as my late mother is with me when I am cooking, Loelie is with us still at mealtimes, when I'm setting the table with her Dutch silverware and laying out her batik napkins. A good word *gezellig*, and even though I can't pronounce it properly, it remains the spirit of my evening preparations for my wife's homecoming.

Out in the material world, people are doing material things with material consequences; but in the hermit cell these deliberations are absent and time loses its measured tread. And since you are no longer much engaged with it, the material world pretty much gives up on you, the rarity of a telephone call like a jolt from deep hypnosis, an alarm bell ringing, last orders please.

A Buddhist once told me that to live a healthy life you must meet at least eight people a day. I don't know whether he was quoting scripture or making it up, but it seemed a sensible assertion. For a long time now I've been in this hermit cell, and there's been many a period wherein I've exchanged no word with anyone but my wife at the start and end of her working day. This line of thought can insinuate a wee nag of doubt into the serenity of the hermit's life.

So I have been reading the portents, my friend, and must accept that my days in the cell are up ... all things must pass. I have to get back on the road, it is written, and I know there's some toughening up to do and messages to be sent ahead. I look around at these book-lined walls, at the wrinkled maps, the curios from treasured times, all in the calm solitude of this shell of contemplation and know this place will not be easy to forsake. I will have to extract my mind like a deep-rooted molar from this gummy content. With a shove from whimsy, I recall again the *kasikasi* evictee of Makuluva, and wonder what new shell awaits.

Another memory gives me pause. It is a sunlit morning a few years ago now; I am drinking coffee at the breakfast table in the courtyard of our Darlinghurst home, and I am as content as a body can be. It is then that I spread open The Sydney Morning Herald and read a report that changes my day. It tells of a man in the deepest of trouble before the Australian courts. His crime was that he'd assisted his wife to end her life. She'd been trapped in a terminal world of hideous disease and pain, beyond the help of doctors, and she'd begged him to help her put an end to it all. There was a book he'd acquired that told him how to fulfill her request with a helium bottle, a plastic bag and a length of hose.

He then drove her to their caravan on a block of land at Phillip Island, where he helped her die. 'Her very last wish,' he told police, 'was that she wanted to lay down in nice clean pyjamas in a nice clean bed and cuddle up under the doona.' He rang a funeral director, then lay with his wife. Police arrived soon after.[162]

When my tears were sufficiently dried from that searing glint of love and death, I scissored the report from its page and pasted the cutting where I could read the man's words when the mood took me. He speaks for me, and others like us, who cosy up under the covers. We spoon the one we love to love, in gentle respite, cuddling up under the doona as storms of circumstance hammer at our doors, putting off the day when Time's awful blast drives all to dust.

Doonas are not a feature of the open road, so when we take to it again, my friend, we should steel ourselves like Seneca. Let Fate find us ready, primed for the realities of an arduous pilgrimage,

> Winter brings on cold weather, and we must shiver. Summer returns, with its heat; and we must sweat. Unseasonable weather upsets the health; and we must fall ill. In certain places we may meet with wild beasts, or with men who are more destructive than any beasts … And we cannot change this order of things … it is to this law of Nature that our souls must adjust themselves, this they should follow, this they should obey … That which you cannot reform, it is best to endure.[163]

Here's to the glory of the brief respites and gracious reprieves! We know there are no refuges in the material world that are for keeps, so pilgrims all, while the road gods beckon, let us burn moxa on our knees and share a last tale or two.

Hah! The hooded man bids me see the hour if we're going to gain the timely inn.[164] Okay then, since these pages are dwindling fast, let me write quickly what my lips would say.

What have we seen on our journey, my friend? Rainforests once filled with precious endemics, have gone the way of precious topsoil, flowing away in red rivers. The silted waterways are disgorging at the coast, choking life from coral on the bleaching reefs. The great life-sustaining trees have gone overseas, they have dissipated like the money passed to shady politicians and the so-called guardians of the land. They have sold them away for a handful of silver. We have seen that it has become the way of the world to litter the land, to choke the air, slay the wildlife and foul the waters.

In the wider world, humanity's profligacy has bought a bad dream upon us all, from which we shall not awake any time soon. Global-warming is no longer a fearful conjecture, its reality and its consequences are upon us. The national plans of the Pacific Islands, must now contend with the purport of eroding shorelines, expiring coral reefs, acidifying ocean and hurricanes of unprecedented ferocity. Rising sea levels will send low-lying atoll nations the way of Atlantis.

Along our voyage we've seen that only the raked beaches fronting the resorts are free of the refuse of the tide - tangled plastic washed in from who knows where. The streets of our harbour-towns are now clogged with profusions of greenhouse gas emitters; urban ills assail us, poverty, pox, pollution, and we bar our windows, for they look out on shanty-towns that are hide-outs for the criminals of the night. We understand the implications of the pictures, from the high jungles of Melanesia, of men in penis-gourds draping Kalashnikovs from their shoulders.

Where do we make our stand? There remains no shortage of beauty and truth in the Islands and we are agreed that those who serve those ideals faithfully can turn the tide on hopelessness. As wild vanilla is my totem, I will stay true to them, and I will walk the road ahead with faith, hope and love, for I have no real choice other than to do so. In the very month I have brought this collection of stories to a close, my first grandchild has arrived

354

in this world. I must thus join with others who rise to safeguard this planet, for my little Grace and all those who come after. This is the inescapable obligation and heavy blessing of the continuity.

How would Seneca counsel us? Of course we must endure, and of course this world was never a paradise lost and thus there is not one to be regained. As ever we will adapt to the times, we'll learn to deal with the new conditions, harsh as they might be. We will enjoy the brief respites, the refuge of snugs, where and when we can, for they will be harder to find in what lies ahead. Where land is to be flooded by ocean, we may like the Dutch build dykes. Where the deserts engulf the grain-lands, our tribes will migrate, with all the intense hardships that process involves. Where countries are drowning, we may erect citadels on reefs as bastions of culture and oceanic stewardship, as guardians of conservation, to police the over-exploiters of our oceans. And we will begin to correct our crimes - to refuse the disposing world of plastics, planet-poisoning non-renewables, the crazed consumption of crap, the destruction of biodiversity, unsustainable rates of human reproduction, with all the while the suicidal combustion of fossil fuels sending greenhouse gases to new life-threatening levels.

Will a one-sided global order, overweening greed and entitlement, mindsets of ethnonationalism, the clashings of rival Semitic belief systems, or Hollywood superhero solutions turn us from the bleakness of the vision ahead? Obviously not. We will have to lend our hearts and minds to the wheels of Science and rational solutions if we are to restore the balance that will allow our species to survive.

And we need a new story, one that makes sense of all we have learned, a story that explains what is required of us if we are to have a future on this best of planets. We can make a good start by rejecting the celebrity dumb-down culture currently oppressing the communal intellect. If every era must generate a new opiate for the masses, we can do better than that.

And so my friend, the time has come for us to part. You have many more roads to travel, you have made your plans, and I ... I have to leave this hermit cell. I see you've loaded pens under the rubber-band strapped around your

355

carnet de voyage, just the way I used to do; and I see your pack sitting at the door like an eager hound panting to be gone. I'm still rustling my affairs into precarious order, or I would walk you the first leg of your journey; so no dithering procrastination, let us make a bold adieu.

Thank you for the gift of your companionship through these pages. Weary travellers two, at the moonlit door it was you who knocked as I called out to those within. We have sailed southern realms of gold, sensed the virginity of first landfalls, and you have stoically endured all my follies.

On the first page of this book, I bowed at the shrine of Basho before we set off on our journey and now as we approach its last pages, I do so again. You will recall how I related that after sweeping clean his hermit cell, the poet-priest footed away on the narrow road to a far northern province of medieval Japan. What I did not mention, was that his dear friend Sora was stepping faithfully at his side as they wandered away with the swallows,

> Through fragrant fields
> Of early rice we went, beside
> The wild Ariso Sea.[165]

But all things pass, and the day came when the companions were compelled to go their separate ways, with an ailing Sora bound to see some relatives in Nagashima, and Basho keeping to his poetic quest. Before taking leave of Basho, Sora wrote these lines of farewell,

> A solitary rover,
> If I fall, then let me die
> Amid bush clover.

Basho put the poem into his travel journal, adding this explication,

> With the sadness of the one who goes and the grief of the one who is left behind, we were like a pair of wild ducks parted from each other and lost in the clouds.

Before I step into this passing cloud, dear companion, I present you one last story. Please take it as a memento of our journey. It is the story of a Melanesian prophet, a long-standing cargo cult, and very strong kava.

Ni moce mada. Fare thee well.

Hold Firm for John Frum

'Bro, we need a new religion for all this stuff!'

My friend was feeling over stimulated, not so much by the empty stubbies of Fiji Bitter on the table between us, as by the rocket-ride of discovery we'd been on. The sun had given up on us and the rest of Fiji, melting over the rim of Bligh Waters in the direction of Melanesia. The twenty-first century was now a couple of years old and we'd been talking about all that had been revealed since our benighted days hanging about the bicycle sheds of Suva Grammar School some fifty years hence: DNA, gene-splicing, the expanding cosmos, global warming - all the stuff our teachers knew nothing of back in those days.

'Uh-huh?'

'Forget writing, bro. We have to start a religion.'

'Another one!'

'But bro, none of them knew all this stuff we been talking about.'

I shook my head as he slapped the table searching for a name, 'Just like that basket ... y'know the fullah ... y'know ... Huppet?'

'Hubbard. You mean the one who dreamed up Scientology?'

'Thass the one. Fullah was too smart again.'

'Is that a religion?'

He ignored my question, having a boisterous point of his own to make. 'That fullah was a writer too. One day the fullah wrote, if you want plenty *paisa*, start a religion.'[166]

'So what's your big idea?'

'I dunno. You the one to do it ... you the writer.'

One shot of my Bounty Rum chaser and I rose to his bait. 'Okay. But first we're gotta have a revelation ... something with a sting to it.'

'Yeah, that's it, bro! String! A piece of string!'

'String? No, I said sting.'

'No, that's it, bro ... string.'

'Why?'

'What you said before 'bout the thing called Superstring.'

'String theory?'

'Thass the one! If they believe that, they believe anything.'

I tried to shush him, but he'd knocked back more Bounty than me, 'What you said before, bro ... everything is just like ... what you say? Like loops of string ... see ... and the string is vibrating through all the dimentias... even the dimentias we don't know 'bout. Thass gonna be our big revelation.'

'Trust me, we're gonna need more than that.'

'Plenty more. Instead of Garden of Eden, we gonna have Big-Bang. The Devil, he's in a Black Hole and he has all the dark matter. Our temple gonna be the Internet. But the big, big thing ... thass gonna be String. Superstring. All people in our religion gonna wear some green string 'round their wrist.'

Any minute now he'd be getting to the tithing formula, so I cut him short. 'Good idea, bro. But the next thing our religion's gonna need is a martyr and I know just the right fullah to sacrifice.'

People like me know how easy it is to be led up the garden path. I'm talking about those of us who bow to the great deity of Science without actually understanding the mysterious utterances of its high priests. The more virtual, cryptic and nanotech the world becomes, the more we must take leaps of faith to remain within the flock. We hear the mighty revelations on the mysterious grainy nature of inner space and the specific properties of the billions upon billions of the expanding universe's stellar expressions, and we nod with open mouths. We take in the new truths before returning to the mundane diversions of our daily lives, humming a little tune as we go: in my case, 'life is a cargo cult, old chum, life is a cargo cult'.

As a demonstration of my continuing faith in Science, when faced with the long ocean crossing to Vanuatu some months after my friend's failed attempt to launch a Superstring cult, I flew there in an aeroplane. This I did in preference to paddling or sailing, in spite of my complete and utter ignorance of the workings of jet engines and all the causes and effects of the array of flashing lights spied beyond the cockpit door.

Like a sardine astronaut in a volatile tin missile, I sat up there, way, way up there in the jet-stream, with my little sachet of peanuts and daggy airline socks, shoulder-to-shoulder with a hundred other sardines, all of us trusting to the glory of Science. I had the faith, and no doubt most of my fellow sardines had it too.

An interlocutor once explained that the force which keeps those massive conglomerations of metal, aviation fuel, alcohol, processed food, bulging baggage racks and mammalian flesh-and-bone airborne, is the occult Law of Aerodynamics. So many times I've entrusted my life to the L of A, experiencing doubts only at those moments when an urgent intercom voice announces severe turbulence ahead, or the palm tops of Savusavu airport are clipped by landing wheels. It's at these moments that I notice a great number of my fellow sardines praying to deities reputably more potent than the Lords of Aero-Science.

I used to think I knew a little bit about the bigger picture, but earlier this year I read a book by Sir Martin Rees, the Astronomer Royal, and when I put the book down, I realized I knew nothing.[167] From what I've read elsewhere, Rees is one of our leading space scientists and knows more about black holes than pretty much anyone else, which becomes relevant when you hear that the centre of our galaxy is probably a giant, star-gobbling black hole.

Something I read in that book has had me muttering ever since. In commendably clear English, the Astronomer Royal says that parallel universes are no longer the exclusive intellectual property of science fiction enthusiasts. Forging ahead into the twenty-first century, Rees reveals that parallel universes have become serious science, along with string theory, time loops and an infinite number of extra dimensions. What's more, some of the baffling paradoxes of quantum physics may only be clarified by our achieving a rudimentary understanding of the parallel universes of which we are but one. I use 'our' in the loosest of senses, as it will only be those in the elite cabal of science-priests who will be *au fait* with the workings of all this stuff - at least we presume they will be.

Incredible to quietly consider that there is an ensemble of universes around us, an infinite ensemble, what Rees calls a meta-universe. But in the act of opening ourselves to this new reality, straining meagre mental resources to probe at the deepest nature of time and space, it dawns on us that even with the assistance of yet-to-be-invented quantum computers, we as a species are probably just too thick to ever comprehend it all. Not only are our senses too limited to grasp the microstructure of the parallel spaces right in front of our noses, but we're also lumbered with a physical design far too cumbersome to cross all those extra dimensional boundaries, let alone travel the confines of our relatively tiny solar system.

Of course for many people this 'new' information comes as no surprise. The lucky ones have been crossing over for a while now and some of them hold that they hail from those other dimensions. You can learn this courtesy of the Internet. Google forth and you'll find there are swaths of the voting public who say they're from somewhere else: the Greys, the Elohim, the Pleiadians. They talk to each other in virtual chat-rooms, discussing essentials such as the Pleiadian physics prostitutes who will trade sex for secrets of nature. Makers of the brazen serpents and golden calves of the New Age, these creatures aren't living in the cult-caves of a desert wilderness, they're manning your supermarket tills and decorating your cars with parking tickets. You've probably already picked up on this, probably noticed the tang of otherness given off here and there by various TV news-presenters and the people who appear in hair-product commercials.

I'm bemused. Since reading Rees, I have a sense that all I thought I knew for sure is somehow tarnished and rather primitive. My feet are in water, galactic water, and I'm feeling a little perplexed, for it is clear that things are not what they seem. Forget alienation from popular culture, organized religion and the daily grind of commercialized sport; now it's an infinity of parallel universes we're excluded from. Conditions are ripe for a cargo cult, a breakthrough providing sufficient explanation for all that is hidden.

This story is on its way to Tanna, the great spirit-island of the wondrously metaphysical archipelago of Vanuatu. Ever since I studied cargo cults back in the dark ages of my undergraduate years at Auckland University, I've harboured a desire to go to Tanna to hang out with the kava-swilling John Frum cargo cultists. It's taken a while, but here I am in 2006, with my Tannese pilgrimage finally under way.

You can't think about the Pacific Islands with any kind of completeness, without contemplation of our colourful swath of cults and religions, and the revolutionary roles of all the missionaries, the evangelists and the prophets. Most of the island countries are possessed by religion with a passion comparable with, say, Europe at the time of the Reformation, or the manner in which fundamentalist Iran or America is possessed today. From beautiful limestone churches in the Cook Islands to tumble-down thatched mission huts in Melanesian mountain valleys, from the Methodist Bible-thumpers of Fijian *coups d'état* to Tanna's mystical Prophet Fred, the people of the Pacific Islands are touched by fervent versions of the Christian faith.

When the rest of the world thinks of the islands, they fantasise about grass-skirted dancers with flowers in their hair. But when most Pacific Islanders picture themselves at their best, they're covered in cloth from wrist to ankle, standing in the swelling ranks of church choirs, suited up for Bible study or busily making more collections for church causes. Far more so than traders, administrators and anthropologists, it is the nineteenth-century missionaries who have coloured the culture of the Pacific Islands. For while the pan-island trading firms and colonial governments have gone the way of the whalers and sandalwood sailors, throughout the great spread of islands, every Sunday, cities, towns and villages resonate with the sound of devotional hymns.

The work of the Christian missionaries began in earnest with the arrival of the good ship *Duff* in Tahiti in 1797. On board were representatives of the London Missionary Society, sprung from Britain's evangelical revival, fired up by the parting command of Christ that they go out into the world and preach the Gospel to every living person.

Their critics would say these evangelists spent the next two hundred years filling the islanders' heads with as much hell-fire and damnation as they did the love and grace of Christ. True, they overcame cannibalism and widow-strangling, but in the process many cultural activities that had filled island nights with laughter and creativity were proscribed. Places like the Marquesas Islands were virtually stripped of their indigenous culture, in their case through laws imposed by earnest representatives of the Church of Rome.

Glorious gospel triumph is how Christians have described what happened in the islands in the spreading wake of the *Duff*. But if the next century witnessed a sweeping victory of Christianity over animism, it would be remiss not to mention the at-times bitter struggle witnessed by the islanders between the forces of Protestantism and Catholicism. And then within

Protestantism, there were divisions too, so that a sort of gentlemen's agreement had to be put in place for areas of mission activity: Vanuatu for the Presbyterians, Solomon Islands to the Anglicans, Fiji the Methodists, Samoa the Congregationalists, and so on.

But nothing stays the same, and with the end of colonialism and post-colonialism, the islands have become abuzz with the arrival of evangelical missionaries from previously unheard-of churches, preaching, prophesying, proselytising, praying and playing their electric guitars in a whole new wave of millennial fervour. To some it was disturbing to see rural Fijian villages, previously happily united under the leadership of their Methodist *talatala*, become splintered by the inroads of evangelicals just off the plane from Australia and America. But then you can never suppress the exchange of ideas, and when you get down to it, what could be more fundamental to life than people making their own choices on the subject of ultimate reality.

The animistic religions of old may have been expunged from Fiji and Polynesia, but in Melanesia, conversion to Christianity was less conclusive. The missions of Melanesia, manned in the early days by Europeans and Polynesians, had their work cut out for them; and though Christianity dominates today, there are many parts of Melanesia where the old religions and intermittent cargo cults reign on.

On many a moonlit Melanesian night, an abiding rumour had been spreading. Something in the story was missing, for it seemed the white man was hiding something from the black man. The suggestion circulated for a century or more was that an all-important first page had been torn from the Bibles distributed by the missionaries to the canny islanders.

The islanders may have been wrong on that one, but I sympathise with them. When I consider the tranquility of my pre-parallel universe state of mind, and ruminate on how unsettling it is to still have this fundamental knowledge hidden from me, I foresee how completely seductive it will be when someone arrives offering me plausible enlightenment. If aliens ever do show up on Planet Earth, it'll mean they've got a better grip on reality than we do, for to get here they'll have had to flip through dimensions we can only vaguely imagine. And if the aliens are proselytisers, there'll be a rush of us ready to convert to whatever the religion is they're offering, even if it turns out that their almighty deity goes by the name of String.

Please excuse me if on our way to Tanna, we make a brief diversion to Suva. Let us turn for just a moment to Fiji's breezy capital where it sits on a thumb of land declining from a fist of emerald volcanic mountains into the bright blue wash of the South Pacific.

These days when you approach the city along the southern coast of Viti Levu, you're struck by the sight of a large white edifice overlooking the harbour. It rises from the uppermost heights of the ridge that climbs up from the harbour-city to the mountains at its back, and as you get closer you see the edifice is a bunker-like building surmounted by a soaring pillar topped with a golden image.

The first time I caught sight of this bold enhancement to our city's profile, I thought it a monument to the leaders of Fiji's various *coups d'état*, something perhaps in the heroic style of Kim Il-Sung. But on closer inspection, I found the hovering gold figure flashing above in the afternoon sun was Moroni, a trumpet-playing angel from America. From his place on high, Moroni surveys all the tropical deviations of my complex home-town, his pillar rising from within the security gates of the temple of the Church of Jesus Christ of Latter-Day Saints, hallowed place of worship for Fiji's growing Mormon population.

At first it was surprising to me that Mormons were active in a Melanesian country like Fiji, for until 1978 'Negroes' were banned from joining the Mormon priesthood; the most commonly advanced reason for the ban being that their race was stained with 'the Curse of Cain.' Then I found out that everything was copacetic for Melanesians, as the ban had not been on all black people, only those of 'Hamite' lineage, which I'm informed is Mormon-speak for Africans. Melanesians, Australian Aborigines and Filipino/Indonesian 'Negritoes' were outside the aforementioned ban, which must have been nice for them at the time.

I've followed this controversial material over the years, because when the missionaries knocked at my door, I had them in for cups of tea. The Jehovah's Witnesses, the Scientologists, the Rajneeshis, the Mormons, I've engaged with them all, asked my questions, heard what they've had to say.

More than a decade after the launching of the civil rights movement in the U.S.A., the Mormon church was still defending its ban on the Hamites, saying it wasn't their Church's fault, for it wasn't they who'd imposed the ban, but God. I forget exactly what year it was that Cain committed his dreadful deed, but it was definitely a long time ago, so it was with relieved smiles all around that after 'much negative media attention', on 1st June 1978, God communicated with President Spencer W. Kimball in Utah's Salt Lake Temple to duly overturn the ban on Hamites.

Like Scientology, the Mormon faith is a salutary reminder that to be a burgeoning religion you don't need to have your origins in the so-called Holy Land. The founding prophet of the Mormon religion, Joseph Smith, was walking through the woods of up-state New York when God and Jesus Christ revealed themselves to him. In these same leafy New World byways, subsequent heavenly messengers and Old Testament prophets appeared to assist Joseph in restoring the true Church to this Earth. This he did with the help of a 'seer stone', which allowed to him to translate the 'reformed Egyptian' text inscribed on a set of golden plates he discovered in the fecund soil of America. The golden angel flying high over Suva in the up-draught of the southeast trades, is the same one who showed Joseph Smith where those golden plates were hidden in the fields of upstate New York.

A down-trodden product of post-colonial hardship, living in a time of fundamentalist religious fervour, Joseph drew a following of people with the same hard-times history. At first they were little more than a wandering cult with a belief in divine guidance and a prophet-in-the-flesh. Then they began moving westwards in search of a better life, to build the new Zion in the state of Illinois. As mentioned, I know of these details because I paid attention to the missionaries at my tea parties.

Some call it the Land of Lincoln, others the Sucker State, either way the Illinois militia took exception to Joseph's occult and some would say womanizing ways and proceeded to assassinate the New York prophet. After their prophet was martyred by the Suckerites, a St. Paul figure arose to lead the Mormons forth. His name was Brigham Young, a man of great vigour and will power, defender of polygamy and Hamite exclusion, who fathered the faithful on their wagon-train exodus out of the pharaonic Midwest to the promised land of Utah.

Today Joseph Smith's religion, over nine million strong and vastly wealthy, dominates the Rocky Mountain States of the Union. No longer downtrodden outsiders, these are not-to-be-messed-with citizens of the most prosperous nation on Earth, with hymnbooks in their hands and nuclear weapons in their back pockets.

In the Book of Mormon we learn that America was settled in about 600 BC by an Israelite patriarch by the name of Lehi and that Christ subsequently visited these New World Israelites after his resurrection from the dead. Amongst them was a bunch known as the Lamanites, whose unrighteousness had led to their begetting dark skin. In the fullness of time, the Mormons came to teach Native Americans and Polynesians that they were the descendants of the Lamanites and that they would only be restored to righteousness through the fullness of the Mormon gospels.

Even before the evidence of mitochondrial DNA, the origins of the Polynesian people were well and truly settled on linguistic and archaeological evidence as being Southeast Asian, which is a long way short of Israel when you're traveling by canoe. But as with the great majority of religions, the Mormon story came before the discovery of DNA, and besides all that, it was only human to see that signing up to the new orthodoxy carried possibilities of educational scholarships and tickets to America. Today Mormon spires arise from Pacific Island villages where Polynesians have presumably accepted their Lamanite origins, and burgeoning communities of Maoris, Tongans, Samoans and Hawaiians live out their days in Utah, riding the fast-food wagon train of the American way of life, restored in the process to an alternative righteousness.

All the while, young Mormon men cover the wide Pacific in their missionary work. Clean-living, strong-minded, going two-by-two down island lanes in white shirts and sensible ties, spreading the words of Joseph Smith and evidently finding many receptive listeners along the way. When I saw two of them on the spiritually turbulent island of Tanna, walking through the religious hot-bed of Sulfur Bay like a pair of vacationing crusaders in Mecca, I marveled at their tenacity, even if they seemed quite superfluous to the needs of Tanna.

So there we were, descending through tumultuous clouds to Tanna, our faith strengthened in the exalted truths of aerodynamics, even if we all privately rejoiced as soon as our plane's wheels reconnected with solid ground. All that time up there in the skyways, I'd been in meditation. I'd declined offerings of foil-wrapped food. I'd turned my face from the incomprehensible rituals of in-flight duty-free sales, and kept my thoughts focused on the teachings of John Frum and what I might learn from Prophet Fred. The famous cargo cult fomenter John Frum, a spirit man not seen for some time now, had emerged from the forests of Tanna in the Second World War. But Prophet Fred was still walking the shores of this Vanuatuan outpost, and I was determined to meet him and hear his syncretic message.

Tanna is like a magnet for missionaries. One of the attractions must be that a good part of the twenty thousand people living there have not converted to Christianity, choosing instead to follow *Kastom*, the pidgin descriptor for customary tribal beliefs and practices that have evolved over four thousand years of human habitation in these islands.

After a week on the island, I made a list of all the churches currently active on Tanna: the Presbyterians, the Roman Catholics, the Seventh Day Adventists, Assemblies of God, Holiness Fellowship, Baptists, the Church of Christ, a church called Four Square, Jehovah's Witnesses, not to forget the Bahais, the Mormons and some other establishments that appeared to represent the ambitions of individual Australian and American evangelists. If they're ever looking for a new headquarters for the World Council of Churches, Tanna must be a consideration; although the members of the John Frum cargo cult might have something to say about that.

At the Tanna airport I was introduced to one of Vanuatu's Members of Parliament, a wild-eyed, loose-limbed, highly articulate John Frummer by the name of Keasipai Song. I asked him whether there might be too many churches competing for the attention of the limited number of Tannese and he agreed, saying the big news was that a mosque had just opened on the island.

I asked him whether matters had settled down since the 2004 spear-chucking battle between the John Frummers and the followers of Prophet Fred. He rolled his eyes enigmatically, flapped a hand in the direction of the hinterland and said that some people had made some big mistakes, but they were being given time to reflect on the error of their ways. Later when I was at the John Frum headquarters, I asked about Tanna's John Frum MP and was told the old men who gave him power had withdrawn it, so he was finished now.

Tanna is completely rural. You just can't call Lenakel, the island's administrative centre, urban. The gas station is a hut dispensing fuel by hand-pump from drums. The roads aren't sealed and dusty fields separate Lenakel's single-story buildings.

The island is mountainous, about forty kilometres of broken volcanic ridges running north to south. It seems underpopulated, as if numbers haven't recovered from the days when blackbirders mined Tanna of its men. The islanders are overtly friendly, but there is a wary air of suspicion and many a furtive sideways look. Nothing, it seems, is as it seems.

The island is beautiful. Freshwater streams tumble from verdant volcanic mountains to sustain villages strung along surf-washed shores. Its forests are filled with echoing birdcall, its food gardens lush with fruit and flowers. Amidst this Eden walk the people of Tanna, and they have all the rich diversity of Melanesian ethnicity, from really dark melanin hue, to milk-chocolate skin with orange hair. Language is complex, for no country in the world has as many distinct languages per capita as Vanuatu, with more than a hundred indigenous languages in the archipelago. Most people on Tanna understand the pleasantly rhythmic pidgin of Bislama, which along with English and French is one of the three official languages of Vanuatu. But there are many amongst the animists in the mountains of Tanna who do not.[168]

There are some things one needs to know about John Frum's chosen island. Firstly, the American war machine did not come to Tanna during the Pacific War, as it did to most of the islands of Vanuatu to the north. This fact is related to you on the island in tones of regret, for the Americans have a good name on Tanna and America has a part to play in the wonderful story of John Frum. That being said, the American role should not be over-stated, as has been done in some books written about the cult, for John Frum is quintessentially Tannese.[169]

Another introductory note is that the bibliography of Tanna's John Frum cargo cult is extensive, rivaling that of any Pacific Island phenomenon. But it's important to register that the written record comes from colonial administrators, missionaries, anthropologists and wandering scribes like me, all with their own fat to chew. It is therefore fair to assume a suspicion that none of us has ever got the saga quite right. For their part, the John Frummers of Tanna have kept the story oral and very much alive.

Okay, it's time, so with humble acknowledgement to all those writers who've set it down before me, here goes with my attempt at a summary history of the John Frum cargo cult.[170] Let me begin in 1939, when there were signs of disturbance amongst the people of Tanna. Clandestine meetings were being held, from which women, Europeans and their agents were excluded. There were rumblings along the coast that the strict regime imposed by Presbyterian missionaries had produced little practical gain for the islanders, Copra prices were falling and the traders and colonial administrators weren't doing anything to correct the situation. Rumours spread the word; it was time for a change.

That year at Green Point on the southwest corner of the island, John Frum made his first appearance to an assembly of men. He appeared as a white man, described as 'a mysterious little man with bleached hair, high-pitched voice and clad in a coat with shining buttons.' He supposedly used 'ingenious stage management', only coming before the men of Tanna in the faint light of evening campfires when they were suitably stoned on kava. John's message was peaceful. He discouraged idleness and spoke in favour of communal gardening and cooperation. His great point of difference with the missionaries was his decree that there should be a return to the old ways of dancing and kava drinking.

Then came the prophecies. There would be a cataclysm, after which John Frum's rule would commence. The Europeans would be brushed from Tanna and all the immigrants from surrounding islands would return from whence they'd come. Customs prohibited by the missionaries would be restored; in particular, proper respect for the place of kava. The people would get back their youth; there would be no need for pigs, gardens or trees. It would be a time of bliss.

Since Friday was the day on which the millennium was going to occur, that became the new holy day for the people, with Saturdays to be dedicated to dancing and kava. Tanna was hit by a sudden orgy of spending to use up the soon-to-be-useless money issued by the Government, for it was all going to be replaced by John Frum money with a coconut stamped on it. People threw hard-won savings into the sea, and the churches and the mission-run villages were abandoned.

By 1941 the British agent on Tanna had had enough. He arrested the John Frum luminaries, leading them away under guard, followed by a menacing crowd chanting, 'Hold firm for John Frum! Hold firm for John Frum!' The cult leaders were sent to jail on the island of Efate, eighty kilometres to the north of Tanna, from whence one of them began writing about John Frum being the King of America, saying the mountains of Tanna would soon be covered with cargo-bearing aeroplanes sent by John Frum. Rather mysteriously, it was revealed that the aeroplanes, and presumably therefore the cargo, would be invisible.

Now the three dark-skinned sons of John Frum began activity on Tanna. After reportedly landing by seaplane in 1942, they began 'junketing', which seemed to have meant partying down in preparation for John Frum's imminent arrival. The sons' names were Isac, Jacob and the rather casually named Lastuan (last one). Youths were dedicated to Frum's sons and lived together with them in communal dwellings, bathing ritually by day, dancing by night and going on picnic-pilgrimages to Green Point. The junketing was groovy, but the British agent judged it to be getting out of hand and moved in, charging the three sons with incest and adultery. They too were packed off to the Efate jail.

When the American troops arrived on the island of Efate in 1943, there were sufficient John Frummers present, in prison and out, to witness the benevolent might of the warriors of the Land of the Free. More people from Tanna made their way north to Efate, happy to provide the Americans with labour in the great cause of fraternal Americo-Tannese relations, and the presence of black soldiers in American uniforms is said to have been a revelation to South Pacific natives ruled by years of Anglo-French colonialism.

Towards the end of 1943, a Tanna man named Neloaig proclaimed himself John Frum, King of America and Tanna. He organized an armed force on the island and the construction of an aerodrome for USAF Liberators to land on in order to discharge consumer goods already earmarked for Tanna by John Frum's father. But it was Neloaig himself who was airfreighted, he too consigned to the Efate jail and later to the island's lunatic asylum. People on Tanna shook their heads. Of course neither Neloiag nor any of the other arrested men was John Frum. John was a spirit and couldn't be contained by the dimensions in which the Government authorities operated.

The next in line claiming to be John Frum was a man by the name of Iokayae, who said he received orders from Isac at a special place in the bush on Thursdays at sunset. Isac was reported to be dead against the colours red, blue and yellow. No doubt he was a lapsed Presbyterian, for even I know the horsemen of the apocalypse wore breastplates of 'fiery red, blue and sulphur yellow.' The cult was in good shape, with visions of the dead, of Isac and Lastuan, and of a new character called Jake Navy, his name derived from a cigarette brand.

Meanwhile, the mythical manikins who had dwelt in Tanna's mountain ravines for as long as tales could tell, were making frequent appearances; as was Mwayamwaya, who according to some written accounts, is the indigenous God of Tanna. Not to be left out, the Presbyterian Church was making its own momentous moves. By now very much in the hands of local pastors and elders, the church upgraded schools and water supplies, went out of its way to avoid confrontation with the cargo cult, and - smart move - gave the nod to dancing and kava-drinking.

Move forward to the 1970s: having decided the time was right, the Presbyterian Church became a leading advocate for Vanuatuan independence from colonial rule. The church had become the champion of radical change and now it was the turn of the John Frum cult's membership to fall away.

About this time, anti-independence French interests stepped into the breach, encouraging the cargo cult to become politically active, only blanching when they heard that the new John Frum leaders were promising bulldozers, trucks, roads and high wages to their supporters. The newly-politicized cult entered a militant phase under the nominal leadership of Antoine Fornelli, a French veteran of Indochina, whose activities became a rallying point against the government and the Presbyterian missions.

An outbreak of cult militancy, complete with guns and uniforms, culminated in Fornelli's declaration of independence for Tanna in 1974. This was too much for the authorities to stomach, with the result that Fornelli took the cult's well-worn exit route to the ignominy of the lock-up. But islanders say the French attention to the cult's political aspirations continued, their main carrot being the provision of educational opportunities superior to those offered by the Tanna missions.

Since the 1970s, sporadic John Frum revivals have been reported here and there, but the bibliographic trail, or at least my attention to it, had gone a little cold. But here I was with my feet on Tannese ground, equipped only with an open heart and enquiring mind, intent on engaging with the cult if they would so allow. At the very least, my arrival on Tanna was a harbinger of hope, for I was greatly impressed through my airport meeting with Keasipai Song to learn that the John Frummers had representation in the national Parliament. Could this mean the cargo had made it through to the cult?

Ken Niavia drove me away from the Lenakel airport in a venerable yellow Land Rover. He looked like Don Cheadle on a good day, with a mop of frizzy ginger hair tied back in a bun and a gold earring glinting from one ear. Ken, in his early twenties, spoke good English, Bislama and a few of the Tanna indigenous languages. He said our destination, the southeast corner of the island, was an hour and quarter's drive away. Six hours later we arrived. My two conclusions from the day were that I really liked Ken Niavia's company, and that Stevenson was right on when he said it was a better thing to travel than to arrive, not that there was anything wrong with our destination.

The road that snakes up over the mountain ridge running the length of Tanna, is little more than a goat-track, devoid of tar-seal or gravel. The ground is compacted volcanic ash, dusty and highly erodible. There is little to see along the way that is not fascinating, and I had ample time to investigate such things, for Ken spent much of the day on a mat under the Land Rover. He wasn't taking siestas under there; he was doing things like reconnecting the drive-shaft, using wooden pegs he cut from branches in the roadside jungle in the place of iron bolts, telling amusing stories as he did so.

I wandered around listening to the breeze in the trees, spotting crimson birds, hearing rumbles from the volcano, and every hour or so, stopping dead in my tracks when a huge explosion would come from the direction in which we were heading. I met *Kastom* people who couldn't speak Bislama but managed to sell me kava roots by pointing to the number of notches cut into the side of the kava stems to indicate the sale price.

By the roadside I found a recently-used *Kastom* butcher-shop, a circle of branches stuck into the ground inside which banana leaves lay over a floor of ferns. A beast had been slaughtered nearby, its severed parts laid upon the leaves. The butcher stood there, Ken told me, pointing into the circle, selling the meat to the customers gathered at the border of branches.

Ken needed a hacksaw for his repairs. We spotted a grass-skirted woman, bearing a huge bundle of flax leaves on her head. She retreated furtively down a jungle track upon our approach. We followed her in, and after a few minutes the track arrived at a deserted ash-clearing, with a tumble-down grass hut to one side. Ken explained it was a ceremonial meeting ground, a *nakamal*, and I saw where a giant banyan tree at the clearing's edge was equipped with an espaliered man-shelter created within the tree's aerial roots.

Fifty metres further down the track and we were at the edge of a *Kastom* village. Children fled screaming at the sight of my red face and white legs. I sympathised entirely with their first impression of me, and Ken agreed I shouldn't accompany him into the heart of the village. So I remained out there in the track's shady tunnel of trees for half an hour while Ken undertook his unsuccessful search for a hacksaw amongst the *Kastom* huts. As I dawdled out on the trail, curious heads of villagers would pop up here and there, from behind fallen logs, tree-trunks and bushes, to get a quick look at me before withdrawing as quickly as they'd appeared.

Evening was not far off by the time Ken delivered me to the house that would be my home for the week ahead. A little bungalow of bamboo and thatch, its floors were set at all kinds of unexpected angles. On closer inspection, I found that everything in its construction, but for nails, wash-basin and toilet, was cut from the over-shadowing forest.

Ken introduced me to Mary, my ever-humorous Tannese hostess, and as the sun went down she laid a table of food for me that she'd gathered from the surrounding land. Then the generator was turned off, and I was left alone in the darkness of the bay.

In my crazy bungalow I tucked myself within the refuge of a mosquito-net, regretting that I'd omitted to ask Ken and Mary whether there were any poisonous snakes or evil spirits hereabouts. When my night-sight came to me, peering through the open bamboo door and windows, checking the starlit beach for movement, I saw how the big waves that were curling into the bay carried the reflections of other worlds. From the horizon to the top of my rustic door, the night was hung with a storm of stars and they were scattering their scintillations across the dark dancing water. I was close now to the volcano, but its rumblings did not disturb my sleep, for not thirty steps from the doorway, ocean's seething night-swell rumbled its cradle song across an adamant shore-reef.

Vanuatu is a creation of the Ring of Fire, rising from the edge of the Pacific tectonic plate, spitting lava from its string of active volcanoes. On Tanna, the volcano is Mount Yasur, an ash pyramid with two calderas spraying clouds of sulphuric steam and floppy slabs of red-hot lava into the air. Depending on the underworld's mood, every now and then Yasur emits an ear-splitting, body-slamming explosion and fires elemental cannonballs into the air. Seeing these bellicose displays is a reminder of the many reports that John Frum's army is somewhere down there under the volcano, awaiting his call to millennial action.

On my second day in Tanna, Ken Niavia and I stood on the uppermost-rim of the volcano. From up there we could see the whole extent of southeast Tanna and could look out at the table-mountain profile of Futuna Island, way out on the ocean's horizon. Ken pointed to where Port Resolution was tucked into the Tanna coast, where Captain Cook had anchored in 1774. It was Cook who bestowed the New Hebridean name by which the archipelago was known until independence in 1980, when the coined name of Vanuatu was adopted for the nascent nation.

Below us at the foot of the volcano, lay the dried-out bed of Lake Siwi, and I saw how the ash plain was serrated into eroding canyons where the lake had burst its banks and washed out to sea. It was clear from our vantage point what a mighty event that must have been, that day when the bursting flood had swept huge trees and broad swaths of land into the ocean.

Tanna's lake had gone on its wild rampage some five years ago and I'd heard that Prophet Fred, had foreseen the cataclysm. I asked my companion if that was true.

'Yes,' said Ken. 'He prophesied it. He saved many people from being drowned in the flood that day.'

Our backs to the caldera, Yasur chose this moment for one of its major explosions. I was almost blown off the ridge and found myself wide-eyed, clasping at thin air. Ken was quite unperturbed, drawing my attention to a large lump of lava that was flying into the heavens. We watched its ascent and the way it arced back down, landing with a heavy whump a little further along the ridge.

Friday night is the big night for the John Frum cargo cult, when followers troop out of the hills to congregate at their Lemakara headquarters. The village sits in the forest above Sulfur Bay on the slopes of the restless volcano. I arrived at night to find Lemakara lit only by moonlight and the orange pool of one benzene lamp. The lamp was hanging from the beam of an open-sided thatched building in the middle of the village clearing. The clearing was devoid of grass, for grey volcanic ash covered the ground, setting up little clouds of dust as you stepped across it. Around the perimeter of the clearing, campfires smoldered. Smoking men hunched about the fires.

In the low central building a crowd of people sat cross-legged, all facing inwards in a tight dark knot of humanity. In the knot's centre were half a dozen guitar and ukulele players beating out a typically rhythmic island beat, surrounded by a rich-voiced male choir, with a female choir making up an outer perimeter.

I squatted by the building in the dark, listening to the music. The women were in perfect harmony with the male choir, but their shrill vocals, delivered at full volume, soon became monotonous. Song after song was belted out, with no chat in between, and I realised I was listening to well-rehearsed performances. Later in the evening I learned the singers were 'teams' from different villages and when their half-hour repertoire was done, they gave up the floor-space to the next team.

In the lamplight, dancing in the ash at the edge of the building were men and boys, doing the sort of boogie you could see in any Pacific Island dance hall. At the edge of the lamplight's dim pool, advancing in step to the music, twirling their grass skirts coquettishly before retreating back into the darkness, were young women. Their dancing kicked up volcanic dust that mingled with the woodsmoke drifting across the moonlit village to prickle the eyes of whispering onlookers.

I joined a huddle of men by a burning log under a breadfruit tree. They became impressed that I had an apparently endless supply of duty-free cigarettes, and every time I pulled a pack from my backpack, they watched as I ripped off the cellophane and consigned it to the flame. I would pull out a cigarette, light it with a faggot from the fire, and pass the pack to my left, never to see it again.

After a while we were talking about some John Frum secrets, and they were moved by my disappointment when I heard that the village chief, Isac Wan, was not on the island. I told them I'd come all the way from overseas hoping to talk with him, but they said he was in Port Vila preparing to fight in the courts of the Republic of Vanuatu for the ownership rights of John Frum. They said the Green Point people on the other side of the island had incurred his ire by maintaining they were the first John Frum people.

But my disappointment was short-lived, for Chief Isac's son was present, and before the night was over he invited me to return to Lemakara any time on the morrow. In his father's absence, he said others would explain everything to me.

The next day, it was late afternoon when Ken and I returned in the yellow Land Rover to the John Frummers focal village of Lemakara. I was deeply embarrassed to find the villagers had been waiting all day for my return. I had thought the nocturnal invitation had been more casual than that. A man named John Nelaues stepped forward to introduce himself, saying that as he spoke English he would be my informant. At this point Ken and I had to go our separate ways, as he was not a member of the cult and was therefore not allowed to enter the John Frum HQ.

There was tension in the air, for my arrival was dangerously close to sunset and there were ceremonies to get through before dark.

'Let's go,' said John, pointing in the direction of a thatched hut that perched on a ledge of land overlooking the village. We climbed briskly up the path to the hut. As we approached it a man stuck his head from the hut's doorway and blew a pealing blast on a sports whistle. Instantly a complete hush fell over the already subdued village.

In front of the hut I saw there was a line of four flagpoles cut from bush saplings. The pole at one end of the line-up carried the French flag, the one at the far end a tattered remnant of the Australian aboriginal flag. One of the central poles carried the American flag, while the fourth was empty. I was told later that the empty pole was for the Vanuatu flag, but there was no explanation as to its absence.

I ducked after John through the hut's one doorway and a mob of about twenty men and boys followed me in. They took their place on the floor at the doorway-end of the hut, facing a circular table in the centre of the hut. On the table was a miniature American flag and a wooden eagle standing beside a jumble of khaki uniforms. From the tree-trunk beam above the table, dangling on a long piece of string, was a beach-ball globe of the world, along with three pink bracelets, a stone ax and some polished stones.

I was ushered past the table to the far end of the hut by John, who I'd noticed by now had an overly officious tone to his voice and manner. He seemed insecure and angry about something, as if he were an officer giving an operational brief to fighter pilots who were about to zoom off to their doom.

On the end wall of the hut there hung a collection of blackboards covered in chalk writing and it was to these that my attention was directed. The only light in the hut was the dwindling daylight filtering through the bamboo walls, but when my eyes adjusted to the dimness I could read what was on the boards. John instructed me to pay close attention as he was about to tell me the full story of John Frum. He had a long piece of wood in his hand that he used as a pointer.

He pointed at the central blackboard and said with greatest authority, 'First, John Frum came as a pussy-cat.'

On the board was fixed a faded poster of a reclining tiger surveying his domain by the light of a full moon rising from the sea behind silhouettes of tall coconut palms. Superimposed on this moonlit scene, staring inscrutably out at the viewer, was the painting's main subject, a grey domestic cat. After closer scrutiny, I saw the poster was the work of a commercial illustrator and found at its base the title *Daydreams* and the artist's name, Carol Lawson.

Squinting through the gloom, I saw that the illustrator had depicted other tiger in the background of this piece of fantasy art, including one sinking its teeth into a wild pig. But these other tigers were obscured by a naïve chalk overlay that I now learned was someone local's portrayal of a cooked pig.

'John Frum appeared to Nikiau, the father of Chief Isac Wan, here in Sulfur Bay. He told him to cook a pig.' John's pointer went to the chalk drawing.

'When Nikiau had cooked the pig, John Frum came again, this time as a tiger.' As John's pointer tapped the reclining tiger, I nodded solemnly to indicate I was with him so far.

Next the pointer became a walking stick in John's hands as, with wide-open eyes, he mimicked a tiger walking on its hind legs with a stick in its paw, 'And the stick in the tiger's hand was a bright, bright light.'

I learnt how Nikiau and John Frum sat down together and ate the cooked pig, after which John Frum told Nikiau that he would return the following year at Green Point on the other side of the island. This element of precedence was emphasised, no doubt with Chief Wan's current legal challenge in Port Vila in mind. 'So John Frum came to Sulfur Bay first, in 1938, and then he only came once to Green Point in 1939.'

'What did he look like when he appeared at Green Point?' I asked. John became very excited and almost took out my eye with the pointer as he jabbed it toward my face.

'Like you! He came as a white man! He was a spirit, so he could be whatever he liked.'

From the seated congregation three strapping young men leapt to their feet and began donning the khaki overalls from the circular table in double-quick time. I saw that the trouser legs were adorned with red stripes and that badges of office were sewn onto the breasts and sleeves. The men marched out the door and I was instructed to follow, while John and the others remained in the hut.

Outside the three men marched to the base of the three poles carrying flags. One of them blew a sharp blast on the aforementioned whistle. In my travels I've seen many a military flag-lowering ceremony and these three chaps did their cargo cult proud, slowly lowering the flags in unison, hand over hand, folding the flags neatly when they came to hand, all the while standing smartly to attention. Another blast on the whistle and they did a precise about-turn and marched back to the doorway of the HQ, with me bringing up the rear. At this point a polite round of hand-clapping applause came from the villagers peering from the doorways of the otherwise silent huts scattered about the clearing below.

Back inside the hut it was a case of resume positions and my cultic instruction continued. Since this is not meant as an anthropological account, and since I am under no obligation to reveal the full details of knowledge imparted, I'll cut to the chase with a quick summary of some of what's written on the other blackboards inside the HQ. 'Now is the time, choose by the Holy, Holy Stone.' In rough chalk lettering, the statement that money makes man rape his brothers and sisters. 'John Promise America. One Day He'll Be Returning.'

There is a white cross above for Jesus Christ and a red cross for John Frum. 'No Forget *Kastom*. *Them* Spirit.' Smudged chalk makes it hard to read misspelled English and Bislama, but I gather that whole-world peace and unity is the overall aim. '*Bilif* in *Ungan*, In *Kastom* Spirit' is the way to a good life. I learn *Ungan* is the traditional name for God in this part of Tanna and he is bravely depicted in a chalk drawing on one of the boards as a circle of orange dots.

But most importantly, I was informed that, 'We are all in darkness, Peter. Jesus Christ came, but he went back, so we are all in darkness, we cannot see what is real. John Frum came to broom the land clear of evil, to prepare us for the time when God will give back the light.'

By now the sun was setting, and one of the elders said that in the absence of Chief Isac Wan enough had been revealed to me, so it was time to drink kava on the *nakamal*. As we filed out of the HQ building, I realised I'd heard some new information about John Frum. I suppressed sceptical thoughts this might have been created specifically to defend the proprietary rights being asserted in Chief Isac Wan's Port Vila court case. I reminded myself that the stories and directions of Christianity were all over the place until 325 AD when the Council of Nicaea consigned many a reverential tale to the apocryphal waste-bin. I wondered if the Court of Vila could have the same long-term authority as its Nicaean predecessor.

The whole mob of us trooped down past the flagpoles to the village clearing, where we were joined by all the remaining men and boys of the village to make our way further down the slope through the forest. A well-worn path took us to another clearing of volcanic ash, the *nakamal*, this one the size of a tennis court ringed in by thick bush and overhung with the branches of giant trees. People were parking their arses in the dark grey ash around the perimeter of the clearing and I did the same.

Fires were lit to provide us with light and keep the mosquitoes at bay. John was sitting next to me and at his suggestion I made a speech which he translated as I spoke. I talked about how humbled I was by the honour they had done to me that day and told them I had once been a kava farmer in Fiji and was pleased to be able to share kava with them this day. Next I presented one of the elders with two green kava roots I'd brought from the *Kastom* man in the hills, together with a roped bundle of local tobacco leaf I'd picked up in a Lenakel store.

A white-haired elder came forward to accept my presentation and responded with words that John translated for me, 'Kava is the key to *Kastom*,' he said. 'Every secret can only be revealed through kava and *Kastom*.'

A John Frum minstrel took up a position on the grassy bank above the *nakamal* and began strumming his guitar. Pieces of newspaper, so old they looked like silk, were being passed around to make long, thin cigarettes from cuttings of my rope-tobacco presentation.

John explained that while the kava was being prepared, the musician would sing John Frum songs that had come to him from the spirits. He said that we could talk freely on the *nakamal* until we drank the kava, after which we must be silent or talk in whispers to show respect to the kava spirits.

For another half hour in the fleeting dusk, as the minstrel played and the volcano on whose flanks we were sitting belched and rumbled, we talked more about our cult. John pointed out various people seated around the *nakamal* who were family members of the three original chiefs of the cargo cult, Nikiau, Tomi Nambas and Tom Meles, now all passed on into the spirit world.

When I asked him about the American flag John said, 'Only America is the brother. America believes in spirit like *Kastom* people. Don't spoil the life of black people.' He told me that when the three John Frum chiefs were taken to Efate by the colonial authorities in 1941, they were put in prison for seventeen years. But when the American forces arrived there in 1942, they released them, giving them an American flag as a symbol of friendship and saying, 'You have won your freedom.' Not for the first time, the thought came to me that our prevalent histories are not what actually happened, but a fluid collection of transitory stories that help explain the evolving present.

The last of the dusk-light had died in the treetops above the ash clearing. Night was upon us. An old man began telling us a story about various *nakamal* up in the sky, which pulled together the heavens and could be seen at various star-stations above. All the young men looked on with open mouths and expectant eyes, but the story lost its momentum and petered out.

I asked what the local name was for the Milky Way, but nobody knew. In pursuit of my question, I took a stick, and in the ash before me drew a picture of the night sky to illustrate what I meant. Men gathered around in the firelight to regard my drawing with suspicion.

What the hell, I decided to launch into a brief exposition of my received version of the make-up of the cosmos. So, trying my darnedest not to sound like a proselytizer of any ilk, I gave it my best shot. First, to get our bearings, I took a stick and drew a diagram in the sand to my right. This speck was Tanna, this collection of specks Vanuatu, Fiji, New Caledonia, Australia, this little circle the whole world, here the moon, there the sun and our sister planets, along with our asteroids and comets, making up the place we call the solar system.

Drawing a bigger circle to the side, I held that this was our galaxy, the Milky Way, the same I'd just been asking about, and waved with my stick up at the white pathway smoking across the sky. Within my depiction of the galaxy circle of the Milky Way, I made a dot saying that was the place of our solar system, one of a few hundred billion stars spinning around the bulging centre of the Milky Way.

Then I drew an even bigger circle in some unsullied ash to my left and dubbed it the universe, making another small dot therein to represent our now diminutive Milky Way. John was getting apprehensive but I persevered with my skeptical audience, telling them that thanks to the observations of the telescopes the Americans had sent up into space, we know the universe is made up of about 125 billion galaxies, each made up of billions of stars grouped into superclusters separated by yawning galactic voids that put into considerable doubt the adequacy of the human scale.

I knew my credibility was shot, but much as I baulked at it, I could not avoid the subject of the Big Bang, so away I went. First I came clean with what I understood to be scientific orthodoxy, saying that even the most cautious of our scientists are now confident they can grasp the outline of our universe and what it is comprised of. I said that fourteen billion years ago there were no stars, that there was only a seed of infinite energy and that the time came when an intensely hot genesis-event caused a very big explosion. The first microsecond of that event was still shrouded in mystery, but everything that has happened since then, the emergence of our incredibly complex cosmos, was the outcome of laws our scientists could now understand. Just as geophysicists have worked out the processes that made the oceans and sculpted the continents, so astrophysicists now understand how it is that our Sun and its planets, and indeed all the other stars, have come to be where they are.

I was hitting my stride and some of the younger men were hanging in there, so I gave it one last push. While the wondrous effect of gravity held us to the surface of our spinning planet, as it does the planet to our rotating solar system, as it does all the stars of all the swirling galaxies, I told them gravity's force was not yet enough to counteract the explosive effect of the Big Bang. By studying over time the direction of background microwave radiation, scientists have come to see that the universe is still expanding. Fourteen billion years later, the galactic superclusters are still flying away from where the Big Bang event took place.

John had stopped bothering to translate my words and even the young onlookers had drifted away now. He looked a little disappointed in me and said, 'Peter.' His hands went up into the air. 'You have your telescope to look through, but we only have our *Kastom*.'

He was right. I'd said too much. I'd wanted to move on, to tell them about the implications for all of us arising from the discovery of DNA, but my delivery skills weren't up to it. Likewise, dishing up some regurgitated material on parallel universes had been on my mind, for I thought cargo cultists might relate to that material better than most. But there was another sort of regurgitation going on around me on the fire-lit *nakamal* that demanded my full attention.

All this while, the men had been preparing the kava. This process I had been observing with considerable interest from the corner of my eye, as I suspected I was destined to drink the first bowl when it was ready. The kava I'd presented was whole fresh roots, meaning it had been recently pulled from the ground with roots and stem-base intact and only the stems and branches cut from the plants.

As I looked around I saw the kava was being skinned, rubbed with coconut coir, chopped into thumb-sized bits and distributed around the *nakamal* for the congregation to chew upon. Imagine the difficult task of chewing a fibrous ginger corm and you get the picture: hard work on teeth, drooling gums and aching jaw muscles. After a prolonged session of this mastication, I noticed the chewers were standing up, taking their mouthfuls to the centre of the *nakamal*, and hoicking the resulting wads of spittle and vegetable matter onto a large communal banana leaf.

For reasons of hygiene, the missionaries had stamped out kava-chewing in most of the Pacific Islands, back in the nineteenth century; but over the years I'd picked up hints that there were still isolated parts of Melanesia where kava was prepared in the old way. I'd heard that unlike pre-missionary Fiji and Polynesia, where the chewing was done by young virgin women, in these places it was young men that did the chewing, since women were not allowed anywhere near the Melanesian kava.

Now as I looked around, I saw that this *nakamal* was much more democratic, for young and old were having a go at the task. All the while there built a kecking cacophony of throat-clearing and rattling nasal air-sucks. Indeed, the din of it all made it difficult to continue conversations between those of us not engaged in chewing.

Squatting near me was a skinny, ash-covered, old chap whose collection of teeth must have numbered no more than half a dozen. He was dribbling badly as he chewed. I watched as he struggled to his dusty feet and tottered on bandy legs to the centre of the *nakamal* to spit the results of his laboured mastication onto the banana leaf. As he shuffled back to resume his place beside me, I thought, 'We shall be joined by the communion of the tribal saliva, even so the residue of the cavities of these many teeth.'

The assembled kava sludge rose like a weeping hillock on the glistening banana leaf, until the last of the fibrous residue had been spat into place and the hillock was slid from the leaf into a large wooden urn. In this deep dark bowl it was mixed with water by means of a stick wielded by three young men.

Behind us a boy began beating loudly on a wooden drum and John said, 'When the women hear the tam-tam they will send us the food.' Sure enough, a few minutes later little bowls of food began materialising around the *nakamal*, carried by boys who deposited them here and there on convenient logs or upon the dusty ground.

John leant towards me and stage-whispered, 'Peter, now you must drink the first bowl of kava.'

Watched by every eye on the *nakamal*, I walked slowly over to the kava and was given a large coconut-shell full to the brim with the feculent brew. This was what in Fiji we call *yaqona drokadroka* or green kava, much stronger than the sun-dried, pounded kava drunk in most Pacific Islands. I expected this bowl to have a kick.

Accepting the bowl Fijian style, I gave a soft clap of my hands before gagging back the mushy liquid in contiguous gulps. The kava was what would be described in Fijian as *rui sosoko*, thickly concentrated, with bits of kava fibre and other pulpy bits catching in my teeth.

I returned the coconut to the communal urn, and picking inexplicables from my mouth, made my way unsteadily back to the perimeter. An ancient palm-leaf, roughly plaited had been laid in the ash for the benefit of my backside. I lowered myself onto the dusty palm leaf, but just as I was beginning to contemplate the effect on my innards of what I'd just imbibed, John leant over again and pointed towards a food bowl to one side of the *nakamal*.

'That is your bowl,' he said. 'You must eat it.'

Food was the last thing I needed right now, but I went dutifully over and extracted a few pieces of manioc from a battered red plastic bowl of acrid fish stew. My cutlery consisted entirely of a rusty but sharply pointed hunting knife, its handle bound by grimy string.

Enough was enough; the effects of the kava were setting in. I took the stew back to where I'd been sitting, put it behind me and forgot about it. I was sitting there cross-legged on my palm leaf, like a stoned Buddha, when John whispered in my ear, 'If you're feeling drunk, they will bring you your second bowl here.'

I mumbled, 'Shnf ... shndgrdtmi,' and another deep bowl of kava came over to hover in front of my eyes. I clapped, took the bowl and sent the swill down my gullet with half a dozen big gulps.

Silence fell over the *nakamal*. Men helped themselves to draughts of kava from the urn and drifted off to sit by themselves around the perimeter to commune with the kava spirits. Pigs wandered about looking for scraps. Limping skeletal dogs, a couple of them three-legged, cringed around the food bowls.

Moonlight began to assert itself, for a gibbous moon was creeping through the treetops, causing the grey floor of the jungle clearing to become dappled with wavering shadows. Moonbeams transformed smoke-wisps curling from the glowing embers of a campfire into ethereal, silver-blue suggestions. Intermittent rumbles from the volcano above were now as natural as human breathing. I heard a night-bird call. Time seemed to have slowed to a crawl, but perversely the hours flew by. I was as content as a frog on a lily pad. John was long gone. I heard a strong breeze leave the sea and work its way up from the coast a mile away. It moved through the jungle a little to the side of us and continued on up towards the caldera.

Most of my drinking companions seemed to have wandered off, but still here and there I could pick out the glow of tobacco where men sat smoking by themselves in the surrounding bush. One villager squatted at the edge of the *nakamal* staring intently at the tree-trunk a hands-breadth from his nose; another sat by a smoldering campfire repeatedly wafting its smoke over his head with his hands. Motionless on a log to my left, an old fullah was perched like a raven, his silver head to one side studying me. Everyone was waiting for ... something. A thought elbowed its way into my drifting consciousness, 'So this is man, this is us, these are my brothers.'

Ritual and magic are everywhere on Tanna. One day I was sitting on a rocky foreshore with some islanders who answered my question about the forked sticks festooned with green leaves that were jammed into rocks along certain sections of the coast. The signs were a warning against swimming and would only be removed when the feast of the first yam harvest was held in April. Prior to that feast, they said swimming would be very perilous in those places. The same reason was given for why I should not go and bathe in Fekel, the island's big waterfall.

Before we'd touched a drop of kava, one man on the John Frum *nakamal* had told me he could control the weather. He said the people came to him when they wanted rain for the crops. I was going to ask him if he could do something for drought-stricken Australian farmers while he was at it, but then I figured his powers would be confined to Tanna and perhaps a few adjacent islands. How much could be reasonably expected of just one man?

I met a man who told me he and his family owned all the breadfruit on Tanna. No one was allowed to eat the new season's breadfruit until he had taken one, baked it in a fire on the *nakamal*, and eaten it. After that everyone could eat. I said that I hadn't eaten any breadfruit since coming to Tanna and he gave me a piercing look. '*Yu no wari*,' he said, I could eat the breadfruit if I wanted to.

When I asked Ken what the breadfruit man had meant, whether all the trees really belonged to his family, he said that every family had a special thing. By way of example he explained his family totems: his mother's the black and white sea snake we call *dadakulaci* in Fiji, his father's the rocks. He said some people put sickness on others by using their totem and only people who shared the same totem could lift the spell from the sick.

One day a group of us near Sulfur Bay were rattling away about John Frum and Prophet Fred, as enthusiastic and opinionated as a bunch of Kiwis talking about rugby in a local pub. One of our number I knew to be Ken's father and I presumed he didn't understand English or my bastardized Bislama, because he just sat there with a big grin on his face looking from talker to talker, saying nothing himself. He had soft brown smiling eyes and his full head of hair and beard were snowy white. I guessed he was in his eighties.

As we got up to go our separate ways, Ken's father came to me and in beautiful English introduced himself as Nalau. He told me that he was a carpenter and happily showed me his smooth broad carpenter's hands, his thumbs looking bent but supple from a lifetime of handling wood. He said he'd spent many years working for the missions and had accompanied the Presbyterian missionary Ken Calvert during the decade or so he was on Tanna. He'd named his son Ken after his missionary companion, and his daughter, Anne, was named after Mrs Calvert.

Nalau said if I was interested in Prophet Fred, I should make my way to Sulfur Bay on Sunday, because people from all over the island were coming there for a Unity meeting and Prophet Fred would be addressing them. The next day I heard reference to Deacon Nalau and realised the speakers were referring to Ken's gentle father.

So Sunday morning found Ken and me walking for two hours from my crazy beach-bungalow, along the rocky coast to Sulfur Bay. This was a foreshore of fishermen, yet not a single fibreglass or aluminium hull was to be seen; instead in every little bay, dragged above the high-water mark were outrigger canoes made of the trunks of breadfruit and mango trees. It was proving to be hot going as we worked our way among the black volcanic rocks. But I held back from suggesting we paddle one of these canoes to our destination, for I'd noticed this stretch of the coastline was sign-posted with many forked sticks entwined with leaves.

Towards the end of our trek, we climbed up onto a plateau of forest and food-gardens and Ken showed me where the battle between the forces of John Frum and Prophet Fred had occurred the previous year, I believe in 2004. The battle had been fierce with one man nearly expiring when his back was opened up by a machete. Another had his foot smashed by a *petanque* ball and a Presbyterian pastor collected a spear that went right through his leg.

Ken pulled a *lastic* from his back pocket, a wooden catapult, the scourge of Vanuatu for all young Tannese males have one and the birdlife suffers accordingly. He said the *lastics* came out during the battle, and that small pieces of iron had been used as their ammunition. It was after this torrid battle that Isac Wan and the rump of the John Frummers moved from Sulfur Bay up to Lemakara village, the place where I had drunk green kava with the men of the cargo cult the week before,

At the edge of the forest plateau, we came to an escarpment and below us lay the bright blue of Sulfur Bay, a deep indent in the Tanna coast facing the southeast trades. Around a broad grey paradeground, the bamboo huts of the large village spread from the coast some two hundred metres inland. Between our escarpment and the village I looked down on a broad rocky riverbed, through which shallow water was flowing, and could see people the size of matchsticks down there, bathing in the river's hot pools.

Ken pointed inland to where Lake Siwi had broken its banks and come raging down the riverbed, taking all the forest along its old banks out to sea. It was about five o'clock when the prophesied cataclysm occurred, he told me, and many people would have been in the river pools washing clothes, doomed to drown had Prophet Fred not come and summoned them to higher ground.

Ken stood with his arms outstretched, 'Prophet Fred was like this. Facing the flood. Keeping the water away from the village.'

Apart from pecking chickens and soporific pigs, Sulfur Bay village was deserted when we walked into it. Then we came across a simpleton sitting on a branch, happily waggling his skinny legs, who knew enough to send us in the direction of the hill above the village.

Under gigantic banyans and rain trees, we climbed up an ash path until we came to a ledge of land upon which hundreds of people were gathered beside a half-built church. Seated in this shade-dappled glade, every one of those dark brown bodies was clothed in scarlet, a stunning sight amongst all the greenery.

It seemed an open-air service was under way, so Ken and I made our way around to the back of the crowd and sat down upon the grass in the company of some people he knew. With loud whispers, I was introduced and handshakes were exchanged all round. The atmosphere back there was quite casual, like the boys at the back of a very big class, or more realistically, those on the fringe of a crowd gathered on a New Testament hillside.

I saw the congregation was being addressed in Bislama by an elderly man. In full flight, he was covering such matters as the Lord's Prayer and the Ten Commandments. I asked who he was and learned it was Elder Kition Nambas of the Presbyterian Church. It was expected Prophet Fred would speak after him.

On the grass next to me lay Tom, a man in his thirties, a good-looking guy with black woolly beard and deep chocolate skin set off by his bright red tee-shirt. He was a relative of Ken's by marriage and Ken asked me to show Tom the copy of *Kava in the Blood* that I carried in my camera bag. The fact that I was the book's author, that I had been a kava farmer, that I was from Fiji, and that there was a photo of me on the cover drinking kava with some Fijian friends, was an entry pass wherever we went on Tanna. Ken was forever asking me to pull it from my bag.

Tom told me that he was brought up believing in John Frum. He said he used to be the number one composer for John Frum - he could beat anyone from all over Tanna in composing John Frum spirit songs. But as soon as he heard Prophet Fred preaching, he had changed over and joined the Unity movement.

Tom said an American man, an ex-military man called David, had given the money for them to build the church beside whose half-built walls we were stretched out in the grass. He said that when they finished the church they were going to put a sign above the door saying, 'Headquarter for the USA and Unity' and underneath that it would say, 'Presbyterian Church, Sulfur Bay.'

Over the woolly heads of the crimson crowd, Elder Kition Nambas launched into a hymn. Though no-one but Nambas seemed to know the words, he soldiered on for another six verses before taking his seat amongst a line of dignitaries seated on chairs facing the congregation. Now a murmur spread through the people upon the grass, heads waggled about, adjusting for better views and Tom said, 'Now Prophet Fred will speak.'

A man came humbly forward to address the crowd and from where I sat I had a clear view of this latter-day prophet from his waist upwards. Like everyone else he was clad in red, but draped over his shoulder was an Omo-white scarf. I fitted a telephoto lens to my camera and zoomed in for a closer look. Prophet Fred had a broad handsome Melanesian face, with a rather saddened look to his eyes and mouth. A scraggy black beard fell to his upper chest and the thick black hair of his head was twisted up in careless tufts.

The prophet's voice was clear and calm and as he spoke he lifted up his open hands to gesture peacefully at the gathering. I was reminded of St Paul's letter to the Corinthians on the matter of spiritual gifts. Paul questioned the usefulness of speaking in tongues, for only God would understand what all the ecstatic babbling was about, but he encouraged his fellow Christians to engage in prophesy, saying that it should be done decently and in order.

As far as I could make out, nothing Delphic was going down today. Prophet Fred's five-minute address was basic housekeeping: telling the people what colour they'd be wearing at the next meeting, conveying news about the march they would soon undertake to the other side of the island, and wrapping up by saying that they should all move down the hill to the village to conclude the meeting.

Kicking up a cloud of dust that rose high into the fern-festooned branches of the giant trees, the red sea descended the ash-path to Sulfur Bay. On the way down, I met Elder Nambas and then the pastor who'd suffered the spear through his leg.

Word must have got around that I was there to meet the prophet, for as we were milling around the now-crowded village, a soft-spoken man approached me and introduced himself as Thomas. With sincere coal-black eyes and slightly self-deprecating manner, Thomas said that he was a teacher. He said that he would translate for me if I wished to speak to Prophet Fred.

I gladly accepted his invitation and followed him through the crowd to a small hut with waist high reed-walls and a floor of leaves and roughly-plaited bamboo. We stooped to enter under the doorway's thatched lintel and I was offered a seat on a wooden bench set against a wall. As I sat down I noticed there were two boulders in the middle of the floor, one grey, the other composed of pink igneous rock. I was later told, without further explanation, that the rocks represented the two main indigenous languages of the island.

Against the wall adjacent to mine sat the prophet, on a long slab of rough stone. He looked distinctly uneasy about my presence and avoided eye contact, other than giving me a couple of furtive glances. I noticed that his left eye was weeping badly and that his hair was matted like a Rastafarian's. I believed he had every reason to be suspicious of the motives of a white stranger, so through Thomas I quickly explained my purpose. I said I was writing a book about the Pacific Islands and wanted to go into the subject of religion in one of the book's chapters. I said I had come to Tanna to learn about the religious activity on the island, in particular Prophet Fred's Unity movement. I said I had walked over the hills of Tanna today in order to hear his message.

The prophet nodded a shy, conditional assent and Thomas looked to me for more *tok-tok*. With the kindly teacher working away at my side, a thirty-minute interchange ensued. To break the ice, I asked about the various colours the Unity movement wore and Prophet Fred and Thomas enthusiastically listed them all: red for the blood of Jesus on his cross, black for the soil and *Kastom*, yellow for the light of the church, green for the weather, and white for the spirit of healing and prediction whose power comes from the sun.

I knew from what I'd heard elsewhere on the island, that the prophet's full name was Fred Nase, that he was about forty-four years old and that he'd had a John Frum upbringing in Sulfur Bay. I wanted to know how he'd received his calling to prophethood and he readily explained that he had procured a job in Vila working on a Taiwanese fishing boat. After a long time at sea, one night they were out in the Indian Ocean's maw, yes, the Indian Ocean, and he was praying out on the deck. Then he noticed one of the stars in heaven becoming brighter and brighter, and its light began shining down all around him. He heard a voice, the voice of the Lord, telling him that he must return to Tanna and bring unity to the people, bring together the *Kastom* people and the John Frum people and the Christian people, '*Unitem* John Frum, *Kastom, mo* historical church *blong kam* wan in God.'

He leant forward in the middle of his story and water poured from the chalice of his bad eye as if it would never stop. He sat up and dabbed the edge of his eye, shook his ragged head and continued the story. He told how eventually he returned from the fishing boat to Port Vila, spent all his accumulated wages on buying stores for the people of Sulfur Bay, then hired a landing craft to carry the stores and a boatload of Tanna people back to the island for the great homecoming.

As soon as he was back on Tanna he began preaching his message of unity, and then with his epiphanous revelations came miracles and prophesies. The Sulfur Bay area had suffered from intense volcanic activity during the previous five years, volcanic dust had coated the southeast corner of the island; but through the powers of the prophet, the dust clouds departed. '*I stopem long* 2nd May 2000.'

Next came his prophecy of the Lake Siwi cataclysm of 2000, through which people saw the divine gift Prophet Fred had received. After that he moved with his followers to a mountain village to fast and augment his spiritual powers. When he came down from the mountain these powers were greatly increased and he could heal the sick and control the weather. '*I kam* down *blong stopem* poisons, *controlem* weather, *healem* sick, *protectum* steal history, *mo plante moa.*'

He began touring the whole island on his evangelical mission, curing the cursed and the infirm, preaching unity and encouraging the building of Presbyterian mission churches. Instead of John Frum's observance day of Friday, he instituted Wednesday as the Unity day, supplementary to the Christian Sunday.

At this stage of my audience, we were joined by a handsome new face, a man by the name of John, who took his seat beside Prophet Fred on the stone bench. Handsome John was the Unity movement's spokesman. He looked like he'd make a good middleweight boxer, like St Paul, a hard-hitting enforcer. While the prophet looked absently at the ground of the hut, dabbing his eye with a cloth wrapped around his fist, John began haranguing me about the mighty powers of the man beside him. I should know what I was dealing with, he warned me; this prophet had the power to control the volcano and the weather. A year ago, he prophesied that not just Tanna, but all of Vanuatu would have no hurricanes for five years. He was using the powers God had given him to hold back the tropical cyclones so the people and their food gardens would not be caused further suffering.

Handsome John gave Thomas a printed piece of paper to read to me, said I could have it, then that I couldn't, then that I could. He said that I should use it to spread the word of the Unity movement. I said that I was not a journalist, but I would use it in my account of our meeting, that I would write about it in my book.

Perhaps John was encouraged by my genuine humility, because he cranked up his assertiveness. Belligerently poking the air with his finger, he told me the Unity movement had started here in Sulfur Bay and would move out into the world. We may be one big family, he said, but the founding people of the world were here on Tanna.

The paper John gave me was written in Bislama, but the English phrase, 'United we stand, divided we fall,' appeared in several places in the text. He said this was Unity's motto. John proclaimed that after Prophet Fred had united Tanna, he would move out and unite all the people of Vanuatu, and after that the whole world. The gist of the text was that Unity required commitment from us all. 'Unity *I fesem fulap* challenges from *ol* man.' But salvation was on the way thanks to the 'plan *blong* God,' and we will be rewarded, for if we '*Unitem* in God, *oltaem blong hemi giveim moa long yumi.*'

Prophet Fred brought up his ragged head and John fell silent. In an urgent, nervous tone the prophet said, '*Taim kam yumi no unitem, wata I ronaot long laif.*' Thomas looked at John who was now brooding. Thomas hesitated, in case I'd not got the gist of it he leant towards me to softly translate, 'If we don't unite, the water will run out of life."

Directly outside the hut, a John Frum stringband's spiritual sing-song had been meandering along. But now it was giving way to a *Kastom* dance. The dance built with enthusiasm, making the ground shake with the rhythmic thuds of a hundred dancers leaping up and down in time. I asked if I might take a photograph and being encouraged to do so, stood and shot the dancers through the half-wall of the hut. The dancing was joyous, men in the centre of the tight swirl of humanity, women at the outer, circling, moving in and out, chanting and clapping hands. All the while the thumping of feet on the ash ground was creating a great cloud of dust that rose from their scarlet mass like steam from Mount Yasur's lava.

At the conclusion of the *Kastom* dance the entire congregation, young and old, men and women, came together in the clearing under the banyan tree in a two-hundred-strong crimson choir and began singing Christian hymns with a harmonious power that made me weak at the knees. Again it was a scene full of joy and I caught sight of my friend, Deacon Nalau, hanging on halfway up the banyan's commodious trunk with a bunch of his friends singing their hearts out. And as I watched that white head, with its smile as wide as Sulfur Bay, going from side to side, and the grinning responses of all those his happy eyes fell upon, I knew I had to record what I saw in that moment and what I recall now with a clarity that fills me with the benevolent spirit of Nalau, a man who was truly living his life in love.

Before we parted, Prophet Fred suggested through John and Thomas that I might like to help them with their forthcoming march. On 15th December a great gathering would take place on the other side of the island, to give thanks for the first year's anniversary of Prophet Fred keeping Vanuatu free of hurricanes. The people of this side of the island would march across the mountain road to attend the meeting.

I asked what sort of help I could give and a sack of rice was suggested. I was happy to have the opportunity to help with the victuals of the pilgrims and replied that I would purchase the rice before I left Tanna. Then John said they had no photos of the Unity movement, could I take a shot, have it framed and send it to them? Yes, I would be honoured to undertake that task, so John shouted instructions and the congregation gathered again under the banyan tree for me to capture the scene on film.

John took his place amongst the throng for the photo, but Prophet Fred declined and went off to sit with a pair of old men surveying the scene from a distance. In one of the Gospels there is an account of Jesus being so hemmed in by a crowd that he could hardly breathe. Among the crowd was a woman who had suffered haemorrhages for many years and nobody had been able to cure her. She came up behind Jesus and touched the edge of his cloak and instantly her haemorrhaging ended. Jesus said, 'Who has touched me?' No one owned up and Peter said, 'Master, the crowds are hemming you in, they are pressing upon you!' But Jesus said, 'Someone did touch me, for I felt that power went out of me.'

I flew out of Tanna with a new story in my head, melding with the lessons of our kirk in Suva's Goodenough Street and the pronouncements of the Astronomer Royal. I was mixing in the drift of the words of Boston's professor of physics, Chet Raymo, who wrote, 'I hunger for a faith that is open to the new cosmology.' The sense of self, the sense of other, the sense of unfathomable mystery that has been with us since the first spark of consciousness ignited a human mind: those senses remain the open door to the divine said Raymo. We got ourselves into our present muddle by naming the unknown sources of these intuitions, then confusing the names with external reality. The Boston professor should go and discourse with the receptive minds of Tanna. He and the Tannese would have much to talk about.

On my way home I flew first to the island of Efate, where I had a few hours idling in Vanuatu's capital, Vila. The capital's full name is Port Vila and is one of the world's great little harbour towns. I asked an airport taxi driver to take me to the bustling market on the waterfront, for I wanted to purchase beautiful Futuna baskets for my beautiful wife back home.

The driver told me he was from Tanna and I replied that I'd just been spending time there with the John Frum people and with Prophet Fred. I was a little taken aback when he cackled a derisive laugh. But as we drove on, he turned out to be a pleasant and honest fellow, if a little narrow-minded, and we arranged that he'd pick me up in two hour's time outside the market to drive me back to the airport.

As I got out of the car, I put my head through the window and asked him what religion he followed. With a confident smile he said, 'SDA.'

Two hours later we were driving back to the airport and I said, 'So you're a Seventh Day Adventist.'

'Yes, I went to the SDA school on Tanna.'

'You don't listen to Prophet Fred?'

'No, no, I'm not interested. Let him say what he likes.'

My driver was a man of progress, we were men of progress together, progressing to the airport in his taxi. I changed the subject, 'Have you heard about the SDA college in Avondale, in New Zealand?'

'Oh yes, I heard about that.'

'And the big Adventist hospital in Sydney.'

He gave a hesitant affirmative.

I told him I'd seen it and it was a very good hospital. Then I looked across at him and said, 'Battle Creek, Michigan, eh!'

'What?'

'Battle Creek, that's where the SDAs really got going.'

He looked at me suspiciously.

'They had a sanatorium at Battle Creek, you know a health place, like a hospital. That's where the Sanitarium name comes from on the Weet-Bix packet.'

'*Yu tru?*' What I was hiding from him? What was I tricking him into? 'Weet-Bix?'

'Sanitarium Weet-Bix. You must have heard of it, the SDA church owns it.'

'Oh yes,' he said unconvincingly.

I had no ulterior motives, all I was doing was story-telling. 'Y'know, an SDA man called Dr Kellogg used to work at the Battle Creek sanatorium. He was a very clever fella. He developed Corn Flakes there, but then his shoe-salesman brother persuaded him to go private with the product and they set up the Kellogg's cereal company.'

The driver narrowed his eyes and said, 'What's Corn Flakes?'

I left off the subject, feeling that these breakfast cereals would reveal themselves to my driver only if and when they ever became relevant to him. In the meantime, he was probably better off without all the collateral milk and white sugar. He certainly looked healthy and that's what the SDAs like to see.

I'm back in Sydney now, finishing off this story. I've just been down for a walk around the green cricket oval, under the flowering jacarandas of

Rushcutters Bay. I lolled for a while on the waterfront's sandstone wall watching slick black cormorants diving for sprats. Above me the massive branches of a giant fig tree extended, and I was looking up at one of these limbs when a plump dove alighted on it. A spangle of light played on the bird's pink breast, bright deflections of sunlight from wavelets lapping the wall below. Once more I found myself waiting for something more to be revealed. It has been a familiar reaction since that evening communing by firelight with the green kava spirit on the side of John Frum's volcano.

Something *is* hidden from us. Not what was torn from the first page of the Bible, but something that is tantalising all around us. Yes, you get hints of it in the light, they call it Wordsworth's dwelling, that place where the sense of something far more deeply interfused rolls through all things. It was in Einstein's mind too, the deeply embedded, mysterious intangible, the fundamental beautiful truth we all seek to penetrate but perhaps will always be too thick to perceive.

Professor Raymo says we'll only be emotionally at home in the universe of the galaxies and the cosmos of DNA when the new story invigorates our spiritual lives, when at last, knowing and believing come together again. So I too say, 'Hold firm for John Frum!' You can have your *Kastom* and look through the telescope my friend.' And I join with those who believe, '*Unitem* we stand, divided we fall.'

We are drifting on in the mist of being, shimmering droplets suspended at the lip of a vast waterfall that is thundering away to eternity. Science tells a saga of incredible discovery and the selective consequences of complexity, but it is not the full story. That we are ephemeral is self-evident, but sufficient scatterings of hints, some mystical, some not, suggest our lives are not without consequence.

I close with a prayer. I pray with those who have faith in reason, take inspiration from nature and have hope in progress.

402

My prayer is for us all, that we may empower those who search on our behalf for cosmic knowledge without limit, those who have the power for good and the awareness of mystery. And I pray with those who teach us to be bound by love for all creation, and to peacefully accept our union with the absolute.

Even as each day, dawn's light breaks from the rim of dark ocean, and lagoons flood with evening's farewell, may we be satisfied. And may we be one with the light that shines from the eyes of all living things. May we truly know the love-light of our meeting hearts.

Let us give thanks for being. Let us face the awe with courage, with faith in the continuity. And when we consider the fast-expanding sum of all that the human mind has discovered, may our response be fortified by humility.

I pray that we find entry to the sacred clearing again. I pray we will ever hold to love for this world. May we always be true in our agreement to travel well on this journey, dear friend. And let us pray that like Prophet Fred, people will ever treasure the land and the sea and the place of the creatures therein, so that the water never runs out of life.

By the keening cliffs of Hane

P.T. & M.V. Aranui

Travellers' Notes

The Moon over Matsushima

[1] Basho quote from *A Haiku Journey*, translated by Dorothy Britton, Kondansha International, Tokyo, 1983.

[2] From *Gilead* by Marilynne Robinson, London, 2004.

[3] From *Michael* by William Wordsworth, London, 1800.

[4] The Kaunimakoni place-name is not much known by Suva people today. Adi Lady Lala Mara, the late paramount chief of the part of Fiji in which Suva lies, used to like reminding me that my family came from Kaunimakoni. In the Fijian language *kau* means tree, *ni* means of, and *makoni* is the phonetic for the inventor of long-distance wireless, Marconi. It is common in Fiji for place-names to reflect the dominant tree-cover of the area, in this case the towers of iron erected to transmit wireless signals.

[5] The description of the Kearsley sisters is from *The Years of Hope* by Philip Snow, London, 1997

Getting Off the Rock

[6] *Daveta* are the broad passages through the main sea reefs of Fiji.

[7] The verse on self-will is from an 1869 hymn by JE Bode.

[8] With apologies to William Shakespeare for mangling the Saint Crispin's speech of *Henry V.*

Yo-ho-ho

[9] *Noqu i tau* translates from Fijian as 'my friend'.

[10] From *Treasure Island* by Robert Louis Stevenson, Edinburgh, 1881.

[11] From *Union Line* by Sydney Waters, Wellington, 1952.

[12] *Dreich* translates from Scots to English as dreary, and *lum* as chimney.

[13] From *St Matthew* chapter 6, verses 24 to 29, King James version, *The Holy Bible.*

[14] The prefix RCS is a rare one. It stands for Royal Colonial Ship and was the moniker of the *Viti* in the years she was the governor's motor yacht. Launched in Hong Kong in 1939, under later manifestations she carried the titles HMFS, HMS and MV. The last I heard of her in the 1960s, she was a tramp steamer working the small coastal towns of the South China Sea.

[15] See *From a South Seas Diary 1938-1942* by Sir Harry Luke, London, 1945.

[16] See *The War Years* by Sir Ian Thomson, Canberra, 2004.

[17] See also *Fiji in the Forties and Fifties* by Sir Ian Thomson, Auckland, 1994.

[18] Adi Lala was the wife of Ratu Sir Kamisese Mara, the long-serving prime minister and president of Fiji. In her own right Adi Lady Lala was the Roko Tui Dreketi, head of the Burebasaga confederacy, and as such one of the three most high-ranking chiefs in Fiji. My father's friendship with her father, the previous Roko Tui Dreketi, Ratu George Tuisawau, arose from their being fellow officers in the Fiji Infantry Regiment during World War Two. Inheriting the leadership of the Burebasaga confederacy from his father, Ratu George Tuisawau was through his mother the great, great grandson of the famed Ratu Cakobau, King of Fiji; as indeed were first cousins Ratu Sukuna and Ratu Edward Cakobau through their mothers' lines.

[19] From The Fiji Times, 21st November 1966.

[20] From *Regular Soldier* by Frank Rennie, Auckland, 1986.

[21] *Vaka bogi drau* refers to the ceremonies of lifting of mourning that occur one hundred nights after the death of a chief.

[22] Students of Fiji history will find frequent reference to my father as JS Thomson. On his birth certificate his name is John Sutherland Thomson, but all his life he was called Ian, the Scottish diminutive of John. When he was knighted by The Queen in 1984 at Holyrood Palace in Edinburgh, he was dubbed Sir Ian Thomson. In answer to an often asked question, Thomson St in Suva was not named after him, but Thomson Crescent in Lautoka was.

Inwrought with Affection

[23]   The Evan's quote is from *Daniel Deronda* by George Eliot, London, 1876.

[24]   Translation of some Fijian words used in this and the next two paragraphs: *rai* means to see, *cakau* means reef and *rorogo* refers to sound; *voivoi* refers to the pandanus plant from the dried leaves of which Fijian floor-mats are made; *dalo* is the Fijian name for the taro plant and *rourou* is the name for its cooked leaves; *duruka* is the edible flower-bud of an indigenous species of cane; *baka* is the name of a local species of banyan tree and *ivi* is the Fijian name for the Tahitian chestnut. *Talanoa* translates as telling stories.

[25]   For further insight into Brett Whiteley's Fiji period, see *Brett Whiteley Art & Life* by Bryan Robertson, Barry Pearce and Wendy Whiteley, London, 1995.

[26]   See *Divided We Stand* by Ropate Qalo, Suva, 1984, for a concise description of Fiji's local government system and the make-up of the provinces and districts.

[27]   *Sevusevu* is essentially the ceremony of the presentation of first fruit, which in a formal Fijian ceremony of welcome involves the presentation of a whole kava tree. In everyday urban practice, a *sevusevu* is usually the presentation of a bag of prepared (powdered) kava as a symbol of respectful introduction or welcome. In everyday Fiji, this latter meaning might be informally extended to the gift you take to someone's house as a token of thanks for the hospitality about to be received, and might sometimes materialise as a bottle of Scotch.

[28]   *Nuqa* is a flat fish, excellent eating, fried, poached or steamed. Its English name, Vermiculate Rabbitfish, is rarely used in Fiji. In the traditional Fijian calendar, the lunar month at the beginning of the year was *Vula ni Nuqa Levu*, the month when the *nuqa* were plentiful.

[29]   *We Three* was a song Meli picked up from his army days. I believe it was first sung by the American group, the Inkspots.

The Dawn Anchor-Watch

[30]   See *Turaga. The Life and Times and Chiefly Authority of Ratu Sir Penaia Ganilau* by Daryl Tarte, Suva, 1993.

[31]   For a full description of Cikobia see *Na Ciri Kalia* by Bruce Biggs, Auckland, 1975.

[32] *Sautu* means peace and plenty. In accepting a whales-tooth tribute, a Fijian dignitary will often call for well-being in the countryside by uttering the invocation, '*Sautu na vanua!*', meaning, 'May there be peace and plenty in the land'.

[33] I believe there are few better tales of sailing the ocean than *The Saga of Cimba* by Richard Maury, London, 1939.

[34] See *South Sea Bubbles* by The Earl and The Doctor, London, 1872.

[35] From *Silktail. A Fiji Ecothriller* by Max Lacrosse, Charleston, 2008.

[36] Verse from *The Rime of the Ancient Mariner* by Samuel Taylor Coleridge, London, 1834.

[37] My thanks to Catherine Morgan for access to the interviews she recorded with her husband John Morgan and Manasa Bulivou in Suva in August 1994.

Heaven Lies About Us

[38] *Too Young to be Married* was written by Tony Hicks and performed by the British pop group The Hollies. It was a number one hit in Australia and New Zealand in 1970.

[39] The 'heaven lies about us' verse is from William Wordsworth's ode, *Intimations of Immortality*, London 1807.

[40] *Belo* is the Fijian name for a reef heron, *Egretta sacra sacra*.

[41] *Bogi walu* means eight nights in Fijian. In this context, it refers to the approximate time a tropical depression, with its lashings of wind and rain, takes to move by the island.

[42] *Satsumo imo* is Japanese for sweet potato and *furio shimbun* means rubbish newspapers. In the domestic streets of Tokyo, little trucks would drive slowly around with loudspeakers nasally chanting one or other of these expressions. The former denoted the sale of sweet potatoes, baked in charcoal in the back of the truck; the latter announced the collection of used newspapers, presumably for recycling.

Where You Cannot Come Again

[43] From *A History of Fiji* by RA Derrick, Suva, 1946.

44 *Bêche de mer* are sea slugs or sea-cucumbers, a lagoon creature that is gutted, boiled, dried and sold for use in East Asian cuisine.

45 From *Wrecked on the Feejees* by William Cary, Nantucket, 1887.

46 See *United States Exploring Expedition* by Charles Wilkes, Philadelphia, 1845.

47 From *King of the Cannibal Islands* by Adolphe Brewster, London, 1937.

48 See Kipling's 1902 poem, *Sussex*.

49 From *Memories of Fiji* by Arthur G Griffiths, Sunnyvale, California, (unpublished) circa 1935.

50 See *South Sea Reminiscences* by TR St-Johnston, London, 1922.

51 The Milton Craig material is derived from *The War Years* by Sir Ian Thomson, Canberra, 2004, *Near the Beach* by Philip Snow, London, 1967, and *Mainly About Fiji* by Sir Leonard Usher, Suva, 1987.

52 From *Out of Africa* by Karen Blixen, London, 1937.

Follow Me

53 *A Pattern of Islands,* by Arthur Grimble, London, 1952.

54 *In The South Seas,* by Robert Louis Stevenson, London, 1890.

55 The *maneaba* are immense meeting houses, surmounted by lofty thatched roofs and supported by low coral pillars. For a good description of one, go to *Islands of the South Pacific* by Sir Harry Luke, London, 1962

Guam Survivor

56 The lyric 'and ice cream castles in the air' is from the 1969 song *Both Sides Now* by Joni Mitchell.

57 Winston Churchill's eulogy to Neville Chamberlain was delivered in the House of Commons on 12th November, 1940.

58 The *Kempei Tai* were the military police of the Imperial Japanese Army. They had special responsibilities for the IJA's prison camps during the war, in which their peculiar enthusiasms for torture and cruelty were revealed to Allied POW's.

59   The infamy of the POW camps of the IJA can be summed up in one statistic - it was seven times more fatal for an Allied prisoner to be incarcerated in an IJA camp in World War Two, than it was to be held in a NAZI one.

60   From the unpublished memoir in my possession *Stars Over Ambarawa* by Loelie Wijnberg.

61   From *Stars Over Ambarawa* by Loelie Wijnberg.

62   Belonging to the Sydney company Burns Philp, MV *Bulolo* ran the mail steamer service between Australia and Melanesia in the 1930s. With the outbreak of World War Two, she was taken over by the British Ministry of War Transport, was converted into an armed merchant cruiser, and undertook convoy and patrol duties as HMS *Bulolo*. She participated in the Normandy landings as a headquarters ship, and later in South East Asia where she was used as the ship for taking the Japanese surrender in Singapore. She returned to merchant service with Burns Philp in 1948.

63   *Hongi* is the ceremonial Maori greeting involving two people mutually grasping hands and pressing noses together. In the *hongi*, the breath of life, the *ha*, is exchanged.

My Home Town

64   *Sulu* is the Fijian word for clothing in general, but more specifically refers to a male sarong. Since colonial times, the uniform of the Fijian military and police has incorporated scalloped *sulu*. *Yavu* are the raised house-foundations built of earth and lined with rocks that were traditional features of Fijian architecture. Chiefs' houses and pre-Christian temples were constructed on particularly high *yavu*. For photographs of *yavu*, see pictures 65 to 68 in *Fiji in the Forties and Fifties* by Sir Ian Thomson, Auckland, 1994.

65   I loosely translate the words of the Suva song as follows:

> Let me show you the heart of the city
> Lights twinkle, forever and ever
> In Toorak, Baniwai and Naiqaqi,
> To old Suva my spirit is falling,
> Yes, it's falling, it's falling.

66   The derivation of the name Naiqaqi, the foreshore locality north of Suva's Government Buildings is as follows. *Qaqi* is the Fijian verb 'to crush' and

since the short-lived Suva sugar mill crushed cane, the locality took on this name from that time. Until recently, a rusted wheel from the 1873 mill used to be propped against a wall of one of the modern buildings of Naiqaqi.

67 AB Brewster eventually became a provincial commissioner in Fiji and is the author of *Hill Tribes of Fiji,* London, 1922, a book that was formative in my interest in the bibliography of Fiji and is the foundation copy of my collection of some 600 Fiji books.

68 The quote is from *King of the Cannibal Isles by* AB Brewster, London, 1937.

69 For background on Brewer and Joske's Naiqaqi mill, see *An Historical Sketch of the Sugar Industry in Fiji* by JC Potts in the *Fiji Society's Transactions and Proceeding for the Years 1958 and 1959.*

70 See an etching of the mill in Fiji's Times by Kim Gravelle, Suva, 1981.

71 From *Rupert Brooke: The Collected Poems,* London, 1918.

72 *Ivi* is the Fijian word for a Tahitian Chestnut, *Inocarpus fagiferus.*

73 For more on the Suva Triangle, see *King of the Cannibal Isles* by Brewster, and the booklet *Suva – A History and Guide* by AJ Schütz, Sydney, 1978.

74 *Faipa* is the Fijianisation of fibre and hence the abbreviation of fibreglass. Since the 1980s the dominant low-cost fishing boat of Fiji has been a fibreglass work-boat of Yamaha design, known locally as a *faipa.*

75 *Broomsala* is the old Suva slang for a street-sweeper. *Sala* means a path or a road in Fijian and its combination with broom is straightforward enough; but *sala* can also be used in Hindi as a mild rebuke with sexual connotations. From such word-plays slang and patois are born.

76 See *With Hook, Line and Snorkel in the South Pacific* by Rob Wright, Sydney, 1969.

77 See *The Education of Young Dunstan* by Christina Slade in Meanjin, Vol 66 - Vol 67, 2007-2008, University of Melbourne.

78 For the quote on Fijian debts see *Tuimacilai: the life of Ratu Sir Kamisese Mara* by Deryck Scarr, Adelaide, 2009. For further insight into nineteenth century Fiji, refer to *Fiji. A Short History* by Deryck Scarr, Sydney, 1984. The author is particularly grateful to Deryck Scarr for reading a very early manuscript of *Wild Vanilla* and his pointing the way to correction of some of its looser historical interpretations.

Makogai

[79] The correct pronunciation of Makogai is: ma as in 'Mars', ko as in 'Korea', g as in the ng of 'singer', and ai as in 'aisle' – Ma-ko-ngai, with a slight emphasis on the ko.

[80] The Bali-ha'i quote is from *Tales of the South Pacific* by James Michener, New York, 1947.

[81] Much of the information in this story is from the book on the Makogai leprosy hospital, *Makogai - Image of Hope* by Sister Mary Stella, Christchurch, 1978. This seminal record is still available for purchase from the Pacific Leprosy Foundation at www.pacificleprosyfoundation.co.nz

[82] In *The Old Testament* there is the third book of *Moses* called *Leviticus*. Between the 13th and 16th chapters of *Leviticus*, there are a total of 149 verses specifying God's instructions concerning those made 'unclean' by leprosy. The quoted verse is from *Leviticus*, ch. 13, vs. 45-46, from the Authorized King James version of *The Bible*.

[83] From *The New Testament, St John*, ch.15, vs.13.

[84] For the full story of Tokoriri's marlin, see *With Hook, Line and Snorkel* in the South Pacific by Rob Wright, Sydney, 1969

[85] From *Makogai - Image of Hope*.

[86] From *Makogai - Image of Hope*.

[87] Dr Desmond Beckett, was the medical superintendent of Makogai from 1957 to 1961. With his first wife and three young sons he lived on Makogai for the duration of those four years, tending to the island's patients. In 1988, as an Auckland widower and by then the medical superintendent of Auckland Public Hospital, he married my mother-in-law Loelie Wijnberg. Desmond Beckett is a member of a famous Dublin family, the 'swimming Becketts', and his first cousin Sam was awarded the Nobel Prize for literature.

[88] The quote from Dr Beckett is from *The Fiji Society Transactions and Proceedings for the Years 1966 and 1967*, Vol. 11, Suva, 1971.

[89] From *The War Years* by Sir Ian Thomson, Canberra, 2004.

[90] See *From a South Seas Diary 1938-1942* by Sir Harry Luke, London, 1945.`

[91] For more on the Ramacake legend, view the video released as part of FijiTV's *Noda Gauna* series, Disc 15, 2006.

⁹² *The New Testament, St John,* ch. 8, verses 1 to 11.

⁹³ *Viti* is the original name for Fiji and is still its name when speaking in the Fijian language. The English version of the name came about as a result of the early European explorers and traders hearing the Tongan pronounciation of *Viti*. Before Cession, the names Fichi, Fidgi, Feegee, the Feejees and such sonant variations were all in use, both in parlance and on charts, as were such early designations as Prince William's Islands, Bligh's Islands and the Cannibal Islands, so that in 1874 the British Government had to decide on a definitive name for the new Crown Colony. Prime Minister Disraeli presented a paper on the subject to Queen Victoria, including such sycophantic suggestions as the Windsor Islands, and she decided that 'Fiji' was the correct form to take, a decision reaffirmed by Fiji's leaders at independence in 1970. I know of Queen Victoria's written directive, because a senior member of the Fiji Foreign Service, Sir Josua Rabukawaqa, was shown the paper in question when he was a weekend guest of Queen Elizabeth's at Windsor Castle. In 1978, I was Sir Josua's deputy in Fiji's Protocol Division when he related the story to me.

⁹⁴ For a detailed account of Queen Elizabeth's visit to Fiji, see *Royal Visit* by Joseph Sykes, Suva, 1954.

⁹⁵ Formal Fijian ceremonies of welcome, *veiqaravi vakaturaga*, vary according to the part of Fiji in which they are performed. The ceremonies enacted on behalf of all Fijians to welcome The Queen on Albert Park in 1953 were as follows: *tama*, the acclamation given on the arrival of chiefs of high rank; *qalowaqa*, a rarely-performed ritual of welcome accorded to ladies of high rank (signifying the ancient custom of swimming out to the visiting lady's canoe and placing a whale's tooth of welcome on its bow); *qaloqalovi*, the presentation of whales' teeth broadly equivalent to the granting of 'freedom to the city'; *luvanitawake*, the presentation of further whales' teeth with an invocation for peace and goodwill; *sevusevu*, being the presentation of an intact uprooted *yaqona* (kava) plant, signifying the giving of the fruits of the land; the *yaqona* ritual during which kava is ceremonially prepared to the sound of ancient chants and served with greatest decorum for consumption by the honoured visitor; *vakamamaca*, the presentation of more whales' teeth along with tapa cloth, mats and other handicrafts; *wase ni yaqona*, by which huge quantities of food are presented (the cooked food to be eaten by

those present, the uncooked pigs, turtles and root-crops to be taken away by the guests); *meke*, being light entertainment by way of dance performances (on the day in question a war-club dance from Tailevu, a spear dance from Cakaudrove, and a graceful action-dance from Lau called *lakalaka*). In the act of drinking the ceremonial *yaqona*, The Queen was formally installed as Tui Viti, Fiji's supreme chief. Once she had done so she was expected to make a brief address to the assembled chiefs and people, and this she did, promising to constantly watch over the promotion of their welfare and prosperity in the years to come.

[96] If something is repeated enough and is not challenged, it becomes orthodoxy whether it's true or not. I challenge! From travel websites to political history books, there are three Fiji furphies cemented into place by lazy repetition. One such is that Sir Arthur Gordon was the first governor of Fiji, another that Pope John Paul said Fiji was 'the way the world should be'; a third that Fiji's colonial administration had a divide and rule policy when the islands were a British colony. In fact, Sir Arthur was the second governor of Fiji, Sir Hercules Robinson being the first from 1874 to 1875. In 1986, the words of His Holiness were that Fiji was 'a symbol of hope in the world'. It was the Fiji Visitors Bureau's advertising campaign of the era that said Fiji was the way the world should be. Finally, the colonial administration did not pursue a divide and rule policy in Fiji. It didn't need to, for two reasons. Fiji did not require division in order for it to be ruled, so such a policy was far from the administration's thoughts. The colonial administration ruled at the invitation of the Fijian chiefs as signified by the Deed of Cession, and in 1970 it departed from Fiji of its own volition. Secondly, hard as it is for orthodoxy to swallow today, the racial communities of Fiji were divided in the main not by their rulers, but by their own choices. Putting aside the inherent racialism of colonialism, no one decreed that races in Fiji could not intermarry, no one said they couldn't speak each others' languages, adopt each others' cultures, or take up each others' religions. The fact is that in modern Fiji's formative colonial era, the majority chose not to. Most schools were not integrated, but that was how most communities wanted them to be in those times. With the benefit of hindsight, and in the context of preparing Fiji for nationhood, was that short-sighted policy by Fiji's authorities? These days we would all probably answer, 'yes'. But for the majority, separate paths of development were the reality of the times, and it might have been

unacceptably provocative had the colonial administration endeavored to enforce a single syncretic one. And it is also factual especially if you look at Fiji's electoral and education systems, that those separate paths continued after Independence. Thus the Fijian model the Pope was extolling in his 1986 speech, was one where an ethnically diverse nation had peacefully and prudently developed its democracy over a period of sixteen years of sovereign independence, in a manner suggesting decency, balance, respect, tolerance of difference, and an apparent celebration of national diversity. Sadly the decency of that democracy would be gone within a year. And looking back on it now, one can say with clarity that the many who throughout that century of separate development chose to come to the syncretic centre, who overcame the limitations of race and culture, embracing and celebrating all the delightful gifts of diversity that are so freely part of Fiji's national fabric, were the ones who were truly blessed by their choice.

[97] Southern Cross Road is named for the aeroplane that Sir Charles Kingsford-Smith piloted from North America to Australia – the first ever trans-Pacific flight by man. In the course of this epic flight, on 5th June 1928, the *Southern Cross* made a precarious landing on Albert Park. Having landed, it was judged the park was too short to permit a fully laden take-off; so the *Southern Cross* was stripped to allow it to depart the field with virtually empty fuel tanks. The aeroplane took off, made a short flight across Laucala Bay, and landed again on the long beach of Naselai at the mouth of the Rewa River. Meanwhile, the plane's gear, two of the crew, and drums of fuel were shipped around to Naselai on the Government's work-horse coastal cruisers, the *Pioneer* and the *Adi Beti*. Suitably equipped, the *Southern Cross* took off from Naselai on 7th June made a fly-over of the Suva waterfront to the cheers of Suva crowds, then turned away for its stormy run to Queensland.

[98] The bibliography of the 1987 *coups d'état* is extensive, including: *Bavadra* co-edited by Atu Bain and Tupeni Baba, Nadi, 1990; *Broken Waves* by Brij Lal, Honolulu, 1992; *Fiji. The Politics of Illusion* by Deryck Scarr, Sydney, 1988; *Fiji. Shattered Coups* by Robert Robertson & Akosita Tamanisau, Sydney, 1988; *From the Mangrove Swamps* by Tomasi Vakatora, Suva, 1988; *Kava in the Blood* by Peter Thomson, Charleston, 2008; *Letters from Fiji 1987-1990* by Len Usher, Suva, 1992; *Rabuka of Fiji by* John Sharpham, Rockhampton, 2000; *Rabuka. No Other Way* by Eddie Dean

and Stan Ritova, Sydney, 1988; *The Pacific Way* by Ratu Sir Kamisese Mara, Honolulu, 1997; and *Turaga* by Daryl Tarte, Suva, 1993.

[99] *Na roko vakacegu* means the retired *roko* (provincial administrator). In rural Fiji, people of note, such as teachers, doctors and administrators, are often known by their occupation rather than their name, as it is respectful to do so. Ratu Kitione Kubuabola had been a highly respected and long-serving provincial administrator, and when I was district officer on the island of Taveuni from 1977 to 1978, he was always referred to as the *roko vakacegu*. He was a senior member of the Ai Sokula, the chiefly clan from which the paramount chieftain of northern Fiji is chosen; and like many of these high chiefs, the Tongan genes of warring forbears showed in his features and bear-like physique.

[100] In the Fijian language, the letter b is pronounced 'mb' as in the English word rambunctious, and u is pronounced 'oo' as in the English word zoo. Thus Rabuka's name is pronounced Ram-booka. It took little time for the Rambo nickname to be taken up by the foreign media.

[101] This note is made to set the record straight, not for any petty reason of slighted pride. I'm forced to make the point because in some Fiji *coup* books, my role at Government House is variously described as Ratu Sir Penaia's 'personal secretary' or his 'private secretary'. Describing my 1987 posting at Government House as such is quite erroneous, as I was throughout this time the permanent secretary to the governor-general, duly gazetted as such by the Public Service Commission. Many readers might be unfamiliar with the 'permanent secretary' nomenclature - it derives from the British system and is the job-title of the civil servant who is the chief executive officer of a ministry, appointed from the senior ranks of the civil service by the Public Service Commission. The word 'permanent' signifies the office is one held by a career member of the civil service, who has worked his or her way up through the civil service. The post is therefore supposedly not subject to the vagaries of political elections. He or she runs the ministry concerned and reports to a minister, who has been selected by the prime minister of the day from the elected ranks of parliamentarians. For the record, prior to my time at Government House, I was the permanent secretary for information in the government led by Ratu Mara and had just been appointed permanent secretary for trade, industry and tourism in the Bavadra government.

[102] For a fuller appreciation of Fiji's great chief, read *Ratu Sukuna. Soldier, Statesman, Man of Two Worlds* by Deryck Scarr, London, 1980; and *Fiji: The Three-legged Stool* edited by Deryck Scarr, London, 1983. See also the two chapters on Ratu Sukuna in *Mainly About Fiji* by Len Usher, Suva, 1987.

[103] Before being posted to Fiji as a cadet in the Colonial Administrative Service, my father had completed both his Master of Arts degree at Glasgow University and his military officer's training course at Dunbar in Scotland. This was in fact critical to his Fiji posting, arising as it did from a decision by Churchill's War Cabinet to post to the war-threatened colonies a handful of university graduates who had already received military training.

[104] From *Ratu Sukuna. Soldier, Statesman, Man of Two* Worlds by Deryck Scarr.

[105] See *Fiji: The Three-legged* Stool edited by Deryck Scarr.

[106] For published accounts of Fiji's *coup d'état* of 2000 see *Speight of Violence by* Michael Field, Tupeni Baba & Unaisi Nabobo-Baba, Canberra, 2005, and *Coup* edited by Brij Lal & Michael Pretes, Canberra, 2001

[107] A word or two about the new parliamentary complex. It was built during the years of the unelected government that ruled Fiji between 1987 and 1992, and was opened in time to receive the parliamentarians elected by the people in 1992. Many thought the old parliamentary chambers at Naqaqi were adequate for the job, but there were also those who felt the old chambers were forever cursed by the events of 1987 and they did not want to return there. The new complex is elaborate, laid out like a Fijian village surveying the reefs that surround the Suva Peninsula, with the high-roofed central building of the complex being the parliamentary chambers. The land from the southern tip of Suva's peninsula, up to the hill on which the new Parliament stands, is known as Veiuto - the breadfruit grove. When I was a pupil at the newly-opened Suva Grammar School on Veiuto's foreshore, my friends and I would often walk through the dense grass under the breadfruit trees to go up to the abandoned gun emplacements of the Suva Battery, now within the grounds of the parliamentary complex. The walls of the massive concrete emplacements were charcoal-scrawled with primitive pornographic graffiti, which we prepubescent boys naively studied as we smoked our cigarettes. Equally fascinating was the housing for the two six-inch naval guns that had been installed there. Capable of firing eleven miles out to sea in defense of Suva, the guns were removed in 1944, but the concrete

emplacements remain as a haunting reminder of the planned Japanese invasion of Fiji in 1942.

[108] *Kailoma* is the Fijian word for people of mixed indigenous and foreign descent. The prefix *kai* denotes where a person is from. If someone is from Suva like me, they are *Kaisuva*. A New Zealander is a *kainiusiladi*, an Indian a *kai-idia*, a Chinese a *kaijaina* and so on. *E loma* means inside or in-between, but *lomana* means to love, so the *kailoma* nomenclature is heavy with positive meaning. America has a *kailoma* president in Barack Obama. The term is so preferable to Fiji's official designation of this demographic sector of the population as 'Part-European', as encountered on immigration arrival forms and census results, that speaking as one with many *kailoma* relatives, I wish it would become an officially adopted term.

[109] The late Dr Apenisa Kuruisaqila played representative rugby for Fiji and served as president of the Fiji Rugby Union. He was a paediatrician, was minister of health in a succession of governments, and was known throughout as an honourable man.

[110] *Kunekune na yaloka ni dilio* is a Fijian proverb, said of something that is very difficult to find. The *dilio*, or Pacific Golden Plover, is a wading bird common along the coasts of Fiji in summer months. During Fiji's winter months it flies north to enjoy the northern hemisphere's summer along the balmy shores of Alaska and Siberia, which is where the *dilio* lays its elusive eggs.

[111] *Koro makawa* means 'a village of long ago'. The house mounds of these abandoned villages can be found all over Fiji, if you trek beyond the ordinary ways.

[112] Major-General Mead was the general in charge of New Zealand troops in Fiji in 1942, who was tragically lost off Tonga that year when his plane went down. Sir Kenneth Maddocks was a governor of Fiji in the 1960s.

[113] *Liu muri* is a slang Fijian phrase literally meaning 'in front-behind' and refers to the various practices of back-biting, saying one thing and doing another, getting others to do your dirty work, and provoking from the rear.

[114] For Robert Keith-Reid's interview of Commodore Bainimarama see the article *Frankly Speaking*, in Islands Business magazine, June, 2003.

[115] For the Chaudhry quote and more on the 2006 *coup d'état*, see *From Election to Coup in Fiji; The 2006 Polls and Their Aftermath* by Fraenkel and Firth, Suva, 2007.

The Pious Princes

[116] In the first half of the twentieth century, amongst many other duties, Sir Harry Luke was Commissioner of Paphos in Cyprus before going on to be Lieutenant-Governor of Malta. Lawrence Durrell knew him in Cyprus and in his book *Bitter Lemons* describes Sir Harry as a man 'whose gentleness and magnanimity of soul were married to a mind far-reaching and acute, who was fantastically erudite without ever being bookish, and whose life had been one of travel and adventure.' From 1941 to 1942 when my father was *aide de camp* to Sir Harry, he lived and worked at Government House in Suva, taking his daily meals with the governor, whose family did not accompany him out to Fiji. There was a world war on, so things were pretty hectic, with Suva being described at the time as the 'Clapham Junction of the South Pacific', and with Government House finding itself at the centre of all the comings and goings. After his first nine months in residence at Government House, my father and Sir Harry calculated that only once during those months had they sat down to a meal solely in each other's company, for the stream of houseguests was endless, and formal dinners for visiting political and military leaders were par for the course.

[117] See *Queen Salote and Her Kingdom* by Sir Harry Luke, London, 1954.

[118] From the poem *To a Louse* by Robert Burns.

[119] *Ratu* is the Fijian honorific prefix accorded to males of chiefly rank. The female equivalent is *Adi*.

[120] The book *Mission to Viti* was published in London in 1862, its full title being *Viti: An Account of a Government Mission to the Vitian or Fijian Islands in the Years 1860-61*. Born and educated in Germany, at the age of nineteen Berthold Seemann commenced work as a gardener at Kew in England. The Admiralty's appointment of Seemann as naturalist on HMS *Herald* resulted in his first visit to the Pacific in 1847. On his return to Britain he was responsible for the publication of the classic *Narrative of the Voyage of HMS Herald, being a Circumnavigation of the Globe and Three Cruises in the Arctic Regions in Search of Sir John Franklin*. When the British Government sent a mission to Fiji to examine the offer made by the Fijian chiefs to cede the islands to the British Crown, Dr Seemann (he had by then been conferred a PhD by the University of Gottingen) accompanied the expedition as its botanist. As well as *Mission to Viti*, Seemann's 1860-61 sojourn in

419

Fiji resulted in his beautiful botanical folio *Flora Vitiensis* and the enduring nomenclature of many of Fiji's plants. He died of a fever in 1871 at the age of forty-seven, while pursuing wild flora in Nicaragua.

121 From *The King of the Cannibal Islands*, AB Brewster, London, 1937.

122 *Ekdum khalas* is Hindi and translates as 'absolutely finished'. It's a good example of Fijian English's borrowing universally understood words and phrases from *na i vosa vakaviti* and Hindi.

123 *Vale vakaviti* is the correct term for a traditionally constructed Fijian house, *vale* meaning house and *vakaviti* meaning in the manner of Fiji. The word *bure*, widely used in the tourist industry to describe a thatched house, has a more specific origin. It is a shortening of *bure ni sa* and describes the house that used to exist in each village for the accommodation of unmarried men and travellers.

124 *Turaga Bale* is a respectful term of reference to the high chiefs of Fiji. The quote comes from a letter my father wrote from Scotland, in November 2000, to the chairman of the Constitutional Review Committee in Suva.

125 See *A Personal Perspective* by Joni Madraiwiwi, Suva, 2008, for more on Fijian attitudes to governance.

126 For students of Fijian idioms, the classic text is *Na i Vosavosa Vakaviti e So* by Anare Raiwalui, Melbourne, 1954

127 *Lewe ni vanua* translates as 'flesh of the land' and is how many indigenous Fijians refer to themselves in the context of their tribal affiliations.

The Money-Bird

128 *Tokelau. A Historical Ethnography* by Judith Huntsman and Antony Hooper, Auckland, 1996.

129 *Ki Te La, Shine the Sun*, is a track on the Te Vaka CD of contemporary music released by The Pacific Nation Record Company, Auckland, 1997.

Tahitian Turks

130 For a rather fantasised account of the artist's time in Tahiti, see *Noa Noa* by Paul Gauguin, New York, 1920 (English translation).

[131] For a first-hand account of the artist's shenanigans and views on the world, see *The Intimate Journals of Paul Gauguin* translated by Van Wyck Brook, London, 1953.

[132] See *Gauguin in the South Seas* by Bengt Danielsson, New York, 1964.

[133] For more on the artist's profligate treatment of women and his homo-erotic proclivities, see *Paul Gauguin: An Erotic Life* by Nancy Mathews, New Haven, 2001.

[134] Gauguin's 12 ft long, 1897 painting, *Whence do we come? What are we? Where are we going?* was painted as a final statement before the artist attempted suicide in Tahiti.

[135] From the *The Intimate Journals of Paul Gauguin*.

[136] *Marae* is the Maori word for a tribal meeting ground. In the Marquesan language the same word is spelt and pronounced *me'ae*.

[137] *Tiki* are carved representations of dead people, usually ancestors of great renown, often deified.

[138] Refer further in the author's story in Australian Gourmet Traveller magazine, Sydney, January 2009.

[139] *Ivi po'o* are decorative tubes carved from human leg bones. For background and illustrations of *ivi po'o* see *Art and Artefacts of the Pacific, Africa and the Americas* by Steven Phelps, London, 1976.

[140] *Poe* in this case is pounded banana pudding in coconut milk.

[141] From *Typee* by Herman Melville, London, 1846.

[142] From *The Saga of Cimba* by Richard Maury, London, 1939.

[143] See *White Shadows in the South Seas* by Frederick O'Brien, New York, 1919.

Scribbles in Sand

[144] From *Typee* by Herman Melville, London, 1846.

[145] From *Rupert Brooke: The Collected Poems,* London, 1918.

[146] From *Mystic Isles of the South Seas* by Frederick O'Brien, London, 1921.

[147] The sonnet is written to Miss Asquith, later Lady Violet Bonham-Carter, from 'somewhere in the mountains of Fiji', presumably Namosi. It can be found in Edmund Marsh's memoir in *Rupert Brooke: The Collected Poems.*

[148] See *The Tragedy of Pudd'nhead Wilson* by Mark Twain, Hartford, 1900.

[149] From *Following the Equator* by Mark Twain, Hartford, 1897.

[150] My thanks to Salesia Ikaniwai of the Fiji Government Archives in Suva for forwarding me a copy of the story in The Fiji Times of 14th September, 1895 concerning Mark Twain's visit to Fiji.

[151] See the 'nonsense poem' *The Hunting of the Snark* by Lewis Carroll, London, 1898.

[152] Jack London material from *Memories of Fiji* by Arthur G Griffiths, Sunnyvale, California, circa 1935.

[153] *By Reef and Palm* by Louis Becke, London, 1894.

[154] The words for the song *Sai Levuka Ga* were penned by the prominent Fijian academic Dr Rusiate Nayacakalou, author of the books *Tradition and Change in the Fijian Village*, Suva, 1978, and *Village Life in Fiji*, Wellington, 1959. The quoted verse translates loosely as:

> I remember you Levuka
> From those days of yesteryear
> All those happy fleeting times
> Are still so sweet and dear.

[155] See *The Beach of Falesá* by Robert Louis Stevenson in *Island Nights' Entertainments*, London, 1893.

[156] From *A Writer's Notebook* by Somerset Maugham, London, 1951.

[157] Refer to *Vailima Letters* by Robert Louis Stevenson, Edinburgh, 1897.

[158] See *Tales of the South Pacific* by James Michener, New York, 1947. Note that Bali Hai, as it has come to be in popular culture, was spelt Bali-ha'i when Michener's juices and pen were flowing free.

[159] For insight into the rewards of flattery, amongst other witty forays, read *Tales of the Tikongs* by Epeli Hau'ofa, Honolulu, 1994.

[160] From *The Happy Isles of Oceania* by Paul Theroux, London, 1992.

The Hermit Cell

[161] The Reef Stone Fish *Synanceia verrucosa* is highly camouflaged to blend in with the coral. It is the most venomous fish in the sea, injecting its toxic poison by way of thirteen stout dorsal spines.

[162] The Sydney Morning Herald, 25th June, 2003.

[163] From *Moral Epistles* by Lucius Annaeus Seneca, the Roman Stoic philosopher (circa 4 BC – 65 AD).

[164] With reference to Scene 3, Act 3, *Macbeth* by William Shakespeare, London, 1606.

[165] From Basho's *A Haiku Journey*, translated by Dorothy Britton, Kondansha International, Tokyo, 1983.

Hold Firm for John Frum

[166] *Paisa* is Hindi for money.

[167] See *Our Final Century* by Martin Rees, London, 2003.

[168] The word 'bislama' is supposedly a corruption of *bêche de mer*, or its Portuguese equivalent *bicho do mar*, referring to the sea-slug that was the main item of trade in the early days of European contact with Melanesia.

[169] The post-colonial anthropologists who wax lyrical on the liberating effect the attitudes of American forces had on Melanesians in the Pacific War, usually omit any reference to the back-of-the-bus treatment that dark-skinned people were subject to in the American military at the time. Nor do such enthusiastic scribes mention the concurrent impact in 1943 of combat battalions of dark-skinned Fijians fighting shoulder to shoulder at the sides of their white-skinned colleagues in the jungle battles of Melanesia.

[170] For more on the written record of John Frum's legacy, see *Mambu* by Kenelm Burridge, London, 1960; Ken Calvert's essay in *Paradise Postponed* edited by Mamal and McCall, Sydney, 1978; *Cargo Cult* by Lamont Lindstrom, Honolulu, 1993; and *The Trumpet Shall Sound* by Peter Worsley, London, 1957.

Other Books by Peter Thomson

Kava in the Blood. First published by Tandem Press in 1999. Second edition published by Tandem Press in 2000. Revised edition published by Booksurge Publishing in 2008.

On Paths of Ash (edited by). Published by Murdoch Books in 2009.

Fiji in the Forties and Fifties (edited by). Published by Thomson Pacific in 1994.

To purchase mail-order copies of **Wild Vanilla** and **Kava in the Blood**, go to www.amazon.com

Vinaka vaka levu na veitokoni.

Made in the USA
Columbia, SC
11 February 2018